Plotinus

Plotinus (AD 205–270) was the founder of Neoplatonism, whose thought has had a profound influence on medieval philosophy, and on Western philosophy more broadly. In this engaging book, Eyjólfur K. Emilsson introduces and explains the full spectrum of Plotinus' philosophy for those coming to his work for the first time.

Beginning with a chapter-length overview of Plotinus' life and works which also assesses the Platonic, Aristotelian and Stoic traditions that influenced him, Emilsson goes on to address key topics including:

- Plotinus' originality
- the status of souls
- Plotinus' language
- the notion of the One or the Good
- Intellect, including Plotinus' holism
- the physical world
- the soul and the body, including emotions and the self
- Plotinus' ethics
- Plotinus' influence and legacy.

Including a chronology, glossary of terms and suggestions for further reading, *Plotinus* is an ideal introduction to this major figure in Western philosophy, and is essential reading for students of ancient philosophy and classics.

Eyjólfur K. Emilsson is Professor of Philosophy at the University of Oslo, Norway. He is the author of *Plotinus on Sense-Perception* (1988), *Plotinus on Intellect* (2007) and (with Steven K. Strange) of a translation and commentary, *Plotinus: Ennead VI.4 and VI.5: On the Presence of Being, One and the Same, Everywhere as a Whole* (2015). He has published numerous articles on Plotinus and other ancient philosophers and translated Plato's *Republic* and other Platonic dialogues into Icelandic.

Routledge Philosophers
Edited by Brian Leiter

University of Chicago

Routledge Philosophers is a major series of introductions to the great Western philosophers. Each book places a major philosopher or thinker in historical context, explains and assesses their key arguments, and considers their legacy. Additional features include a chronology of major dates and events, chapter summaries, annotated suggestions for further reading and a glossary of technical terms.

An ideal starting point for those new to philosophy, they are also essential reading for those interested in the subject at any level.

Also available:

Hobbes	A. P. Martinich
Leibniz	Nicholas Jolley
Locke	E. J. Lowe
Hegel	Frederick Beiser
Rousseau	Nicholas Dent
Schopenhauer	Julian Young
Darwin	Tim Lewens
Rawls	Samuel Freeman
Spinoza	Michael Della Rocca
Merleau-Ponty	Taylor Carman
Russell	Gregory Landini
Wittgenstein	William Child
Heidegger	John Richardson
Adorno	Brian O'Connor
Husserl, second edition	David Woodruff Smith
Aristotle, second edition	Christopher Shields
Kant, second edition	Paul Guyer
Hume	Don Garrett
Dewey	Steven Fesmire
Freud, second edition	Jonathan Lear
Habermas	Kenneth Baynes
Peirce	Albert Atkin
Plato	Constance Meinwald

Eyjólfur K. Emilsson

Plotinus

LONDON AND NEW YORK

First published 2017
by Routledge
2 Park Square, Milton Park, Abingdon, Oxon OX14 4RN

and by Routledge
711 Third Avenue, New York, NY 10017

Routledge is an imprint of the Taylor & Francis Group, an informa business

© 2017 Eyjólfur K. Emilsson

The right of Eyjólfur K. Emilsson to be identified as the author of this work has been asserted by him in accordance with sections 77 and 78 of the Copyright, Designs and Patents Act 1988.

All rights reserved. No part of this book may be reprinted or reproduced or utilised in any form or by any electronic, mechanical, or other means, now known or hereafter invented, including photocopying and recording, or in any information storage or retrieval system, without permission in writing from the publishers.

Trademark notice: Product or corporate names may be trademarks or registered trademarks, and are used only for identification and explanation without intent to infringe.

British Library Cataloguing in Publication Data
A catalogue record for this book is available from the British Library

Library of Congress Cataloging in Publication Data
Names: Eyjólfur Kjalar Emilsson, author.
Title: Plotinus / by Eyjólfur K. Emilsson.
Description: New York : Routledge, 2017. | Series: Routledge philosophers | Includes bibliographical references and index.
Identifiers: LCCN 2016032746 | ISBN 9780415333481 (hardback : alk. paper) | ISBN 9780415333498 (pbk. : alk. paper) | ISBN 9780203413159 (e-book)
Subjects: LCSH: Plotinus.
Classification: LCC B693.Z7 E945 2017 | DDC 186/.4--dc23
LC record available at https://lccn.loc.gov/2016032746

ISBN13: 978-0-415-33348-1 (hbk)
ISBN13: 978-0-415-33349-8 (pbk)
ISBN13: 978-0-203-41315-9 (ebk)

Typeset in Joanna MT and Din
by Saxon Graphics Ltd, Derby

Contents

Acknowledgements   vii

Chronology   ix

Introduction   1

One
Life, works and philosophical background   8

Two
The world according to Plotinus   37

Three
The One and the genesis of Intellect   70

Four
Intellect   104

Five
Soul   144

Six
The physical world   185

Seven The human being I: The soul–body compound		228
Eight The human being II: The higher soul and we ourselves		269
Nine Ethics I: Virtue, happiness and the ethics of everyday life		296
Ten Ethics II: Mystical experience, theodicy, freedom and beauty		335
Eleven Plotinus' legacy and influence		373
Glossary		381
General bibliography		388
Index		405

Acknowledgements

In writing this book, I have enjoyed the assistance and goodwill of several friends and colleagues. It is meant to be Plotinus made understandable to those not yet initiated but curious. I have benefited from comments and questions from a number of such people, who despite knowing a lot about many things, including the history of philosophy, would take no insult in not being counted among the Plotinus experts. I have found their reactions highly instructive because it is people like these I have had in mind in writing the book. So many thanks to Arna Mathiesen, Ambra Serangeli, Hallvard Fossheim and Pétur Knútsson, who each read and commented on parts of the manuscript at an early stage. To this list would also belong my former teacher, colleague and friend, Páll Skúlason, former rector of the University of Iceland, who during his terminal illness was an eager reader of my early chapters, expressing hopes that he would be able to see a draft of the whole. Sadly, that did not happen.

Friends among Plotinian scholars have read and commented on parts of my drafts. In this regard I would especially like to thank Damian Caluori, who carefully read drafts of the first half of the book and with whom I have had long and intense conversations about the Intellect and Soul; Pauliina Remes, who read and commented on Chapters 7 and 8; Julia Annas who read and commented on Chapters 9 and 10; and Dominic O'Meara who gave me comments on Chapters 6, 9 and 10, and has in addition been an inspiration and a great conversation partner over the years. James Wilberding, Riccardo Chiaradonna and Paul Kalligas have advised me on some points and been helpful in providing materials not readily available to me. There are many others. I feel very privileged to have as friends and acquaintances a large number of Plotinian scholars from many different countries. This community is characterized by respect and friendliness that I think is becoming rare in the academic world. I wish to express my gratitude to all these friends and colleagues from whom I have learnt a lot. The three anonymous readers for Routledge offered useful comments of different kinds. Thanks are owed to them too.

I also wish to thank my department, the Department of Philosophy, Classics, the History of Art and Ideas at the University of Oslo, and especially its present chair, Mathilde Skoie, who has always been understanding and ready to provide assistance, financial and otherwise. Many thanks to Lars Gjøvikli, Gina Green and Inger Bakken Pedersen for a splendid job with the bibliography and other finishing touches.

Last but not least: thanks to my whole family for their support and patience. Our puppy, Ulven, who has endeavored to tear and chew my books (he finds my copy of Numenius especially tempting) during the past months and has in many ways been a nuisance, does not receive any thanks on that score. He has, however, been effective in keeping me from being entirely sedentary and is at any rate easily forgiven almost everything.

Chronology

205	Plotinus is born in Egypt.
232	Plotinus begins his eleven years of study with Ammonius Saccas in Alexandria.
242	Plotinus sets out with emperor Gordian on a military expedition against the Persians with the goal of acquainting himself with the philosophers of Persia and India.
244	Plotinus settles in Rome and takes up teaching philosophy there.
246	Amelius joins Plotinus' school in Rome and stays with him till 269.
253	Plotinus begins to write his treatises.
254–268	Gallienus emperor. Plotinus was on friendly terms with him and his wife, Salonina.
263	Porphyry, arriving from Greece, joins Plotinus' school in Rome. Plotinus had then written twenty-one treatises.
268	Porphyry departs from Rome to Sicily. Plotinus has written twenty-four treatises in addition to the first twenty-one.
269	Plotinus leaves Rome for Campania. He sends five treatises to Porphyry in Sicily.
270	Porphyry receives four additional treatises. Plotinus dies.
301	Porphyry writes the *Life of Plotinus*. The Porphyrian edition of the *Enneads* appears.

Introduction

This book is no replacement for reading Plotinus himself. Yet it is my hope that either by reading it first or along with reading the *Enneads* the reader who wishes to familiarize himself or herself with Plotinus' philosophy, will find it helpful. It is also my hope that some parts of it at least can be of interest to the more advanced students of Plotinus, even if I have not particularly striven for novel interpretations. Still, there may be a fresh take on a number of points.

    Plotinus' world is large: I have tried to do justice to all the most relevant parts and aspects of it in a way that I hope is comprehensible to any curious reader. Such a task is not so easy: Plotinus' philosophy is backward-looking even if it is often original. He sees Plato as an authority, and he uses or alludes to others, pre-Socratics, Aristotle and followers, the Stoics, and previous Platonists, in all his writings. How could one present Plotinus without telling the whole history of the whole of previous ancient Greek philosophy? Were such an account to be given, Plotinus himself would drown in reports of what others have held. Yet, a route into his thought that totally ignores the historical setting and his dependence on previous thinkers would seem to be doomed to fail: Plotinus' thought cannot be understood unless we get a sense of the problems he saw, and these are to a large extent given to him by his predecessors. In this situation I have tried to take some sort of middle course: to explain enough of the background to be able to present Plotinus' views as a reasonable alternative in the situation he found himself in. The main focus is, however, on his own texts, which are often quoted and commented on at considerable length. Whether this course is successful is for the reader to judge.

It is possible to enter Plotinus' world by different paths. As we shall soon see, this world may be likened to a pyramid, where the top represents the first principle on which all else depends. One way is to start at the very top. This is, for instance, what Gerson (1994) opts for. Another way would be to do as Rist (1967) does, namely to present Plotinus through a number of topics that he thought important without ever trying to present the whole of his philosophy systematically. I believe this way may be more suitable for a book aimed at readers who already have a considerable familiarity with Plotinus. A third way is taken by O'Meara (1993): to start so to speak in the middle with something familiar to everyone and ascend from there to the principles and ultimately to the single first principle, the One; then to go down again from there.

The route chosen here resembles O'Meara's at least in its main outlines: first ascending and then descending. When I started the project of writing this book I naturally gave some thought to the mode of presentation and concluded that this would be the best way—or let us rather say, be the one that seemed most congenial to me—and decided not to let O'Meara's example influence me negatively in this regard. Our books differ greatly in many other respects, as any reader of both will be able to verify. The much greater bulk of the present work alone turns it into a rather different kind of introduction to Plotinus than O'Meara's.

The ascent taken here is rather steep: after presenting Plotinus' life, works and philosophical background in Chapter 1, the second chapter takes us from the world of everyday experience to the One. In this I follow the lead of one of Plotinus' own treatises, *Ennead* V.1. "On the three primary hypostases," where Plotinus does the same. In this second chapter some recurring basic features of Plotinus' thought are also introduced and explained. The One is the topic of the third chapter and from there the way goes down the Plotinian hierarchy, ending with considerations of ethics.

I have previously written and published on a number of the topics discussed here; on others, I have not written before. I have made use of several of my previously published writings. Sometimes this is merely a matter of reusing thoughts with entirely new wording; at other times, I have lifted whole paragraphs with little change. This holds for Chapters 2, 3 and 4, where materials from Emilsson (2007) have come in handy, and for Section 6 on sympathy in Chapter 5 and parts of Section 3.3 on the emotions in Chapter 7, where I have excerpted from Emilsson (2015) and (1998), respectively.

Conventionally, references to the *Enneads* are often given only in numbers: V.3. (49) 2, 14–16, for instance, means "5th *Ennead*, 3rd treatise (which is number 49 on Porphyry's chronological list of Plotinus' writings), chapter 2, lines 14 to 16." I try to follow the practice of giving the full title of a treatise along with its number when it is first introduced for discussion in a given context but subsequent references only refer to its numerical place in the *Enneads*. With a few exceptions I follow Armstrong's translations of the titles.

There are many references to classical authors other than Plotinus, to Plato and Aristotle in particular, but also to a number of others. These references are given according to established standards, which are shown in all good editions and translations, for example, in the complete translations of Plato and Aristotle listed below and in the texts and translations in the Loeb Classical Library, which has most (but not quite all) of the other authors referred to.

Text, translations and commentaries

The standard edition of Plotinus' Greek text is:

Plotini Opera I–III (*editio minor*, with revised text), edited by P. Henry and H.-R. Schwyzer (Oxford: Clarendon Press, 1964–82).

There is an older edition by the same editors, *Plotini Opera* I–III (*editio maior*), edited by P. Henry and H.-R. Schwyzer (Paris: Desclée de Brouwer et Cie, 1951–73). The Greek text of this edition is available electronically in the database Thesaurus Linguae Graecae.

What must count as the authoritative English translation of Plotinus is:

Plotinus: Enneads, 7 vols., Greek text with English translation and introductions by A. H. Armstrong, Loeb Classical Library (Cambridge, MA: Harvard University Press, 1966–82).

In this book Armstrong's translation is generally followed, sometimes with modifications that are not necessarily noted. There is an older English translation of Plotinus by Stephen MacKenna. This translation is renowned for the beauty of its style but is not as accurate as Armstrong's and often uses different expressions for central notions from those customary in contemporary scholarship. MacKenna's translation, which first appeared in the first half of the previous century, is now available as:

Plotinus: The Enneads, translated by Stephen MacKenna, abridged with an introduction and notes by John Dillon (Harmondsworth, Middlesex: Penguin Books, 1991).

The edition and French translation of Émile Bréhier,

Plotin, Ennéades: Texte établi et traduit par Émile Bréhier (Paris: Les belles lettres, 1924–38)

is still valuable. Even if the text and translation are not always reliable, Bréhier's introductions ("Notices") to each treatise are very helpful and informative.

Furthermore, there is an edition and German translation, which sometimes has alternative readings of the text and interpretations:

Plotins Schriften, with Greek text with German Translation and Commentary by Richard Harder, Robert Beutler and Willy Theiler (Hamburg: Meiner, 1956–71).

There is an ongoing project at Parmenides Publishing, led by John M. Dillon and Andrew Smith, of translating the whole of the Enneads into English with philosophical commentaries. The following volumes have appeared so far:

Ennead II.5: On What Is Potentially and What Actually, translated with an introduction and commentary by Cinzia Arruzza (Las Vegas: Parmenides Publishing, 2015).

Ennead IV.3–4.29: Problems concerning the Soul, translated with an introduction and commentary by John Dillon and Henry J. Blumenthal (Las Vegas: Parmenides Publishing, 2015).

Ennead IV.4.30–45 and IV.5: Problems concerning the Soul, translated with an introduction and commentary by Gary M. Gurtler SJ (Las Vegas: Parmenides Publishing, 2015).

Ennead IV.7: On the Immortality of the Soul, translated with an introduction and commentary by Barrie Fleet (Las Vegas: Parmenides Publishing, 2016).

Ennead IV.8: On the Descent of the Soul into Bodies, translated with an introduction and commentary by Barrie Fleet (Las Vegas: Parmenides Publishing, 2012).

Ennead V.1: On the Three Primary Levels of Reality, translated with an introduction and commentary by Eric D. Perl (Las Vegas: Parmenides Publishing, 2016).

Ennead V.5: That the Intelligibles Are Not External to the Intellect, and on the Good, translated with an introduction and commentary by Lloyd P. Gerson (Las Vegas: Parmenides Publishing, 2013).

Ennead VI.4 and VI.5: On the Presence of Being, One and the Same, Everywhere as a Whole, translated with an introduction and commentary by Eyjólfur Emilsson and Steven K. Strange (Las Vegas: Parmenides Publishing, 2015).

In addition there are the following translations with commentaries on individual treatises:

Kieran McGroarty, *Plotinus on Eudaimonia: A Commentary on Ennead 1.4* (Oxford: Oxford University Press, 2006).

James Wilberding, *Plotinus' Cosmology: A Study of Ennead II.1 (40): Text, Translation, and Commentary* (Oxford: Oxford University Press, 2006).

Barrie Fleet, *Plotinus: Ennead III.6: On the Impassivity of the Bodiless, with a Translation and Commentary* (Oxford: Clarendon Press, 1995).

Wypkje Helleman-Elgersma, *Soul-Sisters: A Commentary on Enneads IV 3 (27), 1–8 of Plotinus* (Elementa 15) (Amsterdam: Rodopi, 1980).

Michael Atkinson, *Plotinus: Ennead V, 1: On the Three Principal Hypostases* (Oxford: Oxford University Press, 1983).

Henri Oosthout, *Modes of Knowledge and the Transcendental: An Introduction to Plotinus Ennead 5.3 [49] with a Commentary and Translation* (Amsterdam: B. R. Grüner, 1991).

P. A. Meijer, *Plotinus on the Good or the One (Enneads VI, 9): An Analytical Commentary*, Amsterdam Classical Monographs 1 (Amsterdam: J. C. Gieben, 1992).

General works

A very substantial part of the best literature on Plotinus is in languages other than English—French, German and Italian, in particular. I do refer to such works in the text, as seems fit, but here as well as in the recommended readings that follow each chapter with rare exceptions I list works in English only. Those readers who wish to pursue the scholarship further may use the references given in the main text or trace the references given in the recommended readings, which normally are not restricted to works in English.

The main general, single-author introductory books on Plotinus in English are:

John M. Rist, *Plotinus: The Road to Reality* (Cambridge: Cambridge University Press, 1967).
Dominic J. O'Meara, *Plotinus: An Introduction to the Enneads* (Oxford: Oxford University Press, 1993).
Lloyd P. Gerson, *Plotinus* (London: Routledge, 1994).

All three works are intended as general introductions to Plotinus' thought but a newcomer to Plotinus is likely to benefit most from O'Meara's book. The following are two French classics on Plotinus that have been translated into English:

Émile Bréhier, *The Philosophy of Plotinus*, translated by Joseph Thomas (Chicago: University of Chicago Press, 1958), appeared originally as *La philosophie de Plotin* in 1928.
Pierre Hadot, *Plotinus or the Simplicity of Vision*, translated by Michael Chase (Chicago: University of Chicago Press, 1998), appeared originally in 1963 as *Plotin ou la simplicité du regard*.

There is a valuable commentary on the *Life of Plotinus* and on the first three *Enneads* in:

Paul Kalligas, *The Enneads of Plotinus: A Commentary*, vol. 1, translated by E. K. Fowden and N. Pilavachi (Princeton: Princeton University Press, 2014). Originally published in Greek, 1991–2004. The second volume will hopefully appear soon.

The following are very readable introductions to Neoplatonism, including Plotinus, of course:

Richard T. Wallis, *Neoplatonism* (London: Duckworth, 1972).
Andrew Smith, *Philosophy in Late Antiquity* (London: Routledge, 2004).
Pauliina Remes, *Neoplatonism* (Berkeley and Los Angeles: University of California Press, 2008).

Considerably more difficult is:

Anthony C. Lloyd, *The Anatomy of Neoplatonism* (Oxford: Oxford University Press, 1990).

The following collections contain valuable and mostly accessible articles on Plotinus and his predecessors and successors:

A. H. Armstrong (ed.), *The Cambridge History of Later Greek and Early Medieval Philosophy* (Cambridge: Cambridge University Press, 1967).
Lloyd P. Gerson (ed.), *The Cambridge Companion to Plotinus* (Cambridge: Cambridge University Press, 1996).
Lloyd P. Gerson (ed.), *The Cambridge History of Philosophy in Late Antiquity*, 2 vols. (Cambridge: Cambridge University Press, 2010).
Pauliina Remes and Svetla Slaveva-Griffin (eds.), *The Routledge Handbook of Neoplatonism* (London: Routledge 2014).

For Plato and Aristotle, see:

Plato: Complete Works, edited by John M. Cooper (Cambridge, MA: Hackett Publishing, 1997).
The Complete Works of Aristotle: The Revised Oxford Translation, 2 vols., edited by Jonathan Barnes (Princeton: Princeton University Press, 1984).

One

Life, works and philosophical background

In the English-speaking world everybody who knows even a little about philosophy is familiar with the names of Socrates, Plato, Aristotle, Descartes, Locke, Hume, Kant, Hegel and Mill. Someone who knows who these philosophers are and has some notion of what they stand for will in all likelihood be familiar with a host of others: Heraclitus, Parmenides and Epicurus, for example, to name just three from classical antiquity. On the other hand, unless one has done some serious reading in ancient philosophy, one is likely to be quite in the dark about Speusippus, Strato, Cleanthes, Damascius and quite a few others.

Whether or not a past philosopher is a household name in our time does not, or at least does not merely, depend on the sheer excellence or the great impact on posterity of his or her thought: some thinkers may sink into oblivion as a result of somewhat arbitrary traditions concerning the writing and teaching of the history of philosophy; it depends also on the intellectual moods and fashions of the times and on other factors that do not reflect the philosophers' objective importance, cleverness or depth.

After his day in late antiquity and during the Italian Renaissance, and for quite some time thereafter, Plotinus definitely belonged to the really illustrious—he is for instance in all likelihood conspicuously present in Raphael's great painting, *The School of Athens*.[1] Today he probably falls somewhere between the categories of the really famous and the obscure. For many Plotinus' name and a vague association with something called Neoplatonism are familiar but little more. In virtue of the subtlety of his thought at its best and his enormous historical influence, Plotinus really deserves better coverage than he

Life, works and philosophical background

has had today. This is not least so in the English-speaking world, probably less on the European continent. As a matter of fact, Plotinus is the thinker who has contributed more than anyone else to the consolidation of what has come to be known as Platonism, both as a set of dogmas and as a set of values and attitudes. I am excepting the founding father, Plato himself, of course. But then it should be noted that not everyone takes Plato to be a Platonist in this traditional sense.

What one gathers about Plotinus from overviews, philosophical dictionaries, book blurbs and the like are typically claims such as the following:

- Plotinus (AD 205–270) was an Egyptian philosopher, writing in Greek, who lived and worked in Rome.
- He was the founder of Neoplatonism.
- He maintained that there were three hypostases, the One, Intellect and Soul.
- Everything emanates from the One.
- The sensible world is a mere reflection of the intelligible one comprising the three hypostases.
- The One is beyond being, unthinkable and unknowable.
- A human being may, however, be unified with the One in a mystical union, an experience that transcends thought.
- The One is good, so are Intellect and Soul; matter is evil and so is everything that has a share in it.
- Though he claims to follow Plato, Plotinus' philosophy is really a mixture of Platonism, Aristotelianism and Stoicism, with some idiosyncratic features of its own.
- Plotinus' writings are called the *Enneads* and they were compiled by his student, Porphyry.
- Neoplatonism, the movement Plotinus started, was the dominant philosophy in late antiquity and deeply influenced early Christian and later Muslim and Judaic thinkers.
- Plotinus greatly inspired thinkers and artists of the Italian Renaissance.
- Plotinus is an extremely difficult author.

It will be our task in the chapters to come to explain, fill out, and in some cases modify or even correct these claims. And in so doing we shall have occasion to consider other aspects of Plotinus and his philosophy that do not appear on this list.

Porphyry, Plotinus' student who was just mentioned as the compiler of his works, actually edited Plotinus' treatises and gave them the form they have come down to us in. Not only did Porphyry prepare an edition, he prefaced this edition with a biography, *The Life of Plotinus and the Order of His Books*—a piece of some forty pages in a modern edition—where he, in addition to biographical material and some anecdotes, gives an account of the chronology of Plotinus' writings and the principles of his edition.[2] This biography is a quite remarkable source, not only for Plotinus and his life and writings but also for philosophy in the Roman Empire around this time. As is common with biographers, Porphyry may have had an agenda to portray Plotinus in a certain way, very favorably in fact. As we shall see, he subtly presents him so that he comes out as a kind of third-century Socrates. Some of the stories Porphyry relates about him show signs of superstition and are incredible. Despite this, *The Life of Plotinus* (hereafter *Life*) is a unique account by someone who personally knew his subject and the intellectual arena in which he worked. In what follows, I shall use the *Life* to introduce our main character and his works and also use it as a springboard to say something about the background to his thought.

1 Plotinus' life and personal traits

Porphyry indicates that Plotinus did not talk much about his early life. He knows that Plotinus was sixty-six years old when he died and calculates that he was born in the "thirteenth year of the reign of Severus," which means in AD 205 (*Life* 2, 36–37). The only incident from Plotinus' childhood that Porphyry was able to relate is his not giving up baring the breasts of his nurse for sucking till he was eight and had already started school (*Life* 3, 2–5). In his twenties Plotinus was in Alexandria, along with Athens the greatest intellectual center of the Roman Empire at the time. After searching around for a teacher, he met a certain Ammonius and was immediately convinced that this was the right man for him.

We do not know very much about Ammonius.[3] He left no writings and what later reports there are have questionable authority.[4] Even if committed to Platonism, he may well have been, as Karamanolis (2006: 196–215) argues, an independent thinker who sought the underlying truth behind texts, uninterested in school polemics. A reconciliatory attitude towards Aristotle, as Ammonius is reported to have had, fits well with this. Shadowy though he is, Ammonius must count as a significant figure in the history of philosophy: not only was he Plotinus' teacher, he also supposedly had as students two illustrious figures each named Origen—one pagan, the other Christian. The latter especially, was a very important early Christian thinker whom subsequent generations continued to discuss and use, even if some of his doctrines were stamped heretical.

Plotinus was twenty-eight years old when he came to Ammonius and stayed with him for eleven years. He "acquired so complete a training in philosophy that he became eager to make acquaintance with the philosophy of the Persians and that prevailing among the Indians" (Life 3, 14–17). In the pursuit of this Plotinus joined Emperor Gordian on an expedition against the Persians in 242. He did not, however, reach very far east for Gordian was killed by his own men in Mesopotamia. "Plotinus escaped with difficulty," Porphyry tells us in Life 3, 22, "and came safe to Antioch" (today on the Turkish coast close to the Syrian border). After this he settled in Rome and started a school there. We shall have a closer look at the school activities shortly.

Plotinus stayed in Rome almost for the rest of his life. He lived in the house of a woman, Gemina. He suffered for a long time from an illness or a set of illnesses. Porphyry says that he often suffered from a disease of the bowels. Whether related to this illness or not, in the end he developed several other symptoms, including ulcers, blindness and a disease of the throat which affected his voice (Life 2, 13–15). Porphyry says that he "had the habit of greeting everyone by a kiss" (Life 2, 17) and that for this reason towards the end of life his friends avoided meeting him such as his condition had become.[5] He retired to Campania for the last year or so of his life and died there in 270 at the age of sixty-six.

Porphyry does not tell us where Plotinus was born, who his parents were or what was his ethnic background. A later source, Eunapius, says that Plotinus came from Egypt and that his birthplace was Lyco (Eunapius, *Lives of the Sophists* 455). Another source, David, gives Lycopolis as his birthplace. This may be a town of that name in Upper Egypt. This information is somewhat suspect: it is hard to see what good evidence Eunapius and David may have had that isn't found in Porphyry's *Life* though it must be admitted that many possible sources, including much of Porphyry's writings, have been lost. What we have, however, points to Egypt as Plotinus' native land and nothing points against it.[6] Plotinus' name, however, is Roman and he wrote in Greek as was common practice among philosophers in the Roman Empire at the time. He was without doubt a very upper-class citizen. He joined the emperor on an expedition, as we have seen, and the latter's murder put him in danger. This may suggest a close affiliation with the emperor. In any case, in Rome Plotinus was an associate of people from high society. The emperor Gallienus and his wife, Salonina, were among his friends and admirers, and so were other prominent citizens, including several Roman senators (*Life* 7 and 12). All this suggests that he and his family were well connected with the Roman elite.

Porphyry tells an amusing story about Plotinus' friends who wanted to have his portrait made (*Life* 1, 4 ff.). Plotinus would not consider sitting for a painter or sculptor and responded to his student and friend, Amelius, who was urging him: "Why, really, is it not enough to have to carry the image in which nature has encased us, without your requesting me to agree to leave behind a longer lasting image of the image, as if it was something genuinely worth looking at?" In this remark there is an obvious allusion to Plato's rebuttal of imitative arts as imitations of an imitation in Book X of the *Republic*. Amelius did not give up, however. He had "Cartesius, the best painter of the time" (*Life* 1, 11–12) come to the meetings of the school, which were open to anyone, to study Plotinus' appearance and in the end he had an excellent portrait of Plotinus.

Porphyry portrays Plotinus as wise, mild and modest. He would nevertheless stand firm on what he believed correct and carry out his duties meticulously. Porphyry's aim in *The Life of Plotinus* is to create an impression of an other-worldly philosopher who, however, could deal with practical affairs with ease, wisdom and authority. Though Porphyry is eager to show his hero in a favorable light, there is no reason to doubt that Plotinus actually had these characteristics. There were many children in the house of Gemina because

> many men and women of the highest rank, on the approach of death, brought him their children, both boys and girls, and entrusted them to him along with all their property, considering that he would be a holy and god-like guardian ... He patiently attended to the accounts of their property ... and took care that they should be accurate ... Yet, though he shielded so many from the worries and cares of ordinary life, he never, while awake, relaxed his intent concentration upon the intellect. He was gentle, too, and at the disposal of all who had any sort of acquaintance with him.
>
> (Life 9, 18–20)

These personal characteristics were also evident in Plotinus' teaching:

> When he was speaking, his intellect visibly lit up his face: there was always a charm about his appearance, but at these times he was still more attractive to look at: he sweated gently, and kindliness shone out from him, and in answering questions he made clear both his benevolence and his intellectual rigor.
>
> (Life 13, 5–10)

Porphyry says that Plotinus had a surprising insight into character (Life 11). In support of this he relates an incident about the theft of a valuable necklace that had been stolen in the house. The slaves of the house were assembled before the eyes of Plotinus who looked at them, one by one, and finally pointed out one and said that this was the thief; this turned out to be quite correct, of course. A more serious incident he relates to prove his point about Plotinus' insight into character has to do with Porphyry himself. Porphyry tells that he had been depressed and was thinking of taking his own life. He had not told anyone about this but one day Plotinus visited him unexpectedly in his house and told him that "this lust for death did not come from a settled rational decision but from a bilious indisposition." And he "urged me to take a holiday," Porphyry says. Porphyry complied and travelled to Sicily and did not see Plotinus again. He adds that this cured him of his bleak thoughts.

Plotinus was above all a philosopher but he was not uninterested in other matters. Porphyry says that "he studied the rules of astronomy, without going very far into the mathematical side" (*Life* 15, 21–23) and that "no proposition of geometry, arithmetic, mechanics, optics and music escaped him but he was not disposed to apply himself to the details in these subjects" (*Life* 14, 7–10). This fits the impression we get from the *Enneads*: Plotinus shows some interest in scientific knowledge and there is ample indication that he is well informed by the standards of his time, but he does not discuss other sciences in detail. He showed an interest in astrology and divination and studied the methods of the casters of horoscopes but became very critical of them and "did not hesitate to attack many of the statements made in their writings" (*Life* 15, 25–26). Still, the *Enneads* show that he had a reserved belief in both divination and magic (see IV.4.30–45).

2 Plotinus the philosopher and teacher

Porphyry calls Plotinus "a master" (*didaskalos*) and frequently talks about "lectures" (*diatribai*) and seminars (*synousiai*) in the *Life*.[7] Clearly, school-like activities took place over an extended period. Yet, for reasons that we shall see there is some doubt that Plotinus' institution in Rome fully qualifies as a school. Porphyry never uses that word for it. I shall, however, stick to custom and talk about Plotinus' school.

It seems that the school was open to anyone (*Life* 1, 13–14) and many of those attending were enthusiastic amateurs rather than people wishing to become professional philosophers. Porphyry distinguishes between hearers (*akroatai*), who he says were many, and followers (*zēlōtai*), who were brought together by enthusiasm for philosophy (*Life* 7, 1–2). Porphyry gives an account of the latter group which included three medical men, three senators, a poet and a banker. It seems that these were followers in the sense of opting for a philosophical way of life rather seeking to become real philosophers (see Goulet-Cazé 1982: 234–236). He mentions three women too, which shows that the school was not a "men only" club: Gemina, in whose house Plotinus lived and kept his school, her daughter by the same name and Amphicleia, who later married the son of the philosopher Iamblichus. All three women were greatly devoted to Plotinus and to philosophy (*Life* 9, 1–5). Only three followers are mentioned, however, who can be called professional philosophers: Amelius, Porphyry himself and the medical man Eustochius. Amelius and Porphyry had both received a philosophical education before they came to Plotinus and were quite mature when they converted to his version of Platonism. Amelius was Plotinus' close associate in the school almost from the start, whereas Porphyry, after receiving a thorough education from Longinus in Athens, came to him in 263, when Plotinus had been teaching in Rome for almost twenty years. Eustochius attended Plotinus in Campania during his terminal illness. Porphyry says about him that he came to know Plotinus late but "acquired the character of a genuine philosopher." The composition and nature of Plotinus' audience suggest that his lectures and seminars were not, or at least not primarily, intended as philosophical education for future professionals.

Porphyry reports that there were in Plotinus' time "Christians and others, and sectarians who had abandoned the old philosophy" (*Life* 16, 1–2). He goes on to list the schools these people adhered to and authors they held in high regard. Porphyry does not say so directly but the fact that Plotinus refers to some with a weakness for Gnostic views as his friends (II.9.10, 3) indicates that such people attended the meetings of the school. The people Porphyry speaks of here were indeed Gnostics, to whom I shall briefly return later in this chapter. Plotinus "often attacked their position in his lectures, and wrote the treatise to which we have given the title 'Against the Gnostics.'" He urged Porphyry and Amelius to follow suit and the latter "went to forty volumes in writing against the book of Zostrianus" (*Life* 16, 12–14). Both Porphyry and Amelius were prolific writers; all of the latter's and much of the former's work are lost.

Only after ten years of teaching did Plotinus "start writing on the subjects that came up" (*Life* 4, 10–11). This presumably means "came up in the meetings of the school." Given that his treatises reflect his lectures, we must suppose that they had been fairly advanced: Plotinus' treatises are hardly stuff for beginners. This is somewhat surprising in light of the fact that the audience, as we have seen, consisted mostly of enthusiastic amateurs. Presumably, the writings do not reflect the lectures very directly.

Porphyry tells an interesting story about a visit in the school by a certain Thaumasius (*Life* 13, 10–17). At the time of the visit, Porphyry had been questioning Plotinus for three days about the soul's presence to the body. Thaumasius wished to hear a more general lecture apt to be published and couldn't bear listening to Porphyry's questions and answers. Plotinus responded that if he couldn't resolve Porphyry's questions, he wouldn't have anything to put into the treatise. This and other remarks suggest that in his teaching Plotinus resembled Socrates in fostering open philosophical discussions. He was very far from the magisterial professor type. Porphyry's account of this indicates that Plotinus may have been rather unconventional by the standards of the times.

According to Porphyry, Plotinus' manner of writing was more than a little unusual and his account is worth quoting in full:

> When Plotinus had written anything, he could never bear to go over it twice; even to read it through once was too much for him, as his eyesight did not serve him well for reading. In writing he did not form the syllables correctly, and he paid no attention to spelling. He was wholly concerned with thought; and, which surprised us all, he went on this way right up to the end. He worked out his train of thought from beginning to end in his own mind, and then, when he wrote it down, he wrote as continuously as if he was copying from a book.
>
> (*Life* 8, 1–8)

In light of this and the previous quote from Porphyry, it is perhaps no wonder that Plotinus is considered a difficult author. Even in antiquity, complaints were raised about his writings. One of the most noted philosophical contemporaries of Plotinus, Longinus of Athens, had received copies of some of Plotinus' works from Amelius and complained that Amelius had not corrected the scribes' mistakes. He evidently didn't realize that the copies were accurate and faithfully preserved what Plotinus himself had written (*Life* 19–20). We do not have to rely on the judgment of the ancients on the question of Plotinus' style: we have got his writings. As a matter of fact, it is easy to agree with Porphyry that Plotinus is concise and, so to say, "abounds more in ideas than in words" (*Life* 14, 2). His style is often extremely compact and even elliptical. Sometimes it is unclear what Plotinus' pronouns refer to in the context. The "tone of rapt inspiration" mentioned by Porphyry is also easily recognizable. Such a tone is, however, not a general trademark but on occasion Plotinus bursts into an elevated language of excitement, even exclamations. Porphyry's statement that Plotinus wrote continuously from his mind and did not even read through what he had written, though perhaps somewhat exaggerated, rings true as well. One often gets the feeling of being confronted with a piece of writing that could benefit from a little polish.

Am I not just evading the conclusion: "The *Enneads* of Plotinus are really a collection of poorly connected incomprehensible sentences with occasional fits of frenzy?" Not at all. Actually, Plotinus' thought and writings are usually quite structured, though little aid is given to the reader for detecting the structure. Introductory or bridging remarks are used sparingly. Most of the time, however, he is either considering a specific question from different angles or arguing for a specific claim, sometimes with excursions into related topics in passing. Moreover, his arguments are often quite powerful but they tend to be very concisely stated, not spelled out at all with explicitly stated premises, inferences and conclusions. Much work is left to the reader.

Even if his writings may indeed be said to be unpolished, Plotinus can write quite beautifully. Perhaps it is connected with the way he wrote that his style is agreeably personal and unaffected. We get an impression of someone who sincerely cares about the issues he writes about and has thought deeply about them. Moreover, when we read Plotinus we easily come to believe that the thoughts are being recorded as they occurred in the thinker's mind, unembellished and unedited. This is undeniably charming and works surprisingly well most of the time. But if it is indeed the case that the *Enneads* record thoughts more directly than is usual with writings, Plotinus' mind must have been quite orderly.

Porphyry is aware of the fact that Plotinus is in danger of being unfairly and fallaciously judged. Many remarks in the *Life* are clearly intended to prevent and to pre-empt such accusations. Porphyry's strategy, which is on the whole quite successful, is to show an understanding of why such misperceptions of Plotinus might arise and at the same time to explain them or even turn the grounds for them into Plotinus' credit. The account of the manner of his writing is to be seen in this light. In the *Life* he cites long passages from his former teacher Longinus, a highly respected scholar, and also a former student of Ammonius Saccas, where he shows how Longinus at first failed to understand Plotinus and then came to appreciate his philosophy deeply, even though he didn't convert to it. The implication clearly is that Plotinus is difficult but very much worth the effort—a judgment that is still valid. Similarly, Porphyry addresses and seeks to dispel rumors spread by some people from Greece when Plotinus started teaching that he was plagiarizing Numenius, a slightly earlier (second–third centuries AD) Platonist/Pythagorean philosopher. In response to this, Amelius wrote a book entitled *On the Difference between the Doctrines of Plotinus and Numenius*. Much of Numenius is lost but we do have a number of fragments. There is indeed a resemblance in that Numenius, like Plotinus, posits three divine principles, the Good or Intellect, a second intellect and the cosmos. These are, however, not the same as Plotinus' principles and so far as the evidence permits us to judge, Amelius and Porphyry, who knew Numenius' works in and out, were quite right in objecting to this charge. Longinus, cited by Porphyry, concurs (*Life* 21, 1–9).

3 The *Enneads*

According to Porphyry, Plotinus entrusted him with the arrangement and editing of his treatises (*Life* 7, 50–51; 24, 2–3), which Porphyry did but not until about thirty years after Plotinus' death. This edition, the *Enneads*, is essentially what is preserved of Plotinus and presumably contains everything he wrote.[8] Excepting philosophical commentaries, this is one of the largest corpuses we have of any ancient philosopher (approximately 1,000 pages in an average book in translation) and one of very few that can be said to be complete (Plato is another and also larger). The Aristotelian corpus is much larger but it is not complete: Aristotle's dialogues are for instance missing.

Porphyry arranged the treatises according to subject matter into six sets of nine treatises, i.e. six "enneads" (an "ennead" is a set of nine), and gave them the titles they still bear. Porphyry counts fifty-four treatises. That does not mean that Plotinus actually wrote fifty-four treatises. Porphyry arrives at this number, which he finds pleasing for numerological reasons (Life 24, 14)—54 = $3^3 \times 2$ or 6×3^2—by splitting several treatises. The treatises Porphyry cut into parts are mostly consecutive in the Enneads. One treatise is, however, actually split into four, which ended up in three different Enneads, each with a different title.

The Life is written as a kind of introduction to this edition. As noted above, Plotinus had been teaching for several years in Rome and was approaching fifty when he began to write. When Porphyry comes to him, Plotinus is fifty-nine years old and has written twenty-one treatises. During the six years Porphyry stayed with him, he wrote another twenty-four. And after Porphyry had left, he wrote nine more, in all fifty-four treatises. Porphyry actually gives us the chronology of all the treatises (Life 4–6). He also offers an evaluation of the three writing periods: those treatises Plotinus had written before he came "show a slighter capacity," those he wrote while he, Porphyry, stayed with him "reveal the power of his height," while those he wrote after Porphyry left "were written when his power was already failing" (for this division into three epochs see Life 4–6). While the early treatises are arguably in general simpler and easier to follow than the middle and late ones, it is impossible to agree with this assessment by Porphyry, who seems to be guilty of a little conceit here. Some of the late treatises must count among Plotinus' philosophically best. The Enneads were written during Plotinus' last seventeen years or so. He started writing late in his life when he must have been quite mature in his thought. We should not expect a drastic change of view nor is there one to be seen.

The Enneads are supposed to be thematic, starting from the less difficult subjects and proceeding to the more difficult (Life 25). Thus, the first Ennead contains mostly treatises dealing with ethical matters—Porphyry evidently thought that this is an easier subject than cosmology or metaphysics. In the second and the third the physical universe is in the limelight. In the fourth, the soul is the focus of attention and in the fifth Intellect and the One. Porphyry doesn't give us a theme for the sixth Ennead; in several but not all of the treatises in this Ennead the One (or the Good), Plotinus' first principle, is extensively discussed. Porphyry didn't have an easy task with a thematic division of the *Enneads*, because quite typically Plotinus has things to say about several levels of reality in each of them.

The treatises vary greatly in length. Several are less than ten pages. These often deal with one specific question or topic, e.g. I.9, "On going out of the body" (about whether suicide is legitimate; a little over one page), and II.8, "On sight, or how distant objects appear small" (four and half pages in Armstrong's translation), but large topics also sometimes receive a cursory treatment: the two treatises called "On the essence of soul (I) and (II)," IV.1. (21) and IV.2. (4), are short, one and six pages respectively. Other treatises are very long: the one that Porphyry cut into four is altogether about 100 pages, and "On the problems of soul (I), (II) and (III)," IV.3–5. (27–29) is about 140.

It is difficult to single out some treatises as the most important ones. Any shortlist made leaves one with a bad conscience on account of what is left out. I shall, however, venture to present a list here. Others would no doubt make a different selection.

The very first treatise of the *Enneads* but chronologically late is "What is the living being and what is man?," I.1. (53). It may be the best presentation of the essentials of human psychology and it contains the fullest account Plotinus' notion of the self.

"On beauty," I.6, is Plotinus' earliest treatise. Here he discusses beauty, both sensible and intelligible. It should be read together with V.8, "On the intelligible beauty." "On beauty" is no doubt Plotinus' best-known treatise. It has had a great impact in aesthetics and inspired many artists and poets, including Michelangelo and Goethe.

The treatises "On virtues," I.2. (19) and "On happiness," I.4. (46) are Plotinus' most important ethical treatises. In the former he presents his doctrine of grades of virtue, which came to be very influential, and in the latter he offers his views on the nature of happiness and describes the character of the sage, his ideal human being.

In I.8. (51), "On what are and whence come evils" Plotinus argues for his radical and somewhat paradoxical doctrine about matter as at once absolute evil and formlessness, in a sense nothing. This doctrine was highly controversial already in antiquity. His views on the nature of matter are also expounded in two other significant treatises, "On matter," II.4. (12), and "On the impassibility of things without body," III.6. (26). The first five chapters of the latter treatise also contain an account of the emotions and their relation to the soul. They partly cover the same topics as I.1.

The treatises or, better, treatise—Porphyry cut it in two—"On providence (I) and (II)," III.2–3. (47–48), contain Plotinus' views on providence—a very traditional topic in Greek philosophy. Though lacking in clear organization, this treatise vividly expounds Plotinus' theodicy, which, as we shall see, is interesting for several reasons.

"On eternity and time," III.7. (45), gives Plotinus' most systematic and detailed account of the topics referred to in the title and contains a critique of Stoic and Aristotelian views on time. His own view is an elegant and philosophically sharp interpretation of Plato's account in the Timaeus, which holds time to be an image of eternity.

The treatise called "On nature and contemplation and the One," III.8. (30), is the first part of what has been called the Großschrift. That is the Plotinian treatise mentioned above which Porphyry split into four and spread out in different Enneads. The others are "On the intelligible beauty," V.8. (31), "That the intelligibles are not outside Intellect, and on the Good," V.5. (32), and "Against the Gnostics," II.9. (33). Each of these "treatises" would, I think, be on anybody's list of Plotinus' important treatises and taken as a whole the Großschrift contains most of Plotinus' characteristic doctrines and views. The previous parts all build up to the last one where Plotinus directly addresses and attacks the Gnostics' doctrines, in particular their totally negative view of this world.

Another long treatise is Ennead IV.3–5. (27–29), "On the problems of soul (I), (II) and (III)." This treatise deals with soul in general. There are parts containing crucial information about Plotinus' views on human psychology, sense-perception and memory, for instance, but the focus of the work is not limited to that. It is the status and system of souls in the universe that Plotinus discusses here.

The treatises "On the three primary hypostases," V.1. (10), and "On Intellect, the Forms and being," V.9. (5), are early. Each of them contains important information about Plotinus' doctrine of the intelligible realm. Moreover, these treatises are, for the most part, relatively easy reading and as such not a bad start for the Plotinus reader.

"On the cognitive hypostases and what is beyond," V.3. (49), and "How the multitude of the Forms came into being, and on the Good," VI.7. (38), are treatises where Plotinus among other things expounds his views on the relationship between the One and Intellect and the nature of Intellect. These treatises are not an easy read but they contain Plotinus' metaphysical thought at its best.

"On the kinds of being (I), (II) and (III)," VI.1–3. (42–44), yet another split treatise, can be said to have being as its topic, both intelligible and sensible. The first, VI.1, is a critical discussion of Aristotle's doctrine of categories, which Plotinus took to be about the kinds of being, and of Stoic categories. The second is Plotinus' positive doctrine of being based on Plato's *Sophist*, and the third a kind of revised Aristotelian doctrine as a theory of sensible being.

The treatise "On the presence of being, one and the same, everywhere as a whole (I) and (II)," VI.4–5. (22–23), contains Plotinus' most penetrating account of the relationship between the two realms, the sensible and the intelligible.

"On autonomy and the will of the One," VI.8. (39), is for several reasons among the most remarkable treatises. Here Plotinus gives an account of human autonomy and discloses his views on what we would have to say about the One, if we could speak about it, which, as a matter of fact, we cannot.

Finally, "On the Good or the One," VI.9. (9), is like V.1 and V.9 an early treatise and relatively simple. It is the first extensive treatment of the first principle, and is a natural place to start for readers who wish to acquaint themselves with his views on that topic.

4 The background to Plotinus' philosophy I: Pre-Plotinian Platonism

Even if we really know better, in our imagination classical antiquity tends to shrink into relatively short periods of Athenian and Roman greatness. We are liable to forget, for instance, that the first recorded Greek philosopher, Thales, lived in the late seventh and early sixth century BC; and Emperor Justinian closed the pagan schools in Athens in AD 529—an event often used to mark the end of classical ancient philosophy.[9] This span of continuous Greek philosophical activity is longer than that which separates us from William the Conqueror (1027–1087) or such arch-medieval thinkers as St. Anselm of Canterbury (d. 1109). A lot happened in philosophy during these 1,100 years.

We can, crudely, divide this span up into five periods: the pre-Socratic period from about 600 to 450 BC, followed by the classical period with Socrates, Protagoras, Plato and Aristotle as the main agents till about 320 BC. After the conquests of Alexander the Great we speak about the Hellenistic period. During this time the Epicureans and Stoics enter the scene and eventually skeptics of different sorts. These schools, especially the Stoics, became very influential in the first centuries of the Roman era but are fading out by Plotinus' time. Additionally, there is the so-called Middle Platonism, which is the Platonic philosophy of the last three centuries before Plotinus, coexisting with the Hellenistic schools. There were Aristotelians too. Given Aristotle's great impact in the high Middle Ages and his relevance and fame still today, it may be hard for us to imagine that his was not a very major school of philosophical thought in antiquity. There were followers, to be sure, but by no means as many or as influential as the Stoics and Platonists. There was, however, a revival of Aristotelianism in the second century AD with Alexander of Aphrodisias as a major protagonist. In the fifth period, there is Neoplatonism, the philosophy that dominated late antiquity and of which Plotinus is said to be the founder. The kind of systematic Platonism characteristic of Neoplatonism was already under way with some of the Middle Platonists before Plotinus' time.[10] Even if Plotinus is original in several respects there is no clear breach with the previous Platonic tradition and at the time he surely did not suppose he was starting something "Neo."

Plotinus knows the previous philosophical tradition. Plato has indeed a privileged status for him but other thinkers make an appearance (often unnamed) in various ways: some appear as adversaries, others he uses to develop his own thought. It actually happens that the same ones are used and criticized, e.g. Aristotelians and Stoics. Naturally, fellow Platonists and especially the above-mentioned Middle Platonists, who are closest to Plotinus in time, are the philosophers he has most in common with. Let us, therefore, have a brief account of Platonism in antiquity with a special focus on the Middle Platonists.

Philosophy claiming Platonic lineage has a curious history. When we consider the nature of Plato's own writings, this is perhaps not so surprising. On one reading, Plato is primarily a metaphysician, who lays down definite theories about the world we see as a mere reflection of another world of everlasting, unchangeable Ideas. The former is the sphere of volatile, unreliable sense-perception and opinion, whereas the latter is the sphere of secure knowledge, which is attainable for human beings through ardent scientific and ultimately philosophical training. Plato uses this foundation to erect theories about human beings and society, the basic idea being that we should both as individuals and in society seek to imitate the perfection of the world above to the extent the materials allow. On the other hand, we might note that Plato's main philosophical hero, Socrates, claims to be ignorant and that moreover, this is reported with apparent approval by Plato himself, e.g. in *Socrates' Apology*. We might note too that Plato wrote dialogues and never, if we disregard the letters whose authenticity was questioned already in antiquity, speaks in his own name. In addition, it may be noted that even the metaphysical Plato with Socrates or someone else as a mouthpiece is full of caveats about the views put forth, views which in any case are by no means in perfect harmony with one another from dialogue to dialogue.

The first generations of headmasters in the Academy after Plato (427–347), starting with Plato's nephew, Speusippus, followed the metaphysical Plato with grand theories about the visible universe, the principles behind it and their application to human concerns. Then, from the headmastership of a certain Archesilaus (c.316–241) on, the Academy came to be dominated by people who admired the searching, probing, Socratic Plato who was very hesitant to put down definite doctrines except with all sorts of caveats. These people, of whom Carneades (c.214–129) is the most illustrious, actually turned Plato's Academy into a bastion of skepticism. After Philo of Larissa (c.159–84 BC), who softened the skepticism of his predecessors, one branch of diehard skeptics, no longer tied to the Academy, gave rise to so-called Pyrrhonian skepticism, which in most ways continued the radical skepticism of Archesilaus and Carneades. Sextus Empiricus (second–third centuries AD, thus nearly Plotinus' contemporary) was a Pyrrhonist who records much about earlier ancient skepticism in writings that have come down to us. Through them and Cicero's *Academica*, which reports on skepticism in the Academy, we are relatively well informed about ancient skepticism. At first sight, one might think that skepticism, whether

Academic or Pyrrhonist, is quite antithetical to Plotinus' thought. As we shall see in later chapters, however, there are certain features of Plotinus' thought that may be best understood as a reaction to and a defense against skeptical arguments such as those presented by Sextus. There is indeed an affinity between Platonism and skepticism especially as regards claims to knowledge of the sensible world.

The word "Middle Platonist" is a label given to various Platonist thinkers in different places in the Roman Empire from Antiochus of Ascalon (c.125–c.68) to Plotinus. They are as one might expect a very mixed bunch, although there are certain common trends. They emphasize the existence of a non-physical level of reality, the human soul's affinity with this non-physical level, and the immortality of the soul. What we often see happening in these thinkers are attempts at systematizing Plato: the goal was to make Plato's philosophy appear as a coherent body of doctrines comparable to contemporary systematic schools. Since Plato wrote dialogues and never presented his whole system, if he had one, Platonists were faced with the formidable task of constructing one out of bits and pieces in Plato. They would of course do so using the current philosophical language of their own time, which might include Stoic and Aristotelian notions. And they were liable to look to either of these schools for support of what they perceived to be the true Platonic point of view, seeing aspects of Aristotelian and Stoic doctrines as developments or explications of what is latent in Plato. Some, however, would take a firm anti-Aristotelian stance, such as Numenius and especially Atticus—both studied in Plotinus' school. Others such as Alcinous, the author of the extant *Handbook of Platonism*, adopt a dose of Aristotelianism both in doctrine and vocabulary.

The Middle Platonists emphasize other aspects of Plato and sometimes interpret him differently than is customary today. The importance of Plato's *Timaeus* for them cannot be overemphasized. This work was very central to the Middle and Neoplatonists—the central work, one might almost say. In the barest outline: Plato describes here, in the form of a myth, the creation of the world and the principles behind this creation; a supreme, benevolent divine mind, the so-called divine Craftsman or Demiurge, imitates the eternal Platonic Ideas to create the World-Soul and other souls according to mathematical principles, and finally makes an orderly, visible, ensouled cosmos out of a pre-existing chaos. The result is as good as anything generated can be, because *aphthonos ho theos*, "the god is ungrudging."

The Middle Platonists faced the task of demythologizing this account, fitting it into what they saw as Plato's doctrines elsewhere and dressing it in respectable philosophical language. And as might be expected, they did not agree on how to do this: for instance, on the crucial point of whether to understand the creation aspect literally and hence as implying a temporal beginning of the world, some thought it did, others not. Plotinus did not believe in a temporal beginning of the world and evidently took this aspect of the story to be due to its mythical form and not to be interpreted literally. As we will have occasion to note every now and then in subsequent chapters, the *Timaeus* is deeply ingrained in Plotinus' thought.

In the Middle Platonic period, some Platonists saw themselves as Pythagoreans as well as Platonists or even saw Plato as a follower of Pythagoras. The latter is for instance the view of Numenius (cf. fr. 24, 57–60). That Plato had a certain affinity with the Pythagoreans is in fact obvious and is asserted by Aristotle. Here the term "Pythagoreans," rather than Pythagoras should be emphasized: we do not know to what extent the doctrines attributed to Pythagoras actually were held by him. The scholars of the field generally ascribe them to later generations of followers rather than the master himself. The Pythagoreanizing Platonists are notable for having interpreted the second part of Plato's *Parmenides* as a piece of pure metaphysics.[11] As we shall see, Plotinus adopts the same interpretation. This is quite significant for the whole of his thought and for posterity: we have here the germs of what later came to be called the *via negativa* or negative theology. More on this later (see Chapter 3, p. 80). Even if Plotinus is unquestionably entitled to the claim of being the first metaphysical monist in the history of philosophy in the sense of being the first thinker to present an elaborate philosophical theory of a first principle and to derive from it absolutely everything, neo-Pythagorean Platonists may have been precursors in this regard (see Dodds 1928 and Dillon 1977: 342–383). A passage citing Porphyry, preserved by Simplicius' commentary on Aristotle's *Physics* IX, 230, 34 ff., ascribes to the neo-Pythagorean Moderatus (first century AD) a scheme of hypostases that closely resembles Plotinus' and which, moreover, is monistic in the sense that everything, including matter, derives from the One. It is debated, however, to what extent this passage reflects Porphyry's own views or Simplicius'. Hubler (2010) argues persuasively that the evidence of this passage—the only passage that may give support to a pre-Plotinian doctrine of the One—has been highly overrated.

Mention should be made of what John Dillon (1977: 384), a leading scholar of this period, has called the Platonic Underworld: Gnosticism and Hermeticism. These are Platonistically inspired quasi-religious movements. The texts that have come down to us often exhibit a blend of mythological and philosophical forms of presentation. The Gnostics believed that the world was an evil or failed creation in which the human soul, which is of divine origin, is trapped. Salvation is, however, possible through esoteric, spiritual knowledge (*gnōsis*) of higher divinities. As noted above, Christians and Gnostics are mentioned among Plotinus' listeners in Rome (Life 16)—perhaps the Christians he speaks of were of the Gnostic variety. Plotinus wrote against the Gnostics in a harsher tone than he is wont to use. He resented their absolute rejection of the goodness of the sensible world and accused them of fabrication and confusion. This Platonic Underworld, which thrived in Plotinus' environment in Alexandria and apparently in Rome too, may however be quite relevant as "background music" in his philosophical formation. Such a background can have considerable effects, even if it is impossible to pin them down exactly.

The only writings Porphyry explicitly mentions as subjects of study in Plotinus' school are commentaries on Plato and Aristotle by the Middle Platonists/Pythagoreans and Aristotelians. He does not mention Plato's or Aristotle's texts as being directly studied in Plotinus' seminars. Presumably, however, this goes without saying: what would be the point of studying a commentator in the absence of the primary text? We know that Plotinus did in fact write a substantial critique, which is a kind of commentary, on Aristotle's *Categories* (VI.1.1–24). In any case, there is no hint that Porphyry holds his list to be exhaustive of what was read in Plotinus' school.

Despite the use of commentaries, neither Plotinus' writings nor his teaching took the form of a commentary: "he did not just speak straight out of these books [the works of the commentators that have been mentioned] but took a distinctive personal line in his consideration," says Porphyry (*Life* 14, 14–16). Plotinus is most of the time dealing with what he perceives as substantial philosophical questions. He evidently believed that for answering such questions the correct understanding of the tradition, Plato in particular, is necessary. Even where there clearly is a Platonic text underlying the discussion—*Timaeus* 35a on the constitution of the soul is for instance pervasive—Plotinus' treatment is not exegetical, except in a much extended sense of exegesis.

However, he occasionally argues against a particular interpretation of a Platonic passage or remark. For example, the first eight chapters of the large treatise "On the problems of soul (I), (II) and (III)" (IV.1–3) are an attempt to solve the question in which sense our souls come from that of the world, as Plato says in *Philebus* 30a. In dealing with this Plotinus argues against what he considers an incorrect (Stoic?) conception of the relation between our souls and that of the world. Perhaps such a view was expressed in a commentary or other kind of writing that was read in a seminar in the school. It is typical, however, that the bulk of the discussion of the question is philosophical rather than exegetical. Not only are the Stoics and Aristotle's *Metaphysics* hidden in the *Enneads*, Plato is fairly hidden too. There are many short Platonic citations and allusions that easily escape the notice even of readers well versed in Plato.

5 The background to Plotinus' philosophy II: Plato, Aristotle and the Stoics

Let us now again turn to Porphyry's *Life* and the *Enneads* themselves for what we can find about Plotinus' relation to the main authors and schools before him. He was well versed in previous Greek philosophy generally. Plato and Aristotle, and the previous interpretations of them, he evidently knew in depth. He does not, however, mention many names: Plato is mentioned by name fifty-six times in the *Enneads*, Aristotle four times, other predecessors even less often. Frequently he refers to some unnamed "they" who he is arguing against. Depending on context, these may be the Aristotelians, Stoics or Platonists he disagrees with. Strangely, Porphyry says nothing directly about Plotinus' relation to Plato;

perhaps this was for him a matter too obvious to discuss. Plotinus himself, however, has this to say:

> And [it follows] that these statements of ours [about the three hypostases, the One, Intellect and Soul] are not new; they do not belong to the present time, but were made long ago, not explicitly, and what we have said in this discussion has been an interpretation of them, relying on Plato's own writings for evidence that these views are ancient.
> (V.1.8, 10–14)

The point Plotinus is making here regards the doctrine of the three hypostases, which he claims to have Platonic authority for. I shall have more to say about this in the chapters to come. His remark here that this doctrine is not explicit reveals a general trend in his attitude towards Plato: just like Ammonius was said to have done, Plotinus seeks to go under the surface and elicit the true philosophical content of the text. The result sometimes looks far-fetched and implausible from the viewpoint of contemporary Plato scholarship, at other times, more often than not, in fact, Plotinus' interpretations deserve serious attention. We shall see examples of this in the following chapters.

The authoritative modern edition of the *Enneads* by Paul Henry and Hans-Rudolf Schwyzer has an *index fontium* (index of sources) at the end of the third and last volume, a list of passages of previous authors cited or alluded to by Plotinus. A glance at this index shows indeed that, of Plato's works, the *Timaeus* and the *Parmenides* are much cited, especially the former. This is in accordance with Middle Platonic attitudes. It would not be a great exaggeration to say that Plotinus' interpretation of these two dialogues yields the essentials of his whole philosophy. Other often-cited dialogues are the *Phaedrus*, *Republic*, *Phaedo*, *Philebus*, *Laws*, *Sophist* and *Symposium*. We cannot go into the details of the actual use Plotinus makes of these texts without accounting for his own thought in a systematic way. That task lies ahead of us and I shall have occasion to remark on Plotinus' understanding of some of these texts in later chapters.

We may note, however, that if we look closer and see which Platonic passages Plotinus uses and for what purposes, we discover that metaphysical passages or passages taken to have metaphysical import predominate: Republic VI, 509a–b on the Idea of the Good and Phaedrus 45c on the soul's self-motion are, for instance, cited a great number of times. It has been said that Plotinus is Plato without Socrates (Bröcker 1966). Now, it is true that Socrates was first and foremost interested in ethical questions. Plotinus is not uninterested in ethics. He wrote, for instance, a treatise on the virtues, two treatises on happiness and a great deal in several treatises on the nature of evil. One could even say that his whole metaphysics is value-laden—it is no coincidence that the first principle, the One, is also called "the Good" and that the lowest opposite principle, matter, is evil. However, on reading his ethical treatises we soon see that this interest leaves out one central aspect of Socrates' and in fact Plato's ethical concerns: the notion of justice. As a philosopher Plotinus took little interest in justice as a virtue governing interpersonal relationships or the set-up of society. Porphyry's Life suggests that as a person Plotinus was indeed quite concerned with being just but this did not motivate him philosophically. One might speculate that he lived in such an environment and had by formation become such that questions relating to interpersonal relationships or possible reforms of society that so engaged Plato didn't appeal to him intellectually. Presumably that is so. It should be noted, however, that in this Plotinus differs in no way from his Platonic predecessors and successors. Such topics were not what preoccupied philosophers at the time. His philosophical-ethical interests lie elsewhere.

Right after mentioning Plotinus' "tone of rapt inspiration" in Life 14 (see p. 17), Porphyry asserts that "[Plotinus] states what he himself really feels about the matter [at hand] and not what has been handed down by tradition. His writings, however, are full of concealed Stoic and Peripatetic [i.e. Aristotelian] doctrines. Aristotle's Metaphysics, in particular, is concentrated in them." The index fontium indeed contains many references to Aristotle's Metaphysics and quite a few to other works of his and to the Stoics.

Many of us were taught that Aristotle is an antithesis of Plato: whereas the latter was a rationalist believing in a world of which the sphere of the senses is but a shadow, the former was an empiricist of sorts for whom the physical world is fully real. Contemporary scholarship generally rejects such a simple picture of their relationship. Few, however, maintain that Plato and Aristotle are in complete agreement. As was noted above, there were Platonists before Plotinus on whom Aristotle or his school made a distinct impact, and the Neoplatonists from Porphyry on generally took Plato and Aristotle to be in agreement.[12] Plotinus adopts a great deal of Aristotelian vocabulary: "substance" (*ousia*) and "attribute" ("accident," *kata symbebēkōs*), "forms" (*eidē*) (of bodies and in the soul); "power" ("potentiality," "potency," "faculty," *dynamis*) and "act" ("activity," "actuality," *energeia*); divisions of psychological faculties into "rational," "perceptive" and "vegetative." And there are various others. This does not necessarily indicate that he picked such terms directly from Aristotle's writings. In most cases they were probably already part of the school jargon and in any case he uses them to express Platonic rather than Aristotelian views.

Some of Plotinus' views, however, reflect a direct use of Aristotle: aspects of his psychology and his views on the divine Intellect in particular. It seems fair to say that he interprets the *Timaeus* myth about the divine Craftsman and his vision of the realm of Ideas with the help of Aristotle's account of the divine mind as expressed in *Metaphysics* XII and what he says about the active intellect in *On the Soul* III. Again, further discussion must be postponed until later chapters.

We should not conclude from this that Plotinus considered Plato and Aristotle to be in perfect agreement. His attitude towards Aristotle is ambivalent. As already noted, he wrote a very critical account—a kind of commentary—on Aristotle's *Categories*, mentioned above, and on several occasions he explicitly rejects or distances himself from well-known Aristotelian views such as Aristotle's hylomorphism of the soul–body relation and the view that the first principle of everything is an intellect.

As already noted, Porphyry also says the *Enneads* contain a lot of Stoicism. The Stoics were materialists believing that everything that exists is a body. Plotinus, of course, didn't concur; in fact he strongly opposes such views, e.g. in IV.7, "On the immortality of the soul," and in IV.2, "On the essence of soul." On occasion he argues explicitly against the Stoic views. It is, however, not these anti-Stoic passages that Porphyry has in mind in his remark. Rather, this is Porphyry, the historian of philosophy,[13] noting Stoic influences on Plotinus' thought. One thing is beyond any doubt in this connection: Plotinus' use of the notion of *logos* ("rational formula") shows a clear influence of Stoicism. The Stoics thought that God is *logos* in the sense of a rational principle or rational formula that governs the cosmos and every part and detail in it. The *logos* in Stoicism is an internal, constitutive principle, bringing order, harmony and reason into the world. The Stoics believed that the world's rational behavior is determined by immanent *logoi* (plural of *logos*) which are a part of God, God carrying out his plans for the world, in fact.[14] The Stoic *logos* is, however, a physical phenomenon—hot air, *pneuma*, in fact. In Plotinus there is a pervasive use of *logos* as a causal principle that bears a great resemblance to the Stoic concept and is without doubt a Stoic import, though Plotinus naturally rejects its corporeal basis. Also in the sphere of ethics—the denial of external goods and evils, the character of the sage, the nature of providence—Plotinus is clearly under Stoic influence. The actual views in question may in all cases be in agreement with passages in Plato but it is evident that Plotinus expresses them with a Stoic slant.[15]

Some scholars of Plotinus see widespread dematerialization of Stoic concepts going on in the *Enneads*: they see Plotinus as taking Stoic notions and patterns, which for the Stoics are physical phenomena, and giving them an immaterial, spiritual interpretation in harmony with his Platonist leanings.[16] There may be something to this but the matter is hard to judge, one reason being that Plotinus' language is generally much more Platonic–Aristotelian than Stoic, another that the Stoics themselves owe a great deal to Plato and Aristotle, a third that our information about Stoic theory is quite fragmentary. It seems fair to say, however, that Plotinus is liable to sway his Platonic and Aristotelian material in the direction of Stoic patterns, though definitely without the Stoics' materialism. Nevertheless, it is hard to see Plotinus consciously adopting a Stoic line.

6 Plotinus' originality

Looking again at Henry and Schwyzer's index of sources, we see that Plotinus in fact not only cites Plato, Aristotle and their commentators, most of the important pre-Socratics such as Parmenides, Heraclitus and Anaxagoras are there as well. Though a Platonist, he actually appropriates much of previous Greek philosophy into his thought in one way or another. He has this great, long tradition at his disposal. He at once comments on it, uses it and takes it further in innovative ways. The most innovative aspect is presumably Plotinus' doctrine of the One—the necessary first principle of everything, which is "beyond being" and beyond description and thought. It is, however, by virtue of his whole approach—the breadth and depth with which he tackles the topics and problems handed down by the tradition—rather than by virtue of any particular view that Plotinus' work constitutes a landmark in the history of philosophy.

There are, however, two issues mentioned by Porphyry in his *Life* that might lead us to doubt Plotinus' originality. These are the rumors, mentioned above, that he plagiarizes Numenius and his possible debt to his teacher, Ammonius Saccas. We have dealt with the former already and found that the rumors were unsubstantiated. Let us consider the latter.

Is there reason to believe that he just passed on what he had learnt without significant independent contributions? We do not know and will never know with certainty the extent to which Plotinus reflects Ammonius, who wrote nothing and is indeed a quite shadowy character. Once Origen (certainly the pagan Origen), also a former student of Ammonius, came to Plotinus' seminar in Rome. Plotinus blushed and said he didn't like to speak in front of someone who knows what he is going to say (*Life* 14, 20–25). Origen would presumably have heard Plotinus' talk before from Ammonius. In a passage already quoted above, Porphyry remarks in connection with the commentaries that he says were read in the school that Plotinus "did not just speak straight out of these books but took a distinctive personal line in his consideration, and brought the mind of Ammonius to bear in the investigations in hand" (*Life* 14, 14–16). This sounds as if Porphyry at once praises Plotinus for his independence and points to his reliance on Ammonius.

We should not be overhasty in concluding from these passages in the *Life* that Plotinus just reflected Ammonius. After all, Porphyry in the same breath praises him for a "distinctive personal line." The topic discussed on the occasion of Origen's visit may, for instance, have been exceptional in its dependence on Ammonius' teachings. Moreover, as we have seen Porphyry portrays Plotinus as a very modest person. The story of Origen's visit may above all be meant to underline his modesty. As to his bringing "the mind of Ammonius to bear on the investigations," even if true, this is compatible with quite an original take on the issues. It presumably means that Plotinus addressed the problems in the spirit of Ammonius rather than that he adopted his specific doctrines. The essential aspect of this spirit, it is tempting to conjecture, is that of delving under the surface of what is stated in the literature. Actually, so far as we have any indications about Ammonius, these suggest that Plotinus' views must have gone well beyond what he taught. Plotinus' independence as a thinker is also confirmed by Longinus' evaluation cited by Porphyry (Life 21, 1–9). As a former student of Ammonius, Longinus was familiar with the latter's thought. Yet he praises Plotinus as an independent thinker and does not at all seek to reduce him to the status of a puppet of Ammonius. To this we may add that the probing spirit of much of Plotinus' writings that we have already noted is very unlikely to be a copy of anyone.

It should be made clear that in any case Plotinus did not seek to be original. Originality was not a particularly esteemed virtue in the third century AD. As we have seen, his principal doctrine about the three hypostases, the One, Intellect and Soul, was in his view not new at all. Even if Plotinus did not seek to be original, it is difficult to avoid the conclusion that he nevertheless was—almost despite himself.

7 Chapter summary

Porphyry's *Life of Plotinus* contains very valuable information about Plotinus' life and character, school activity, and writing, and also about philosophical activity in the Roman Empire in the third century AD. Even if some of what Porphyry says cannot be believed as the exact truth and even if the reader should be aware that he is consciously drawing a very favorable picture of Plotinus, there is no reason to doubt that the *Life* generally gives us a truthful impression of Plotinus and his context. The *Life* depicts an in every respect honorable person who was agreeably undogmatic and open to probing philosophical discussion. We have considered the background to Plotinus' thought. The conclusion is that he is above all a very faithful follower of Plato, even if his views are sometimes dressed in a language different from Plato's and even if his interpretations of Plato may sometimes differ from what seems reasonable according to contemporary standards. What is beyond question is that Plotinus managed to give new life and philosophical depth to what is very recognizably Platonic philosophy.

Further reading

Primary sources

Porphyry, The Life of Plotinus. A translation of the Life is printed in the first volume of Armstrong's Loeb translation of Plotinus. Indeed, all serious editions and translations of the Enneads include the Life.

Secondary sources

The best and most complete modern account of Plotinus' life and surroundings is to be found in the two volumes edited by Luc Brisson and others, Porphyre: La vie de Plotin, 2 vols. (Paris: Vrin, 1982 and 1992).

John M. Dillon, The Middle Platonists: 80 B.C. to A.D. 220 (London: Duckworth, 1977) gives a fine account of the main actors and doctrines of Platonism in the centuries before Plotinus.

Philip Merlans, "Greek Philosophy from Plato to Plotinus," in A. H. Armstrong (ed.), The Cambridge History of Late Greek and Early Medieval Philosophy (Cambridge: Cambridge University Press 1967), 14–134, may in some respects be superseded by more recent scholarship but it gives an accessible and intelligible account of Plotinus' philosophical roots.

Notes

1 It is convincingly argued by Reale (2005) that the figure in red standing alone under the big statue on the right is Plotinus.
2 The text, French translation, textual notes and various studies relating to The Life of Plotinus are presented in Brisson et al. 1982 and its sequel Brisson et al. 1992. A detailed commentary is provided by Kalligas 2014.
3 A good overview of Ammonius Saccas and scholarship relating to him is given by Schroeder (1992) and by Karamanolis (2006).
4 The main source is Hierocles (fifth century) as excerpted and cited by Photius. The texts are translated and discussed by Karamanolis (2006).

5 On theories about Plotinus' illness, see Grmek 1992.
6 On the question of Plotinus' birthplace, see Kalligas's (2014) excellent commentary *ad loc*.
7 A very detailed and sensible account of Plotinus' school is to be found in Marie-Odile Goulet-Cazé 1982. I am indebted to this work in the account given here.
8 A qualification is needed here: five chapters included in modern editions as *Ennead* IV.7.8^1–8^5 in the treatise "On the immortality of the soul" are preserved in Eusebius and are not contained in the manuscripts of the *Enneads*. They have either fallen out of the archetype manuscript or were never contained in it. There was another ancient edition of Plotinus' writings by the doctor Eustochius. If Porphyry's edition for some reason did not contain these chapters, Eusebius may have had them from Eustochius' edition. The division of Plotinus' treatises into chapters, which is universally followed by modern editors, is the work of Marsilio Ficino, whose Latin translation of the *Enneads* from 1492 is the first printed version. Hence, the different marking of the passages from Eusebius.
9 Plato's Academy was founded around 387 BC. It is a commonly repeated falsehood that this institution stood without interruption till AD 529 when Emperor Justinian ordered the pagan schools in Athens closed. It disintegrated in the first century AD. The later Neoplatonists considered their school in Athens (probably started by Plutarch of Athens in late fourth century AD) as a revival of Plato's Academy.
10 The term "Neoplatonism" originates in eighteenth-century German scholarship (see Catana 2013). It was at the outset loaded with negative associations and the philosophy of Plotinus and subsequent late ancient Platonists and was not considered to be true Platonism. While much of the negative associations may have worn off with a better historical understanding, some may still linger on. Mainly for this reason some scholars object to the use of the term. It seems to me, however, that it is often handy to have a single word for the thought of just these thinkers and the word "Neoplatonism" is deeply ingrained. Let us just hope that it soon becomes a fully neutral term, if this has not already happened.
11 See Dillon 1977: 341 ff.
12 Karamanolis (2006) discusses in detail the Platonists' attempts at reconciling Plato and Aristotle. Porphyry played a decisive role in establishing the harmony between the two thinkers as a given fact for subsequent Platonists. Gerson (2005) exemplifies a contemporary sympathetic attitude to a reconciliation between Plato and Aristotle.
13 Porphyry wrote a history of philosophy of which only fragments survive.
14 See e.g. Aetius I.7.33 = Long and Sedley 1987: 46A; Diogenes Laertius VII, 135–136 = Long and Sedley 1987: 46B.
15 On Stoicism in the *Enneads*, see Graeser 1972. For Plotinus' appropriation of the Stoic *logos*, see Brisson 2000a.
16 Such interpretations are for example pervasive in Hadot's monumental study, *Porphyre et Victorinus* (Hadot 1968).

Two
The world according to Plotinus

In this chapter we shall have an overview of the main tenets and central notions of Plotinus' philosophy, "the basic logic of the system," so to speak, which should be useful to have at the start. This is not a summary of the chapters in the book, however. The main tenets presented here in outline are more fully dealt with in Chapters 3, 4 and 5 in reverse order and continue to be relevant for the topics covered in later chapters.

The treatise *Ennead* V.1, "On the three primary hypostases" (a title given by Porphyry, as all the others), is among Plotinus' earlier treatises, the tenth on Porphyry's chronological list. It is the first treatise in which he reveals his grand picture in a continuous manner.[1] Admittedly, the sensible sphere is only very cursorily treated here but we do get a good insight into what sort of reasoning Plotinus is liable to use in connection with the three intelligible principles, Soul, Intellect and the One, and our relation to them.[2] In this overview we shall use this treatise as a guide, following Plotinus' train of thought in it and citing and commenting on some of the things he says. Other material not found in this treatise will be added as needed.

First, a note about the term "hypostasis" that occurs in the title of the treatise. It is common to refer to the levels in Plotinus' hierarchical picture of reality, in particular the One, Intellect and Soul, as hypostases, and this will sometimes be done here and in the following chapters. It is Porphyry, however, who introduces this specific use of the term; Plotinus does not use it this way, at least not systematically. The term has several meanings in non-philosophical contexts, the most relevant for this philosophical use presumably being "foundation," "sediment."[3]

1 The status of souls

Plotinus starts the treatise V.1 by raising the question what "has made the souls forget their father, God, and be ignorant of themselves and him, even though they are parts which come from this higher world" (ll. 1–3). He goes on to say that by some kind of audacity, a wish to belong to themselves, the souls leave that higher world and forget about their origin. They descend into the sensible sphere and become captivated by earthly things. Several comments on this are in order.

First comment: A fundamental divide between two realms is hinted at here: the sensible and the intelligible. Plotinus is in accord with Plato and the tradition in drawing a sharp line between these two realms. Originally, the words translated as "sensible" and "intelligible," *aisthēton* and *noēton*, meant "what can be perceived by the senses" and "what can be grasped by thought," respectively. This sense of the words is sometimes alive in Plotinus but often they are used more freely. The first principle, the One, is as we shall see, not graspable by thought but it is included in Plotinus' notion of the intelligible realm, *to noēton*. Likewise, matter, which underlies bodies, is in itself non-perceptible but it may be included in the notion of the sensible realm. So the sensible realm consists of matter, bodies and their qualities such as colors and shapes. Its main characteristic is spatial extension and temporal dispersion. The One, Intellect and Soul comprise the intelligible realm.

The soul spoken of here is the individual human soul. As the lines cited indicate, the soul originates in the intelligible realm but descends into the sensible. More precisely, this descent means that soul becomes embodied. The embodiment does not mean, however, that the soul comes to share in the body's nature and becomes corporeal or sensible. It retains its non-corporeal intelligible status even in this condition. Thus, Plotinus is a dualist with respect to soul and body in the sense that the soul can exist independently of the body and doesn't even depend on it when embodied. The soul is an independent, separable substance. It is, however, set over the living body it ensouls in the sense that it is in charge of it. This means that it takes care of the body, sees to it that it is nurtured and unharmed. The danger Plotinus alludes to in our passage is that the soul becomes so preoccupied with this task and its accompanying pleasures and agonies, that it ignores its true origin and nature. This is in essence the human condition. The role of philosophy is to awaken the soul, make it turn its focus away from body and the sensible and towards the intelligible.

Does this mean that Plotinus despises the sensible sphere as worthless and evil? He may seem ambivalent on this point. At times he sounds as if this realm is totally worthless and even an evil place for the soul. A great deal of what he has to say about the sensible realm is, however, non-evaluative and there are passages that clearly recognize beauty and value in sensible things. In the treatise II.9, "Against the Gnostics," he scolds the Gnostics for their hostility towards this world and insists that the true Platonic position recognizes its value. Presumably, Plotinus' position in this regard is very close to Plato's: the sensible world is indeed not worthless. It is caused by truly eminent principles which it to some extent reflects. Its value is, however, small compared with that of these principles and it is a fatal error to suppose that its value is all the value there is.

Plotinus speaks here of "father, God." What is the import of that? Are we about to enter the sphere of religion? Not really. Plotinus not infrequently calls the members of the intelligible world, the One and Intellect, and even the souls of stars and the Earth, gods and divine. This is no innovation on his part, many of his predecessors expressed similar views. There is no doubt that he really meant that in some sense the One, Intellect and Soul are gods but it does not follow that we are dealing with religion rather than philosophy here. At least much of what we strongly associate with religion is missing. There is, for instance, no appeal to faith as opposed to reason in his discourse. Plotinus evidently sees his discourses on these matters as proceeding by appeals to sound reasoning. Second, the gods he speaks of are not the focus of rituals or offerings or other such worship as is typical of religions. They are called gods presumably because they are regarded as something greater and more venerable than we are and on whom we also depend. He also occasionally identifies traditional deities of the classical Greek religion with "philosophical" elements of his system. Zeus is, for instance, sometimes identified with Intellect but also with Soul (cf. IV.4.10, 1–4; V.3.5, 21). We thus see some tendency to give allegorical, philosophical interpretations of traditional myths. Plotinus, however, does not take this very far. This trend is sporadic and hardly systematic. The later Neoplatonists carried such allegorizing much further.

As Plotinus moves on in *Ennead* V.1, he proposes to reveal to the human soul its own nature: "Let every soul, then, first consider this, that it made all things itself, breathing life into them, those that the earth feeds and those that are nourished by the sea, and the divine stars in the sky" (V.1.2, 1–4). His strategy is clearly to make us realize that the human soul is of the same kind as that great power which makes and animates the whole sensible universe. Like Plato, Aristotle and the Stoics, Plotinus thought that the sensible world— the earth, heavens and the heavenly bodies—is a limited, spherical whole. As opposed to the Stoics and in agreement with the other two—assuming with Plotinus' that Plato is not to be understood literally where he speaks in the *Timaeus* of a temporal beginning of the world—Plotinus thought that the sensible world is eternal, with no beginning and no end. Furthermore, in agreement with Plato and the Stoics he believed that the sensible world is ensouled, a living being.

The sensible world is animated by a World-Soul—a part of Plotinus' Platonic heritage, especially the *Timaeus*. Not only does this World-Soul animate the body of the world, it continually sustains it. Even the matter underlying bodies is its product. The regular, orderly patterns we see in the sensible universe are all the work of the World-Soul. Moreover, the World-Soul does all this by some kind of thought. It would be premature to seek to explain this at the present stage. Let us just note this fact, we shall come back to it later (see Chapter 5, Section 1, "Soul's Thought"). Soul unifies living bodies and makes them persist over time. We may find this strange: do not ordinary organic bodies, at least, rather persist by nourishment, their capacities to grow and heal and suchlike? What has the soul got to do with it? Actually, according to the ancient Greek thinkers the soul has everything to do with it. For many Greek thinkers, notably Aristotle and at least sometimes Plato, soul is the general principle of life, that in virtue of which organic bodies are alive. Hence, such capacities as those of growth or nourishment are capacities of soul just as much as the power to sense or to reason. Plotinus clearly holds, however, that the lower capacities depend on thought and that their activities can even be seen as a low mode of thinking (III.8.4).

Though the soul was widely agreed to be a principle of life, the Greek thinkers didn't agree about its nature. Some were materialists, notably the Epicureans and the Stoics, and thought that the soul is a body of some sort. They would then hold that it is by the presence of that special kind of body that other bodies are alive. Aristotle maintained a different sort of theory according to which the soul is the form of the body; it is nevertheless not a separable form which enters into the body from elsewhere; it is rather an inseparable form of its body like the form which makes a piece of wood and a piece of iron an axe (see Aristotle, *On the Soul* II, 1). Plotinus stands firmly in this tradition which held soul to be the principle of life in general. He differs, however, from both the materialists and Aristotle in his views on the nature of the soul. As has been indicated, according to him it is an entity of a different order. He holds that what we see of harmony, beauty and unity in the sensible realm must be caused by something other than the bodies of this realm, in fact by something that possesses these characteristics to a higher degree than the bodies themselves. The life itself that the bodies take on is a feature imposed on them, not something they could give rise to by themselves.

Plotinus' main purpose in the passage quoted above from V.1.2 is to make the human soul think well of itself by pointing out that "our soul is of the same kind [as that which makes and rules the world], and when you look at it without its accretions and take it in its purified state you will find that very same honorable thing which is the nature of soul" (V.1.2, 44–46). So our souls and that of the world are on a par. He elsewhere indicates their parallel status by calling the World-Soul and our souls sisters (II.9.18, 16; IV.3.6, 13). The accretions spoken of here are the body and the psychic powers related to the soul's embodied state, such as sense-perception and the affections. One may wonder whether the World-Soul itself isn't just as immersed in body as our souls and hence no purer even if it has a larger domain. This is not the case, however: the World-Soul does not "descend" like ours (see e.g. IV.3.6, 11–13). Although parallel with ours as an entity, it is in many ways much better off. We shall consider the reasons for this in Chapter 5.

As remarked above, there is not much in V.1 about the details of the sensible world or about the nature of human beings. As already noted, the World-Soul generates the body of the universe and sustains it, and endows it with life. It is, however, possible to do as Plotinus frequently does, namely to abstract from the organic nature of the sensible cosmos and consider it as lifeless, which it is in itself. A certain structure of the lifeless then emerges: there is, at the bottom, so to speak, matter. Plotinus' notion of matter may at first sight appear very strange: it is void of any features of its own; in and of itself, it is nothing. The Plotinian matter has the same name as Aristotelian and Stoic matter, *hylē*, but it owes more to Plato's notion of the receptacle of sensible forms in the *Timaeus* 51a ff. It may also be influenced by the Stoic notion of matter with which it shares the feature of being void of qualities (Diogenes Laertius, *Lives of the Philosophers* VII, 134). But even if it is nothing, Plotinus maintains that matter is the root of evil; it actually is absolute evil, as he explains in I.8, "On what are and whence come evils." We shall consider this view in Chapter 6. Being without any determinate size or quantity, matter is not to be identified with space. Yet, as we shall see in Chapter 6, it is responsible for spatial dispersion.

The first determinate entity in the Plotinian ontology—counting from below—is body. The bare notion of body is that of a determinate spatial magnitude. Dispersion in space and time is the prime characteristic of bodies and the sensible realm generally. On top of these magnitudes come corporeal qualities such as colors and shapes, which are less dispersed, less "plural," than the bodies themselves but still count as sensible rather than intelligible items.

Living bodies such as our own share in the nature of the sensible, as just described. They are, however, organized so as to be able to receive life, which they indeed do receive. Sometimes Plotinus speaks as if our own, individual soul is that which animates our bodies, sometimes he suggests that the lower, biological functions are due to the World-Soul and our individual soul is imposed on top of that. In any event, soul and life are something imposed on the body and in principle separable from it. This dualism does not prevent Plotinus from adopting a great deal of Aristotelian conceptual machinery in his account of the incarnate soul.[4] He uses a basic Aristotelian taxonomy of the incarnate soul that distinguishes between reason, sense and a growth-principle (to phytikon). Sense-perception and the growth-principle are psychic functions that essentially involve the use of bodily organs. Many details of Plotinus' theory of sense-perception have a clear Aristotelian flavor. See Chapter 7, Section 3 ("The Functions of the Living Being").

In the preceding paragraphs the term "principle" has been used several times. We have described the One, Intellect and soul as principles and just recently talked about the growth-principle. The Greek word for principle, archē, means "origin" or "beginning" and in philosophy it is often synonymous, or nearly so, with "cause," aitia. Both principles and causes are in Plotinus as in Aristotle certain real things—in a wide sense of "thing" according to which e.g. forms are things—that are appealed to to account for something else.

Plotinus holds, echoing Aristotle (Nicomachean Ethics IX, 1166a16–17) that we ourselves are mostly at the level of discursive reason (dianoia) (cf. I.1.7, 17; V.3.3, 35). Discursive reason is our everyday reason, the faculty by which we estimate our present situation, plan our future and reflect on the past. In the literature on Plotinus the "we" at the level of discursive reason is sometimes referred to as the empirical self. It was said earlier that in V.1 Plotinus' aim was to boost the human soul's self-esteem by showing it its kinship with and likeness to the soul at large. Actually, Plotinus holds that we, every one of us, have intelligible roots and that something of us remains in the pure intelligible realm: see Chapter 8, Section 4 ("The Soul and We Ourselves"). We may call this our intelligible or noetic self as distinct from the empirical one. So our task in life is not merely to inspect and appreciate the intelligible as foreign tourists: doing so involves going to our own roots, raising the empirical self to the level of the intelligible one.

2 The Principle of Prior Possession and priority of unity

As a life-giving principle, the soul must itself possess life. This may sound innocent enough. Underlying this claim, however, is a view that can be found in one form or other in much of Greek philosophy and of which Plotinus holds a rather extreme version. We see an instance of this view for example in ancient physical theories of the elements: fire is hot; it is by the presence of fire that other things become hot—not only is fire actually the hottest thing, it is hot in a different and we might say superior way to other things. We might say that fire is hot by itself, hot just in virtue of being what it is, namely fire. Its hotness is in need of no further presence of anything that makes it hot. Other things, arguably, need something else, i.e. fire, in order to be hot. The general claim that the principle invoked to explain something else has itself the feature it is intended to explain, and has it in such a way that the question does not arise why it has the feature in question, we may call the Principle of Prior Possession. We see it at work, for instance, in Plato's theory of Ideas in the view that the Idea of anything is itself that of which it is the Idea, that e.g. the Idea of Man itself is a man of sorts. This is what has been called the self-predication of the Ideas in the scholarly literature on Plato. The principle is also found throughout Aristotle's writings in the claim that "actuality is prior to potentiality," that something potentially such and such becomes actually so by the agency of something which already is actually so—"a human being begets a human being" is Aristotle's standard example. And we see this principle in Plotinus' view of soul as a rational, organizing, life-giving principle.[5]

The Principle of Prior Possession, which is at work throughout the Plotinian hierarchy, is in evidence in his views on the relation between body and soul: as a principle of the life of bodies, the soul itself must live. Moreover, its life must be better, more perfect than the borrowed life of living bodies. "Better" or "more perfect" in such a context means "more complete," "more a whole," in a word more "unified." We see an expression of this in the account of the World-Soul in V.1.2:

> One body lies in one place and one in another, and one is here and another there; some are separated by being in opposite parts of the universe, and others in other ways. But soul is not like this and it is not by being cut up that it gives life, by a part of itself for each individual thing, but all things live by the whole, made like to the father who begat it in its unity and its universality.
>
> (V.1.2, 32–38)

Thus, even if it makes and sustains bodies, the soul is not subject to division into spatially different parts as bodies are. The things that live by the soul, live by it as a whole, not part by part. This in turn signifies that the soul itself is more unified than the bodies it animates. This observation leads us to another basic characteristic of Plotinus' thought: the principle responsible for a feature F not only itself possesses F but possesses it to a higher degree, which in turn means in a more unified way than that which depends on the principle.

This leads us to the notion of unity, which is indeed a very central notion in Plotinus—the key notion, we might even say. The principle invoked to explain anything is more unified than that of which it is the principle. We shall see this more in detail later in this chapter, but let us at this stage simply note that Plotinus' world is stratified according to degrees of unity and plurality: souls have a higher degree of unity than bodies and bodies themselves have a higher degree of unity than the matter which underlies them. As we shall see, Plotinus' version of the Principle of Prior Possession demands an ultimate principle which is sheer unity.

3 Logoi and forms, paradigms and images

Unified though it is in comparison with the sensible realm, the soul is not the ultimate principle of unity, far from it. Even if the soul does not partake in the spatial divisibility of bodily nature, it is the intelligible principle which is directly involved with the sensible. This indicates that it must itself be significantly plural. As already noted, the soul is essentially a thinking thing. The thought that is characteristic of soul is, however, not the most perfect unified kind of thought. In our treatise, V.1, Plotinus says:

> For, although [the soul] is a thing of the kind our discussion has shown it to be, it is a kind of image (*eikōn*) of Intellect; just as an uttered rational formula (*logos*) is an image (*eikōn*) of the rational formula in soul, so soul itself is a rational formula of Intellect, and its whole activity and the life which it sends off to establish another reality; as fire has the heat which remains with it and the heat which it gives. But one must understand that the activity

on the level of Intellect does not flow out from it, but the external activity comes into existence as something distinct.

(V.1.3, 6–12)

Plotinus is here describing how soul's thought is not the original thought but the expression of another more perfect form of thought, that of Intellect. I shall postpone addressing the nature of Intellect and its kind of thought and for the time being focus instead on the general features, as they emerge from the account given here, of the relationship between Intellect and Soul. For in these few lines Plotinus manages to incorporate several ideas that are central not only to his account of the relationship between soul and Intellect but to his philosophy generally.

Let us start by considering what is called here a "rational formula" (*logos*). Already with Plato this word, *logos*, had acquired a number of meanings and shades of meaning. When we come to Plotinus' time its uses are even more complex because it has been a key term in most of the philosophical schools in the intervening centuries. Among its translations in philosophical literature we find "reason," "account," "formula," "explanation," "statement," "discussion," "utterance," "argument," "law," "word" and so forth, all depending on context. Presumably, the ancient Greek-speaking philosophers saw just one concept here with so many shades of meaning. We find most of these senses in the *Enneads* but the most common and the characteristic use of *logos* is such as we find in V.1.3: *logos* is the *logos* of something. The *logos* of X is something that expresses the content of X but in a more detailed and explicit form than this content has in X itself.[6] This use fits Aristotle's sense of *logos* as an account or formula making explicit what something is. As noted in the previous chapter, as a metaphysical and cosmological notion the Plotinian *logos* also owes much to Stoicism (see pp. 31–32).

Logos appears at every intelligible level in the hierarchy except the One. Intellect is the *logos* of the One, and Soul the *logos* of Intellect. Within the level of soul there are also *logoi* of different degrees of generality: the *logoi* that produce bodily qualities are less unified and more specific than those at the level of undescended souls. Where *logos* is the productive agent for the features of bodies, Plotinus is apt to speak of *logoi poiētikoi*, often called "formative (rational) principles," for example in Armstrong's translation of Plotinus. As the passage in V.1.3 suggests, the *logos* of something is a rationally arranged intelligible structure which is a more manifold, inferior expression of a higher, more unified entity. But in general the *logoi* are not merely intelligible structures: Plotinus holds that they are thoughts (see Chapter 5, p. 185 ff.).

Another pervasive term in Plotinus is "form" (*eidos*, plural *eidē*). *Eidos* is one of Plato's words for the Platonic Forms or Ideas (*ideai*). It is also Aristotle's word for the principle opposite to matter. As such, form in Aristotle is close to essence (*to ti*) and substance (*ousia*) and nature (*physis*): the essence and substance of anything Aristotle identifies with its form. Aristotle also speaks more loosely of forms, for instance when he says that in sense-perception the sense-organ receives the form of the object without the matter (*On the Soul* II, 424a17–19). Here the form is the quality of the thing perceived without the underlying matter, not its substance and essence. Form can also exist in the soul according to Aristotle: an artist has, for instance, the form of the object to be made in his soul before and while he makes it. Plotinus takes over all these uses of "form" in addition to the Platonic. Thus, there are, for example, forms in matter—identified with qualities and shapes of bodies—and there are forms in soul and the Forms in Intellect. These forms constitute a hierarchy or a series such that the same form can exist at different levels: starting from the Platonic Form of Man, we have the human form at the level of soul, and the same finally at the corporeal level.

It will not have escaped the reader's notice that the preceding account of forms resembles that of *logoi*. The two notions are indeed closely related and *logos* and "form" seem often to refer to the same thing, even if they differ in their history and connotations (cf. III.8.2, 22 ff.). In fact speaking of "form" and *logos* together or even identifying them goes back at least to Aristotle (see *On the Soul* II, 414a9, and *Metaphysics* III, 996b8). Both exist at different levels of unity from Intellect on, and both imply form, order and rationality. There is one notable difference, however: whereas *logos* seems to be restricted to the intelligible sphere in the broadest sense, including all levels of soul, Plotinus is willing to speak of sensible qualities and shapes as forms in matter or corporeal forms.

In the passage from V.1.3 cited at the beginning of this section, Plotinus also speaks of images: soul is an image (*eikōn*) of Intellect as well as a *logos* of it. We have here yet another pervasive notion in Plotinus, for which he has a number of terms: imitation (*mimēma*), shadow (*eidōlon*), trace (*ichnos*), in addition to *eikōn*. There is a tendency to limit "shadow" and "trace" to images in the sensible world. I shall use "image" as the general term. Images are of course images of something: ultimately the images of things have paradigms in Intellect, the Platonic Ideas. The forms and *logoi* we have considered fit into a pattern of images and models: the less unified *logoi* and forms are images of more unified *logoi* and forms. Thus, to reuse the example of the human being, the Idea of Man is the archetype, of which the human being in soul is an image, of which the corporeal human being is an image in turn. It goes without saying that this talk of paradigms and images is a part of Plotinus' Platonic heritage.

4 Emanation and double activity

Nothing has been said so far about how all these different stages of images, forms and *logoi* come to be. Plotinus' general answer to that question is adumbrated in our passage from V.1.3 quoted above. He says here that "as fire has the heat which remains with it and the heat which it gives. But one must understand that the activity on the level of Intellect does not flow out from it, but the external activity comes into existence as something distinct." As the context shows, this is an explanation of how the soul is a *logos* and image of Intellect. He is here alluding to his theory of emanation and double activity, which is also a pervasive aspect of his thought. Every level in the hierarchy consists in a characteristic activity, which may be referred to as the internal, self-contained activity of that level. Plotinus' term for this is "the activity of the essence (*ousia*)," even if he applies this term to other things than essences strictly speaking, for instance the One itself (see Chapter 3, Section 4, "The First Emanation from the One: Viewpoint of the One"). Each such internal act, except matter and immanent forms at the lowest level of the hierarchy, are accompanied by an external one, which constitutes the beginning of the next stage below. This is the "activity from the essence." We may say that this notion of double act or activity describes in philosophical terminology what emanation metaphors render in a more pictorial language.

Plotinus frequently uses physical metaphors or analogies to describe how a higher level generates a lower one: fire and the heat it emits such as we have here in our passage from V.1.3 (cf. also V.4.3, 30) or a source of light and the light it radiates (see V.1.6, 28–30; V.3.12, 39–44). Elsewhere, we see references to other physical phenomena: sources of water and the water that flows out of them (e.g. V.2.1, 8; III.8.10, 5), snow and cold, the source of smell and scent (e.g. V.1.6, 30 ff.). The sources of heat, light and water, or what have you, of course, stand for the causes, the internal acts, and what proceeds out of them for the lower level that comes into being.

It is the appeal to such physical phenomena that has given rise to the notion of emanation. There is no single word in Plotinus, however, that is naturally translated as "emanation." His most common general way of speaking about so-called emanation is in terms of process (*proodos*): the external act proceeds from the cause. But talk of process or emanation may, however, mislead in so far as it suggests that the cause spreads itself out. Plotinus consistently maintains that the intelligible causes remain unaffected and lose nothing by giving away. Our passage refers explicitly to this feature of the causes: "the activity on the level of Intellect does not flow out from it."

The analogy of the fire and heat that we see here may suggest that Plotinus conceives of ordinary physical fire in the same way: in our passage from V.1.3 quoted above he distinguishes between the heat that remains in the fire all the while that heat is going out from it (cf. V.1.6, 34–37). Indeed, without this distinction the fire–heat analogy would not convey the desired idea (cf. Lloyd 1990: 100). There is, however, a notable difference between the physical phenomena and the intelligible causes and effects they are invoked to explain: ordinary fires and springs of water will eventually burn up and dry out. Not so with the intelligible causes.

Before proceeding any further, let us consider the notion of activity (*energeia*, plural *energeiai*) more closely. Plotinus borrows this notion from Aristotle and it is at least as central for him as it is for Aristotle. *Energeia* in Aristotle[7]—variously translated as activity, actualization, act or actuality depending on context and interpretation—is no simple topic, and a superficial account of it will have to suffice here.[8] We have already come across this notion in connection with the Principle of Prior Possession in Section 2: what is potentially F becomes actually F by the agency of something which already is actually F. An actual human being begets another human being, an actual fire makes a fire out of what is potentially a fire. Aristotle also speaks of activity/actuality as the exercise of a capacity or as we might say, the activity of a capacity: when a person who can swim is actually swimming, the capacity is active. Aristotle makes heavy use of the notion of activity in his metaphysics: the being of anything can be identified with the actuality/activity characteristic of the being in question.

Neither for Aristotle nor Plotinus does activity imply that that which is engaged in activity undergoes any change (cf. III.6.1, 8–13). Aristotle distinguishes between activities and changes or motions (kinēseis).[9] When a builder builds, for instance, the building activity does not constitute a change in the builder. This is not to deny the obvious: surely some changes take place as a result of the building, in the house that is being built, for instance, and the builder himself may become tired. As a builder, however, he is not essentially changed by building. As Waterlow (1982: 187) puts it in connection with Aristotle: "[The activity of building] is not a process of acquiring a new property." On the contrary, in building the builder is realizing his or her nature as a builder. That is not a change but becoming fully what one already is. Though Plotinus criticizes Aristotle's distinction between activities and changes, he retains this aspect of Aristotle's account: to be activated is not to be changed.[10]

So Plotinus takes this notion over from Aristotle but he does not follow him in every detail.[11] Double activity is pervasive in Plotinus. Each stage in the Plotinian hierarchy from the One downwards is characterized by an internal activity which in turn is accompanied by an external one. The internal activity constitutes the given stage, while the external one constitutes the basis for the next stage below. At the metaphysical level, such a process of internal and external activities continues until a level is reached where there is no more productive power.

Plotinus emphasizes the identity of the internal cause and the activity: it is not the case that the Intellect or Soul is something which happens to be engaged in some sort of activity—Intellect *is* its characteristic activity and the soul is its characteristic activity. A question naturally arises about the internal activity of the One. Given that the One is beyond any positive attribution, can we still attribute activity to it? Plotinus sometimes attributes activity to it (V.4.2, 27 ff.; V.6.6, 8–11, VI.8.20), sometimes he denies it because this would compromise the absolute unity of the One. See Chapter 3, Section 3 ("Thought, Activity, Will, Power and Freedom of the One").

Every such internal activity is accompanied by an external one, illustrated in our passage by the heat the fire gives to its environment. The external activity is what is often described in terms of physical metaphors suggesting emanation such as we have here with fire and heat. Plotinus emphasizes that the internal act is self-contained. It is not defined in terms of its effects. It is, as he occasionally puts it, absolute, independent, free (*apolytos*) (VI.8.20, 4–8). This raises questions about the exact relation between the internal and the external act: if the internal act is self-contained, we may wonder how it could have any external effects. The answer is that Plotinus conceives of the external act as a by-product: it is neither intended nor in any way essential to its cause; the internal act would be just as it is, even if there was no external one.

A crucial difference between Plotinus and Aristotle appears in Plotinus' conception of the external act: whereas for Aristotle humans beget other human beings rather than some inferior humanoids and in general what is actively F produces something which is just as fully F as its cause, in Plotinus the external act is always inferior to the internal one: it is less unified and weaker in its powers. Thus, the doctrine of the two acts is combined with the Platonic doctrine of paradigms and images: the internal act is the paradigm which gives off an imperfect image of itself. It follows that the soul is an external act of Intellect, and Intellect an external act of the One. It follows also that the different levels of *logoi* and forms described in the previous section are to be seen in this light: the lower strata of *logoi* or forms are in general external acts of their higher counterparts. The distinction between internal and external activity runs through every Plotinian principle down to soul and is crucial for an understanding of causation in the Plotinian system (see e.g. V.3.12; V.4.2).

There has been considerable speculation about the origin of the theory of double activity and emanation: Plato, Aristotle and the

Stoics have all been mentioned. While the Stoics are not a relevant influence in my view, Aristotle and Plato both play a widely recognized role.[12] Not only the language, but many of the crucial ingredients of the double activity scheme have antecedents in Aristotle's account of agency. Double activity may indeed be seen as an application of the Principle of Prior Possession, which certainly is Aristotelian—though, as we shall see, also Platonic (cf. Makin 1991; Sedley 1998). There are interesting deviations from Aristotle, however. It is not only that the external act involves a loss. We do not see in Aristotle—despite his commitment to the Principle of Prior Possession—the same sort of emphasis on the self-containment of the prior *energeia* as in Plotinus on the self-containment of internal act: Plotinus tends to present his agents, the internal activities, as inessentially agents, i.e. as we have seen, their acts on other things are necessary but incidental in the sense that the effects do not enter into the account of what their causes are. To conclude, Aristotle surely plays an important role in the development of the double act doctrine, but there are very significant differences.

Let us then turn to Plato. Several suggestions have been put forth about individual passages in Plato that may have inspired Plotinus' notion of the double act: Gerson (1994: 23–24) mentions three such. First, there is the famous passage about the Idea of the Good in *Republic* VI, 508e–509b. Whatever the Idea of the Good is doing privately, as it were, and the truth it infuses into the other Ideas correspond, according to Gerson, to the internal and the external acts, respectively. Second, there is *Timaeus* 29e, the celebrated passage about the Demiurge's ungrudging nature, which may be interpreted as an everlasting overflow of benevolence and was so interpreted by the tradition in the doctrine, *bonum est diffusivum sui* ("the good is self-diffusive"). Third, Gerson mentions Diotima's speech in the *Symposium* (see especially 212a–b), where the possession of the Beautiful itself is said to result in the production of beauty. The idea is that the possession of the Beautiful in itself brings about beauty in other things.

Plotinus draws on all these passages. If we consider actual occurrences of the double act theory in the *Enneads*, two other passages stand out as being at least as important as these, however. One is *Timaeus* 42e4–5 where Plato says that the divine Craftsman "*remains* in his customary way of life" while the lesser gods are carrying out his orders. Plotinus quotes this passage several times. For him the passage contains a general message about causes: even if they act on other things, they *remain*. Apart from those passages in Plotinus that obviously reflect this *Timaeus* passage, the *Enneads* abound in talk of remaining (*menein*) in contexts having to do with causes: the causes remain. All these passages can claim this *Timaeus* passage as their authority.

Another passage I have in mind is *Phaedrus* 245c–d, the celebrated passage about the soul's self-motion. Here Plato says:

> Every soul is immortal. That is because whatever is in motion is immortal, while what moves, and is moved by, something else stops living when it stops moving. So it is only what moves itself that never desists from motion, since it does not leave itself. In fact, this self-mover is the source and spring of motion in everything else that moves.

So the soul, any soul, moves itself and others, and it does so without leaving itself. In other words, the soul moves itself and others while remaining. "Not leaving itself" is another expression Plotinus frequently uses to convey the idea of remaining. And again he applies it not only to the soul but to causes generally. In this context it is worth noting that at least as regards intelligible entities "motion" and "activity" amount to the same thing for Plotinus. He reinterprets Platonic passages speaking of non-physical motion as Aristotelian activity.

The same general idea about remaining is again to be found in the *Symposium* 212b, one of the passages cited by Gerson, using still more expressions that recur in Plotinus' account of causes. Socrates (Diotima) says the following about Beauty itself: "But itself by itself with itself, it is always one in form; and all the other beautiful things share in that, in such a way that when those others come to be or pass away, *this does not become the least bit smaller or greater nor is it affected at all.*" Beauty itself is responsible for whatever beauty there is in others, but it is not in the least affected by this nor is it lessened. Plotinus employs both expressions.

While there may not be fully fledged emanation metaphors in Plato, there surely are some passages Plotinus cites that may have led him to such ideas. There is the Analogy of the Sun in *Republic* 509b, which clearly suggests that something comes from the Good to the objects of knowledge like light from the Sun which shines on sensible objects. And the *Phaedrus* passage cited above also describes the soul's self-motion as "the source (*pēgē*) and spring (*archē*)" of all other motion.[13] The phrase "source and spring" is cited several times in the *Enneads* and not only in connection with the soul but especially in connection with the One's productive activity (see I.9.1, 41; I.7.1, 15; VI.7.23, 21). In III.8.10, 2–5 we find the following passage: "But what is above life is the cause of life; for the activity (*energeia*) of life, which is all things, is not the first, but itself flows out, as it were, as if from a spring (*ek pēgēs*)." The use of the word *pēgē* in such a context is no doubt an allusion to the *Phaedrus* passage, which Plotinus here and in the lines that follow develops into a full-blown emanation or flow metaphor. Moreover, what "flows" from the "source" is the external activity of the One. So in this way this *Phaedrus* passage is clearly linked to the double act doctrine. If we take into consideration that *Phaedrus* 245c–d also contains the feature of self-containment of the cause, it becomes tempting to regard this passage as quite crucial as background for the double act doctrine.

Interestingly, Plotinus also interprets Plato's views on virtue in terms of the double act doctrine. In the *Republic* 443c–d Plato says about true justice that it consists in doing one's own "not as regards one's own external action (*peri tēn exō praxin*) but as regards the internal one since it truly concerns oneself and what belongs to oneself." Plotinus obviously has this passage in mind where he says in connection with autonomy that "so that also that which is autonomous (*autexousion*) and depends on us (*eph' hēmin*) in actions is not referred to the acting (*to prattein*) or the external activity but to the internal one (*eis tēn entos energeian*) and the thought and contemplation of the virtue itself" (VI.8.6, 19–22). Plato is of course not discussing autonomy in this passage of the *Republic*. Plotinus may, however, have taken the phrase "concerns oneself and belongs to oneself" to refer to what "depends on us," as he understands the latter. In any case, external virtuous action is here described as an external act of the internal activity of virtue itself. Plotinus evidently thought that the virtue itself is there as a condition of the soul quite independently of any overt actions (cf. VI.8.5 and Emilsson 2012). This passage is also discussed in Chapter 10, Section 2.2 ("Freedom and What Is Up to One").

I find it likely that this list of Platonic passages that may be seen as containing some elements of Plotinus' double act scheme could be lengthened considerably. Rather than pursuing this further, however, I would like to raise some questions about the topic in general. First, is Plotinus reading back into Plato something that he basically has from elsewhere—Aristotle and Alexander for instance—and believes on independent grounds? Or is his fundamental motivation Platonic (by his lights)? Second, if it is fundamentally Platonic, how is it so?

It seems to me that the literature on the sources of the double act doctrine generally proceeds on the assumption that there must be a passage or two somewhere in Plato, Aristotle, the Stoics or someone else that gave Plotinus an idea which he then generalized or "blew up," one might even say. This, however, needn't be the case at all. First, we have noted that Plotinus sees salient features of his double act doctrine in several Platonic passages that are, at least superficially, quite different. Not that he sees all the features in every such passage, but each passage gives Platonic authority to some of the features. Admittedly this is compatible with his mostly having the doctrine from elsewhere but finding it appropriate to give it some Platonic flavor. It is in my view more plausible, however, to suppose that he saw the double act doctrine as an interpretation of Plato on causality or "how intelligible principles work." Let us see briefly how such an interpretation makes good sense.

Plato describes the relation between his primary causes, the Ideas, and what depends on them in terms of participation or imitation. Plotinus and the other Neoplatonists also employ these concepts. Both participation and imitation are notions which, so to speak, see the matter from below, from the viewpoint of the caused: it is the lower, caused item that formally is the agent in participation or imitation. It is clear, however, that for Plato the participants or imitators play a passive role in the sense that it is the participated or the imitated which has the main responsibility for the outcome: in participating or imitating, the lower is or becomes such and such because of the higher item, though the nature of the recipient also plays a role. In Plato there is, however, very little to be found about how this happens from the viewpoint of the cause. In a famous passage in *Phaedo* 100a–e the Ideas are said to be "causes" in which other things participate and in virtue of which they come to have certain features, but nothing is said about what, if anything, the Ideas do in order to bring this about. Passages such as the analogy of the Sun in the *Republic* or the account of demiurgic activity in the *Timaeus* may give us certain clues, but considerable interpretive work is required to elicit the message. The so-called doctrine of double activity and its accompanying notion of emanation are meant as an attempt to do just this, i.e. to account for Platonic causes from the viewpoint of the causes themselves rather than the effects. Thus, what is described in terms of emanation is not meant to be anything different from participation or imitation. Rather, what from the viewpoint of the subordinate items is called participation or imitation may be described in emanative language from above.

Second, even if Plato is brief about the causality of his causes, Plotinus sees several hints. For instance, by being causes of other things Platonic causes do not lose anything, nor are they affected in any way. In fact Platonic causes are something in their own right without regard to the effects they may have. Nevertheless, they have certain effects. The doctrine of double activity is intended as an explanation of how this happens. So I take it that the doctrine is an interpretation of Plato's views on causality. If this is so, the question of which particular Platonic passage gave Plotinus the idea that this is how Plato is to be interpreted seems to me a fairly pointless one: Plotinus sees evidence of this all over the place, different pieces of the doctrine in different contexts. The interpretation, however, actively makes use of Aristotle's understanding of activity. It provides the doctrine with some of its key terms and notions. The modifications of Aristotle it involves, however, are all in the direction of what one might justly suppose was Plato's general account of causation, if he had one.

It may be worthwhile to pause here and comment on the notion of cause involved. There may be a simple explanation of Plato's reticence about the activity of the Ideas. Even if Plato occasionally calls the Ideas "causes" (*aitiai*) and frequently implies that they have the status of principles, it does not follow that they are causes in the sense that they *do* something, that they exert themselves in any way. In fact it has been plausibly argued by Frede (1987) that the notion of cause in Plato and Aristotle is rather different from ours especially in that their notion does not imply agency. Thus, when Plato's Ideas or Aristotle's end, form, matter and mover are called causes it is not to imply that these are agents that do something or other in order to bring about their effects. Rather, according to Frede, they are called causes because they figure in explanations of the features of which they are said to be causes.

In light of this, one may wonder whether the search for the agency of Ideas or an account of it such as I have just attributed to Plotinus is not highly mistaken, at least in so far as his account is taken to be an interpretation of Plato. Let us note in response that whatever the facts about Plato's notion of a cause may be, the notion of paradigm/imitation is quite naturally interpreted as involving some activity on the part of the paradigm. Of course the paradigm is not supposed to do something extraordinary in order to bring about its effects. Quite the contrary, one would suppose that simply by minding its own business in "its own abode," a paradigmatic cause at the same time molds, impresses or influences (or whatever causal verb may be appropriate) the imitator. Moreover, in between Plato and Plotinus the Stoics had conceived of a different notion of cause as that which is responsible for a particular event or state of affairs, as that which brings about this event or state of affairs (cf. Frede 1987). It is quite conceivable that Plotinus' double activity doctrine as applied to Platonic causes is influenced by the new Stoic conception of causation, which may make understandable his interest in the mode of action of the intelligible causes.

5 Conversion

Not only are there internal and external activities, there is also some kind of conversion (*epistrophē*), a looking back towards the source by the external act that has left it. This is not evident in our passage from V.1.3, but immediately afterwards Plotinus says:

> Since then [the Soul's] existence derives from Intellect, soul is intellectual, and its intellect is in discursive reasonings (*logismos*),

and its perfection comes from Intellect, like a father who brings to maturity a son whom he begat imperfect in comparison with himself. Soul's establishment in reality, then, comes from Intellect, and its thought becomes actual in its seeing of Intellect.
(V.1.3, 13–17)

Even if the technical term "conversion" (*epistrophē*) or its cognates are not used here, we see a typical account of the phenomenon. Plotinus characteristically changes his metaphors when accounting for the conversion: real heat or light do not show any tendency to go back towards the fire. The physical metaphors have now been replaced by psychological ones: those of need and longing (not evident here) and vision. The "efflux" needs its source and "looks" back in an attempt to capture it. As a result it is filled and becomes fully itself. As Plotinus puts it in the passage of V.1.3 we have been using: "Soul's establishment in reality, then, becomes actual in its seeing of Intellect."

Conversion does not mean "reunion"—in that case nothing new would come about. Rather the idea is that the outward process distinguishes the product from the original, whereas the conversion establishes their identity, which, however, is incomplete since what assumes the character of the source in the conversion is something which by proceeding is already other than the source. The Plotinian conversion is a tending of thought. After all, every activity below the One, including the operations of nature, is a kind of thought (III.8. (30)). We may compare this to a teacher and pupil: the teacher's knowledge emanates from her in the form of speech and gestures. As every teacher knows, this is not enough, however: the pupil must direct her mind to what has been sent out. As Plotinus does not posit any kind of pre-existent matter as the recipient of form, what becomes informed must come from the informing source. Thus, the outgoing aspect functions as a material or receiving principle, the conversion aspect as the informing of it.

The phenomenon of conversion corresponds to imitation in Plato, and love and desire as cosmological principles in Aristotle: the latter says in *Metaphysics* XII, 7, 1072b3, that God, the unmoved mover, moves other things as an object of their love. Thus, for both Plato and Aristotle there is a kind of striving towards the causes that is supposed to explain the effects. The Plotinian conversion is also of this kind and no doubt inspired by kindred notions in his eminent predecessors. Thus, there is an emanation from the One which is turned towards its source and thereby becomes the fully actual Intellect; a similar process takes place in the generation of soul from Intellect.

Emanation and conversion are not temporal processes and hence neither is temporally prior to the other, even if they are often so described. Instead of conceiving of emanation and conversion as temporally distinct events, a better way to think about it is to imagine the emanation as always facing the source; the emanation, so to speak, departs from its source facing it. It follows that it is incorrect to conceive of the emanative aspect merely as the establishment of a receptacle which, later, is to be informed: what goes out is already informed, already an image of the source.

Double activity and conversion are pervasive in Plotinus' thought. We have seen that they are at work in the generation of the three intelligible hypostases. Also, the sensible world itself is an external act of soul. In this case, there is no conversion, however. Conversion is essentially a kind of thinking activity. The merely sensible sphere is as such lifeless and does not think: the ability to convert is the mark of belonging to the intelligible realm, the realm of thought.

6 Intellect and the One (the Good)

Although my intention has been to present themes in an orderly way and only minimally employ terms of art without proper introduction, it has been unavoidable in previous sections to refer to Intellect and the One a few times. As these previous references make clear, the principle above soul is Intellect, which in turn depends on the One, alternatively referred to as the Good. Let us first briefly discuss Intellect. Two questions immediately arise with respect to this Intellect: why is the principle behind soul an intellect, a thinker? And how is Intellect more unified than soul?

Each of these questions can be tackled in different ways. One way is to give a historical explanation: Plato in the *Timaeus* proposes that the Demiurge grasps the realm of Ideas and fashions from his vision the structure of the world, the World-Soul and other souls, which in turn organize the sensible world. Aristotle had suggested an intellect as the ultimate principle of everything: his God, the unmoved mover, is a thinker, eternally engaged in the activity of thinking. Moreover, being pure activity without matter, eternally and changelessly thinking itself, God is as unified as anything can be (see *Metaphysics* XII, 7 and 9). Plotinus' more immediate Platonic predecessors such as Alcinous and Numenius also maintained an Intellect as a principle above soul. For them it was in fact the ultimate principle. So we might say that Plotinus just follows suit: positing an intellect above soul was a well-established norm in his tradition. This is indeed so and Plotinus might not have come up with his Intellect and all its features at this stage independently of the tradition. This does not mean, however, he could not have given philosophical reasons for Intellect and its properties. What reasons might he have given?

The philosophical answers to the two questions will indeed turn out to be interrelated because the perfection evoked in the first turns out to be the same thing as the unity mentioned in the second. We shall see the reasons for this in Chapter 3. One reason Plotinus gives for Intellect being the principle above soul is that even if soul is essentially a thinker its thinking is seen to fall short of the supreme kind of thought. This is the point of the quote from V.1.3 on pp. 57–58. Soul's activity is a thinking activity and soul, we have seen, is an image. The Principle of Prior Possession implies that that which it is an image of is a more perfect kind of thinking activity. That settles the first question.

As to the second question, about how Intellect is more unified than soul, the first and main thing to note is that Intellect's thought is all at once of everything at once. It is non-discursive or intuitive, whereas soul's thought is discursive, which means that it divides what otherwise exists as a whole in intuition. The object of Intellect's thought is the Platonic Ideas which Plotinus, naturally for a Platonist, identifies with being (*to on*) or with what really is (*to ontōs on*). These are also very frequently referred to as "the intelligibles" (*ta noēta*), though the latter may include also items at the level of soul. We shall postpone until Chapter 4 the discussion of the details of the structure of the realm of Ideas on his account. Plotinus surely builds on what he sees as hints in Plato but the outcome is in several respects different from what most contemporary readers of Plato expect the

Platonic intelligible world to look like. For one thing, Plotinus emphasizes much more strongly than Plato the holistic nature of the realm of Ideas:[14] Intellect grasps this whole realm in a single timeless intellectual gaze. This is not the kind of thought that moves from premises to conclusions. As Plotinus puts it in V.1.4: "[Intellect] thinks by having, not by seeking" (l. 16). It does not seek, it possesses. It is a non-discursive, a timeless grasp of everything at once. What is "everything" here? Everything that really is, which for the Platonist Plotinus, is of course the Platonic Ideas.

Aren't the Ideas then yet another level or principle in addition to the Intellect? No, not exactly: the Ideas exist as the objects of the thought of Intellect, not as an independent reality that exists in its own right outside Intellect. Soul, by contrast, breaks up this whole. In our treatise and elsewhere the dispersion involved in soul's thought is connected with time: "For around Soul things come one after another" (V.1.4, 19). Plotinus' accounts of this vary somewhat, however: there often seems to be room for timeless thought of undescended souls that is distinct from the intuitive grasp of Intellect. This topic will be resumed in Chapter 5.

But what is this claim that Intellect's thought is of the things themselves? In V.1.4 we find the following relevant statement: "But each of [the intelligibles] is intellect and being, and the whole is universal Intellect and being, Intellect establishing being in thinking it, and being giving Intellect thinking and being by being thought" (ll. 26–28). The meaning of this statement is of course far from transparent. For now, let the following elucidation suffice: beings (Ideas, intelligibles) exist in the thoughts of Intellect. Plotinus adopts here aspects of Aristotle's ideas about the active intellect in *On the Soul* III and God's thought in *Metaphysics* XII. Even if the Ideas are internal to Intellect, it is not the case, however, that the Intellect simply makes up the Ideas from nothing: as the lines just quoted indicate there is mutual dependence between Intellect as a thinker and the Ideas. This doctrine constitutes a significant deviation from standard interpretations of Plato according to which the Ideas, though graspable by minds, exist in their own mode of being independently of any mind. This is indeed what Porphyry believed before he came to Plotinus. He resisted Plotinus' view at first but he was thoroughly convinced after several exchanges with Amelius, whom Plotinus had given the task of setting Porphyry straight on this issue (*Life* 18). As *Life* 18 and 20 testify, this interpretation was controversial also in Plotinus' time.

The weightiest philosophical reasons Plotinus gives for placing the Ideas inside rather than outside Intellect have to do with epistemology: the Ideas are what is real. Intellect considered as a thinker is what grasps the real, if anything does. He believes that if the Ideas are placed outside Intellect, problems will arise about how Intellect can know the real as it is in itself. If the Ideas are really outside, how can Intellect grasp anything but some kind of impression of them (see V.5.1)? Evidently, he thinks that if the Ideas and Intellect considered as a knower are from the start one thing rather than two, a better sense can be given to the notion that Intellect grasps the real as it is. We shall take this issue up in greater detail in Chapter 3, Section 5 ("The Emanation from the One: Viewpoint of the Emanation").

Yet, as the preceding account indeed suggests, Intellect is not wholly one: there are many Ideas and there is a subject who thinks them that is at least notionally distinct from what it thinks, even if these two are also one and the same in the sense that they necessarily come as a pair. In fact Plotinus insists that it is in the nature of thought, even the intuitive thought he attributes to Intellect, to involve plurality. Here Plotinus differs from Aristotle, where God's thought must have a simple object. Actually, the plurality thought involves is of two kinds: the duality between thinker and what is thought and a plurality internal to what is thought: no object of thought can be something undifferentiated because if it were, there wouldn't be anything to think about it. So the high level of unity Intellect possesses turns out to be an imposed feature: Intellect as the whole consisting of a thinker and a variegated object of thought cannot be the primal source of unity.

This necessitates the supposition of a more unified principle above Intellect. The Intellect is indeed supremely unified as compared with other things, yet it is not wholly one: its unity is an imposed feature which it must have from elsewhere. This is what Plotinus calls the One or alternatively the Good. Because the One is totally simple and, hence, entirely undifferentiated, it cannot be captured by thought, not even by Intellect's kind of intuitive thought. For as we just noted, any thought presupposes differences: a difference between the subject and the object of thought and a variegated object of thought. Not even Intellect can have a thought of something totally seamless. Perhaps some kind of experience of such an entity is possible, but that experience would not be an experience of thought.

It also follows from the simplicity of the One that the One itself does not think (or desire, love, hate or anything of the sort): a thinking or desiring thing involves a distinction between the subject who thinks or desires and what it thinks or desires. A totally simple thing couldn't even think itself, for that would presuppose that it saw some distinctions within itself. But there aren't any, so it could not think itself. Nevertheless, Plotinus seems to suppose that in some sense the One isn't void of mental life. It is just not the kind of "mental life" we have or even Intellect has. At other times Plotinus denies any sort of mental life to the One. We shall address this apparent inconsistency in the next chapter.

In any case, the One cannot be thought and does not think at all or at least not in any way that is remotely familiar to us. Another claim about the One Plotinus several times makes is that it is "beyond being" (*epekeina tēs ousias*). The phrase comes from Plato's *Republic* VI, 509b9, in the famous passages where the Idea of the Good is likened to the Sun. The Idea of the Good is said to be beyond being. This passage in Plato along with the first hypothesis of the *Parmenides* 137c–142a is Plotinus' main Platonic source for his notion of the One. Plato treats the Idea of the Good as an Idea, even if it has a special status among the Ideas. Plotinus denies that the One (the Good) is an Idea. The One is beyond being in the sense that there is nothing we can say that it is: if we said it was just or brave or whatever, we would, Plotinus thinks, be presuming distinctions within it. Nevertheless, the One is the source of everything and in that sense it contains everything there is but in an indistinct form.

The One is not only so called, it is also called the Good. The reason for this is that in Plotinus' view unity and goodness are ultimately the same thing. Goodness means perfection. Nothing which isn't unitary is perfect, complete. The underlying assumption here is that any plurality is a sign of imperfection, a lack that needs to be amended. This may seem like a strange supposition. Something of the same kind is, however, presumably present in the contemporary drive for a unified theory of physics. Why should we not be content with several irreducibly different fundamental forces in nature?

7 Plotinus' language

Even if attempts at detecting a radical change of mind in the *Enneads* have largely been unsuccessful, this does not prevent Plotinus from saying different and at least prima facie incompatible things about the same subject from time to time.[15] It is just that these cannot so readily be connected with the chronology of the treatises. So if these apparent inconsistencies reflect changes of mind, we would have to suppose that Plotinus changed his mind on some topics rather often. This may occasionally be the case, but presumably by and large the apparent inconsistencies are to be explained in a different way.

Let me give a few examples. Plotinus sometimes speaks as if it is quite natural to attribute a kind of activity (*energeia*) to the One (V.4.2; VI.8.20); at other times he seems to reject the legitimacy of such an attribution (VI.7.17; VI.8.16). Sometimes he emphatically denies that Intellect undertakes any kind of search for knowledge (*zētēsis*) (V.9.7, 9–11), it possesses its object; on occasion, however, he attributes a search for knowledge to it (V.3.10, 49–50). He sometimes speaks without any reservations as if Intellect's thoughts can be rendered by sentences. Admittedly, these sentences do not constitute any ordinary shop talk, they are rather philosophical and abstract, but ordinary sentences nevertheless (V.3.10; V.3.13); at other times he suggests that these thoughts are of a kind that our discursive reason employing its ordinary sentences is incapable of expressing (V.8.6). He sometimes suggests that the One and Intellect, in proceeding, give something of themselves to what follows upon them; at other times he says that they do not. And so forth.

The problems such apparent inconsistencies give rise to must of course be tackled one by one in context. It turns out that the inconsistency can often be explained away as purely superficial, depending, for instance, on what Plotinus is comparing and contrasting on each occasion. Thus, he might attribute a search for knowledge in a certain sense to Intellect when contrasting it with the One, but deny that Intellect searches for knowledge when comparing it with the embodied soul. It is a question of being a search of a different sort.

There is, however, a certain pattern in Plotinus that is not to be overlooked. On many delicate issues it is as if he wishes to say both "yes" and "no," or in a way "yes," in another way "no." Sometimes he says both "yes" and "no" virtually in the same breath. Occasionally this may be a matter of style more than anything else. When for instance he says of a cause that it "gives itself and doesn't give itself" (IV.9.5, 4), he might have explicated himself, as he often does elsewhere, by saying that the product arising from the cause is to some degree similar to it and to that extent the cause must have given something of itself to the product. On the other hand, he also believes that the principle is not in the least affected by this act of image-making and that it loses nothing of itself by it; in this sense it doesn't give itself. In this and other similar cases the air of contradiction can easily have been eradicated—even if the doctrine behind it may remain something of a puzzle.

In some other cases, however, the apparent contradiction lies deeper: Plotinus is trying to say things that he thinks cannot be properly expressed in ordinary language. This is surely the case for instance about his statements about the internal activity of the One. Strictly speaking neither activity nor anything else can be ascribed to the One. Nevertheless, he thinks that if one were *per impossibile* to describe the One as it is in itself, it would be correct to attribute activity to it. More or less the same goes for the apparent contradiction mentioned above about Intellect speaking discursively: intellect thinks but it doesn't use words or sentences in its thinking (on the issue of talking and writing about the non-discursive, see Rappe 2000). Plotinus, however, when accounting for Intellect's thought not only uses words to describe it (that goes without saying), he also attributes words and sentences to it. He even says that Intellect "says" certain things. Here he is expressing in language thought that, according to him, is essentially independent of language: linguistic expression of it is at best an inferior image of what it really is (cf. V.8.6). In any case, Intellect is supposed to be atemporal and non-spatial. Our reasoning capacities are adapted to describing the sensible world, which is crucially different in these and other respects (see VI.5.2, 1–5). This means that in his accounts of the supra-discursive sphere, i.e. Intellect and the One, Plotinus often uses words metaphorically as a hint and they cannot be taken at face value. But in what sense then are they to be taken? Obviously, none that can be rendered by alternative words.

Plotinus' attempt to say, using words and sentences, things that cannot be adequately expressed in language becomes especially problematic in his accounts of the generation of Intellect from the One. There is no shortage of passages that state in clear terms that the intelligible region is timeless and non-spatial. Yet, the whole of the language Plotinus employs to talk about this abounds in spatial metaphors and in the language of events, which, one would presume, presupposes time. Evidently, he is trying to say something his tools of communication are not suited for. There are in fact indications that Plotinus takes our discursive reason, and thereby presumably language, to be based in the realm of bodies (see VI.5.2). It is a pressing question, which I shall, however, not address here, what meaning we can give to Plotinus' discourse on the intelligible realm without presupposing the world of time and space that this discourse undeniably invokes at the same as it rejects. Presumably, he wants us to think of "something analogous to events but not events" and "something analogous to space but not space." The question is what such a "something" could be.

8 Chapter summary

We have now got a glimpse of the stages of Plotinus' view of reality: from matter and bodies, to Soul, Intellect and, finally, the One. Some ideas or patterns pervasive in his thought have been introduced: there is the Principle of Prior Possession and the idea that the principles are realities in their own right independently of what they bring about, i.e. the notion of a self-contained internal activity. Furthermore, the central notions of unity and plurality have been introduced: Plotinus' version of the Principle of Prior Possession implies that the principle of anything possesses what it is the principle of in a more unified form than the effect. We have further seen how talk of *logoi*, images, emanation and external acts can be seen as a part of this general picture.

All this suggests the picture of a pyramid-shaped hierarchy with an absolute unity at the top and then stages of increased plurality the further down we go, reaching in the end the ultimate plurality of pure matter. The "pyramid" comes in distinct steps or levels (in that respect, it resembles an Aztec pyramid) and in a sense the same things exist at the different levels: somehow, everything is in the One but there it is totally indistinct and undifferentiated; in Intellect, these same things have come to light as distinct but still as a part of a very unified whole; and in Soul, the distinctions are clearer but it is still a unified whole. When we come to mere bodies everything has become more individuated and less a part of a whole. While Plotinus on the one hand emphasizes the enormous difference between, say, Intellect and mere sensible bodies, there is nevertheless a sense in which the same things exist at both levels: bodies are the things in Intellect at a certain stage of development.

The extremities of the system, the One and Matter, are no doubt meant to be limiting cases: Matter is not just "very plural" and the One "very simple," they are, respectively, the most plural possible and the most simple possible. There is reason to believe that Plotinus considered each different level to be characterized exactly by a given degree of unity/plurality and that every possible degree is actually instantiated. He is explicit about this as concerns the three hypostases: the One, Intellect and Soul. Again, picking up on Plato's *Parmenides*, he describes the three hypostases as respectively "one," "one–many" and "one and many." At least once he continues to give similar formulae for the sensible sphere (IV.2.2, 53–55). Nevertheless, whatever he may exactly have thought about this, he nowhere systematically tells his readers in what each degree of unity consists. The following, however, seems reasonably evident. The One is the limiting degree of unity that cannot be exceeded. Intellect involves a subject/object distinction and a distinction between different intelligible objects (Ideas). Despite these distinctions, Intellect is a tightly knit whole, whose components all presuppose each other. As regards Soul, the chief difference between it and Intellect is that soul's thought is discursive. This means that instead of the non-discursive grasp of the whole in Intellect we have the whole broken up in soul. A power of the World-Soul thinks in temporal succession and Plotinus says that the life of this power of soul is time. This successive thought in turn causes the movement of the spheres by which we measure time. This will be dealt with in Chapter 5, Section 7 ("Soul and Time").

Time and space are to be seen as instances of increased multiplicity the further away from the One it gets. Things that are in Intellect in a non-spatial and atemporal unity are temporally and spatially separated in the sensible sphere. Plotinus sometimes uses the analogy of a seed and the plant that grows from it to illustrate this (IV.8.6, 9; IV.9.5, 9). Think of the seed itself in the place of Intellect or that of the undescended soul, and of the plant in the place of the sensible world. Then we may note that the features of the plant are all together in the seed and in a way timelessly (nothing is going on in the seed while it remains a seed). The features of the plant develop in a temporal order: first the root and sprouts, then stem and leaves, then flowers and fruits—or whatever the exact manner of reproduction is. These are temporally separated events and the different parts of the plant are spatially separated as well. In the seed, Plotinus insists, they were all together. One might try to object: even if the seed is much smaller than the plant, the seed still has distinct parts that must give rise to the different parts of the plant. But no, Plotinus would respond, all the parts of the plant are potentially present in each; it is possible to cut off a branch and make it develop roots.

Further reading

Primary sources

Ennead V.1. (10) "On the three primary hypostases." There is a translation with commentary by Atkinson (1983).

Secondary sources

The general works listed at the end of the Introduction above may be consulted for an overview of Plotinus' thought.

Notes

1 There is an English translation, Greek text and useful commentary on *Ennead* V.1 by Atkinson (1983).
2 The words "the One," "Intellect" and "Soul" are written with initial capitals here when they are used to refer to the hypostases, i.e. the levels of reality in Plotinus' system.

3 For the history and meaning of "hypostasis," see Dörrie 1955.
4 On the Aristotelian features of Plotinus' psychology, see Blumenthal 1976.
5 There are apparent notable exceptions to the Principle of Prior Possession: God, the first mover is according to Aristotle necessarily unmoved. And Plotinus' first principle, the One, which is the cause of being and knowledge, is itself none of these things. Strictly speaking the One, the supreme principle of unity, cannot even be said to be one, because to predicate one of it is to presume a distinction between the One and its being one. These exceptions are, however, probably more apparent than real. Especially in Aristotle's case it is clear that though unmoved, the unmoved mover nevertheless imparts its own features onto things moved by it, things whose motion imitates or represents features of the unmoved mover. That is why its first effect is eternal, circular, uniform motion, which is as close as anything bodily can come to the eternal activity of thought, which is what Aristotle's God is always doing (cf. *On Generation and Corruption* II, 336b ff.). In the case of Plotinus' One, it is more debatable whether the exception is merely superficial—I happen to think though that ultimately it is. I shall postpone the discussion of that till the next chapter.
6 For a good concise account of *logos* in Plotinus, see Remes 2007: 68–72. See also Kalligas 1997, Brisson 2000a and Gerson 2012.
7 Aristotle also uses another word, *entelecheia* ("being in a state of completion") apparently interchangably with *energeia*.
8 There is immense literature on Aristotle's notion of activity/actuality. For a recent comprehensive study, see Beere 2009.
9 See *Nicomachean Ethics* X, 1174a19; *Metaphysics* IX, 1048b23–35; *On the Soul* II, 417b5–9.
10 See VI.1.16; VI.1.18, 1–3; VI.1.19, 1–8; for a discussion of this criticism with further references, see Chiaradonna 2002: ch. 2, and Emilsson 2007: 34–42.
11 On the Aristotelian roots of Plotinus' double act, see Rutten 1956, and Lloyd 1987: 167–170; 1990: 98–101. A more detailed comparison between Aristotle and Plotinus on activity is given by Emilsson 2007: 52–59.
12 Hadot (1968: 229) and Narbonne (2001: 61–79) argue for a Stoic influence. So does Armstrong (1937: 61–66; 1967: 240) in a different way. Rutten (1956) and, in the latter's footsteps, Lloyd (1987: 167–170; 1990: 98–101) take the doctrine to be a modification of Aristotle, whereas Gerson (1994: 23–24) points to Plato. For a further discussion, see Emilsson (2007: ch. 1 §§7 and 8), from which the present account is excerpted.
13 The word *archē*, here translated as "spring," is the same word that in Aristotle and in the tradition after him is usually translated as "principle."
14 In the earlier Platonic dialogues featuring the Ideas such as the *Phaedo* and the *Republic* the Ideas tend to be presented as solitary. In later dialogues such as the *Sophist* it is suggested that they are interwoven. Plotinus relies heavily on the *Sophist* in his account of the realm of Ideas (see Chapter 4, Section 2) but he definitely takes further the notion that all the Ideas make up a unified whole.
15 This section is a modified version of part of my introduction to Emilsson 2007.

Three

The One and the genesis of Intellect

1 The notion of the One or the Good

In the treatise "On the cognitive hypostases and what is beyond" (V.3. (49)), we find the following argument for an absolutely simple first principle:

> But we now have to add this further point, that, since in things which are generated it is not possible to go upwards but only to go downwards and move further towards multiplicity, the principle of each kind of thing is simpler than it. Therefore, that which makes the world of sense could not be a world of sense itself, but must be an intellect and an intelligible world; and that which is before this and generates it could not be an intellect and an intelligible world, but simpler than intellect and simpler than an intelligible world. For many does not come from many but this [intelligible] many comes from what is not many: for this would not be the principle of it if it was also many itself, but something else before it. There must therefore be a concentration into a real one outside all multiplicity and any ordinary sort of simplicity, if it is to be really simple.
>
> (V.3.16, 5–16)

We have here an explicit statement of what we could label "the Principle of Prior Simplicity." That is to say, it holds for any principle that it must be simpler than that of which it is the principle. Most of Plotinus' philosophical predecessors—Xenophanes, Parmenides,

Anaxagoras, Aristotle and the Stoics came up with a mind or intellect (*nous, logos*) as the first or at least as a member of a pair of first principles of the world. This is, for instance, Aristotle's position and Plotinus' Platonist predecessors concur on this point. Indeed, they thought that this intellect is one (both in the sense of there being only one highest intellect and in the sense of having unity in the highest degree), perfect, and self-sufficient. It has, in fact, many of the same characteristics as the Plotinian One. In the passage above, Plotinus does not really argue that there must be a principle above "Intellect and the intelligible world." He rather assumes that since there is plurality in Intellect it needs a further principle, and argues that this principle must be of a different kind. Behind this assumption lies his view that "Intellect and the intelligible world" do not have the right kind of unity and are in fact something unified rather than unity itself. Elsewhere we find abundant arguments for the plural nature of any intellect. We shall consider them in detail later in this chapter and in the next. Let it suffice to note here that any thought, even the timeless, holistic, intuitive thought of the second hypostasis, Intellect, is multiple.

The logic of Plotinus' reasoning here is fairly simple and recognizably Platonic: nothing that is at all unified but yet plural can be the ultimate principle because its unity is something mixed with plurality and not pure. Any plurality demands a simpler principle. This sort of reasoning will inevitably lead to a first principle that is absolutely simple, sheer unity. While the notion of "sheer unity" may strike us as strange and on the verge of incomprehensibility, aspects of Plotinus' thought about these matters are familiar and have a clear intellectual appeal. Often, at least, diversity is seen to need explanation and the explanation consists in subsuming the diverse phenomena under one law or concept. Eminent philosophers of science have argued that as a rule good scientific explanations consist in unification and simplification (Friedman 1974; Glymour 1980). There may be a general presumption holding that plurality needs an explanation that makes some kind of unity out of the plurality. Such an assumption seems also to be at work in contemporary physics, which seeks to unify the different partial theories of nature in one ultimate theory of everything. We may see Plotinus' concept of the One and the argument behind it as this kind of reasoning carried out to the extreme. In his view the One "must be alone by itself if it is also to be seen in other things. ... for that which is unable to be simple will have no foundation (*hypostasis*), and the composite of many parts will not exist if the simple does not" (V.6.3, 10–15). Put succinctly: the fact of composites demands something which is one, pure and simple.

Not only is the One simple, it is also unique: "A reality of this kind [i.e. absolutely simple and self-sufficient] must also be one alone: for if there was another of this kind both would be one" (V.4.1, 15–16). Thus, Plotinus evidently thinks that not only is the principle of all things absolutely simple, there cannot be more than one absolutely simple thing because any absolutely simple and self-sufficient entity would be identical with the One. We do not see much of a direct argument for the latter claim. Clearly, however, the supposition that there are two "Ones" leads to some strange results. If "the other One" is a principle of unity for our world just like the One, there would be two independent principles of unity. How would one distinguish them? Plotinus indeed has a point when he says that "if there was another of this kind both would be one."

We might suppose, however, that this "other One" was totally unrelated to this world. It would then be the principle of unity for another world that is unconnected to ours. At least prima facie this is not an inconsistent supposition but presumably Plotinus assumes the uniqueness of this world and intends his uniqueness claim about the One to be understood as saying that there is only one entity of the nature of the One behind this world: if we imagine another one like it, it would, both internally and in its effects, turn out to be indistinguishable from the One. In other words, we were not really conceiving of a different entity after all.

We do not see this explicitly claimed in the *Enneads* but Plotinus might also have questioned the supposition that there is another world "unrelated to ours." At least he is likely to have queried what is meant by this: if this other world is conceived of as something of the same kind but not included in our world, Plotinus would have reacted by saying that the supposition does not make sense; if that other world is "of the same kind" it is really included in the conceptual framework of our world and our reasoning about this totality and its conceptual framework would lead to the same, unique One. If, on the contrary, this other world shares nothing with ours, Plotinus might have rejected the hypothesis as nonsense: in what sense could we speak of a world that shares nothing with our world?[1]

Plotinus also calls the One the Good—he refers to it almost as often by the latter name. This designation reflects the perfection and self-sufficiency he attributes to the One: the One is not in need of anything, does not lack anything, doesn't desire anything. Actually, these two characteristics, unity and perfection, are according to Plotinus ultimately one and the same. This point is well brought out in the following passage from "On the One or the Good":[2]

> For when you think of [the One] as an intellect or a god, it is more; and when you unify it in your thought, here also the degree of unity by which it transcends your thought is more than you imagined it to be: for by itself it is without any attributes. But one could also think of its oneness in terms of self-sufficiency. For since [the One] is the most sufficient and independent of all things, it must also be the most without need; but everything which is many is also in need unless it becomes one from many. Therefore, its substance needs to be one. But the One does not need itself: for it is itself.
> (VI.9.6, 12–20)

The underlying reasoning in this passage is that whatever is not the One, and hence is in some way many, needs the One. The fundamental need of anything is the need for unity, and the One is the only thing that has, or rather is, perfect unity. Therefore, it does not have the fundamental need: as our text says, the One does not need itself. On the other hand, whatever is at all many needs to be unified. This expresses a deep conviction in Plotinus' philosophical tradition: being and unity go hand in hand, to be is to be some one thing (cf. Aristotle, *Metaphysics* IV, 1003b23). In Plotinus, however, even if being needs unity, unity does not need being, at least not determinate being (cf. p. 63). Beings are in general composite, i.e. "many" or plural, and are in need of unification. The One is of itself, self-sufficient (or good, perfect) just because it is perfect unity. If we say, perhaps illegitimately and misleadingly according to Plotinus, that the One is one we are not ascribing a property to something that is different from the property.

The One is good in the sense of being perfect, lacking in nothing. It follows that it is not in need of the things that come after it:

> But a principle is not in need of the things that come after it, and the principle of all things needs none of them. For whatever is in need is in need as striving toward its principle; but if the One is in need of anything, it is obviously seeking not to be one; so it will be in need of its destroyer; but everything which is said to be in need is in need of its well-being and its preserver. So that there is nothing good for the One; so then it does not wish for anything; but it transcends good, and is good not for itself but for the others, if anything is able to participate in it.
>
> (VI.9.6, 34–42)

As this passage suggests, though the One does not need the things that come after it, they need it. In that sense too the One may appropriately be called "the Good": it is the preserver and source of well-being for everything else. There is, however, nothing which is good for it in the sense that it would be better off by having this good.

The absence of need for what comes after the One Plotinus comments on here is an indication of a characteristic feature of his thought quite generally. As he says in our last quote: "a principle is not in need of the things that come after it." It holds for the One but also for the lower principles that they in no way need what comes after them. This is connected to the logic of double activity: the internal activity of anything is self-contained. It is concerned with itself and what is prior to it. Its external act does not arise from any need or imperfection. It is simply an overflow, a bonus, so to speak. It follows from this that the One (or any other principle) does not want, wish or will anything that comes after it. The Judeo-Christian notion of a supreme God who is deeply concerned about his creation is alien to Plotinus: it would have struck him as a sign of imperfection incompatible with the self-sufficiency of the first principle. That this is so, is borne out by his claims about the will of the One in VI.8: this will is not concerned with anything outside itself (see p. 85).

We may summarize what we have seen so far about Plotinus' first principle: he holds, more or less following the Platonic–Aristotelian tradition, that there must be a single first principle on which all else depends. He agrees with the tradition about some of the first principle's important characteristics such as unity and self-sufficiency. In insisting on the absolute simplicity of the first principle, however, and the drastic consequences of this for the ontological and epistemic status of the One, he takes a crucial step beyond his predecessors—unless, of course, Plotinus was right in holding that his own doctrine is Plato's too, which in my view is unlikely. We shall consider these consequences in the next section.

2 The One is beyond being and beyond thought

Plotinus frequently describes the One as "beyond being" (*epekeina ousias*) clearly echoing Plato's *Republic* (509b9) where Plato says that the Good is beyond being (I.8.6, 27–28; V.1.8, 8; V.3.17, 13; V.4.2, 40, etc.). It is noteworthy that even if Plato in the context speaks just of "the Good," this is clearly the same thing as he elsewhere in the *Republic* calls "the Idea of the Good." Plotinus, however, takes the One (the Good) to be beyond the Platonic Ideas. Thus, in V.1.8 he writes:

> And the father of Intellect which is the cause he [Plato] calls the Good and that which is beyond Intellect and beyond being. And he also often calls being (*to on*) Idea. So that Plato knew that Intellect comes from the Good and Soul from Intellect.
> (V.1.8, 6–10)

So Plotinus thought Plato identified Ideas and being, and that since he claims the Good to be beyond being, it must be beyond Ideas too, which, of course, flies in the face of Plato's calling the Good the Idea of the Good (*Republic* 517c). Plotinus nowhere explicitly discusses this deviation from Plato. Presumably, he believed that the status of the Good as described in the *Republic* is so elevated and different from the other Ideas that it is not properly called an Idea at all. For him "Idea" and "being" go hand in hand, and each is taken to be an object of knowledge. This implies that in so far as Plato holds that the Idea of the Good can be an object of knowledge—clearly suggested e.g. by the simile of the Cave, where the released prisoner is in the end able to study the Sun itself—Plotinus deviates from him also on that point: the One itself is not an object of knowledge.

Does the claim that the One is beyond being mean that the One doesn't exist, that it is also beyond existence? Not necessarily, and in fact it cannot mean that. It has been pointed out that Plotinus did not have available a term for existence as distinguished from being.[3] Following a well-established tradition at least since Plato, he takes "being" to be "being something determinate." There is nothing that merely "is" without there being something that it is: to be is to be something. The One is beyond being in this sense: there isn't anything one can say that it is. If there were, the One would not be totally simple. For any determination of being implies a limit: if the One were for instance F, where F is some determinate being, there would also be something that is not-F. So either the One itself would be varied, being both F and not-F, or limited by something else, neither of which is compatible with its nature as the first principle of everything. So the One is beyond determinate being but not thereby beyond existence. According to such a view, the One exists without being anything in particular. This is indeed a possible view and I see no good alternative to it. Plotinus refers to the One, not as if it were some kind of fictional entity, but as very real indeed, since it is the ultimate cause of everything. He is definitely committed to the One's existence, to use contemporary philosophical parlance. It is equally clear that according to him there is nothing that the One can be said to be. If existence without being anything in particular strikes us as a strange kind of existence, we should remind ourselves that the One is no ordinary entity.

Plotinus emphasizes that it would be a mistake to consider the One "one of the all," i.e. as one of the beings (III.8.9, 54; V.1.7, 19, etc.). This is, of course, just an explication of what it means to say that the One is beyond being. This formulation is, however, significant in that it emphasizes the One's transcendence and radical difference from anything else. It is by virtue of claims such as this that a case has been made to differentiate Plotinus from the mainstream of Western metaphysics/theology, which supposedly proclaims a first principle, often but not necessarily identified with

God, that is a kind of super-being or eminent being, perhaps unknowable, but one of the beings nevertheless. So understood Plotinus' One has been compared with Heideggerian *Ereignis*, "the event of disclosure" (Schürmann 1982). It goes together with this interpretation that the One is understood as a kind of event that is a condition of, and not an active cause of, the beings. The comparison with Heidegger is interesting but an interpretation which denies the active causal role of the One in relation to the others, the beings, flies in the face of many passages that clearly indicate the contrary (cf. Narbonne 1999).

The One is thus the single ultimate cause of everything. Plotinus sometimes accounts for this in words suggesting that everything there is comes from the One or that the One is the power of everything (*dynamis pantōn*) (III.8.11, 40; V.2.1, 7–8; V.1.7, 9–10; V.3.15, 33). But if everything comes from the One, does not the One contain everything and how can it then be beyond everything, beyond being? The answer is again that being, as Plotinus understands that term, is something determinate. But the One is nothing determinate and contains nothing determinate. Hence, the One is beyond being, and it contains everything only in the sense that it is the power from which every determinate being derives.

It follows from the utter simplicity of the One that it is not a possible object of thought. The reason for this is that Plotinus holds, rightly in my view, that any sort of thought, even the timeless intuition characteristic of Intellect, must have an object that is somehow complex, multiple: in the totally simple there is nothing to think, know or understand. The One does not think itself either. This is well brought out in a famous passage in "On the cognitive hypostases and what is beyond":

> For if the altogether partless [i.e. the One[4]] had to speak itself, it must, first of all, say what it is not; so that in this way too it would be many in order to be one. Then when it says "I am this," if it means something other than itself by this "this," it will be telling a lie; but if it is speaking of an attribute of itself, it will be saying that it is many or saying "am, am" or "I, I." Well, then, suppose it was only two things and said "I and this." It would already be necessary for it to be many: for, as the two

things are different and in whatever manner they differ, number is already there and many other things. Therefore, the thinker must grasp one thing different from another and the object of thought in being thought must contain variety; or there will not be a thought of it, but only a touching and a sort of contact without speech or thought, pre-thinking because Intellect has not yet come into being and that which touches does not think.
(V.3.10, 33–44)

Parts of this quotation are quite obscure in the details. Plotinus argues here that the One could neither say what it is not nor what it is, in either case it would have introduced a plurality into itself: in the case of thinking what it *is not* this is presumably so because by distinguishing itself from something it is not, it would introduce a duality into its thought;[5] if it has duality in its thought, it is no longer perfectly simple. Thinking what it *is* also involves making distinctions within itself, or else its thought would boil down to something like "I, I" or "am, am," which, as Ham (2000: 196) notes, would be failing to say or think anything at all, mere gibberish.[6] The general reason why the One does not think itself which emerges here is the same as we gave for why the One is not a possible object of thought for Intellect or for us: "the object of thought in being thought must contain variety." Hence, were it to think itself, it would have to be a complex object of thought and any self-thought we may try to imagine on its behalf would introduce plurality into it.

There is another distinction at play here, which would also suffice to make any self-thinker double rather than simple, namely that between the subject and the object involved in any thought. Not only does the object of thought have to be plural, any thought also involves another sort of plurality, the distinction between the subject and the object of thought. This distinction is at stake where Plotinus says "but if it is speaking of an attribute of itself, it will be saying that it is many." In the case of the self-thinking at issue in the passage quoted these two sorts of plurality, the duality of subject and object and the plurality of the object, are really merged. More on this in the next chapter, Section 4 ("Intellect's Self-Thinking").

It goes together with the view that the One cannot be thought, that it cannot be described. Said a bit technically: nothing can be predicated of the One, not even the predicates "one" or "good" can be applied to it, even if Plotinus refers to the One as "the One" and "the Good" (see VI.9.5, 30–33; VI.7.38, 1). The reason is that the statement "the One is one" (or "the Good is good") indicates in Plotinus' view that the One is one thing and its attribute of being one, another. In that case the One would no longer be absolutely one and simple. The One is not a thing that happens to have unity: it is unity itself.

So nothing can be said of the One. Nevertheless, Plotinus says a great deal about it. So have I in the preceding pages. How can this be? The answer to this question lies in a distinction Plotinus makes between different ways of saying something. He says in connection with the One:

> How then do we ourselves speak about it? We do indeed say something about it, but we certainly do not speak it, and we have neither knowledge nor thought about it. But if we do not have it in knowledge, do we not have it at all? But we have it in such a way that we *speak around* it, but do not *speak* it. For we say what it is not, but we do not say what it is: so we speak about from what comes after it.
>
> (V.3.14, 1–8)[7]

He seems to be saying that we know nothing and can say nothing about the One as it is in itself—there is, as we have seen, nothing that it *is* in itself, so there is nothing to say—but we can say something about what it is not and talk about it "from what comes after it."

The remark that we can say what the One is not deserves special notice. Plotinus doesn't mean that we can, for instance, assert the One is not dead, in order to be able to affirm positively that it is in fact alive. The negation applies to both of any pair of contradictory terms. As already said: the One is none of the many, from which it follows that it is neither one of any contrary pair. This idea goes back to, or at least is given support by, Plato, who says about the first hypothesis in the *Parmenides* postulating a "one," that this one is neither in itself nor in another, neither moves nor stands still, and so forth (*Parmenides* 137c ff.). Presumably only a minority of scholars today would say that by this first hypothesis Plato had in mind anything resembling the Plotinian One. It should be noted, however, that Plato says about this same one that it "is not named or spoken of, nor is it the object of opinion and knowledge, nor does anything that is perceive it" (*Parmenides* 142a). So it is no wonder that Plotinus and other ancient Platonists saw a deep metaphysical meaning here. Perhaps they were even right.

What then about negative statements such as "the One does not think," which the *Enneads* are full of? Would this not simply be true of the One without a supplementary "thinks," i.e. without being a part of a neither–nor statement? The answer is presumably that it follows from the One's nature that it does not think just as, though for opposite reasons, it follows from a stone's nature that it doesn't think: the One is "above" thinking, the stone is "below." Arguably, terms such as "thinking" or "living," which are constitutive of the very hierarchy of reality would be exempt from the generalized "neither this nor that" claim: there must be a sense in which "the One does not think" is to be understood simply and absolutely. Yet, in the case of the One there is a further reason why it does not think, namely that no predicate, negative or positive, is true of it in so far as any predicate implies a limitation: "does not think" taken in the most direct and ordinary way, suggests that the power of the One is limited in such a way that given the class of all things, it falls into the subclass of the non-thinking ones. Plotinus repeatedly warns against putting the One together with what comes after it in this way. This is signified by the already familiar expressions affirming that the One "is not one thing among the beings" and that it is without form and boundless (V.5.6). So after all the neither–nor formula also applies to the One in the case of thinking and other such systemic predicates.

This idea of "neither *A* nor not-*A*" types of statements formed the basis of what came to be known as negative theology (*via negativa*, apophatic theology) in the medieval Christian, Muslim and Judaic traditions. Humans, it was believed, can approach and reach a certain insight into the deity by denying every term of it. They will of course not thereby come to a positive understanding of what the deity is like—that would be affirming something positive about it— but nevertheless by this means it is possible to get a sense of it. Plotinus may not have invented the *via negativa*—it is founded on an interpretation of Plato's *Parmenides* that Plotinus did not invent (see Chapter 1, Section 4, "The Background to Plotinus' Philosophy I: Pre-Plotinian Platonism")—but he is certainly the first preserved thinker in the Western tradition to use it extensively and he played an instrumental role in establishing it as a settled approach.

The One figures also in many other kinds of statements than negations: the *Enneads* abound in remarks to the effect that the One is the ultimate principle and cause of Intellect and everything else (III.8.11, 40; V.2.1, 7–8; V.3.15; VI.8.19, 12–20, etc.)—the productive activity of the One will be dealt with in Section 5. Plotinus also frequently says that Intellect bears resemblance to it and that everything else needs or desires it (III.8.11, 15–16; V.5.12). Thus, there are plenty of remarks indicating the One's status in relation to other things. None of this, however, asserts anything about the One as it is in itself, and it should be counted as "speaking around it," not as "speaking it." Considering the fundamental features of the system, we note the ever-increasing unity the closer to the One we get. This of course gives a certain indication of the nature of the One: Intellect is that which must come closest to it, be most like it; yet, we know that in the characteristics in virtue of which Intellect is second in the hierarchy, the One surpasses Intellect to such an extent that we can no longer talk about "characteristics" or an intellectual grasp.

Plotinus also says that the One is totally unrelated to anything (*pros ouden*) (VI.8.8, 12–13; VI.8.11, 32). How is this compatible with its being the cause of others? The answer is that its causality is not essential to it, that is to say, if we could *per impossibile* define the One, the others which it causes would not enter into its definition at all. Thus, the statement that the One is unrelated is on par with the one we have already met with, that it is in no need of the others. It rests entirely in itself, "isolated" (VI.8.9, 10).[8]

With his doctrine of the One as beyond knowledge and thought, Plotinus becomes the first thinker in the Western philosophical tradition to argue in a sustained manner that there are absolute limits to thought—not just human thought, but any thought—and at the same that in some sense there is something beyond these limits and that that something is of great importance if it is not God himself. Such a view was to have a long history in the West in the

Middle Ages and the Renaissance. In later centuries Immanuel Kant, with his doctrine of the unknowable thing in itself, and the early Wittgenstein of the *Tractatus Logico-Philosophicus*, with his notion of the mystical, express views reminiscent of Plotinus'. By noting this I do not wish to suggest these thinkers' conceptions of the unspeakable or unknowable are the same as Plotinus'—much is actually rather different—or that Plotinus directly influenced them. That there are indirect traces of him at work here, however, seems highly probable: see Chapter 11 on Plotinus' influence.

One significant difference between Plotinus and his ancient Neoplatonic followers has to do with what has come to be known as Plotinus' mysticism: although it is not possible to think or know the One according to Plotinus, it is possible to have an experience of it that transcends intellectual thought. This is what has been called, misleadingly, in my view, the mystical union with the One. That theme will be resumed in Chapter 10, Section 1 ("Mystical Experience").

3 Thought, activity, will, power and freedom of the One

Despite numerous crystal-clear denials that the One can be thought or described, we find in the *Enneads* a number of positive attributions. There are at least two passages where the claim that the One does not think may seem to be compromised. In the early treatise, "How that which is after the first comes from the first, and on the One" (V.4. (7)), he says that the One

> is not like something senseless; all things belong to it and are in it and with it, it being completely able to discern itself. It contains life in itself and all things in itself, and its comprehension of itself is itself in a kind of self-consciousness in everlasting rest and in a manner of thinking different from the thinking of Intellect.
>
> (V.4.2, 15–19)

In the much later treatise, "On autonomy and the will of the One" (VI.8. (39)), he attributes to the One some kind of "thought transcending thought" (*hypernoēsis*) (VI.8.16, 32).[9] In the same context he ascribes to the One both activity (*energeia*) and a kind of will (*boulēsis*, *thelēsis*) and being or substance (*ousia*). It should be noted, however, that in this treatise Plotinus warns that he is breaking the rules. He says about these attributions that "it was not correct to use them, because one must not make [the One] two, even for the sake of forming an idea of it; but now let us depart a little from correct thinking in our discourse for the sake of persuasion" (VI.8.13, 2–5). He then proceeds to speak about the One much more positively than anywhere else. Often he qualifies his positive word or statement by the word *hoion*, which may be translated as "kind of," or even "as if," "quasi-." Indeed, he remarks that one should take all his expressions here to be qualified by "kind of," "as if" (VI.8.13, 47–50). This is Plotinus' standard way, not at all restricted to this treatise or topic, of indicating that what he is saying is not to be taken at face value.

It is not easy to judge what we are to make of this. Some scholars take it that Plotinus really intends the One itself to be utterly beyond anything mental or psychological.[10] Thus, they play down the significance of these passages. The former passage is early and the first principle is referred to as "the intelligible" here, which is unique. (Clearly, however, he is talking about the first principle, prior to Intellect; in most respects what he says about it here is the standard doctrine of the One.) As to the chronologically later passages in VI.8, one might say that the "kind of" qualification indicates that Plotinus is speaking metaphorically or wilfully saying something he doesn't really mean. I shall return to the question of the compatibility of this kind of positive attribution to the One with the negative approach at the end of this section.

Plotinus also ascribes activity (*energeia*) to the One. In discussing problems involved in holding that the One makes itself, he imagines someone objecting that "if [the One] makes itself, it is not yet, in so far as it is the object of the making; but in being the maker, it is already before itself, since itself is the product" (VI.8.20, 2–4). To this he responds:

> Against this it must be said that [the One] is not to be ranked as product but as agent; we hold that its making is absolute (*apolytos*), not so that something else should be accomplished from its making, as its activity does not aim at accomplishing a product, but it is entirely it.
>
> (VI.8.20, 4–8)

Several comments on this activity attributed to the One are called for. We should note that when Plotinus, with qualifications, ascribes being (*ousia*), activity and will to the One, he is not ascribing three different things to it: "and its activities are its, kind of, being, and its will and its being will be the same thing" (VI.8.13, 6–8). It may be a consolation that the simple One does not turn out to be three different things but how can Plotinus even attribute activity to it and still keep it simple? After all, he also says that the One is beyond activity (VI.7.17, 10).

The activity ascribed to the One would not be like that of a builder who begins to build or a thinker who is not thinking and begins to think, thus becoming fully what he or she really is. There is no transition from passivity to activity here, not even of the sort that does not constitute a genuine change. Intellect—we shall see more about this in the next chapter—is characterized as activity par excellence but this does not mean at all that it is constantly changing. So activity as such does not imply change. In the case of the One, there is not even a formal distinction to be made between the agent of the activity and the activity as such or its object. As Plotinus puts it in the quote above: "[the activity] is entirely [the One]." Thus, the activity of the One is different from that of Intellect, which does presuppose formal distinctions.

So, the activity pertaining to the One is of a peculiar sort, identical with the One itself. Perhaps it is a misnomer to call this activity and we are in any case likely to be at a loss about what this means. Actually, as we have seen, it isn't really an activity, strictly speaking, but a "sort of activity." One reason why Plotinus may be tempted to see something like activity in the One is that what the One brings about is a by-product of it, something that behaves like an external activity elsewhere in the system. If the product is the external activity of something, "that something" presumably has got to be something like internal activity (see Chapter 2, Section 4, "Emanation and Double Activity"). And since it is evident from other considerations that "that something" must be utterly simple, it must *be* its internal activity rather than *having* it: no distinction can be made between it and its internal activity.

In VI.8 Plotinus even ascribes a kind of will to the One. This will, however, does not aim at producing anything—this was indeed the point of the lines we quoted above from this treatise. The will of the One is just for itself, and it is an unusual will in at least two respects: it does not involve having alternatives, the ability to do this or that (VI.8.21, 1–3), and what it wills is just itself. In virtue of this will the One is free in the highest possible degree. The intuitive idea here seems to be that the ultimate object of will or desire of anything is the One (the Good). In the case of other things than the One itself, this aim is, however, never entirely fulfilled—if it were, the thing in question would be the One. This is because these other things have completeness as something external to themselves, as an imposed feature they have to win. The Good itself has nothing to gain. Its will is itself as it is. As Plotinus puts it himself:

> So it was all will and there is nothing in it that is not willing—nothing then before willing. So it itself is primarily its will. So then it is also as it willed and of the kind it willed and what follows upon this will, what this kind of will generated—but it generated nothing in it, for it was this already.
> (VI.8.21, 14–19)

The One's will, clearly, is a strange sort of will: it is not directed at anything external to itself and the One is simply its own will! This statement may stretch our sense of comprehensibility. It may seem that in an attempt to render it compatible with the simplicity of the One Plotinus has transformed the notion of willing beyond recognition. In order to see what lies behind the attribution of a kind of will to the One, we must consider this passage's context in the treatise. After discussing human freedom and "what is up to us"—we shall return to this topic in Chapter 10, Section 2.2 ("Freedom and What Is Up to One")—and the freedom of Intellect, Plotinus has come to the conclusion that "[t]he soul, then, becomes free when it presses without hindrance to the Good by means of Intellect, and what it does through this is in its power, but the Intellect is free through itself [because it rests in the Good, cf. VI.8.6, 35]" (VI.8.7, 1–3). So we can be free and so is Intellect thanks to the One—here mostly referred to as the Good. But can the Good itself be said to be free and to have something in its power, even if it is thanks to it that what comes after it is free?

At this point Plotinus presents what he calls a "rash statement" against granting freedom to the Good: "since [the nature of the Good] happens to be as it is and does not have the mastery of what it is, and is what it is not from itself, it would not have freedom, and its doing or not doing what it is necessitated to do or not to do is not in its power" (VI.8.7, 11–15).[11] Most of the remainder of the treatise is to be seen as a response to this "rash statement," which Plotinus immediately characterizes as "absurd." It may seem that the "rash statement" invokes contradictory objections, both chance and necessity: on the one hand the Good just happens to be the way it is and has no responsibility for this, on the other hand it says that it is necessitated to act as it does. There is, however, nothing contradictory in the "rash statement." It is a conditional: if the Good just happens to be the way it is and has no mastery over the way it is, then it is necessitated to act or not to act the way it does. In what follows Plotinus argues against both the antecedent of the conditional and the consequent. The Good neither just happens to be the way it is nor is it not its own master nor is it necessitated to act the way it acts. Let us look at these claims in turn.

It makes no sense to say that the Good just happens to be the way it is. Plotinus gives several reasons for this. He argues in chapter 10 that the Good is what gives the opposite of chance, "reason, order, and limit" (VI.8.10, 11–12), to others. "Chance" and "happens to be" apply to others when what happens "does not come to be as a result of what goes before and consistently, but is mere coincidence" (VI.8.10, 9–11). But nothing comes before the Good. Hence, the way it is cannot be attributed to chance. Terms such as "chance" or "happens to be" are simply not applicable. He continues to argue against the supposition that the Good merely happens to be in chapter 9, now seeking to understand what the person who holds this really means. Unfortunately, the text is obscure (even for Plotinus) and there are some textual issues but here is what I make of the first twenty-four lines: The opponent is saying that if the Good had had a different nature, that nature would have been the first principle—it is tacitly implied that there is no reason why it has this nature rather than that. Thus, the standard for all goodness, and in fact all being, is arbitrary. To this Plotinus replies that nothing else than the Good as it is could have been the first principle, which is as it has to be. For any other principle, however good, would be inferior and hence, by the Principle of Prior Possession, in need of the Good.

Being the master of what one is is another term the "rash statement" denies of the Good. But is the Good its own master? He does say in chapter 9 that the Good "is complete truly sovereign power over itself" (l. 45). Later, however, he qualifies this, saying that "being the master of something" really is a relation implying two terms, "master" and "what is mastered," which does not apply to the Good. Thus, he concludes that "we shall not even admit the 'master of itself' to it, not because something else is its master but because we have allotted the 'master of itself' to substance, and put [the Good] in a more honourable position" (VI.8.12, 28–31). So the Good is something akin to being its own master but superior. Of course, this does not mean that the Good is not its own master in the way, say, a slave is not his own master, i.e. in a sense that implies being mastered by something else.

Plotinus gives less space to the question whether the Good is necessitated to do or not to do what it does. He does say, though, in chapter 10 that "[the Good] is not as it is because it cannot be otherwise, but because being what it is is the best. For not everything has the power over itself to go to the better, but nothing is hindered by another to go to the worse. But that it did not go was due to itself" (VI.8.10, 26–29). It turns out that this "due to itself" means "due to its will," which in turn is the Good itself. So nothing hinders the Good from being different but it is entirely content with itself the way it is. What might it want from worse things? In the final chapter of the treatise, Plotinus, however, asks: "Could it then make itself anything else than it did?" And he responds:

> Now we shall not yet do away with its making itself good because it could not make itself evil. For power to make there is not to be understood as the power to make opposites, but as making with power unshaken and not to be deflected, which is the power to the highest degree when it does not abandon unity: for to be capable of the opposites belongs to incapacity to remain with the best.
>
> (VI.8.21, 2–7)

So the Good could not be any different from the way it is and still remain the Good but this is not so because anything forces it to be the way it is. It could be different in the sense that nothing hinders it from being different. But it is its own will and its will, i.e. itself, is not directed at anything else. So the Good stays with itself.

Could we raise a *Euthyphro* kind of question about the Good? In the *Euthyphro* 10a Socrates asks Euthyphro if pious things are pious because the gods love these things or the gods love them because they are pious. Could we ask about the Good in a similar manner whether it is the Good because it wills itself to be such as it is and the way it is sets the standard for goodness, or does it will itself such as it is because this is the best possible thing to be? The message of VI.8 seems to be that neither question should be answered affirmatively, i.e. it is not the case that the goodness of the Good (and hence of anything else) is stipulated by what happens to be its will, nor is it the case that there is a supremely good object independently of the Good's will and its will is directed at this object. The reason is that the thesis that the Good is its will and is directed at nothing else guarantees that the Good is utterly undifferentiated and self-contained; it follows that it must be the first principle of everything; and it guarantees as well that the will of One is a perfectly good will: there is no better thing that it is possible to want.

Is it the case that while mostly sticking to a negative discourse about the One, "speaking around it," perhaps, but not "speaking it" (see pp. 79–80), Plotinus also presents a positive doctrine about it in VI.8? And if so, are the two approaches compatible? Leroux (1990) discusses this question in his long introductory essay and seems to come to the conclusion that there is a contradiction between Plotinus' standard negative theology and the attribution of will and freedom to the One in VI.8. In a critical discussion of Leroux' work, O'Meara (1992: 248) resists this conclusion. He reminds us of Plotinus' warning and qualifications concerning deviation from correct thinking, and suggests that in the later chapters of VI.8, where we find the positive attributions, "Plotinus proposes a series of persuasive arguments falling short of what is correct (cf. 18, 52–3), yet serving to raise soul up to a better view of things (cf. 19, 1–3). We could describe these arguments as conceptual exercises, a philosophical therapy for the confused soul which is scarcely satisfactory as a discourse about the One."

The negative account of the One is certainly present in VI.8 (see VI.8.19, 13 ff.; VI.8.21, 33 ff.) and Plotinus evidently does not see any conflict in this with his other statements. Of course, Plotinus might be wrong about this; in other words, in fact there might be a conflict but he does not recognize it. It would, however, definitely be more desirable to have an interpretation that does not present him as confused about the import of what he is saying. In what follows I make a suggestion as to how and why the positive attributions are useful or helpful, a suggestion which reveals them to be true at least in a transferred sense of the terms.

The One is beyond everything, every predicate, be it self-knowledge, life, activity or whatever. This is Plotinus' standard position. So why does he deviate from that even in a qualified way as he does in VI.8? The reason may well be that he does not want his students or readers to start comparing the One with something utterly sterile and inactive, a stone or empty space, for instance. On the contrary, we should think of it as mental life at its best or something even better than that. The One is not at all void of mental life but its way of possessing it, or rather being it, is such that if we ascribe our human, mental vocabulary to it we tend to be misled into thinking that the One possesses the attributes in question in the same way as we do. Our mental attributes for the most part contain elements that suggest incompleteness and diversity. The point is obvious in the case of psychological states such as desire or need: all these imply plurality. As we have seen, according to Plotinus this holds for thought too in so far as thought necessarily involves plurality. Even Intellect's intuitive thought is not free from these implications. The fact that Plotinus sometimes thinks it necessary to resort to mental vocabulary when talking about the One indicates that he sees the One as of a "kind of mental kind" whose "kind of life" is, however, free from such implications. I venture to propose that the One is "mental life" without any plurality, without any differentiations. It is no accident that the next stage after the One is Intellect, and this fact may actually give us an inkling of what sort of thing the One is: the One, were it to give up its unity in the smallest possible degree, would degenerate into an entity of the same kind as the divine Intellect.

4 The first emanation from the One: Viewpoint of the One

Why should the One generate anything? If anything else comes after it, it is bound to be worse than it. The best thinkable state of affairs, it would seem, would be that the One just remained itself without producing anything.

We have seen that some answers to this question must be ruled out: it is not because it wants to or needs something that the One has an external product. Instead, Plotinus appeals to the generative nature of what is perfect: "everything perfect generates" (V.1.6, 38), he says. In the same vein he sometimes refers to the One as "father" (V.8.1, 3; V.8.13, 11). It is not altogether easy to assess the significance of this. In Plato's *Timaeus* 29e ff. it is said in explanation of why the Demiurge created the world that he is good and of an ungrudging nature and hence he made something like himself, i.e. good, in so far as this was possible in a created being. Surprisingly, perhaps, Plotinus does not quote this *Timaeus* passage directly but we may speculate that the generative nature of the perfect is somehow a version of this Platonic thought: what the Good brings about is good too, though inevitably less so than the Good itself.[12] So the Good has good effects. This is not at all its intention, however: its external act is just a by-product of its perfection and not its concern. The same holds true at lower levels in Plotinus' hierarchy: the "higher" is generally not concerned with the "lower."

The general metaphorical idea seems to be that there is such an abundance that there is an overflow: "This, we may say, is the first act of generation: the One, perfect because it seeks nothing, has nothing, and needs nothing, overflows, as it were, and its superabundance makes something other than itself" (V.2.1, 7–9). As we noted in the previous chapter (p. 49), he also describes this with the aid of other physical metaphors and analogies: fire and the heat it radiates or light-sources and emitted light.

All these metaphors are part and parcel of the doctrine of internal and external activity discussed in Chapter 2. Let us resume that discussion and see the fullest account of this doctrine, which is actually given to shed light on the creative act of the One. What in this early treatise, "How that which is after the first comes from the first, and on the One" (V.4. (7)), is called "the intelligible" is the first principle, the One. Plotinus has asserted that that which comes into being from the first principle is a "representation (mimēma) and image (eidōlon) of it." Then he continues:

> When, therefore, the intelligible[13] abides "in its own proper way of life" [cf. *Timaeus* 42e] that which comes into being does come into being from it, but from it as it abides unchanged. ... But how, when that abides unchanged, does Intellect come into being? In each and every thing there is an activity of the substance[14] (*ousia*) and one which goes out from the substance; and that which belongs to essence is the activity which is each particular thing, and the other activity derives from that first one, and necessarily follows it in every respect, being different from the thing itself: as in fire there is a heat which constitutes its substance, and another which comes into being from that primary heat when fire exercises the activity which is native to its substance in abiding unchanged as fire. So it is also in the intelligible; and much more so, since while it [the first principle] abides "in its proper way of life," the activity generated from its perfection and its coexistent activity acquires substantial existence, since it comes from a great power, the greatest of all, and arrives at existence and substance: for that other is beyond being.
>
> (V.4.2, 20–37)

A crucial point in this passage is that the One remains unaffected by its productive activity. Plotinus often expresses this, as here, by saying that the principle "remains." We might think that this idea accords badly with the emanation metaphors. Isn't this exactly what happens in the case of fire? It loses its heat. However this may be, Plotinus insists that in the case of the internal acts of the principles there is no loss, no change at all.

Another important point (not explicit here) Plotinus frequently makes about the relationship between the internal and the external act is that the latter is "not cut off from" the former.[15] This means that even if the external act is something distinct from the internal one, it constantly depends on the latter: were the internal act to cease, the external one would vanish like a mirror image or a shadow in the absence its maker. In this respect the relation between models and images at the metaphysical level is different from the relation between a painter, her model and the portrait: in this case the portrait can exist when both painter and model are gone. In the case of the horizontal causation of the hypostases the relation is rather like that between mirror images and the objects that are mirrored, which constantly depend on the originals (see VI.2.22, 34–35; VI.4.9, 36–10, 30; VI.4.10, 11–15).

It is evident from the passage above that the agent of the internal act is the same as of the external one: in the one case it acts internally, in the other externally. Plotinus is not suggesting that one and the same agent accomplishes two unrelated acts. Rather, the point must be that in accomplishing the first act it accomplishes the second. Elsewhere, however, he describes the internal act as totally self-contained and self-directed (VI.8.20; V.3.7). This raises the question how anything that "takes leave of" everything outside itself could be the cause of something outside itself.

Plotinus also uses the metaphor of leaving a trace (*ichnos*) to describe the relation between the internal and the external act (see p. 48). This may seem to fare better than the emanation metaphors in accounting for how the internal act can remain self-contained and at the same time cause something outside itself: think of the One's internal act as a walk and the external one as the trace left by the walk. In this case, there is no affection or loss involved in the cause, still it has an effect outside itself, namely, the trace it leaves behind.[16]

Someone might object to the metaphor of leaving a trace for expressing the generation of the hypostases on the grounds that it presupposes some matter on which to make the trace. Leaving a trace when walking presupposes sand or some other pliable matter to receive the trace. If we are seeking to account for how the One makes anything at all outside itself, we must keep in mind that there is no antecedent recipient on which it may leave a trace. When the One, superbly self-sufficient and self-contained, nevertheless acts externally, there is absolutely nothing on which it can act. Such considerations may well play a part in Plotinus' fondness for emanative metaphors and analogies. For on the surface, emanative metaphors of emitted heat or light, or of the overflow of liquids, may seem to fare better than one of leaving a trace on the ground inasmuch as they do not presuppose a pre-existing receptacle onto which the source acts.

This is not to say, however, that the emanative metaphors manage to do full justice to the case. For just like any other physical metaphors these presuppose a notion of space: we are asked to see the cause as a limited physical object that emits something of itself into its surroundings. We cannot conceptualize this without picturing the source along with its surroundings. This, however, is already too much: as Plotinus himself insists, we should not imagine the One as an object in space (VI.8.11, 13 ff.); it cannot be anything like that at all and what immediately comes after it, the intelligible region, is not in space either.

All this raises deep and intricate questions about the very meaning of Plotinus' language. Given the supposed non-physical, non-spatial and non-temporal nature of the One (or for that matter of Intellect), what can it mean to say, for instance, that it "overflows"? It is not just that this is a metaphor, which in itself is perfectly fine. The problem is that we are at a loss to relate the metaphor to the object it is applied to. I shall not attempt to solve these puzzles. Let me say, however, on a more positive note, that the metaphors do after all suggest a certain structure, namely the basic structure of double activity that we have been considering. That may not be a whole lot but it is not nothing either.

Sometimes Plotinus' notion of double act and emanation is contrasted with the Christian notion of creation out of nothing: emanationism vs. creationism. There is, however, nothing in the idea of creation out of nothing as such that conflicts with emanation or, which is the same thing, with double activity. At least, double activity is not a creation out of *something* as opposed to out of nothing. As already noted several times, Plotinus is a metaphysical monist: the One is the source of *everything* and, hence, it does not make anything from some pre-existing material. There may, however, be at least an apparent conflict between the double act view and common Christian conceptions of divine creation. Christian theology emphasizes that God creates out of his good will and that the creation is His free act that He could have left undone if He so had wished. Thus, a Christian theological critique of the Plotinian account would be that according to Plotinus and the Neoplatonists generally the world is a necessary consequence of the One's nature, not a gift freely given by an act of God's will. Thus, St. Thomas

Aquinas, for example, says that "God makes his creatures, not from necessity but through His intellect and will" (e.g. in *Summa Theologiae* I.19.4). There is an apparent conflict between this and Plotinus' statement in our passage from V.4.2 (see p. 91) that the external act of the One follows the internal one by necessity. The conflict is, however, only apparent. As Gerson (1994: 28) notes, Plotinus could accept Aquinas' statement (with the modification that for Plotinus there is no question of the One's intellect): as we have seen, the One wills itself and is itself nothing other than this will. In so doing, it is not constrained by anything else and not by its own nature either. Any difference of Plotinus and Aquinas on this point would be a false contrast: in saying that the One's act necessarily follows, Plotinus is denying that its act results from deliberation, something with which Aquinas agrees. Once the One's will is determined, which it always is, what the One wills follows by necessity. But so it is for Aquinas too.

5 The emanation from the One: Viewpoint of the emanation

There are several accounts in the *Enneads* of how the emanation from the One is turned into Intellect. Every single one of them may be said to be obscure in its own right. And though there are recurrent ideas that go through many of these passages, they are accompanied by disconcerting differences of detail. In the account that follows, I seek to focus on the common threads and ignore the troubling details.[17]

Plotinus often calls the One's external act simply "intellect" (*nous*) but clearly it is not the full-blown Intellect that comes out of the One. What comes out is something indefinite, whereas the fully fledged Intellect is in every respect defined. This first offshoot or emanation is often referred to in the literature as the inchoate or potential intellect. Its definiteness comes about through a conversion (*epistrophē*) of the external act towards its source, the One. Let us start by taking a closer look at this conversion.

As noted above, Plotinus is a monist in the sense that the One is the source of everything. With the exception of the neo-Pythagoreans mentioned earlier (Chapter 1, p. 26), in the previous Greek metaphysical tradition generally there are most commonly at least two irreducible principles, one formal and one material. The material principle, often called the "dyad," is characterized by indefiniteness, whereas form is what makes the indefinite definite. Even if Plotinus does not evoke two irreducible principles, he nevertheless essentially follows the logic of the tradition in distinguishing between a formal and a material, or receptive, aspect, a distinction to be found at every level of the hierarchy except at the top and bottom. It is just that these aspects are not ultimate principles. In the case at hand, the first product of the One serves as a kind of material aspect for the next stage, that of Intellect.

The conversion is described as a turning of what has come out of the One back towards it. It is an attempt to capture the One in thought. As we have seen, the One is not to be captured by thought and the result of this attempt is some kind of image of the One that does not depict it as it is in itself. We shall consider details of this in due course but let us get two possible misunderstandings out of the way: the conversion is not reabsorption of the emanation back into the One. That would simply bring us back to the initial stage and nothing would have happened. Second, even if Plotinus sometimes talks this way, we should try not to conceive of the emanation and the conversion as different consecutive events (cf. p. 59). As we have already noted more than once, there is no time here, hence consecutive events are out of place. So the conversion is contemporaneous with the emanation. The best way to visualize this may be to think of the emanation as backing out from the One, facing it. The emanation and the conversion may at first sight look like philosophical novelties. We saw, however, that Plotinus sees double activity and emanation as a part of the Platonic heritage. And as also previously noted, we can see how the conversion corresponds to familiar notions in a new dress: imitation in Plato, and love as a metaphysical principle in Aristotle according to which God is a cause by being an object of love. That is to say, the conversion describes the stance of a lower level by which it seeks to comprehend and absorb of a higher one as much as it can.

So the One's emanation is characterized by indefiniteness. Other characterizations that are frequently given are psychological: it is described as "sight not yet seeing" (V.3.11, 5) and as a desire or yearning (III.8.11, 22–24; V.3.10, 49–50; V.3.11, 11–12). Thus, strangely perhaps, what has been described with the aid of physical metaphors as a kind of emanation turns out to be some kind of a psychological entity having desire and, potentially, vision. The sense of surprise may be reduced if we remind ourselves that the One itself is not void of psychological traits: that this should be reflected in its offshoot is really just to be expected.

The details of the story that follows are obscure and debated. What seems fairly clear, however, is that that which has left the One, the emanation, is no longer fully one, self-sufficient, perfect. This loss gives rise to a longing for the perfection left behind and the potential intellect seeks to satisfy this longing by trying to catch sight of the One in an intellectual vision. What also is clear is that there can be no vision of the One as it is in itself: it is beyond any such grasp. Thus, what the emanation, the potential intellect, as it is often called, grasps in its conversion when it seeks to grasp the One, is some sort of image of the One that it multiplies in itself in order to get hold of it (V.1.7, 17–18; V.3.11).

What in particular is debated here is the role of the One in this process. On the one hand, it is noted that in some passages the One plays a direct, active role in informing the potential intellect. Thus, for instance, in VI.7.16, 33–35, he says: "but another principle, in a way external to [the potential intellect], was the one that filled it, from which it received its character in being filled." It is as if first the potential intellect is established by an emanation from the One and then this offshoot, by turning towards its source, gets a refill of content from that very source. But then there are other passages that rather seem to suggest that the One plays no direct role after the original emanation: "so [the potential intellect] desired one thing, having in itself a kind of image of it, but came out having grasped something else that made many in itself" (V.3.11, 6–8). Here it seems that the potential intellect comes out with an internal image of the One and that it is this image that it seeks to apprehend in the conversion (for a more detailed discussion, see Emilsson 2007: 90–101).

Bussanich (1996: 51–55) suggests Plotinus has two incommensurable ways of describing the relationship between the One and Intellect presenting two different points of view. One way is from within the intellect: from the potential intellect's point of view only the One as seen enters the picture—the potential intellect's One is the One as seen by it. Here there is no need to postulate any activity on the part of the One beyond what is given in the establishment of the potential intellect with its image of the One. The other way sees the matter from the outside or from the viewpoint of the One itself. In this case the One is taken to be active not only in establishing the potential intellect but also in informing it. This seems reasonable and would seem to do justice to the different texts. The question remains, however, whether the One is doing something different when it is informing the intellect from what it did when establishing it. In that case, the One turns out to be rather more versatile in its activities than it seems natural to suppose. Perhaps we could harmonize the two points of view by imagining that the potential intellect backs out from the One: viewed from the outside, the One is active both in producing the potential intellect and in filling its vision but this is, as it were, one and the same act. Thus, when the potential intellect turns its gaze towards the One, it in a sense just meets itself but in itself it meets an image of the One that is being produced by the One.

Let me dwell on this theme a bit longer on a speculative note. Here is the story suggested by central passages about this issue: having left the One the potential intellect feels a loss and longing after the unity and perfection of the One. It has an image or impression of the One but the intellect cannot get hold of it because of its simplicity and has to break it up into many.

First, why can the intellect not know the One, since it has got an accurate image of it which reflects its simplicity? There are two reasons for this. One reason, on which I shall have much more to say in the next chapter, is that knowledge, any kind of intellectual grasp, must be of something non-simple. There is nothing to be grasped in something that is totally without distinctions. The other reason is that to know something as it truly is in itself is to know that thing by its internal activity while the only way to know something by its internal activity is by being that internal activity. At the level of the actualized Intellect there is such a merging of the internal act constituting the object of knowledge and that of the knowing subject: the activity constituting the object and the one constituting the subject are one and the same. Since in the case of the One and the potential intellect there is already a kind of subject/object distinction in that the potential intellect has distanced itself from the One (as is evident from the fact that it needs and desires it), the potential intellect hasn't got a chance of grasping the One as it is in itself, even if it were in principle graspable. However good an impression it had of the One, it would not count as knowing the One as it is in itself, for this wouldn't be knowing it through its internal activity. The One in itself, as we have noted, may have a sort of "mental life." But this activity or "quasi-activity" is not that of thought or knowledge. So no thought of anything would capture that activity as it is in itself, for it would fail to be that activity. Thus, the argument makes a tacit appeal to the fact that the internal activity of the One is not an activity of thought; knowing the One itself would be knowing it through this internal activity. But that is impossible, because this internal activity is not of the order of thought or knowing.

This pattern of reasoning is not at all peculiar to the relation between the One and Intellect, but holds quite generally, e.g. for a soul's apprehension of Intellect: so long as it remains soul, the soul's mode of cognition is an apprehension of another and of an image. To a soul which remains a soul, Intellect in itself is, for parallel reasons, as unknown and unknowable as the One is to Intellect.[18] The difference is that Intellect is not unknowable *tout court*: by becoming Intellect, the soul will know Intellect; becoming the One, by contrast, will not result in knowing the One, for knowing is not the sort of thing that goes on there. This difference between the intended object of apprehension, in this case the One itself, which the potential intellect wishes to grasp, and the intentional object of apprehension, which is what it actually grasps, provides the dynamics of the stages in Plotinus' world: it ensures a difference between what a giver has and what is received, a difference which gets the unfolding of reality going towards ever-increasing plurality.

The very notion of the potential intellect gives rise to some difficult questions. We have frequently spoken of the potential intellect as the predecessor of Intellect. We have also said that Plotinus adheres to the Aristotelian Principle of Prior Possession. How can he also maintain that the actual Intellect arises from the potential intellect? Does not the potential intellect clearly fall into the class of potential things? As we shall see more fully in the next chapter, Intellect supposedly involves no potentiality. This is tantamount to saying, on the one hand, that Intellect is not acted on by objects external to itself, on the other, that as subject it always actively thinks, that it never moves from potentiality to actuality. But how are we to square this with the notion of a potential intellect? For what is the potential intellect other than a potential thinker and potential being? And if so, Intellect indeed seems to arise from a potential intellect. Contrary to what passages stressing the actuality and self-sufficiency of Intellect may make one believe, Intellect originates in something that is indeed incomplete and needy. So our question becomes: how can Plotinus claim both that Intellect involves no potentiality and is sufficient to itself and at the same time maintain that it originates in the inchoate intellect, which is anything but actual and self-sufficient?

I believe the answer to our dilemma lies in realizing that when Plotinus insists that Intellect is essentially actual, involving no potentiality, he means that all the intelligibles are fully whatever they are; so far as the character of any one of them is concerned there is nothing prior to it which gives it its form. So the intelligible Horse is not at some stage only potentially a horse and then made into an actual one by some prior horse. It is the first of its kind. The Principle of Prior Possession primarily applies when there is potentiality in the sense of a receptive principle, capable of receiving form. What we have called the potential or inchoate intellect—which, by the way, is not standard Plotinian terminology—is not like that: it is not the case that the contents of Intellect are there, somewhere, ready to impose their character on the potential intellect. This is not to deny that Intellect is actualized by the One. That actualization is, however, not an actualization by means of a prior actuality. The same point is convincingly argued, though in a somewhat different way, by D'Ancona (1996).

6 Chapter summary

Plotinus' first principle, the One (the Good), must count among the greatest but at the same time among the most puzzling notions ancient Greek philosophy ever produced. Although building on earlier ideas, in particular from Plato's *Parmenides* and its previous interpretations, in its richness Plotinus' notion of the One surpasses by far any previous attempts to posit a totally simple, ineffable first cause of everything. General principles of Plotinus' thought lead to the conclusion that there must be a unique first cause that is absolutely simple. It follows from its simplicity that it is beyond being in the sense that there is nothing one can say that the One is. From this it follows that the One in itself is beyond thought, knowledge and language. Nevertheless, the One can be known through its effects.

Even if Plotinus insists that the One is not a thinker and in particular that it does not think itself, in a few passages he attributes some kind of mental life to it. It was argued that these passages are not to be dismissed as aberrations. Rather, the fact that the first descendant of the One is an intellect, shows that mentality is not alien to the One. Our concepts of mental phenomena, which invariably imply plurality, are, however, unsuitable for it.

Although said to be totally self-contained and unrelated to anything that comes after it, the One nevertheless produces something—if it didn't the world would not exist. The manner of its production has given us occasion to consider more fully Plotinus' concepts of double activity and emanation. Even if Plotinus says that the One is beyond activity, he explains the One's production by the model of double activity: the One produces something out of its superabundance without, however, losing anything of itself. This is the One's external act, which Plotinus describes as a potential intellect. The intellect becomes actual when the potential intellect turns towards its source and seeks to comprehend it. The Platonic Ideas arise in the intellectual vision the intellect then has, a vision that, however, fails to grasp the One in its simplicity.

Further reading

Primary sources

Ennead VI.9. (9) "On the Good or the One." There is a commentary in English by Meijer (1992).

Ennead V.3. (49) "On the cognitive hypostases and what is beyond," especially chapter 11.

Ennead VI.8. (39) "On autonomy and the will of the One."

Ennead V.4. (7) "How that which came after the first comes from the first, and on the One."

Ennead VI.7. (38) "How the multitude of Forms came into being, and on the Good," especially after chapter 14.

Secondary sources

Eric Robertson Dodds, "The Parmenides of Plato and the Origin of the Neoplatonic 'One,'" Classical Quarterly 22 (1928), 129–143.

John R. Bussanich, *The One and Its Relation to Intellect in Plotinus: A Commentary on Selected Texts* (Leiden: E. J. Brill, 1988).

Frederic M. Schroeder, *Form and Transformation: A Study in the Philosophy of Plotinus* (Montreal: McGill-Queen's University Press, 1992).

D. J. O'Meara, "The Freedom of the One," Phronesis 37, 3 (1992), 343–349.

D. J. O'Meara, "Scepticism and Ineffability in Plotinus," Phronesis 45, 3 (2000), 240–251.

John R. Bussanich, "Plotinus on the Inner life of the One," Ancient Philosophy 7 (1987), 163–189.

John R. Bussanich, "Plotinus's Metaphysics of the One," in L. P. Gerson (ed.), *The Cambridge Companion to Plotinus* (Cambridge: Cambridge University Press, 1996), 38–65.

Anthony C. Lloyd: "Plotinus on the Genesis of Thought and Existence," Oxford Studies in Ancient Philosophy 5 (1987), 155–186.

Eyjólfur K. Emilsson: *Plotinus on Intellect* (Oxford: Oxford University Press, 2007), ch. 2.

Notes

1 Though not concerning the nature of the One, there is a very interesting thought experiment in Plotinus about another world in "On the problems of Soul (III)," chapter 8 (IV.5.8), where he considers the hypothesis that we are faced with a body outside our cosmos and raises the question of whether we could perceive it. (He has previously argued that external perception depends on the psychic unity we have with our cosmos, hence, it may seem that we could not perceive anything outside this cosmos.) He responds that if what we are confronted with outside is similar to what is inside, the supposition is really self-contradictory: if similar, it must be because it belongs to the same cosmos. The inspiration for what I have speculated here on Plotinus' behalf about the possibility of another world and another One unrelated to ours is taken from this passage.

2 VI.9. (9). Chronologically, it is the first treatise in which Plotinus reveals his whole theory of the One. For a commentary, including on the passage just quoted, see Meijer (1992).

3 On the emergence of the distinction between essence (determinate being) and existence, see Corrigan 1996 with further references.

4 Strictly speaking Plotinus has not yet introduced the One at this stage of V.3: it will unmistakably appear in the next chapter. Here he is talking about anything "altogether partless." Only the One is such, however, and we see from the end of the quote, where he says that "Intellect has not yet come into being," that it is actually the One he has in mind: the One is there "before" Intellect.
5 In fact Plotinus says that the One *must* say what it is not, if it is to "speak itself." It is far from evident why the One would necessarily have to say this. Some speculation about Plotinus' reasoning in this regard is offered by Emilsson (2007: 87).
6 Ham (2000: 196) is right in rejecting both that the formulas "am, am" and "I, I" stand for tautologies and the view of Beierwaltes (1991: 132) and Oosthout (1991: 136–137) that by the repetition in the formulas Plotinus wishes to indicate that even these formulas involve a complexity. Ham also plausibly suggests that behind this lies the doctrine of Plato's *Sophist* 262a–d that a *logos* must contain both a noun and a verb in order to say anything at all. For a more detailed analysis of this passage and its context, see Emilsson 2007: 80–90.
7 On this passage, see O'Meara 1990: 151 ff., and Schroeder 1992: 66–68.
8 The word *monachōs* in VI.8.9, 10 is I believe wrongly translated by Armstrong as "by [the Good's] uniqueness." It means here rather "in isolation."
9 What is said in VI.8 about the will and freedom of the One is of great intrinsic interest. But the treatise also discusses human freedom. Human freedom will be discussed in Chapter 10, Section 2.2 ("Freedom and What Is Up to One"). More will be said about the freedom of the One in that connection.
10 See Armstrong's introductory note to V.4, which suggests that the deviation here from the standard negative stance to the One is to be explained as an early lapse. Halfwassen (2004b: ch. 3) too holds the One to be utterly transcendent and beyond any sort of mental attribute.
11 This "rash statement" (*tolmēros logos*) has received considerable attention: Armstrong (1982) argues that the objection comes from a Christian source eager to maintain the absolute freedom of God's will. Others have suggested the Gnostics (see Leroux's 1990 commentary *ad loc.*). Armstrong's suggestion of a Christian source has been much criticized: see Leroux 1990: 112–122, O'Meara 1992: 345–346 and Frede 2011: 150–151. The way Plotinus introduces the "rash statement" suggests an external source, even if it may constitute an appropriate question to ask in the context: he often invokes an imaginary opponent in his discourse to raise objections that plausibly arise in the context but it is not his habit to label the opponent's statements the way he does here. Perhaps there is no reason to search further than Alexander of Aphrodisias' *On Fate*, as O'Meara (1992: 345–346) suggests.
12 There are, however, a few allusions to the ungrudging nature of the divine: see IV.8.4, 1–10; IV.8.6, 1–18; V.4.1, 34–36. Plotinus, however, qualifies "not grudging" with "as if" sorts of phrases. Noble and Powers (2015: 53, n. 6) plausibly suggest that Plotinus is hesitant to commit himself to the ungrudging nature of the divine because it may imply a wish to go out of itself on the part of the divine.

13 As already noted what is called "the intelligible" (to noēton) in the early treatise V.4 is what normally is called the One or the Good. Plotinus does not use these terms for his first principle in this treatise.
14 Alternatively, one might translate ousia here by "being," as I have sometimes done in previous chapters (and did for this passage in Emilsson 2007), or by "essence." "Activity of the substance" and "activity from the substance" are technical terms, and probably of Aristotelian origin, even if there is no exact equivalent to Plotinus' distinction in Aristotle. Therefore, I have chosen here the more Aristotelian word "substance," which is the traditional rendering of ousia in Aristotle, rather than the Platonic "being." It is because "activity of the substance" is a technical expression signifying primarily that the activity is internal to whatever is engaged in it that talking about the activity of the substance in connection with the One is not to imply that the One is or has a substance.
15 The expression "not cut off from" comes from Aristotle's Physics III, 202b7–8. It is pervasive in Plotinus and invariably used to indicate the constant dependence of the external act on the internal.
16 For a more detailed discussion of double activity and trace, see Emilsson 2007: 42–47.
17 John Bussanich (1988) provides an excellent commentary on all the main passages where Plotinus discusses the generation of Intellect from the One. A penetrating interpretation of the issue is also given by Lloyd (1987). I also provide an extensive discussion in Emilsson 2007: ch. 2.
18 The soul may know that Intellect is there above it, that it depends on it and that it has its rational capacities from it; this is however not to know Intellect from the internal point of view (cf. V.3.4, 15). In an entirely parallel way the Intellect is aware of the One as its principle, knowing it through its works (V.3.7, 1–9).

Four
Intellect

Intellect is the second hypostasis, the level of reality closest to the One but different from it in that it is plural. Being closest to the One, it is nevertheless as unified as anything plural can be. Intellect is in Plotinus' system the locus of real beings (identified with the Platonic Ideas) and at the same time the locus of perfect knowledge. In fact—this may be claimed to be the most essential aspect of his theory of Intellect—knowledge and being coincide, in a way coalesce, in Intellect. We shall consider this and other aspects of the theory in this chapter but let us proceed from where we left off and delve into the intricacies of this second-best hypostasis.

1 The potential intellect and the plurality of thought

We saw in the last section of the previous chapter ("The Emanation from the One: Viewpoint of the Emanation") that the potential intellect feels a loss and longing for the One and that in order to remedy this it seeks to grasp the One in an intellectual vision; the intellect cannot see the One as it is in itself and what appears to it is something it has made many in itself. I shall start the discussion of Intellect by trying to get a firmer grip on how the central notions here—the longing, the intellectual vision and the many that come about—hang together.

The need and longing for the One that the potential intellect feels and the intellectual vision it seeks to have of it are connected in a non-arbitrary way. This is shown by an interesting remark in "On the fact that that which is beyond being does not think, and on what is the primary and what the secondary thinking principle" (V.6. (24)). He says here that "sight's desire is vision."[1] The meaning of the sentence must be that the desire of the capacity of sight is to see actually. Thus, the potential intellect's desire is qualified in the following way: even if it is a desire for the One, and even for the One "in its simplicity," it is a desire to possess the One by seeing (thinking) it. So to put it crudely: the intellect in one way desires the One as it is in itself. Of this it has a certain inkling, thanks to the image it has got; cf. p. 95 in the previous chapter. But because the intellect is after all an intellect, its desire is nevertheless of such a kind that it can only be satisfied by thinking. This is because the potential intellect is of the nature of intellect and it will seek to satisfy its desire according to its own nature, i.e. by an intellectual vision.

Some light is shed on the preceding considerations by a passage in "On the cognitive hypostases and what is beyond" (V.3. (49)), chapter 13. Here Plotinus says: "That which is altogether simple and self-sufficient [i.e. the One] needs nothing; but what is self-sufficient in the second degree [i.e. Intellect], but needs itself, this is what needs to think itself; and that which is deficient in relation to itself achieves self-sufficiency by being a whole, with an adequacy deriving from all its parts, intimately present to itself and inclining to itself" (V.3.13, 16–21). Plotinus wishes to maintain both that the potential intellect needs the One and that it needs itself (V.3.10, 7–14). These are not two unrelated needs: clearly Plotinus thinks that the need for unity would not be there unless the intellect was deficient with respect to itself, i.e. needed itself. So these are different descriptions of the same need. Moreover, the need for self will not be satisfied by the acquisition of the absolute unity of the One but by self-thinking whereby the potential intellect becomes a unified whole. That is to say: of course, if the potential intellect became the One itself, its need would be satisfied. But given that the potential intellect has moved from the One and remains at a distance, it will have to satisfy its need in a different way.

But why is the stage after the One an intellect? It has already been hinted that because of the quasi-psychological attributes of the One the intellectual nature of the second stage should not come as a surprise: if the minimal degree of plurality is added to the One, it will turn into a thinker of the sort Plotinus envisages his Intellect to be. That sort of intellect has the minimal degree of plurality: it is manifold but anything less manifold would collapse into the One. In this connection a short note on the notion of thinking involved may be helpful. The Greek word for Intellect's thinking is *noein* and the corresponding substantive is *noēsis*. The English words are really too wide to capture the meaning exactly: what is involved is a rather special kind of thinking. We shall discuss this in greater detail in Sections 6 and 7 of this chapter but let us note here that the thought in question is intuitive thought, a grasp in one go of a totality. This helps explain why Plotinus thinks Intellect is something highly unified, in fact second to the One in this regard.

Before we fully embark on the discussion of the second hypostasis, Intellect, some further notes on the terminology may be in order. I adopt the convention of most scholars by writing Intellect with an initial capital when this refers to the full-blown second hypostasis. That is Intellect as subject and object of thought at once, both the highest, most general objects and the subordinate ones. I seek to restrict the capitalized word to intellect in this sense. The corresponding Greek word, *nous*, does not always refer to this, however, not even when the second hypostasis is the general topic of discussion. What here has been called the potential intellect is, for instance, most often simply *nous*, and one has to rely on the context to see that this rather than Intellect is what is meant. Sometimes, and this can be tricky to detect, Plotinus shifts the meaning of *nous* so as to refer only to the subject of Intellect's thought. Again, only the context will tell. Furthermore, there is a notion of the universal intellect (*pas nous*), which is, so to speak, at the top of Intellect, the thought of the most embracive Ideas.

How exactly does the plurality come about? Plotinus holds that any thought has a varied object. We can guess his reasons for this from the following lines from V.3:

> Therefore the thinker must apprehend one thing as different from another and the object of thought must contain variety; or there will not be a thought of it, but only a touching and a sort of contact without speech or thought, pre-thinking, because Intellect has not yet come into being and that which touches does not think.
>
> (V.3.10, 40–44)

So that which is simple cannot be grasped by thought. He does not explicitly say so, but there is little doubt that in claiming this Plotinus is appealing to our intuitive understanding of thought as involving plurality: if there are no distinctions whatsoever, there isn't anything to think.[2] Thinking seems always to be relating at least two things to each other. As Plotinus himself puts it: "one must always understand Intellect as otherness and sameness, if it is going to think" (VI.7.39, 5–6). So what is apprehended by thought is necessarily plural.

This, however, is not the only reason why thinking is necessarily plural: not only must that which is thought, the object of thought, contain internal distinctions; there is also necessarily a distinction to be made between the subject of thought and its object (V.1.4, 30–38; V.3.8, 38; V.3.10, 44–48; VI.7.39, 5–7). Arguably, this latter distinction is the more fundamental one: in a way the emergence of the potential intellect, is the emergence of a potential subject.

We may wonder why the mere emergence of the potential intellect with its differentiation from the One and longing for it does not constitute the second stage after the One: some sort of plurality seems already to have entered the scene with the very fact of the difference between the potential intellect and the One. So far as I can tell, the question is nowhere directly addressed but the answer presumably is that the stage of the potential intellect is not stable. I just called it a subject but even that is misleading because it does not apprehend anything yet. So it is at best a potential subject. The potential intellect is an inherently dissatisfied state in search of a settled existence. Plotinus would only count a stable and determinate state as a new level characterized by its own degree of unity.

2 Plurality enters the scene: The five highest Ideas

Plotinus holds that as soon as there is thought a number of things appear. In particular the very first thought will involve the five highest kinds or Forms (*megista genē* or *eidē*) invoked in Plato's *Sophist* 254d ff.: being, otherness (difference), sameness, motion and rest.[3] The distinctness of each of these ensures that there immediately are at least five items present when thought is present. Let us consider one of the passages where he introduces the five kinds in connection with the actualization of Intellect:

> But each of [the intelligibles] is intellect and being, and the whole is universal Intellect and being, Intellect with its thinking establishing being, and being giving to Intellect its thinking and its being by being thought. But the cause of thinking is something else, which also is the cause of being; they both, therefore, have a cause other than themselves. For they are simultaneous and exist together and one does not abandon the other, but this one is two things, intellect and being and thinking and what is thought. For there could not be thinking without otherness, and also sameness. These then are primary, Intellect, being, otherness, sameness; but one must also include motion and rest. One must include motion if there is thought, and rest that it may think the same; and otherness, that there may be thinker and thought; or else, if you take away otherness, it will become one and keep silent; and the objects of thought, also, must have otherness in relation to one another. But one must include sameness, because it is one with itself and so that there be something one common to all; and the difference between them is otherness.
>
> (V.1.4, 26–41)

This passage contains in a concise form a great deal of Plotinus' theory of intellect. We shall dwell on it for quite some while. I shall proceed by commenting on the different ideas contained here.

1   We see that intellect, understood as the thinker, the subject of thought, and being come as a pair: there is no actual subject of thought without an object, without some content that is being thought, and there is no object of thought without a thinker who thinks it. We should note that there is no other object of thought outside the intellect available at this stage: the only other thing there is is the One, which no doubt is the common cause of both intellect and the being mentioned. As we have seen, this is not a possible object of thought even if the One is the intended object of the potential intellect's thought. That

being and intellect come as a pair, where neither of these members can have an independent existence, a unity with distinct parts or rather aspects, is without doubt Plotinus' standard doctrine. There are some passages, however, that may seem to point in a different direction, taking either Intellect or being as primary, and there are scholars who have disputed their coequal status.[4] Since I do not know what sense it would make to maintain that there is being prior to thought given Plotinus' standard account according to which being first arises through the potential intellect's attempt to grasp the One, I have nothing to offer as regards the two passages that seem to maintain this, and shall not address this controversy here.

2   The reference to being provides an occasion for some remarks about being and related notions as applied to Intellect. Being (*on*) is along with motion, rest and the others one of the highest intelligible Forms or genera, as we have seen. Plotinus also refers to particular intelligibles as beings (*onta*). How is being as genus related to the subordinate beings? Plotinus insists that "we must be careful about this, that each genus does not disappear in its species, and that the genus is not only predicated as observed in them, but that it is both in the species and in itself, and must be at once mingled and pure and unmingled" (VI.2.19, 13–16). So Plotinus wishes to leave room for the pure genus of being (and the other primary genera), which is something in its own right above its species and is at the same time predicated in and present to each of the species. The genus of being may be something over and above subordinate species but it will never appear totally unmixed: it will always appear as being in motion (activity), at rest, and so forth (VI.2.15).

3   The question may be raised whether it is not important to keep *on* (being) and *ousia* (being; substance) distinct. Plotinus himself after all explicitly makes a distinction between the two in II.6.1, 1 ff.: being (*on*) is along with motion, rest, identity and difference one of the genera of being (*ousia*) which is the totality of these. He does not, however, follow this proposal in practice, since he continues to say that e.g. motion in the intelligible world is *ousia* and he takes the Platonic phrase "beyond *ousia*" as equivalent to "beyond *on*." As Corrigan (1996: 106) notes, *on*

and *ousia* are generally coterminous. I have chosen as the least misleading option to render both *on* and *ousia* by "being," except when the context demands the Aristotelian sense of "substance" or "essence" for *ousia*.

4   Our passage asserts: "For there could not be thinking without otherness, and also sameness." The otherness that is a necessary ingredient in thought is of two rather different kinds: there is the otherness between the thinker and the object of thought and there is the internal otherness between the objects. Each of these is evident in the remarks about otherness in the passage. Where otherness is first mentioned in the middle of the passage it is in a follow-up on the relation between thinker and object, and no doubt it is the subject–object distinction Plotinus has in mind. In the last line of the passage he means the internal difference within the object of thought. To summarize: thinking involves otherness because there is a distinction between the subject and the object of thought and because the object of thought must be varied—of what is absolutely simple there can be no thought. Sameness (or identity) is there for securing the unity of the thinker and the object as well as the unity of the object itself: there is just one item here, though internally differentiated.

5   Plotinus is brief about motion and rest in this passage. Elsewhere, he explicitly identifies the motion involved with the activity of thought. It is in this act of thought that the subject and the object are united and become something actual. Generally at the intelligible level the terms "motion" and "activity" are equivalent (cf. p. 53). Rest is included "so that it may think the same." This is presumably meant to ensure that the activity that constitutes thought rests on a selfsame object and doesn't just move on without any fixed points.

6   A notable aspect of Plotinus' use of the five kinds is that he takes them to be the highest genera of being or, which amounts to the same, the highest Ideas. This is explicit in "On the kinds of being (II)" (VI.2. (43)), chapter 1, where he makes it clear that the doctrine of the five kinds is meant to replace Aristotle's doctrine of the categories. Plotinus takes the latter to be a doctrine about the highest genera of being and criticizes it for disregarding intelligible being. The doctrine of the five kinds is

thus introduced as an account of the highest, most universal Ideas of the intelligible world. Since the universal is prior to the particular according to Plotinus, these highest Ideas must also be conceived as aetiologically first. They have, of course, not come about temporally before the other Ideas—we must constantly remind ourselves that there is no question of temporal priority at this level—but they are what the lower Ideas presuppose and depend on, not vice versa. In "On the kinds of being (III)" (VI.3. (44)) he proposes a revised version of the Aristotelian category theory as a viable theory for sensibles.

7 The five highest kinds are called Ideas (*eidē*). Yet they do not seem to be standard Platonic Ideas or Forms—these expressions are used interchangeably here. As Atkinson (1983: 94) notes, "movement and rest, for example, like sameness and otherness are both aspects of the act of thinking which is itself the activity of Intellect." Clearly, the status and role of, say, movement, being the activity of thought, is rather different from that of an "ordinary" Platonic Idea such as that of the ideal Horse or Justice. That may be so but I still think Plotinus conceives of the five as bona fide Ideas. Each of them is present in every other as something distinct and hence each will be an ingredient or aspect of every other Idea. This is implicit in our passage and explicitly stated at VI.2.8, 25 ff. Moreover, Intellect thinks each of them (see VI.2.8, 1–5). I take it that this doesn't mean that, say, motion, which as we have seen is the act of thought, has first to be established as a distinct object of thought in order to occur in the act of thought: that would indeed lead to a regress because if there is no thought without the motion, which is the act of thought, motion cannot be established as an object of thought prior to being an act of thought. Rather, in the very act of thought, which has being as its object, motion itself is made manifest and becomes an object of thought, a being, to the intellect. As he remarks elsewhere, Intellect has an intimate consciousness of everything within it (V.3.13). Motion and otherness as aspects of the primary thought are no doubt included.

8 The five primary Ideas are highest in the sense that there are no more encompassing Ideas of which these are species. Nor is any of them subordinate to any other. Yet they mingle: being shares

in motion, rest, sameness and difference, and likewise for any of the others. Thus, being and thought at once involve several things. This is how plurality is established.

9   It was noted above that Plotinus' accounts of the role of each of the five genera in the constitution of Intellect differ. Moreover, allusions to the genera are absent in a number of passages where we might expect them. This has led some scholars to suppose that the genera were not of primary importance to Plotinus (Atkinson 1983: 96, following Nebel 1929: 44). Is this perhaps a somewhat desperate attempt to elevate the five kinds discussed in Plato's *Sophist* to a Platonic alternative to Aristotelian and Stoic categories? While it is true that we do not see a fully fledged theory of the five highest kinds recurring in the *Enneads*, I do think Plotinus attaches great importance to this doctrine. In particular being, otherness, sameness and motion (activity) are quite central to his whole theory of thought: sameness and otherness indicate the unity-in-multiplicity characteristic of Intellect, and motion is the activity and life in which its being is actualized.

10 Many scholars have correctly noted that Plotinus' accounts of the genera differ significantly from Plato's in the *Sophist* (see Atkinson 1983: 95–96; Brisson 1991). It is pointed out that while Plato starts from the distinctness of each genus in order later to arrive at their intertwining, Plotinus takes their unity for granted and proceeds to show their distinctness. And there are a number of differences between the two thinkers' arguments for the differentiation of the genera. The Plotinian passages on the genera do not look like interpretations of the text of the *Sophist*, which he uses very freely and puts into the context of his own theory of Intellect. In the *Sophist* there is, for instance, no evident connection between the greatest kinds and thinking, which is essential in Plotinus' account. Furthermore, it is probably a misunderstanding on Plotinus' part that Plato conceives of these five as an exhaustive list of the highest Ideas. Yet, Plotinus no doubt sees himself as interpreting the *Sophist* and *Parmenides* 145e ff., where the same five kinds are also in evidence. Or shall we rather say he sees himself as bringing out the true message of these Platonic passages, as he understands them, of course? Just before the discussion of the greatest kinds in the *Sophist* and

in direct connection with it, it is established that motion, life, soul and intellect must be present to what absolutely is (*to pantelōs on*). Plotinus understands this as meaning that the intelligible realm of itself has motion, life, soul and intellect. And as mentioned on p. 67, Plotinus takes the second hypothesis of the *Parmenides*, where we find all five kinds employed, to correspond to his level of Intellect. So he sees essential aspects of his view of Intellect in these parts of the *Sophist* and the *Parmenides*.

3 The other members of Intellect

Plotinus thinks that once the highest genera are in place the rest of the intelligible world will follow. Included among these are the standard Platonic Ideas we see in Plato's dialogues and some others as well that are not found there: quality, quantity and number (V.1.4, 41–43). Quantity and quality are of course notions of Aristotelian origin. Plotinus wishes to include them in the intelligible realm because every natural property in the sensible realm has an archetype in the intelligible realm and he does recognize quantities and qualities as items at the sensible level.

The exact way of derivation of the other intelligibles from the primary ones is very cursorily dealt with in the *Enneads*. The key passage is VI.2.21. The line of reasoning there suggests that Ideas such as of magnitude, quantity, quality, geometrical shapes and no doubt a whole hoard of Platonic Ideas see the light as aspects or a kind of spin-off that follows in the wake of the first thought involving the primary genera. What he says about magnitude is perhaps typical: "and with the continuity of [Intellect's] activity you will see magnitude, quietly at rest, appearing to your gaze" (VI.2.21, 13–15). It seems that the continuous activity gives rise to magnitude. So magnitude is there! One wonders what he means by continuity of activity here given that there is no time yet.

The status of Beauty in the intelligible realm is controversial. Interpreters often assume that Beauty is one of the many Platonic Forms (cf. Rist 1967: 53). However, as Stern-Gillet (2000) has convincingly argued, this is by no means clear. There are passages, most notably VI.7.32 and 33, where it is suggested that the beautiful may be yet another name of the first principle itself: "The primarily beautiful, then, and the first is without form, and such is Beauty, the nature of the Good" (VI.7.33, 21–22), and a little earlier he describes the One as "Beauty above beauty" (VI.7.32, 29). This, however, does not exclude there being lower versions of beauty, e.g. in Intellect. Still it is noteworthy that Plotinus does not in general suggest that the very prototype of any Form is to be identified with the One. There must be something special about beauty. Elsewhere, however, he suggests that the beautiful is posterior to the good (V.5.12). Beauty is evidently shared by each of the Forms and by the realm of Intellect as a whole. So is each of the primary genera, but beauty is nowhere suggested as one of them. So where does beauty fit in? The unresolved status of this question presumably reflects Plato's ambivalence on the matter: he comes close to identifying the beautiful and the good, for instance in Diotima's celebrated speech in the *Symposium*, yet leaving us with the impression that some distinction is to be made. Bréhier in his "Notice" to VI.7 (1924–38: vol. 7, p. 61) suggests that primary beauty exists in the relation between the Good and Intellect, a position questioned by Stern-Gillet (2000). We shall return to this issue in the final section of Chapter 10 ("Beauty and the Fine Arts").

In the early treatise, "On Intellect, Ideas and being" (V.9. (5)), there is a fairly systematic discussion of membership in the intelligible world.[5] Plotinus' focus here seems to be on debatable members, standard Platonic Ideas being taken for granted without much discussion. Evidently there were debates about this among his Platonist predecessors. In his *Handbook of Platonism* Alcinous says that the majority of Platonists hold that there are no Ideas of things that are against nature, artificial things, individuals such as Socrates, worthless things or relations such as the greatest and the supreme. This list gives an indication of debated members. Plotinus addresses several of these in his discussion.

He starts this discussion in chapter 9 by noting that since the sensible universe "is a living being containing all living beings" (V.9.9, 3–4), the whole archetype of this universe must be in Intellect. This archetype is the intelligible universe itself which Plotinus identifies with the absolute living being Plato speaks of in *Timaeus* 39e. Everything that exists by nature in the world of sense is derived from the intelligible world and none of the things that exist in the intelligible world are against nature. The Aristotelian categories, qualities, quantities, actions (*poiēseis*), affections and relations are there in so far as these are in accordance with nature, as are numbers and magnitudes, motions and standstills. Time is not there as such but time has an intelligible archetype, which is eternity (see Chapter 5, Section 7, "Soul and Time"). The paradigm of place is the presence of one thing in another in an intelligible mode, as e.g. the Horse is present in Animal.

We see in the case of time and place that the intelligible paradigm of these things is something rather different from sensible time and place, yet it is not too difficult to imagine that were eternity and intelligible presence to be made more plural they would degenerate into time and place.[6] The same holds for the other archetypes: they are something different from their sensible counterparts. Notably, everything in the intelligible realm is substance or being (*ousia*). Plotinus continues his account by saying: "There, then, since all things are together, whichever you take of them is substance [being] and intelligent, and each shares in life, and is the same and other, and motion and rest, and in motion and at rest, and substance and quality, and all of them are substance" (V.9.10, 10–14). We see here the intermingling of the primary genera—substance is here no doubt equivalent to what he often refers to as being. It follows from this intermingling that everything in the intelligible world is being (substance), including the paradigms of what appear as qualities at the sensible level.

This is followed by a discussion of the arts in chapter 11: do the arts belong to the intelligible realm? Plotinus' answer to this is mixed and cautious: in so far as the arts go beyond the mere use of sensible models they have their principles in the intelligible realm and the artists must reach that level in order to practice their art. The mathematical sciences are there and the arts are based on intelligible principles in so far as they make use of these sciences. This holds for example for music, which "considers and contemplates universal proportion in the intelligible" and building and carpentry too, in so far as these make use of proportions. Wisdom belongs to the intelligible realm as well, and arts such as rhetoric, generalship and administration have some part there in so far as they "contemplate intelligible beauty (*to kalon*)" (V.9.11, 22–23). We shall resume the question about the status of the arts in Chapter 10, Section 3 ("Beauty and the Fine Arts").

Plotinus then raises the question of Ideas of individuals in chapter 12. As we noted, Alcinous claims that the majority of Platonists hold that there are no Ideas of individuals. It is unclear where Plotinus stands on this question. Different passages point in different directions, and scholars have had a hard time construing one consistent doctrine in them.[7] As Armstrong remarks in his note to his translation, this chapter in V.9 does not really commit him one way or the other. Plotinus devoted a short treatise, "Are there Ideas of individuals?" (V.7. (18)), to this question and seems to answer it affirmatively. In this connection we should distinguish between two issues. On the one hand, there is the question whether our individual human souls or selves have individual intelligible counterparts. This is not the central question here in V.9 or in V.7, the treatise on Ideas of individuals, and we shall postpone the discussion of it till later (see p. 337).

In the little treatise on the Ideas of individuals the main issue is about natural physical features: do they all have intelligible causes in such a way that the *logos* forming an individual contains all its natural features?[8] Plotinus suggests that features such as an aquiline or snub nose are indeed contained in the *logos*. The idea is presumably that such traits that are natural and in fact inheritable characteristics of whole groups must be carried by the *logos*. There are individual traits, however, that are not due to the *logos* but to the underlying matter, e.g. what type of aquiline nose one has got (V.9.12, 8–9). In V.7 he takes these ideas even further, toying with the idea of a unique, individual characteristic contained in the *logos* (V.7.2). This would mean that there are as many intelligibles, i.e. *logoi*, as there are individuals. What he apparently settles for, however, is the view that even if identical organisms are produced by nature, e.g. in animals that have litters, each of them is produced with an individual difference that is due to the form, i.e. the *logos*. The reasoning behind this is interesting: the number of natural products is not random but fixed in the intelligible realm; hence, the producer in some way keeps count of the number of his products. The carpenter who is making, say, three identical chairs does this by thinking: "Here is one, there is another, and a third!" giving a distinct thought to each.

In nature what corresponds to this distinct thought that keeps the count must be included in their *logos*. According to this treatise, then, there may be *logoi* that are identical in content but nevertheless distinct (V.7.3, 8–10).

We may wonder why the arguments for individual *logoi* necessarily amount to the affirmation of individual Platonic Ideas, as Plotinus seems to assume both in V.7 and V.9. The *logoi* directly responsible for producing organisms are items at the level of soul. Could not the distinct *logoi* first come about at the level of soul without there being distinct Ideas of individuals at the level of Intellect. This is the position of Kalligas (1997) and Aubry (2008), but contrast Tornau and Michalewsky (2009), who argue for human individuality also at the level of Intellect. It is at any rate clear that the realm of the intelligible is much larger than that of Ideas strictly speaking that belong to the pure Intellect. The *logoi* are intelligible as opposed to sensible items but not every intelligible item is a Platonic Idea. It is a different question whether individual human souls exist as individuals at the level of Intellect.

The doctrine of Ideas of individuals does not as such play an important role in the *Enneads*. Nevertheless, the fact that he entertains such a notion reveals something of importance about his conception of the intelligible realm and the differences between this conception and that of Plato. Plotinus' view is indeed a development of Plato's. The *Timaeus* especially is always in the background when Plotinus deals with relationship between the two realms. The subtle changes, however, show strong Stoic influence. The Stoic *logos* is a much more detailed formal principle than Platonic Ideas, at least as we ordinarily conceive of the latter. The Stoic *logos* is of course physical and that aspect of it Plotinus does not want to have anything to do with. But he takes over the formal concept and its functions, including the attendance to detail of the Stoic *logos*.

In chapter 13 Plotinus expresses agreement with the Platonist majority view, presumably not shared by Plato himself (cf. *Parmenides* 130c–d), as regards repugnant things such as those resulting from putrefaction, dirt and mud: they have no place in the intelligible realm. Yet, these things are evidently something, so how do they come about? Plotinus does not give a clear detailed answer but seems to suggest that they are due to the inability of soul to control matter. In later treatises such as "On providence (I) and (II)" (III.2. (47) and III.3. (48)), however, we see that he is willing to include some disagreeable things in the rational structure of the sensible world. I shall return to this topic in Chapter 10, Section 2.1 ("Providence, Fate and Human Responsibility").

4 Intellect's self-thinking

Let us return to the initial phase of Intellect and consider the question what is the content of Intellect's first fully fledged thought. We see two answers to this question in the *Enneads*: Intellect thinks being and Intellect thinks itself. Because the being in question is identical with Intellect itself, thinking of it is the same as Intellect's thinking itself. This short answer is, however, not very informative. What does it mean? Let us first consider self-thinking.

That Intellect thinks itself is a claim we find in most of the accounts of Intellect in the *Enneads* (e.g. II.9.2, 49; V.3.5, 29; V.6.5, 18; VI.2.8, 11). It is not obvious what it means, however. On the face of it, thinking oneself could, for instance, mean thinking about oneself. In a way Intellect may be said to think itself in this sense: surely it thinks about something and that something is identical with itself. The phrase "thinking about oneself" as we normally employ it, however, suggests that the thinker is something distinct from and independent of her thoughts about herself: she is there already and just happens to have certain thoughts, true or false, about herself. In Intellect's case there is a much more intimate connection between the thinker and the thought.

We saw above (p. 105) that the potential intellect is in need of itself and that this need is satisfied by its thinking itself. This suggests, what also is confirmed by several other passages, namely, that the so-called self-thinking of Intellect is also a kind of self-constitution. Prior to its actual thought of being there is no intellect and no being. Sometimes Plotinus sounds as if these two, intellect (subject) and being, are present together in some concealed form in the emanation from the One, and Intellect's first thought involves sorting them out and at the same time keeping them together.

There is a sense in which what Intellect thinks is fairly trivially it itself. We see this in the following lines from V.3: "If then it [Intellect] is activity and its substance is activity, it is one and the same with its activity; but being and the intelligible are also one with the activity. All together are one, Intellect, [its] thought, the intelligible" (V.3.5, 41–44). The central idea here is fairly simple: the activity which constitutes the intellect as a thinking subject is one and the same as the activity that constitutes being. Intellect (subject) is one with its thought because there is no actual thinker prior to the thought; being is one with that same activity of thought because there is no being prior to the thought. So the activity is, so to speak, the median term: both thinker and object are identical with the activity. So in a sense the intellect (subject) is identical with its object of thought.

The reasoning we have just seen is essentially Aristotelian. Plotinus' views on Intellect's thought owe much to Aristotle and his followers, in particular Alexander of Aphrodisias. This has been well recorded and explained by eminent scholars: see in particular Armstrong (1960), Szlezák (1979: 126–135) and Menn (2001). Aristotle and Alexander too speak of God and the active intellect as thinking itself and insist on the identity of the divine mind with its objects of thought. Alexander in fact plausibly identified the active intellect of *On the Soul* III, 5, with the divine mind of *Metaphysics* XII (Alexander *On the Soul* 89, 7 ff.). Plotinus takes over the Aristotelian claim that actual knowledge of things without matter is identical with its object. This aspect of Plotinus' thought is very well accounted for in Menn's article just cited.

There is a problem about the Plotinian version of this account of the identity of the thinker and the object of thought that does not arise for the Aristotelians. For them God the thinker is the very first item at the top of the ontology. There is nothing there that corresponds to the One and what we have called the potential intellect in Plotinus, hence nothing that looks like a move from potentiality to actuality. Plotinus, on the other hand, has the notion of the potential intellect. At the same time he accepts the Principle of Prior Possession (see p. 44) and generally insists that Intellect and everything in it is actual. Nothing is potential there (IV.9.5, 16–17). So the question arises whether the genesis of Intellect isn't a kind of actualization of something merely potential and also the further question, how this is possible given the Principle of Prior Possession and the fact that there are no beings prior to Intellect.

I believe that in order to understand how Plotinus would respond to this, a first step is to recall the difference between Aristotle's version of the Principle of Prior Possession and Plotinus' Platonic version: For Plotinus imitation of something prior comes with a loss. Thus, in this case, in which the potential Intellect imitates the One, the result is not an exact replica—far from it. The result is being and beings, the intelligible world. They are not there in the One *as such*, yet they are an imitation of the One, and, we might say, actualizations at a lower level of something the higher level contains.[9]

So Plotinus endorses the Aristotelian reasons for holding that Intellect thinks itself: the thinker is one with the activity of thinking which is one with the object of thought. So thinker and object are identical; hence, the thinker thinks itself in thinking its object. There is no indication that Aristotle (or Alexander) had in mind any kind of self-reflexive act of thought when they described divine thinking as self-thinking, and there is nothing in their kind of reasoning, which Plotinus shares, that seems to necessitate this. As Sorabji (1983: 147) puts it, "[t]here need be nothing narcissistic in the claim that God thinks of himself, or regressive in the claim that he thinks of his own thinking." Other leading experts seem to agree. Kosman (2000: 323), for instance, argues forcefully and explicitly that Aristotle's notion of God's self-thinking and the description of his thinking as the thinking of thinking in *Metaphysics* XII, 9 "is not the description of an act of reflexive self-awareness." In Alexander this is even more obviously true. For the Peripatetics, then, the intellect is identical with its object of thought because the act of thinking is numerically identical with the object of thought, and the intellect acting is identical with its acts. The divine intellect is essentially an act of thinking and the object of its thought exists in this act. Since Intellect and its objects are identical, it follows trivially that the intellect thinks itself when it thinks its object. It follows that the Aristotelian divine intellect may think itself without knowing at all that it is itself that it thinks.

There are reasons to believe that Plotinus has a more elaborate notion of self-thinking in addition to this Aristotelian one and that the additional elements indeed have to do with reflexive self-awareness. This is strongly suggested by a passage in "How the multitude of the Forms came into being, and on the Good" (VI.7.

(38)), chapter 38.[10] The context is a discussion of the Good (the One). In the previous sections it has been ruled out that one can attach "is" to the Good. So the Good won't entertain any attitudes that amount to saying that it *is* something. This maxim is appealed to in the passage. Here Plotinus is considering an objection to his conception of the Good (the One) as above any sort of thinking: the Good cannot be worth very much, the hypothetical objector insists, if it doesn't even have self-perception or self-awareness.[11] The notion at stake here, the Good's self-awareness, which Plotinus rejects, is understood as the Good's awareness or knowledge *that it is the Good*. So if the Good is to have self-awareness, it must think "I am the Good" or something tantamount to that. The thrust of his argument against this is to force the objector to admit that the Good cannot have self-awareness without the "is"; but the "is" has already been ruled out for the Good. So it cannot think this thought.

Then Plotinus imagines the opponent proposing that the Good only thinks "Good," without any addition: it just thinks "Good." The hypothetical opponent proposes this as a candidate for the self-awareness of the Good which avoids the "is." He responds that if this is what it thinks "it does indeed think 'Good,' but the thought that it itself is this will not be present to it. So the thought [constituting self-awareness] must be 'I am Good'" (VI.7.38, 16–18). So the conclusion is that for a thought to pass as self-thinking it must contain a conscious identification of itself with what is thought.

This whole passage is of course explicitly about the One, something which does not think itself according to Plotinus. It is, however, revealing for our purposes on account of what it says about what the One would be like if it had perception of itself, knowledge of itself or thought of itself, i.e. if the One had that crucial feature which Intellect has and the objector wishes to see in the One. So we can use the passage to become clearer about Plotinus' conception of the self-knowledge or self-thinking of Intellect. So, to put it succinctly, the self-knowledge here denied of the One, is without doubt just the kind of self-knowledge insisted on for Intellect. Plotinus' demand that "the thought that it itself is the Good" must be present to the Good if it were to have self-knowledge is quite telling. It shows that he conceives of the self-thinking of Intellect as including the awareness that the subject of thought is something or other. So according to this passage nothing could "think itself" in the relevant sense without it being the case that the subject of thought conceives of what it recognizes as itself as its object.

Several other indications point in the same direction. It is, for instance, noteworthy that on the few occasions Intellect speaks in its own voice it speaks in the first person making what look like self-identifying statements. In V.3.13, for instance, he says:

> For consciousness (*synaisthēsis*) of anything is a perception (*aisthēsis*) of something multiple, as the term itself bears witness to. And the thought which is prior turns inward to it [the intellect] which is obviously multiple.[12] For even if it only says just this, "I am being" (*on eimi*), it says it as a discovery and plausibly, for being is multiple: since if it had an immediate grasp (*epibalēi*) as if of something simple and said "I am being," it would attain neither itself nor being.
>
> (V.3.13, 21–27)

From the preceding lines it is clear that the word *synaisthēsis* ("consciousness") here replaces "thinking oneself." It is as if Intellect's turning to itself in order to discover itself leads to the thought "I am being." Thus, Intellect's self-thought is represented as a first-person statement about what the subject or thinker of Intellect's thought is. The passage aims at establishing the plurality of self-thought in order to show that self-thought does not pertain to the One. This multiplicity seems at least in part to be established by the duality of subject and object involved in "I am."

This understanding gains further support from another first-person statement in the same treatise, V.3.10, 33 ff., a passage we visited earlier, in Chapter 3, Section 2 ("The One is beyond Being and beyond Thought"). Here Plotinus imagines that something entirely partless (as the One) were to think itself. His point is that this would be impossible because even if it only thought the minimal thought "I am this," the mere duality of "I" and "this" suffices to render the object of what "speaks itself" multiple. We may take Plotinus to be making the same point here in chapter 13: Intellect thinks "I am," and in so thinking it shows itself to be complex, consisting of a subject that thinks and an object that it is thinking.

The foregoing considerations make it tempting to see Plotinian self-thinking as essentially self-identifying and self-constituting thoughts in the first person. The significance of the first person, the "I," is that the subject is thinking about itself in such a way that it knows that the object of its thought is itself. It is self-identifying and self-constituting because there is no object of thought prior to the thinking in which the subject says what it is.

5 The intelligibles internal to Intellect

It is evident from the discussion of the genesis of Intellect in the previous section that the intelligibles are internal to Intellect and not outside it. Plotinus claims this and argues for it in many treatises throughout his career of writing. Porphyry even gave one of the treatises the title "That the intelligibles are not outside Intellect and on the Good" (V.5. (32)).[13] This means that Plotinus does not share the picture of the realm of Platonic Ideas most modern contemporary Plato scholars adhere to, according to which the Ideas are in a *sui generis* realm, neither mental nor physical, yet accessible to the mind and not to the senses.

Plotinus was actually by no means the first Platonist to hold that the Ideas are divine thoughts. We see such a notion in a number of Middle Platonist thinkers. There are, however, distinctions to be made between quite different ways of conceiving of the Ideas as divine thoughts. As Armstrong (1960: 401) puts it: "The writers who put forward the doctrine that the Ideas are the thoughts of God seem very often to be concerned with the questions 'On what pattern did God make the world?' and 'What is the relationship between the Maker and the pattern he used in making?'" He rightly contrasts this with Plotinus who "in formulating his doctrine that the Intelligibles are in Intellect seems to me to be concerned with a question of a different sort 'What is the relationship of eternal intuitive thought to its object (or objects) and how is that object to be conceived.'" Plotinus' version of this doctrine has, however, a clear precedent in Alcinous (as Armstrong fully recognizes). The distinctive feature of Alcinous' version of the doctrine is his embrace of Aristotelian theology, with which he mingles his Platonic metaphysics so as to be able to assert that "the Ideas are eternal and perfect thoughts (*noēseis*) of God."

It is not the case, however, that every Platonist at the time would agree with the claim that the Ideas are thoughts of God and surely not with the Plotinian version of it. In the *Life of Plotinus* 18 Porphyry tells a story of how he disbelieved in Plotinus' account when he first came to Plotinus in Rome and wrote an essay arguing that the object of thought exists outside the intellect. Plotinus asked his long-time student and assistant, Amelius, to enlighten Porphyry, which Amelius did in a substantial treatise (now lost). They kept exchanging treatises on the topic until, finally, Porphyry admitted his error and wrote a recantation. Another skeptic in this regard was the famous Platonist scholar Longinus, Porphyry's former teacher, with whom he corresponded (*Life* 20, 87 ff.).

Plotinus too puts Aristotle at his service in his account of Intellect, no doubt in full knowledge of Alcinous' or similar views. Plotinus' version, however, goes far beyond anything we find in Alcinous. The latter is brief and has hardly any arguments in support of his claims—this goes together with the handbook genre of his work (see Alcinous, *Handbook of Platonism* 163, 14–15). Plotinus, on the other hand, goes on at great length about this topic. As we have seen, he accepts Aristotle's notion of a divine intellect that is an essentially active thinker and whose thinking is self-contained: it thinks itself and is one with what it thinks. Aristotle describes its thought as the thought of a thought (*Metaphysics* XII, 1074b34–35)—a statement whose exact meaning has puzzled commentators since antiquity. Plotinus, who is in this respect in line with Alcinous, gives content to this by claiming that the object of the divine intellect's thought is the array of Platonic Ideas. This is in essence the Platonized Aristotelian legacy in Plotinus' theory of Intellect. There are other elements in the background of this theory, however, most notably skepticism, as we shall see.[14]

Let us consider some of the arguments Plotinus gives for the internality of the intelligibles in V.5, the treatise mentioned above bearing this topic in its title. In the first two chapters of this treatise he contrasts Intellect's thought with sense-perception: a chief characteristic of the latter is that it is of something external to the power of sense-perception itself. It follows from this that the power of sense-perception has to be acted on from the outside. This in turn means that the power only receives an impression (*typos*) or image (*eidōlon*, *ichnos*) of the object. These images are identified with the quality of the thing as opposed to its essence, the thing itself (V.5.2, 1–9).

Intellect, Plotinus insists, is not like that at all. If it were, various unacceptable consequences would follow. Here are those that I find most telling and interesting: (1) Intellect would be dependent on an external object acting on it. This would mean that it might not essentially be an active knower since it depends on something outside itself for knowing. This is incompatible with the essentially active nature of Intellect as Plotinus has conceived of it. (2) Intellect would not know that "this [supposed intelligible it has received] is good or beautiful or just," because the principles of judgement on which it would rely will be outside (V.5.1, 29–32). The point here is that according to any Platonist the Ideas are the ultimate criteria of what is good, beautiful or just; if the intellect does not possess the Ideas innately but receives them from the outside, by what would it judge that this image it has received is, say, the Beautiful? It has no criterion by which it could ascertain this. One might think that some images are so powerful that they, so to speak, bear the mark of authenticity in themselves. Plotinus does not explicitly discuss this possibility but he clearly thinks that no mere image can do this, the reason no doubt being that in the case of images the identity of the activity of the subject with that of the object fails.

But how do internal intelligibles guarantee truth and knowledge? Plotinus' answer to that question lies in the following claim, which culminates his discussion in V.5.2: "So that real truth is also there [in Intellect], which does not agree with something else, but with itself, and says nothing other than itself, but it is what it says and says what it is" (V.5.2, 18–20; cf. V.3.5, 22–26). Several comments on this are warranted.

1 Plotinus refers to truth that agrees with something else and to truth that doesn't and agrees with itself. The truth that agrees with something else is undoubtedly the ordinary truth of thoughts or statements such as "the cat is on the mat," where there supposedly is an agreement between what is thought or said and the fact. The truth in Intellect is different: it agrees with itself.

2 On closer inspection, talk of agreement may be misleading here where the chances of not agreeing are nil: Intellect is setting the standard and cannot go wrong. Nevertheless, it is not the case that Intellect, so to speak, makes up the intelligible according to its fancy: the contents of Intellect are determined by the One without, however, the One's imposing a particular content upon it.

3 Yet, Intellect "says what it is." This means that Intellect somehow declares its content and identity, no doubt to itself—it is, as we have seen, intimately conscious of itself—but also to anyone else who is able to approach it. This is how Intellect functions as a standard for posterior things.

4 Not only does Intellect say what it is, it also is what it says. This means that any particular intelligible, say, the intelligible Horse, is a horse (or equinity) even if it is a thought: this thought is what determines the equine nature by its own example.

5 The "says what it is" part refers to Intellect's knowledge of its contents. This knowledge is true in the sense that it corresponds to the things as they are. When Plotinus, on the other hand, says that "it is what it says" and connects this with "real truth," we seem to have a different notion of truth, namely, truth in the sense of authenticity, the genuine, real article as opposed to an image of it. While we might suspect that he is guilty of conflating two different senses of "true," I think Plotinus would respond by saying that his point is precisely that these two senses coincide in this case: in being what it is Intellect says what it is.

6 The phrase "is what it says and says what it is" expresses the merging of ontology and epistemology and psychology, which is one of Plotinus' most original ideas, a merging that can also be expressed by the equation of being with Intellect's thought. He sometimes cites old Parmenides in support: "For thinking and being are the same."[15] Intellect's thinking X is X itself.

7 One might suspect that making the intelligibles internal to Intellect does not in itself secure authentic knowledge of them. My memories, for instance, are internal to my mind, somehow, but clearly I can misremember. Perhaps, we can even be mistaken about our occurrent thoughts. So how does Plotinus guarantee Intellect's infallible thought about the intelligibles? A

crucial step in appreciating his take on this is to realize that he rejects the model of the Intellect and the intelligibles as a kind of internal spectacle where the intellect (as subject), having gotten the best seat, watches them and proclaims with authority what is what. Rather the intelligible is the active thought itself, which does not have to be matched against any other object.

As several scholars have noted, the specter of skepticism lurks in the background of this merging of ontology, epistemology and psychology. Plato seems to have believed that the Ideas do not fail to impress their true identity on the philosophers' minds, provided they are properly prepared and have proceeded towards them in the right manner. Moreover, sight is clearly the model of knowledge of the Ideas in central passages such as the Analogy of the Sun in the *Republic* and the spectacle of the Ideas on the plane of truth in the *Phaedrus*. The centuries between Plato and Plotinus, however, saw a lot of skepticism about knowledge and about perceptual knowledge in particular. How can we be sure that our perceptions represent an external object as it is? What kind of access can we really have to independently existing objects? Some of the skeptical arguments directed at perceptual knowledge may be applied to intellectual knowledge, if the latter takes sense-perception as its model. Without doubt this threat played a role in Plotinus' insistence on internal intelligibles.

6 Non-discursive thought

As we have seen in the previous section, the kind of thought Plotinus attributes to Intellect is far removed from the kind of thought we engage in in daily life. The latter moves in steps, often even back and forth, before it reaches its conclusion. Thus, we can describe it as inferential and temporal. The kind of thought characteristic of Intellect is non-discursive or, as it is sometimes called, intuitive. It has the opposite characteristics to those we have just been giving to discursive thought. Plotinus' most usual terms for this are *noēsis* ("intellection") and *theoria* ("contemplation").

Plotinus is not the first Greek philosopher to distinguish between higher and less perfect forms of thinking: in *Republic* VI, 509d–511d Plato famously distinguishes between the kinds of thought involved at the two upper levels of the Divided Line: the lower of the two, characteristic of the mathematical disciplines, he calls discursive thought or *dianoia* ("discursive thought"), while the higher one, which is associated with dialectic, is called *noēsis* ("intellection"). Aristotle too makes some such distinction between higher and lower thinking. Though the terminology is not fixed, *nous* and its cognates are used of the higher kind of thought, though they may also be used in a wider sense that covers reasoning and inferences. Thus, it is *nous* or *noēsis* that is involved in the non-inferential grasp of first principles in *Posterior Analytics* II, 19, in divine thinking in *Metaphysics* XII, and in the passages about the intellect in *On the Soul* III, 4–6.

While Plotinus certainly draws on sources such as those just mentioned, it is equally clear that he develops and modifies the Platonic and Aristotelian material to suit his own purposes. Plotinus turned the notion of non-discursive thought into an extremely rich and many-faceted concept that plays a fundamental role in his thought and continued to play a role in the history of Western philosophy. The idea that there are different modes of thought the highest one of which is non-inferential, veridical and vision-like haunts both medieval and early modern philosophy, clear examples being intuition in Descartes and Spinoza, and Kant's notion of intelligible intuition (*intellektuelle Anschauung*) (which Kant rejects, at least for us humans). In our times, this notion is to a large extent lost, at least in professional, systematic philosophy. Some bits and pieces of the ancient notion, however, survive or have been reinvented here and there, e.g. in notions such as "tacit knowledge" or that of "intuition" as in "our moral intuitions" or "our pre-philosophical intuitions." There is, however, nothing in current philosophy that comes close to satisfying all the conditions of Plotinus' notion of non-discursive thought.

Several of the distinguishing marks have already been mentioned or alluded to above but let us now address the matter directly and systematically. First of all, non-discursive thought is all-at-once and of all-together. That is to say: Intellect grasps what it grasps in one go. This could not really be otherwise because as has been noted Intellect is outside time: it cannot require temporal duration to grasp what it grasps. Picking up a phrase that can be found in both Parmenides and Anaxagoras, Plotinus very frequently says that the intelligibles are "all together" (*homou pan* or *homou panta*). By this he not only wishes to deny that the intelligibles are spatially separated but also to indicate that they make up a kind of organic whole, where the whole and the other parts are implicit in each. I shall have more to say about this organic unity in the next section. Let us for now note that the all-at-once and all-together jointly imply that Intellect grasps all its contents at once in a single apprehension of a manifold. That there really is a manifold of distinct objects has been questioned by an eminent scholar of Neoplatonism, the late Anthony Lloyd. I think, however, the *Enneads* leave little doubt that there is, as can be seen from the fact that Plotinus very frequently describes Intellect as "many," in fact as "many-colored," variegated (*poikilos*).

In the previous section we saw that Intellect's thought is veridical and certain, and we discussed how this is conceived. We also saw there how this thought is directly of the intelligibles themselves. Thus, we can continue the list of characteristics: non-discursive thought is the veridical, certain, non-inferential and immediate grasp of many intelligibles at once.

There are still more features to consider. There has been a scholarly debate on whether or not non-discursive thought is propositional. Anthony Lloyd argued (1970: 263; 1986) that for Plotinus non-discursive thought is so unified that it involves no complexity. Non-discursive thought is so unified that it has no distinction corresponding to the difference between the subject and the predicate essential to propositional thought. For Lloyd the "all-together" and the "all-at-once" requirements for non-discursive thought amount to non-complexity and thereby to non-propositionality—for any proposition is composed of at least a subject and a predicate. So, according to Lloyd (1970: 261 and *passim*; 1986: 260), being non-inferential is indeed a necessary, but by no means a sufficient, condition of being a non-discursive thought. In Emilsson (2007), chapter 4, I argue for an alternative view from which the following pages are excerpted with modifications.

Lloyd's position was forcefully attacked by Richard Sorabji (1982, 1983: 152–156; see also Alfino 1988), who argues that the passages that have been taken as evidence of belief in non-propositional thought, not only in Plato and Aristotle, but also in Plotinus, show no such thing. He does not thereby deny the distinction between non-discursive and discursive thought in these authors, but it seems to be reduced to that between non-inferential and inferential thought, both of which, however, are propositional according to Sorabji. So non-discursive thought is always like the grasp of an essence in Aristotle, which indeed is non-inferential in the sense that it is not demonstrated, not deduced from superior premises. The grasp of an essence, however, is the grasp of a proposition expressing an identity, e.g. the proposition "Man is a rational animal."

I shall not enter into the details of this controversy, which ultimately is quite complicated. Let me say though that it seems to me that neither Lloyd's nor Sorabji's account is satisfactory. For details I refer the readers to Emilsson (2007), chapter 4, §2. Lloyd and Sorabji share the assumption that complexity of thought as equivalent to the propositional nature of thought and thereby also, of course, that non-complexity as equivalent to non-propositionality. Lloyd reasons that since non-discursive thought is not complex, it has to be non-propositional. Sorabji, on the other hand, reasons that since non-discursive thought is complex, it has to be propositional. I do not think their common assumption is right: thought may be complex without being propositional. What I suspect is that Plotinus never fully pondered the question whether Intellect's thought is propositional in the present-day sense, according to which propositions differ from linguistic expressions. He explicitly denies that Intellect thinks in terms of the logical expressions of the Aristotelians and the Stoics, which he apparently takes to be linguistic items. It does not follow that he would have refused propositional status to Intellect's thought. Perhaps, we should take a fresh look at the matter.

There are texts that may be taken as indications that Intellect's non-discursive thought is indeed propositional: as we have seen in previous sections, Plotinus assigns truth value to Intellect's thought; it is in fact always true. What sense can we make of non-propositional truth, except perhaps truth as synonym for "real" or "authentic"? But he clearly doesn't limit his notion of truth to that (see p. 126). Moreover, he applies figures of speech to Intellect that may suggest propositions: Intellect "says" what it is, we saw in the previous section. Even if we know that this is a figure of speech because literally Intellect doesn't say a word, these locutions do seem to indicate that something proposition-like is going on.

On the other hand, there is much that points in a different direction. I have in mind the numerous statements to the effect that Intellect "sees" a many-faceted complex of intelligibles. At least that does not square well with how we ordinary humans think in propositions: at best we can manage one by one. Does Intellect perhaps intuit many propositional truths at once? Possibly, but I think that in order to come to better grips with this issue, we must take Plotinus' visual metaphors seriously and inquire what is behind them. In fact, his account of Intellect is awash in metaphorical uses of language pertaining to vision: "to see" (*horan*) and "to watch" (*blepein*), are almost as common as "to think" (*noein*) in the passages describing Intellect.

Plotinus is of course not the first Greek philosopher to employ ocular metaphors in connection with thinking and knowledge. Plato and Aristotle too abound in them. We are here confronted with the famous ocular metaphors that Richard Rorty (1979: 162–3 and *passim*), following Heidegger and Dewey, makes so much of in his account of the history of Western philosophy and how it, in his view, went wrong. It is well known to scholars of ancient philosophy, but apparently not appreciated by philosophers generally, that the perceptual imagery for the mind in the Platonic–Aristotelian tradition is by no means confined to vision. Nor are the metaphors that are called upon to describe knowledge and the methods of getting it all perceptual: they are of all sorts.[16] Although his account of the intellect is primarily modeled on vision, Aristotle appeals significantly to touch as well to account for how knowledge of essences cannot go wrong.[17] The language of touch is also quite conspicuous in some Platonic passages describing our contact with ultimate reality such as *Symposium* 212c, and even more clearly in *Republic* VI, 490a–b. The kind of touch Plato has in mind is fairly explicitly sexual contact: the wisdom-lover's most intimate knowledge of the truly real, the Ideas, is likened to having sexual intercourse with it, and this is naturally a contact that is bound to bear fruit, which in this case is true virtue.

In Plotinus too we find tactual, erotic language, mostly in connection with contact with the One, not in connection with thinking and knowledge as such (cf. V.3.10, 40–44; V.3.17, 25–36; VI.7.39, 15–20; VI.9.11, 24). In light of this, Rorty's (1979: 39) ironical remark, presumably pointing to the arbitrariness of philosophical visual metaphors, that "some nameless pre-Socratic, is responsible for viewing [knowledge of universals] as *looking* at something (rather than, say, rubbing up against it, or crushing it underfoot, or having sexual intercourse with it)," somehow misses the mark. The Greeks had a variety of metaphors to describe "the better sort of knowledge," some of which were indeed fairly explicitly erotic.

So what is the point of this visual imagery in Plotinus? It seems to me that likening Intellectual intuition to vision serves to convey several points: first, for one not in a skeptical mood, sight is the paradigm of being exposed to the things themselves as opposed to some "images" as when we learn about something from a report or by hearsay; secondly, vision seems to be an all-at-once affair: I enter a room and I immediately see the floor, the walls, the ceiling, the window and the furniture in lucid relations to one another. Thus, sight is the best Plotinus can come up with to convey the idea of grasping many intelligibles at once: that must be somewhat like seeing them.

We may become suspicious about this talk of seeing and sight for more than one reason. Didn't I say that Plotinus took skeptical attacks on perceptual knowledge seriously? Why does he then resort to vision as a metaphor for intellection? The answer is that here as often elsewhere we must remember that Plotinus' metaphors have a limited function: they are meant to shed light on certain aspects of what he is talking about, not thereby every aspect of it. Nor should every aspect of the figure (in this case vision) be transferred to the subject under discussion. In employing the vocabulary of vision Plotinus is not at all in a skeptical mood: what he wishes to convey by it are the features mentioned above: immediacy and grasp of many at once. Moreover, he is careful to point out that intellectual and ordinary vision are quite different: not only is intellectual vision of something internal to Intellect itself, the relation of the subject of the cognition to its object is much more intimate than in sensory perception (cf. e.g. V.5.7). Still, it seems fair to say that Plotinus' visual imagery suggests some kind of internal stage on which the intelligibles are "seen." As we have noted, other aspects of his account of Intellect's thought and its relation to being—I have in mind the coalescence of being and thinking we spoke of earlier (see p. 133)—do not go so well with visual language, even if the stage is made internal. He owes his readers a better account than we find in the *Enneads* of how exactly he thinks this works.

Let us return to where we started this discussion: the topic of visual imagery in Plotinus is interesting in itself but the occasion for bringing it up was the question of whether or not Intellect thinks in propositions. It is notably unclear whether ordinary vision is propositional. I may truly say: "I see there is a red spot on my white shirt (probably the pasta sauce)," in which case my vision takes a proposition as an object: "there is a red spot on my shirt." I may also say: "I see a red spot on my shirt (probably the pasta sauce)," in which case there is a direct object: the red spot on my shirt. Plotinus' Greek language and his own theory of sense-perception accommodate both constructions, although the latter suggests that seeing an object is the primary form of vision (see Chapter 7, Section 3.2, "What Do We Perceive?"). In any case, even when a visual experience is reported by a single sentence such as "I see the red spot on my white shirt," it is clear that the experience behind this report is much richer than what is captured by the sentence: I see the shape and shade of the spot, its location and relation to the buttons of my shirt; lots of other things. It would be odd to describe this experience as one of keeping lots of propositions in one's mind at once. Surely, I do not consciously assert to myself that the spot on my shirt is of this or that unnamable shape or that it is between the third and the fourth button from the collar, on the right. I simply see this.

Intellectual vision, I propose, has the same characteristics in this respect: it captures many things at once without necessarily entertaining distinct propositions about this experience. Moreover, just as the ordinary vision of an object can be veridical or not, depending on whether the object is there and has the features and relations that appear in the experience, it makes sense to say that Intellect's intellectual vision of intelligible objects is veridical when it reflects its object as it is in all its relations. The difference is that intellectual vision always reflects its object as it is because there is no external object to match it with that might falsify the vision. There is of course a strong tradition in contemporary philosophy—I am thinking of positivism and thinkers influenced by it—that goes against any such notion of an unfalsifiable experience. Be that as it may, Plotinus thought such unfalsifiable experience was necessary, if there is to be any knowledge of the real.

The fact that Plotinus often renders Intellect's thoughts by simple sentences really does not constitute such a serious objection to the account suggested here: given that Plotinus is in the business of writing and that he wishes to communicate some of Intellect's thoughts to his readers, it goes without saying that he does so using sentences. How else could he do it? It does not follow that he believed Intellect itself thought these thoughts in exactly the same way.

7 Plotinus' holism

Not only is the relation between subject and object more intimate in intellectual than in sensory vision, the connection between the objects of intellectual vision is a much more intimate one. I have in mind here what I mentioned earlier and referred to as the organic unity of the intelligible realm (see p. 129). The following passage from "On the intelligible beauty" (V.8. (31)), which apparently inspired Leibniz's doctrine that each individual substance reflects the entire universe from a certain point of view,[18] gives us an idea of the nature of the interconnectedness of everything:

> For all things there [in the intelligible world] are transparent, and there is nothing dark or opaque; everything and all things are clear to the inmost part to everything; for light is transparent to light. Each there has everything in itself and sees all things in every other, so that all are everywhere and each and every one is all and the glory is unbounded. ... the sun there is all the stars, and each star is the sun and all the others. A different kind of being stands out in each, but in each all are manifest.
>
> (V.8.4, 4–11)

The view expressed here that "each is all" certainly looks strange. It is however perhaps less queer than it may at first sight seem. Plotinus is saying that each of the intelligibles is all the others, but "a different kind of being stands out in each." This is doubtless the same doctrine as he elsewhere expresses by saying that each of the intelligibles implicitly contains all the others (VI.2.20, 20–23). Even if he nowhere gives us all the details, it is not at all difficult to follow his thought here in general outline. He evidently believes in a thoroughgoing holism about the intelligible world. This means that if we were to understand any one item in it, we should have to bring in all the rest. So when he says that the sun is all the stars, he means that an account of what the sun really is would have to bring in the stars: an exhaustive account of the sun, "the sun is ...," where the blank was filled with everything that pertains to the nature of the sun, would include a reference to the stars; the stars are a part of what makes the sun what it is. He is not suggesting that in the intelligible world to be the sun is the very same thing as to be e.g. the Evening Star or that the Evening Star is an attribute of the sun (for this claim seems to imply that the sun would just as much be an attribute of the Evening Star, which is absurd). The claim here must rather be that an account of each thing involves all the others; that "a different kind of being stands out in each" just means that we could put the focus on any one we like and say what it is, all the rest would enter into that account. This is very much the kind of world Leibniz envisaged in, for instance, *Discourse on Metaphysics* 9 and *Monadology* 59. In Intellect, however, not only is it the case that the stars would enter into an account of the sun; in intellectually seeing the sun, Intellect sees the stars.

Plotinus' holism is tied to a certain view about causes or reasons in Intellect. To see how this comes about, let us consider the following lines from VI.7.2:

> For we [with our limited sight of the intelligible] grant that it [Intellect] has the "that" but not the "why," or, if we do grant it the "why," it has it as separate [from the "that"]. And we see man or, if it happens so, an eye, as an image or something pertaining to an image. But in reality there [in the intelligible] there is man and the reason why there is man, if the man there must also be intellectual, and an eye and the reason why there is an eye; or they would not be there at all, if the reason why was not. ... But there [in the intelligible] all are in one, so that the thing and the reason why of the thing coincide.
>
> (VI.7.2, 3–12)

I take it that the main claim here is that the questions "Why is there man?" or "Why does man have eyes?" coincide with the questions "What is man?" or "What is an eye?" Following Aristotle, Plotinus notes that even in the sensible realm there are cases where the "that" (*hoti*) and the "why" (*dioti*) coincide, e.g. in the case of the eclipse: an eclipse is, in Aristotle's words, "the privation of the moon's light by the interposition of the earth" (*Posterior Analytics* II, 90a15–18; cf. *Metaphysics* VIII, 4 1044b9–15). In addition to saying what an eclipse is, this account also states its cause, the reason why there is an eclipse. In the intelligible world everything is supposed to be such that the "what" and the "why" coincide.

The intuitive idea here is no doubt the consideration that an account of what a given object is must bring in the whole of which it is a part. If one is to say what an eye is or what a given type of eye is, one would have to say something about the nature of an animal and, in the particular case, say something about the nature of the kind of animal which has the given kind of eye. Such considerations answer the question what the given kind of eye is. Is it for instance an eye fit for hunting or an eye that catches a wide horizon so as to make the animal fit to notice and flee from a predator? These considerations, however, also answer the question why there is such an eye: this is explained by the kind of animal in question. Now the Intellect as a whole is, according to Plotinus, an organism of a certain kind. So the same sort of considerations that apply to parts and wholes of ordinary animals apply to the intelligibles and Intellect at large. So what is here asserted about animals and their parts holds for the intelligible world at large: the causes or reasons for the parts are immanent in the wholes; so if one knows the wholes, and especially if one knows a given whole and its intelligible context, one knows that it will contain such and such parts.

In the passage from V.8 we started this section with, it was said that the sun is all the stars; it was suggested that this means that the stars would have to enter into an account of what the sun is. In the second passage cited we saw that in Intellect each thing contains its reasons or that the reasons for it are contained in what it is. If we put the two passages together, we get the picture that the way a given intelligible, F, is everything according to the former passage is by having everything else among the reasons for its being such as it is, reasons which in fact constitute what F is. So what F is is determined by F's place in the system of intelligibles, though it also has a character of its own.

Plotinus sometimes uses the analogy of a science and its theorems to illustrate the holism of Intellect: each theorem of a science implicitly contains the whole science (III.9.2, 1–3; IV.3.2, 50–55; IV.9.5, 12–21; V.9.8, 5–7; VI.2.20).[19] In VI.2.20 he discusses this analogy at considerable length. It may be worthwhile to consider what he has to say in some detail:

> Let us then grasp that the intellect which in no way applies itself to partial things and is not active about anything in particular exists, so that it may not become a particular intellect, like the science before the specific, partial sciences, and the science in specific form before the parts of it. No science is [the science of] any of its specific [contents] but the power of all of them; each is actually science and potentially each specific content. And the same is true of universal science: the specific sciences, which lie potentially in the whole, those, that is, which grasp the specific contents, are potentially the whole; for the whole is predicated of them, not a part of the whole; yet it must certainly be pure and independent. Thus, we can certainly say that universal intellect exists in one way—that is the one before those which are actually the particular intellects—and particular intellects in another, those which are partial and filled from all. But Intellect ranging over all of them leads the particular intellects, but is the power of them and contains them in its universality. They, on the other hand, in their partial selves contain the universal intellect, as a particular science contains the science.
> (VI.2.20, 1–16)

This passage seems to invoke three levels of science: (1) the universal science, which is not of anything in particular; (2) particular sciences such as geometry or musical theory; and (3) particular scientific knowledge, or theorems. The relationship between (1) and (2) and between (2) and (3) is such that the more particular contains the more general which is predicated of it; and the more general contains the more particular in the sense of being the power of producing them, or containing them potentially. The same kind of relationship is supposed to hold between the universal intellect and the particular intellects.

Before proceeding any further, let me clarify what is meant by "universal intellect" and "particular intellect" in this passage. The first lines of the next chapter, VI.2.21, make it clear that the universal intellect is the thought that comprises the highest kinds (see p. 112), whereas the particular intellects are equivalent to more particular beings. The question may be raised whether the account of the relationship between the universal science and the partial ones, and the universal intellect and the particular ones doesn't add support to Lloyd's view that at its peak Intellect's thought is undifferentiated and simple; for Plotinus says here in VI.2.20, 1–3, that it isn't about anything in particular; it may seem that differentiation first comes with the particular intellects. But this is not so. The universal intellect may in a sense not be directed at anything in particular. It is, however, per se directed at being as such (see VI.2.8, 14–16): being as such, though, is in a sense nothing in particular. But if the universal intellect is directed at being as such, it also involves the thought of the other primary genera. So the thought of being as such is indeed complex. Plotinus does not expand on what he means by universal science. I conjecture that he has in mind the knowledge of axioms common to all sciences such as Aristotle describes in *Metaphysics* IV, 3.

Two important questions that arise in connection with our passage are in what sense the part is potentially in the whole and in what sense the whole is potentially in the part. The key to the answer to both of them lies in another and earlier passage, where Plotinus uses the science analogy, but this time to explain the relationship between the hypostasis Soul and individual souls, IV.9.5. This latter is in fact closely linked to the relationship between Intellect and partial intellects, so that it is in itself not surprising that the same analogical explanation is used for both (cf. IV.3.2, 50–55). Here Plotinus explains that when a geometer holds a given theorem in his mind, "[a]lso there [in the science of geometry] what is brought forth for use is indeed by its activity/actuality (*energeiai* [dative]) a part, and this stands out; but the others [i.e. the other theorems] follow unnoticed in virtue of the power but they are all there in the part" (IV.9.5, 13–15). He explains this further by noting that holding a particular theorem in mind in isolation from the rest of the science, "will no longer be by art or scientific, but like a child was talking" (ll. 21–22).

It emerges from this that the sense of science Plotinus has in mind is not geometry or grammar abstracted from anybody's mastery of it. On the contrary, it is the science as incorporated into the scientist's soul. Accordingly, the whole is in the part in a sense which brings in the mind of the scientist engaged in the science. But, even so, how are we to think of the whole science as all-at-once actual in the scientist's mind, as Plotinus suggests (IV.9.5, 17; IV.3.2, 50–55)? Christian Tornau's (1998) article sheds much light on this question. What I have to say about the science analogy below largely reflects his conclusions.

Plotinus says nothing very explicit about this, but it could be argued that the mastery of a science constitutes a determinate state in the scientist's soul: the scientist's soul is such that not merely is she prone to think certain particular propositions, she thinks them by virtue of already being active in thinking some other thoughts from which these particular propositions flow. These other thoughts would be something like the thoughts of the principles of the science. By this I do not mean to suggest an express thought of a given axiom or set of axioms of the science from which the scientist deduces the particular thought. Rather I am thinking of a more general state of mind, the state of mind which constitutes general understanding of the principles of the science. To be in such a state is not to think about particular propositions of the science, but to be in a state that allows the scientist to think of any proposition she chooses with scientific understanding.

So, to return to our two questions: for the one who is in the state of mind of mastering a science, the particular theorems are readily available. They can be brought forth at will. This shows that they are present in the mastery of the science in general though they may not be explicitly activated. And conversely, for one who masters the science in this way the entertaining of a single theorem brings with it, for almost trivial reasons, the whole science: nobody who hasn't mastered the whole science could entertain the theorem in this scientific way, with this understanding of it. So the particular thought of this theorem contains the thoughts that constitute the mastery of the science in general, which in turn contains the thought of any other theorem of the science.

Plotinus' remark in VI.2.20 that "[t]he specific sciences ... are potentially the whole; for the whole is predicated of them" is to be seen in light of the same view of science. That is to say, the point is not, or not merely, that geometry is science or a science. It is rather that the one who really masters the science of geometry also masters scientific knowledge in general. If not, his general geometrical thoughts would be like "a child talking." So to master, say, geometry, is to master scientific knowledge in general, i.e. to master geometrical knowledge is to master general scientific knowledge. That is the sense in which science as such is predicated of a branch of science.

As the foregoing account indicates, the universal intellect is not just the apex of Intellect, Intellect's most universal thought, it is also something the subordinate thoughts share in. As our passage quoted above from VI.2.20 suggests: it is something all the subordinate intelligibles can be said to be, and is present in all of them. We could say that it is the thread or glue that runs through the system and unifies it. There does not seem to be anything comparable in Leibniz's system of individual substances, except perhaps God himself. As we shall see in the next chapter, there is something analogous to be found at the level of soul, namely, Soul the hypostasis, as distinct from particular souls.

8 Chapter summary

The second hypostasis of Plotinus' world, Intellect, is the realm of Platonic Ideas and thereby of what Plotinus (and Plato) considers to be the realm of real being. It turns out that as soon as the simplicity of the One has been abandoned, not just two but several things are bound to make an appearance at once, a thinker, the act of thought and the object of thought, each of which presupposes the other, so together they make up a unity. Yet they are logically distinct. Plotinus explains this simultaneous unity and plurality in Intellect with the aid of an interpretation of the five "greatest kinds" in Plato's *Sophist*—being, motion, rest, sameness and difference—out of which all other Forms are interwoven. It goes along with this account that the

Forms are internal to Intellect: they exist as its thoughts. Thus, Plotinus' view of the realm of Forms differs from most contemporary accounts of the Forms in Plato according to which this realm, although knowable by thought, is in some sense entirely extramental. A further feature of Plotinus' account of Intellect is that Intellect thinks itself. In part this is a consequence of the identity that holds between the subject and object of Intellect's thought: because both subject and object are immaterial, the subject of thought, the act of thought and the object of thought are one and the same thing. There is reason to believe, however, that the self-thinking of Intellect amounts to more than this formal identity for Plotinus: the subject of thought is aware of itself as the object of the thought. A final and in no way negligible aspect of Plotinus' of account of Intellect to be mentioned is that its thought is non-discursive and holistic: it is an atemporal all-at-once grasp of the intelligible realm as a whole. Moreover, each of the Forms presupposes or reflects this whole so that the grasp of any one of them involves grasping the whole. The point is not merely epistemological: since the being of each of the Forms consists in a thought, the being of each of the Forms involves the being of all the others.

Further reading

Primary sources

Ennead V.3. (49) "On the cognitive hypostases and what is beyond."
Ennead V.5. (32) "That the intelligibles are not outside the Intellect, and on the Good." There is an English translation with a commentary by Barrie Fleet (see "Text, Translations and Commentaries," in the Introduction).
Ennead V.8. (31) "On the intelligible beauty."
Ennead V.9. (9) "On Intellect, the Forms and being."

Secondary sources

A. H. Armstrong, *The Architecture of the Intelligible Universe in the Philosophy of Plotinus: An Analytical and Historical Study* (Cambridge: Cambridge University Press, 1940).

Anthony C. Lloyd, "Plotinus on the Genesis of Thought and Existence," *Oxford Studies in Ancient Philosophy* 5 (1987), 155–186.

Steven Menn, "Plotinus on the Identity of Knowledge with Its Object," *Apeiron* 34, 3 (2001), 233–246.

Eyjólfur K. Emilsson, *Plotinus on Intellect* (Oxford: Oxford University Press, 2007).

Damian Caluori, *Plotinus on Soul* (Cambridge: Cambridge University Press, 2015), chapters 2 and 3.

Notes

1. V.6.5, 10: *ephesis gar opseōs horasis*. As Bussanich (1988: 62) notes, Plotinus tends fairly consistently to use *opsis* and *horasis* or corresponding verbs to distinguish between the doings of the inchoate or potential intellect and those of the actual one. The word "sight's" (*opseōs*) here must, as Lloyd (1987: 164) maintains, be a possessive genitive with *ephesis* (desire) rather than an objective genitive, "for the sight," as some interpreters have presumed, and it must refer to the indefinite sight which is the potential intellect.
2. As noted by O'Meara (1990: 149) and Remes (2007: 73, 133), the idea that what is simple cannot be grasped by thought may go back to Plato's *Theaetetus* 201d–e.
3. On Plotinus' interpretation of the genera of being, see Santa-Cruz 1997. The "greatest forms" or some subset thereof appear in several other passages. The fullest discussion is to be found in VI.2.1–8 but see also II.6.1, 1–3; III.7.3, 9–11; VI.6.9, 3 ff.; VI.7.13, 4 ff.
4. See especially V.9.8, 8–11 and VI.6.8, 17 ff. Among scholars who argue for a priority of being is Hadot (1996). For a discussion of the issue, see Emilsson 2007: 152–157.
5. There is a fine commentary on this treatise in French by Schniewind (2007).
6. In VI.2.16, 5 Plotinus denies that there is "place" in the intelligible world.
7. A fine account, which also surveys older literature, is given by Kalligas (1997), who argues that so-called Ideas of individuals are in fact items at the level of the undescended soul; see also D'Ancona 2002, Remes 2007: 79, Aubry 2008 and Caluori 2015: 78–86. In an important article Tornau and Michalewsky (2009) argue that human beings as subjects or selves also exist at the level of Intellect.
8. On Plotinus' notion of *logos*, see Chapter 2, Section 3.
9. For a more detailed discussion of this aspect of the causal relation between the One and Intellect, see D'Ancona 1996 and Emilsson 2007: 153–154.
10. For a fuller discussion of this passage and others invoking self-reflexive awareness of Intellect, see Emilsson 2007: especially ch 2, §7.
11. "Perception of oneself" (*aisthēsis heautou*) and "awareness of oneself" (*gnōsis heautou*) are here and in other similar contexts equivalent to "thinking (of) oneself" (*noēsis heautou*); note the shift to *noein* and *noēsis* in the passage quoted.

12 I understand *ton noun* ("the intellect") as implied after *auton* ("itself"). See Henry and Schwyzer's *editio minor*, note *ad loc*.
13 This treatise is part of the Großschrift—see Chapter 1, p. 21—split into four by Porphyry. The title is not Plotinus' any more than other titles of his treatises.
14 That Plotinus' account of Intellect's knowledge is influenced by skepticism has often been noted and is explored to great length and insight by Kühn (2009).
15 Parmenides, fr. 3. Plotinus clearly understands Parmenides' sentence, which he quotes several times, along the lines of the translation given here, see III.8.8, 8; V.1.8, 17; V.9.5, 29–30. Many contemporary scholars translate it differently and, in my view, less straightforwardly and in fact questionably.
16 In Plato the search for the definition of justice in *Republic* II–IV as well as that for the definition of the sophist in the *Sophist* are described with the aid of metaphors from hunting: the search for knowledge is like pursuing a wild animal; getting the knowledge is then presumably like locating the animal, if not killing it. Then there is the famous midwifery metaphor in the *Theaetetus*, which seems to equate the acquisition of knowledge with the birth of a healthy child. In Stoicism the main metaphors tend in the direction of grasping things and getting a solid hold of them, cf. the famous story about Zeno's gestures with his hands reported by Cicero (*Academica* II, 145 = Long and Sedley 1987: 41A). The central term in Stoic epistemology is *katalēpsis*, which contains the root of *lambanein*, "to take."
17 *Metaphysics* IX, 1051b23–24. Cf. also XI, 1072b21, where Aristotle appeals to contact in explaining how thought and its object are the same.
18 See Rodier 1902 and Emilsson 2013 with further references.
19 For illuminating discussions of this analogy, see Tornau 1998 and Nikulin 2005.

Five
Soul

In this chapter we turn to soul, the stage after Intellect and the last of the intelligible levels in Plotinus' world. For a number of reasons soul is the most complicated stage of the hierarchy and hardest to come to grips with—as if the One and Intellect were not difficult enough! There are various reasons for this. One is surely that soul is the most versatile of the three hypostases in its activities: some soul never leaves the intelligible realm and eternally contemplates true beings; some governs the motions of the heavens and produces sensible qualities and quantities, and even matter; some is responsible for functions such as digestion, sense-perception and reasoning in human beings. Moreover, it is my soul that feels the attraction of the higher realms and seeks to approach them. How are we to see a single thing behind all this?

This versatility of soul is part of Plotinus' Platonic heritage: at least as he reads Plato, soul is doing all these things in Plato, except perhaps creating matter. It does not simplify the picture that there are other influences on Plotinus' notion of soul, Aristotle in particular, whose psychological terminology Plotinus largely adopts. In my opinion, despite the magnum opus on the soul, "On the problems of soul (I), (II) and (III)" (IV.3–5. (27–29)), and the sincere attempt we see there to clarify a number of pressing questions, various issues relating to soul remain unresolved. In the present chapter, I shall try to steer a middle course: I do not wish to oversimplify but I don't want to drown the presentation in difficulties, caveats and qualifications either.

There are at least five kinds of soul: the World-Soul, star souls, the soul of the earth, individual human souls, and last but not least the Soul, the hypostasis. The souls other than the hypostasis are individual souls in the sense that they are souls of particular bodies. Following indications in the *Enneads* we shall speak of World-Soul, star souls and the soul of the earth collectively as the divine souls. In practice, however, Plotinus often treats the star souls and the soul of the earth as parts or powers of the World-Soul. In this chapter we shall discuss each of these kinds and also consider some claims Plotinus makes about souls in general. The specific issues concerning the human soul will be dealt with in Chapters 7 and 8. The human soul will in fact be of central concern in Chapters 9 and 10 as well.

1 Soul's thought

Much in the same vein as Plato and the Stoics, Plotinus sees the soul both as an essentially rational thinking being and as a principle of life. Given that soul is the immediate descendant of Intellect and given that both for the ancient Greeks and for us thinking is a paradigmatically psychic activity, it should not come as a surprise that thinking and rationality are essential characteristics of the soul. The account of the relationship between Intellect and soul fits the pattern of the double activity and conversion that was discussed in Chapter 2. We have a clear expression of this in V.1.6, 45–48:

> As soul is a *logos*[1] and a kind of activity of Intellect, just as Intellect is of that other [the One]. But soul's *logos* is obscure—for it is a shadow of Intellect—and for this reason it has to look to Intellect: but Intellect in the same way has to look to that god, in order to be Intellect.

Thus, soul is an image of Intellect. Being an image implies both a resemblance and a difference: an image is always more diffuse and weaker than its archetype. Nevertheless, it is clear that the first stage of the order of soul after Intellect is totally engaged in thought of the intelligibles. In fact, as we shall see more clearly later in this chapter, all souls remain in the intelligible realm. Given soul's productive activities and other involvement with the sensible realm this may seem quite puzzling. We will have some explanations in the course of this chapter. First, however, we must address another difficult question: if the first stage of soul remains in the intelligible realm and is engaged in the thought of the intelligibles, how does soul differ from Intellect, if at all?

What one would expect on general grounds is that the undescended souls' thinking is somehow more dispersed, more plural than that of Intellect. This is indeed so (see III.9.1, 34–37; VI. 4.4). Plotinus distinguishes between the thought of Intellect and the thought of its immediate offspring, soul, by describing the latter's thought as discursive thought (*dianoia*): "the offspring of Intellect is a kind of rational formula (*logos*) and a level of being (*hypostasis*), that which thinks discursively (*to dianooumenon*)" (V.1.7, 42–43). Interestingly, he even describes soul's thinking as reasoning (*logismos*): "[the soul's] intellect (*nous*) is in reasonings (*logismois*)" (V.1.3, 13). This may seem strange in light of the fact that he also contrasts the kind of thought of undescended souls with the reasoning kind of thought that embodied human souls are typically engaged in, which is also called "reasoning," *logismos*. We have an explanation of this in "On the problems of soul (I)." Here, after denying that undescended souls are engaged in reasoning, he qualifies this statement by saying that the term "reasoning" can also be applied to the undescended souls: "But one must understand reasoning in this sort of sense; because if one understands reasoning to be a state of mind which exists in them always proceeding from Intellect, and which is a static activity and a kind of reflection of Intellect, they [the souls] would employ reasoning in that other world too" (IV.3.18, 9–13). For the embodied human soul discursive reasoning is a searching, temporal process. But this is not how undescended souls think (cf. IV.4.15, 13 ff.). So when characterizing their thought as discursive and as employing reasoning, at least Plotinus does not mean a temporal, tentative thinking process. So what does he mean? What is essential to the discursive thought of the undescended souls?

The distinction between discursive thinking (*dianoia*) and intellection (*noēsis*) goes back to Plato's celebrated Divided Line in the *Republic*. There, intellection is the highest form of thought—with discursive thought in the second rank. Among the distinguishing marks mentioned by Plato is that intellection moves "upwards" to ever more comprehensive premises or concepts, whereas discursive thought moves "downwards" from given premises. I suggest that this may provide us with a clue to Plotinus' understanding of discursive thought generally: it is essentially some kind of derivation. That, however, does not mean that the derivation is necessarily a tentative, temporal process, though this may be in the case for embodied souls.

In order to come to better grips with the kind of thought undescended souls are engaged in, a little excursion back to Plato's *Timaeus* and its interpretation will be helpful. This will also put us in a position to see why soul is indispensable in Platonism, at least the sort of Platonism that was prevalent in antiquity. Plato's views on the generation of the sensible world are often presented as if there were just two sorts of things: the Ideas and physical objects that participate in, or imitate, the Ideas. If we only had e.g. the *Republic* and the *Phaedo*, we might easily be led to adopt this simple picture. Human souls are of course prominent in both dialogues but there is no hint that they or any other souls are involved in making or managing the world at large. The *Timaeus* has a more complicated account. We have there the realm of Ideas, which is called the Living Being. We have in addition the character of the divine Craftsman or Demiurge, the maker of the world. The Craftsman fashions the world on the model of the Forms with the help of his children, to whom he gave the final task of "weaving mortal bodies" (*Timaeus* 42d). Before that, he had made the World-Soul and other souls and set the world in uniform circular motion, thereby creating time as "a moving image of eternity."

Plato relates all this in a semi-mythical language that was not meant to be taken literally in every respect. So Plato's ancient followers had the formidable task of interpreting the *Timaeus* so that it made good philosophical sense. Some of Plotinus' Platonist predecessors noted that the Craftsman seems to be engaged in two rather different activities. On the one hand he is engaged in pure intellection of the Forms. In the *Timaeus* the Forms, the Living being, is presented as something external to the Craftsman's mind. On the other hand, the Craftsman must think about what he is about to make and how.[2] This observation gave rise to theories, such as that of Numenius, which split the Craftsman's thought into two: pure intellection and providential thought about the world (Numenius, fr. 11; cf. *Timaeus* 30c). Plotinus follows this trend and takes it further. For him too this providential thought is, so to speak, essential to soul's thinking activity.

How does this providential thought differ from pure intellection? The following is reasonably clear: (1) This psychic thought is less unified than intellection. (2) It is derived from the latter by means of the soul's vision of Intellect in its conversion. (3) It is practical in that it involves making the blueprint for the sensible world according the maxim that it is to be as good as a sensible image can be. (4) Nevertheless, this thought is not a temporal process that involves a search for an unknown conclusion.

What sort of thought could this be? In what way exactly is it more diffuse than intellection? Caluori (2015: 44–51) argues that as opposed to the non-propositional, vision-like thought of Intellect, the first psychic thought is propositional. Admittedly, the evidence for this is thin but the suggestion makes very good sense. Soul's thought must be more dispersed than Intellect's and it is hard to conceive of a way for it to be so without its becoming propositional. As we saw, Plotinus also calls soul's thought *logismos*, "reasoning," and in the case of undescended souls he qualifies this by describing it as a "static activity and a kind of reflection of Intellect." This may indeed count as evidence for propositionality: even if this reasoning is static, hence not inferential, the very willingness to use of the term *logismos* to refer to it would suggest some sort of propositional thought.

However this may be, the thoughts the offspring of Intellect entertains cannot be direct descriptions of the contents of Intellect: Intellect only implicitly contains all the details of the sensible world, not explicitly. So the soul's work cannot consist in straightaway describing this content in propositions. Some mediation must be involved. In comparing embodied and undescended souls, Plotinus notes that "just as in the arts reasoning occurs when the artisans are in perplexity, but when there is no difficulty, the art dominates and does its work" (IV.3.18, 5–7). "Reasoning" here is clearly meant as temporal, searching reasoning. Good craftsmen do not normally need to go through such a process. Their mastery of their art ensures effortlessness. That, however, does not mean that they do not think: on the contrary, they think excellently! Perhaps we can compare the soul's thought with a skilled portrait painter: she will look at her model and start her work without any searching thought process. In this case we may assume that even if resemblance between model and portrait is sought, this is not a matter of exact copying: there are all sorts of constraints imposed by the materials that make that impossible and, moreover, the artist may on purpose deviate from exactness for the purposes of artfulness; the best portrait needn't be the one that faithfully represents every detail. The soul's thought is similarly an effortless elicitation and transformation of the content of Intellect somewhat like the thought of a skilled craftsman or artist.

This analogy with human artists seems to fail in one important respect, however. In "On providence (I)" Plotinus writes: "This universe has come into existence, not as the result of a process of reasoning that it ought to exist but because it was necessary that there should be a second nature; for that true all was not of a kind to be the last of realities" (III.2.2, 8–10). The "true all" here is the transcendent soul and Intellect, the intelligible realm. Unlike most human craftsmen, the soul does not think and act with a certain product as a goal. It is rather like an unusual craftsman who only has the perfection of his art in view. The Stoics indeed thought that ideally craftsmen are like that: at least the sage who practices the art of living only aims at the perfection of her art, not at a given result.[3] In this way psychic activity follows the same pattern as the One and Intellect: the One does not emanate with the production of the Intellect in mind, nor does Intellect wish to produce soul: this just happens as a kind of byproduct of what they are doing. The sensible world presents itself indeed *as* if it had been carefully planned by an intelligent and benevolent being but there was no planning in the sense of goal-directed thought aiming at the sensible world as a result. In that sense Plotinus rejects natural teleology and his notion of providential thought lacks what we may strongly associate with providence, namely the explicit wish to care for the beneficiary of providence.

2 The hypostasis Soul and individual souls

I have so far talked about souls indiscriminately without any distinction between types of soul. As we noted at the outset of this chapter, there are at least five kinds: the hypostasis Soul, the World-Soul, star souls, the soul of the earth and individual human souls. It is time to consider them and their distinctions. The first thing to note is that the souls other than the hypostasis are individual souls. The soul of Venus, for instance, is the individual soul of the heavenly body we can see and recognize as Venus. Even the World-Soul, being the soul of a single thing, i.e. the sensible cosmos, is individual. Plotinus asserts that it and our individual human souls are sisters (IV.3.6, 13), thereby implying that in a sense they are on the same level and have common ancestry. Only the hypostasis Soul is not individual, meaning it is never in charge of a particular body.

What then is this hypostasis Soul? For a long time, scholars did not see a clear distinction between the undescended World-Soul and the hypostasis.[4] It is true that the distinction between the hypostasis and the World-Soul is not often explicitly made. It is, however, clearly there: in "On the problems of soul (I)" Plotinus says: "This then is how it is with the solution of this problem [the question whether our souls are parts of that of the world], and the fact of sympathy does not stand in the way of our account: for since all souls come from the same [soul] from which the soul of the whole also comes they are sympathetic to one another" (IV.3.8, 1–3). It is unambiguously asserted here that there is some one soul from which both the soul of the whole, i.e. the World-Soul, and our souls derive. No doubt the star souls and the soul of the earth are also included in this, presumably as often elsewhere subsumed under the soul of the whole. Why would Plotinus think that there is such a soul from which all the other souls derive?

As so often the case, Plato's *Timaeus* and its interpretative history provides the answer. It was remarked above that Plotinus' predecessors found it necessary to divide the divine Craftsman's thought into two: pure intellection of the realm of Ideas and world-making thought. The *Timaeus* tells us something about the latter though most of it is expressed as a narrative rather than as philosophy in a strict sense. We learn that the Craftsman wished to make the world as good as a perishable being can be and that in doing so he exercised providence (*Timaeus* 30c). And we learn further that the Craftsman makes the World-Soul, the star souls and the individual human souls according to some rigid principles but not at all in the manner of detailed copying of the Forms. The Craftsman's thought seems in the first instance to be concerned with making the souls. Now, as we have seen Plotinus seeks to minimize, even get rid of, whatever results-oriented teleology the *Timaeus* story may suggest. He does, however, retain the idea of providence at least in the sense of a guarantee of an optimal result. The hypostasis Soul, I suggest, consists in the rational thoughts of the totality of Intellect whose content becomes the order of souls.[5] Thus, the hypostasis soul is analogous to the universal intellect discussed in Chapter 4 (p. 138). It is not simply the totality of all the partial intellects but, so to speak, the top of the structure that is present as a whole in all the parts. It is freely admitted that this is somewhat speculative, lacking direct textual evidence. According to this suggestion the particular details of the sensible world are only implicit in this thought. Making them explicit is the job of the individual souls, not least the World-Soul which has the largest task. Still, with the order of souls in place a lot has been achieved.

But how does it come about that the sensible world is as good as can be without any planning that seeks to guarantee this result? One obvious answer is that it is an image of Intellect and ultimately an image of the Good—how could an image of these be other than good? The question is whether the process of image-making by means of the familiar emanation and conversion is sufficient to explain why the cosmos is not only good but optimally good. Caluori (2015: especially 51 ff.) argues that emanation and conversion is not enough: while admitting that neither Intellect nor the hypostasis Soul are engaged in deliberation or aim at a particular result, he nevertheless holds that in order to attain the optimal cosmos the Soul must think about unrealized possibilities. The reason is that so many details of the sensible world, which are expressed not only by necessary theoretical propositions but also contingent ones, are undetermined by Intellect when it comes to making a full-blown sensible world. Caluori argues convincingly that in addition to theoretical thought, the soul must also be engaged in practical thinking about how to construe an excellent sensible world. Also recently, Noble and Powers (2015) have defended an interpretation according to which the making of the sensible world follows the general pattern of double activity (emanation). They argue for this mainly on the basis of the first few chapters of *Ennead* VI.7, "How the multitude of the Forms came into being, and on the Good," where Plotinus resolutely argues against any sort of planning of the sensible world in Intellect. It is true that this passage does not consider the work of the soul directly but neither this nor other passages that describe the genesis of the sensible world invoke any sort of decision-making or considerations of alternatives anywhere in the process; cf. V.8.7.

While I agree with Noble and Powers in that Plotinus sees the making of the world as following the general pattern of double activity, I find Caluori's account as such very attractive. Perhaps his sort of account, which emphasizes that practical nature of the thought that goes into making the world, can be brought into accord with the pattern of double activity, if we take into account Plotinus' view on artistic activity: we noted above that he says in the context of discussing the kind of thought employed by disembodied souls that "just as in the arts reasoning occurs when the artisans are in perplexity, but when there is no difficulty, the art dominates and does its work" (IV.3.18, 5–7). An artisan who is, say, making a table, and does not have to deliberate because "the art dominates and does its work," will nevertheless implicitly be making a lot of decisions. He just does not have to consider the possibilities he rejects because his artistry sees to it that he makes the best choice. I shall not pursue this further but it seems to me that if we adopt such a model, which Plotinus really invites us to do, there may be a way of unifying the kind of account Caluori gives with the general pattern of emanation.

3 The unity of soul

Plotinus maintains the seemingly paradoxical thesis that all souls are just one soul. He argues explicitly for this in an early treatise, IV.9. (8), to which Porphyry gave the title "Whether all souls are one," and the paradoxical thesis appears prominently in the treatise "On the presence of being, one and the same, everywhere as a whole (I) and (II)," VI.4. (22) and VI.5. (23). The hypostasis Soul plays a prominent role in the rationale for this claim. We noted in connection with Intellect that the hypostasis Intellect, which we identified with the "first" thought of being along with the other highest genera, is both something in itself and present as a whole in the particular intellects (see Chapter 4, p. 109). We also discussed the analogy with a science and its branches and theorems that Plotinus appeals to in illustrating the unity of Intellect. Clearly, he conceives of the thesis about the unity of souls as a version of the same doctrine and it is argued for in the same way, by the analogy with the sciences (cf. V.9.5, 12–26). The underlying idea is that just as the hypostasis Intellect embraces the whole intelligible realm in a general way by virtue of being the thought constituting the apex of the intelligible realm from which all the other intelligibles are generated, so the thought of the hypostasis Soul embraces the whole arena of souls in a general way. This must indeed be the general thought that will produce an optimal sensible cosmos. The individual souls, be they human souls or those of the cosmos and the stars, are partial thoughts of this whole and this whole is "in" them in much the way the whole of a science is implicit in a particular theorem being thought by a scientist, cf. Chapter 4, pp. 139–140.

This last point has a corollary: every soul has the same powers as any other, it is just that the same powers are not activated in each. This follows from Plotinus' conception of the unity of souls: if the hypostasis Soul is present as a whole in each of the individual, partial souls, and given that the Soul incorporates all soul-powers, all soul-powers are present in each particular soul.

Does the unity of all souls mean that the unity of souls is just as strong as the unity of intelligibles in Intellect? At least it is clear that the unity of souls *appears* to be weaker: this is evident from the case of our embodied souls that seem to be spread out between different bodies and each one of these spread out between the organs of its own body. As we shall see, Plotinus thinks these impressions are importantly deceptive. Nevertheless, we know that generally speaking the sphere of souls is less unified than that of Intellect. It is, however, evidently strong enough for the thesis of the unity of all souls to apply.

But does Plotinus really mean that all souls are strictly identical? That you have got the very same soul as I? Despite the claim that all souls are one, the relation Plotinus is after is not that of strict identity but a strong relation close to identity: he wishes to maintain that my soul is something in its own right and different from yours. It is even something in its own right at the intelligible level (see VI.4.4, 1 ff.). At the same time he wants to say that my soul contains the whole hypostasis Soul, as does yours; and my soul and your soul are, conversely, both contained in the hypostasis.[6] As we have noted the relations between individual souls and between them and the hypostasis reflect the situation at the level of Intellect but these relations have no parallel in the purely physical world: here every item is totally distinct from any other (see Chapter 6, p. 201). They do, however, have a parallel within the individual soul: each of us has one soul but we also have different soul-powers that are even active in different parts of the body: hearing in the ears, sight in the eyes and so forth. Yet, it is one and the same soul that sees the musician and hears her music. Plotinus makes a lot out of this fact, which we shall return to in Section 8 ("Soul and Body").

4 World-Soul, star souls and the earth soul

When as a student I first came across the World-Soul, in connection with Plato rather than Plotinus, I was baffled: what on earth could lead a supremely intelligent person such as Plato evidently was to believe in such a thing? Anthropomorphism! Plotinus has his notion of the World-Soul from Plato and previous Platonists. It is a central notion in the *Timaeus* and is alluded to in a few other dialogues. In Plotinus the World-Soul appears at length in several treatises and is never far away.

In order to make a case for the World-Soul let us start by noting that not only Plato, Plotinus and other Platonists posited such a being but the Stoics too. For the latter the World-Soul, God and the cosmic Reason (*logos*) are one and the same thing. An important difference between them and the Platonists is that the Stoics were what we would call materialists, i.e. they thought that everything that exists, including souls and Reason, is a body. Another difference is that according to the Stoics Reason is immanent in the cosmos. Though firmly rejecting these aspects of the Stoic view, Plotinus' account of the hypostasis Soul and World-Soul is quite flavored by Stoicism. Now, the number of proponents is not in itself a strong argument for the feasibility of a view. Still, the mere fact that so many ancient thinkers found the notion of a World-Soul quite natural gives us reason to suppose that there was something in their more or less tacit assumptions about the world that renders such an idea reasonable to them.

There are primarily two such interrelated assumptions. One is that these thinkers took for granted a biological model of the world: we best understand the world if we assume that it is a kind of organism. This of course does not mean that the world was thought to be just like any other organism. A very important difference is for instance that the world neither takes in nourishment, nor procreates. And as opposed to ordinary organisms, the world is eternal according to Plotinus and the other pagan Neoplatonists; hence, no "birth" or "death" for this organism. Here the Stoics differ: they thought the world is generated and comes to an end only to start again in exactly the same way (see Long and Sedley 1987: 46).

The evidence for the world's organic nature lies in its regular and apparently coordinated movements, especially of the heavenly bodies, and in the clever arrangement of everything, which makes it possible for lots of living beings to inhabit the world. Secondly, not only is there evidence for mere life, these same facts indicate that the life in question is some sort of rational life or at least that some sort of rational life is behind this life. According to Plotinus, any life, being essentially an expression of rationality, presupposes rational life. In Plotinus' case at least, the organic model is quite thoroughgoing: with the exception of loose stones and suchlike stuff, all bodies are parts of organisms. We may well conclude that this model is ultimately anthropomorphic. We should note, however, that the kind of thinking Plotinus attributes to Intellect and Soul and the divine souls is rather different from human thought. In particular it does not involve deliberation with a certain end in view.

As noted above, Plotinus does not always mean the same when he talks about the World-Soul. In "On the descent of soul into bodies" (IV.8. (6)), he says that "the divine soul is always said to direct the whole heaven in the first way, transcendent in its higher part but sending its last and lowest power into the interior of the world" (IV.8.2, 31–33). Sometimes the World-Soul is this higher part together with all its powers, including the powers of nature that directly fashion the bodies on earth. Sometimes he is only referring to the "commanding faculty" of the World-Soul, which though not strictly speaking located, begins the actualization of its activity from the heavens. As Wilberding (2005, 2006: 53–57) has shown, the "commanding faculty" of the World-Soul is located in the heavens in the same sense as the principle of sense-perception is located in the brain: it is not there as in a place but in the sense that it is from there that the actualization of its power begins (IV.3.23, 10 ff.).

The higher World-Soul does not descend into its body, the body of the sensible cosmos (II.9.7; IV.8.2). This is because the body of the cosmos does not have to deal with any contingencies: there is nothing outside it, nothing that threatens it, no unexpected situations that would require the soul to get directly involved with the body of the world (IV.8.2). So the World-Soul rules the cosmos like a king in a peaceful and orderly kingdom. Plotinus remarks that the World-Soul "needs only a kind of brief command" (IV.8.2, 16) to rule the world. As Caluori (2015: 118–119) plausibly suggests that this "brief command" is the World-Soul's only immediate external act and that it consists in the "order" to move the firmament. This first motion guides the star souls which move accordingly, each according to its own assignment.

Even if the World-Soul itself is thus not much involved in the particular motions within the cosmos, somebody has to get dirt on his hands, so to speak. Caluori (2015: 114 ff.) has shown, helpfully relating Plotinus' views on this to the pseudo-Aristotelian text *De mundo* (On the world), the World-Soul rules the cosmos through agents: primary among these are the divine star souls, whose activities have various effects on earth. This is very evident in the case of the Sun but, as we shall later see, the stars have various less obvious influences. Plotinus counts these as individual souls, no doubt because each of them is an individual thinker. They can think for themselves and are not just puppets of the World-Soul, but as becomes good functionaries of an excellent leader they will do as the World-Soul intends. The stars are bodies and the star souls are embodied souls. Their situation is, however, crucially different from ours: while humans have to deal with ever new situations and even dangers to their bodies, there is nothing that disturbs, not to say threatens, the bodies of stars. Nor do their bodies need any nourishment.

There is, finally, the soul of the earth. Actually, the soul of the earth does not make a prominent appearance in the *Enneads*, and Plotinus raises the question whether to consider it an individual soul in its own right or a mere power of the World-Soul, though he comes to the conclusion that indeed it is an independent thinker and hence an independent soul (IV.4.22, 17 ff.). Often, however, the activities of the soul of the earth are simply attributed to nature (*physis*), which appears as the lowest phase of the World-Soul. The most important function of the soul of the earth is to be the principle of plant life. As such it contributes greatly to the economy of the sensible world as plants play a crucial role for the life on earth and is given a divine status just like the star souls.

All these souls and their acts make up a well-organized system: "[the living cosmos] completes its course periodically according to everlastingly fixed rational formulas ... everything being ordered under one rational formula in the descents and ascents of souls and with regard to everything else" (IV.3.12, 13–19). The single all-embracing rational formula mentioned here is no doubt the thought of the hypostasis Soul. The general picture that emerges is that the tasks and work of the individual souls are predetermined in the grand rational formula. The World-Soul leads on. The other individual souls are meant to behave in accordance with it. The divine star souls and the soul of the earth invariably do so. The human souls can in principle follow suit but being less perfectly rational they often—in the majority of cases—actually fail to do so.

Nothing has so far been directly said about how the bodies, their properties and their matter come about. Plotinus repeatedly asserts that this is the work of soul, more precisely the lowest phase of soul, which he identifies with nature (IV.4.13; III.8.1–5). Admittedly, the origin of matter is disputed but I do not doubt that it too is produced by soul. I shall resume my discussion of the generation of matter and bodies in the next chapter but a few remarks on nature are in order here.

The status of nature in relation to the other souls is in fact somewhat unclear. Plotinus implies that it is an image of a higher soul (III.8.4, 15–16) and confirms that it is a soul, by which he presumably means that it belongs to the order of soul rather than that it is an individual soul in its own right. It is the principle immediately responsible for growth in plants and animals. In IV.4.13, 19–20, he describes nature as that which is reflected from the World-Soul onto matter and elsewhere he says that the World-Soul has already made a preliminary outline on matter before the individual soul-powers enter into it, apparently meaning that this power of the World-Soul has made the bodies which the other souls come to animate (VI.7.7). But as we just noted, he also says that the soul of the earth is the principle of plant life. He does not explain how this is compatible with regarding it as the lower phase of the World-Soul but presumably this is according to the wide sense of "World-Soul," according to which the other divine souls are regarded as merely its powers.

There are some interesting remarks about the activity of nature. In "On the problems of soul (II)," chapters 13–14, he denies all apprehension, consciousness and mental images of it. Its activity consists simply in making. It receives, however, something of the nature of thought from the soul above which enables it to do so. In the treatise "On nature and contemplation and the One," III.8, the first six chapters deal with nature. Here Plotinus attributes some kind of thought to nature, a dim form of contemplation (theōria), which results in production in the sensible realm. We shall revisit these passages in the next chapter.

Some readers have presumably wondered how something like soul, a being that has been described as an essentially thinking entity, can produce anything like matter and corporeal extension. The question is indeed a natural one to ask. We may find it odd that Plotinus never directly addresses it. He does, however, indicate what his answer would be. In chapter 3 of the treatise "Various considerations" (III.9. (13)), he suggests that matter is produced by a soul that is becoming "more indefinite" (III.9.3, 11–12). "More indefinite" means for Plotinus "less unified." This passage and others in the same vein suggest that he regarded both spatial extension and the ultimate indefiniteness that is matter as the results of the activities of a soul which already has become fairly indefinite. In other words, extension and matter are regarded as the next stages after an indefinite soul in a process that started in the unity and completion of the One. This is, of course, not a mechanical explanation of how matter and extension come about from soul. There is no such explanation to be had. But this is an explanation that fits into the familiar pattern of emanation and image-making with a loss of unity at each step.

5 Sense-perception and memory of the divine souls

A considerable part of Plotinus' large treatise "On the problems of soul (I), (II) and (III)" deals with the question of which psychic powers the divine souls are endowed with. In particular, several chapters are devoted to discussing whether they have sense-perception and memory. Surprisingly, perhaps, the fullest discussion of sense-perception in general in the whole *Enneads*, chapter 23 of IV.4, is a preamble to the more specific question whether the earth has sense-perception. We shall consider sense-perception and memory more fully in relation to human psychology in the next chapter. Plotinus' remarks about the divine souls' capacities in this respect are, however, of general interest for his views on the nature of these soul-powers and at the same time complete the picture of his views on the divine souls.

Sense-perception is an activity of the soul using the body: it is a process starting in the external object perceived that acts on an organ of sense; the affection on the organ is transmitted to the soul to which sense-perception properly speaking, consisting in judgment, belongs. The bodily organ and its affection are, however, essential: without this the cognition in question would not count as sense-perception. Furthermore, sense-perception is there for a reason (even if nobody planned this result): it serves the purpose of making the organism aware of its environment for its safety and benefit (IV.4.24, 1–9). Memory, on the other hand, is exclusively the work of the soul without the involvement of a bodily organ: Plotinus rejects the Aristotelian view of memory as residues stored up on a bodily organ (cf. *On Memory* 449b31; *On the Soul* III, 428b10).[7]

Memory belongs to souls that migrate and change their state "for memory is of things which have happened and are past." This means that there is no memory for the divine souls who are always in the same state: the star souls "will not remember that they went around the earth yesterday ... and that they lived yesterday" (IV.4.7, 4–5). Nor will these souls remember their grasp of the intelligibles: they always grasp them. Similarly, these souls do not employ reasoning: for the need to reason is a sign of comparative lack of intelligence: the man who reasons "is like one who is learning in order to know" (IV.4.12, 9), as is clear from the fact the person who reasons stops reasoning as soon as she has found out what she was searching for (IV.4.12, 12). These souls simply don't have to recollect or use reasoning: they simply know.

The divine souls have bodies and could in principle have sense-perception: they may not have sense-organs just like ours but as

Plotinus points out sense-organs vary greatly among animals (IV.4.26, 21–23). From this he concludes that "there is nothing absurd or impossible in the earth's soul seeing" (IV.4.26, 28–29). As to the World-Soul, he says that "we must grant it self-perception, just as we are aware of ourselves, but not perception of a continual succession of different objects; since we too, when we apprehend something in our body which differs from its permanent state, apprehend it as something coming from outside" (IV.4.24, 21–25). As to vision, Plotinus asks why a translucent body such as that of the World-Soul—he is referring to the heavens—should not have the power of seeing. The answer he gives is interesting. The presence of the physical conditions for seeing and sense-perception generally is not enough for there to be sense-perception: "the soul must also be so disposed as to incline towards sense-objects" (IV.4.25, 2–3). The World-Soul is always inclined towards intelligible objects. So even if it had the power to perceive through its sense-organs, it would not do so. It is the same with us too, he says: "when we are strongly concentrating on the intelligible objects, as long as we are in this state, sights and other perceptions pass unnoticed; and in general, when one is concentrating entirely on one thing, all the others are unnoticed" (IV.4.25, 5–8).

While Plotinus' denial of memory and reasoning for the divine souls is definite and unqualified, he is more ambivalent as regards their sensory powers. From the discussion in IV.4.24–27 it seems tempting to conclude that even if they have no need for sense-perception they may have the power of vision and hearing but this power is unactualized because the souls are entirely focused on contemplating intelligibles. He notes "that their awareness of prayers is the result of a sort of linking and a particular disposition of things fitted into the whole." This means, as he goes on to suggest, that their awareness of this is by means of sympathy (IV.4.26, 1–4). We shall deal with sympathy more fully shortly but this remark suggests that the divine souls are not aware of our prayers by hearing them in the ordinary way. A little later, in IV.4.30, he says, however, referring to what has come before, that we gave the star souls the power of sight and hearing and that they hear our prayers. There is no previous mention of active hearing of prayers on the part of the star souls and in general his account that follows of the influences of the heavenly souls appeals to sympathy rather than sense-perception.

This apparent inconsistency can perhaps be resolved: Plotinus thinks that sense-perception involves a passive affection of the organ of sense (see p. 245); in sight and hearing such affections come about by means of sympathy. There is more to a fully fledged sense-perception, however, than this affection. What he may have in mind when he says that the stars hear our prayers is simply the auditory affection effected by means of sympathy. So there is a kind of auditory affection but not thereby an actual hearing. This may be thought to suffice for the star to react accordingly though the prayer at no point reaches the star souls' consciousness.

6 Sympathy

The discussion that follows in chapters 30–45 of "On the problems of soul (II)" (IV.4. (28)) is about the effects of the heavenly beings on things on earth and in particular about the efficacy of magic, divination and prayer.[8] Belief in occult phenomena such as astrology, divination and magic were extremely widespread in antiquity, not least in the Hellenistic and Roman Imperial Era.[9] Some intellectuals, such as Cicero, remained skeptical about such practices but for instance most of the great Stoic school of thought seems to have accepted occult phenomena as natural facts that should be given a natural explanation. Plotinus simply follows suit here. Of the occult phenomena he discusses, the influence of the heavenly bodies receives by far the most attention. This may have to do with the fact that astrology was a particularly ingrained part of Egyptian culture in which Plotinus grew up and received his education.[10] He is skeptical, however, of the theories of practitioners of the occult arts and he thinks their effects are limited. His general stance, which emerges from the above-mentioned chapters of IV.4, is to regard them as a part of the workings of nature, no more mysterious than the influence of the moon on the tides. The notion of sympathy is a central notion in his account of these and in fact also other natural phenomena. We shall consider this notion at some length because it is indicative of how Plotinus thinks the world works.

Commonly Plotinus' notion of sympathy is said to be a borrowing from the Stoics.[11] This may need some qualification. The fact is that much of the background of sympathy as Plotinus conceives of it is to be found in the *Timaeus*. Plato emphasizes here that the physical world is animated by a soul that renders it a unified and unique living being (*Timaeus* 30c–d, 37c–d) of which the ordinary animal species are somehow parts. Human souls are made of the same stuff as this World-Soul, although somewhat more diluted, and are thus akin to the World-Soul (*Timaeus* 41d); Plato notes, moreover, that in fashioning the world, the divine Craftsman made the number of souls equal to the number of stars and assigned each soul to a star (*Timaeus* 41d–e). Thereby he suggests a connection between different parts of the universe, though he does not specify the nature or consequences of this assignment. Plotinus presumably saw his notion of *sympatheia* as a part of the Platonic heritage. As in some other cases where the Stoics seem to build on and develop views expressed by Plato, Plotinus is liable to turn to the Stoics and use their insights to develop what by his lights is essentially a Platonic view.

The word *sympatheia* and its cognates occur in several earlier writers (see Brouwer 2015: 16–19). The basic meaning, suggested by the composition of the word, is that one thing is affected in a certain way because some other thing is affected in a certain, usually similar, way. "Syn" (or "sym") means "together," "along with" (cf. "symphony"), and "patheia" means "affection," "state." An early instance is in Plato's *Charmides* 169b–c, where the phenomenon of contagious yawning is described in terms of "suffering along," *sympaschein*, the verb corresponding to the substantive *sympatheia*.[12]

The Stoics are responsible for making sympathy a kind of cosmic principle. Their notion of it is perhaps best elucidated as an inference from their belief that the cosmos is an organism. Just as in the case of an ordinary organism different parts may be so connected that an affection in one place leads to an affection in another—a bad stomach may for instance be accompanied by a headache though the lungs and the other parts in between are left quite unaffected—so in the cosmic organism distant parts may be affected by one another. The Stoic theory of the soul provided an explanation of such phenomena. According to the Stoics, the soul is *pneuma*, fiery air, that permeates the body as a whole (see e.g. Calcidius, 220 = Long and Sedley

1987: 53G). This *pneuma* is in a state of tension, as a result of which there is continuous wave-like motion back and forth in the organism (see e.g. Nemesius, 70, 6–71, 4 = Long and Sedley 1987: 47J). It appears that sympathy is effected by means of such tensional motion.[13] By means of the tensional motion, the organism is affected as a whole by an impact that hits only a part. It is worth remarking that the tensional motion is neither movement of physical particles from one place to another nor is it the kind of action–affection relation by which the quality of a thing is imparted upon the things adjacent to it. Rather, it seems to be the transmission of a state through the *pneuma* as a vehicle; hence when a change occurs at a given place, this is reflected in the tensional motion and may cause a similar or different affection elsewhere in the organism according to the disposition of these other parts. *Sympatheia* is affection depending on the tension of the *pneuma* that permeates the organism.

The Stoics did not limit the principle of *sympatheia* to familiar organisms. They conceived of the whole cosmos as an organism unified by all-pervasive *pneuma* in a state of tension, and they put the principle of *sympatheia* to various uses on the cosmic scale. They used it, for example, to explain the connection between the moon and the tides, the change of seasons, and the efficacy of so-called occult phenomena, such as divination (cf. H. von Arnim, *Stoicorum Veterum Fragmenta* [Fragments of the ancient Stoics] (1903–) II, 441, 446, 475, 1013).

The Stoic notion of sympathy depends on their view of the unity of soul. Each ordinary organism is of course animated by its particular soul. So is the whole cosmos. The individual souls enjoy a relative unity and coherence but ultimately they are just parts of the great World-Soul. So there is one continuous *pneuma* that pervades everything and it is on this that sympathy depends. Like in the case of the Stoics, sympathy in Plotinus depends on the unity of soul. There are, however, significant differences between his and the Stoic's views of the soul that matter for their respective views on sympathy: Plotinus, of course, rejects the physicalism of the Stoics which underlies their version of the theory and he has a different concept of the order of souls: according to the Stoics the individual souls are parts of the World-Soul and hence entirely subject to sympathetic affects from it, whereas according to Plotinus individual, rational souls are immune to such affects which are limited to the lower soul involved in bodily functions.

It seems that any sort of natural causation and coordination of states and events that is not to be explained as affection through direct physical contact is the working of *sympathy*. In general sympathy can occur without the affection of the parts that stand between those in the relation of sympathy, whereas what is in between may reduce its effect, and similar things are particularly susceptible to sympathetic influence on one another (IV.4.32).

Sympathy turns up in a number of passages in the *Enneads*.[14] In many of these the mention is cursory and hard to make much of but there are two extensive discussions, both in the long treatise "On the problems of soul (I), (II) and (III)" (IV.3–5. (27–29)). More precisely, we have in IV.4, chapters 31–45, a discussion of the influence of the stars, magic and prayer in all of which *sympathy* plays an essential role, and in IV.5, especially chapters 3 and 8, where he discusses visual and auditory transmission. In what follows, I shall be concerned primarily with the first of these passages.

At the end of the previous section we noted in connection with the sense-powers of the divine souls that Plotinus thinks they "hear" our prayers by means of sympathy (IV.4.26, 1,4). Shortly after this in IV.4, Plotinus fully embarks on his account of the occult: the influence of the heavenly bodies and astral divination (IV.4.32–39), and magic and prayer (ll. 40–45). Having rejected bodily causes (*aitiai sōmatikai*) and deliberate decisions as general explanations of what "comes from the sky to us and the other living creatures," Plotinus raises the question of what other explanation there may be. He sets the stage as follows:

> First of all we must posit that this All [the perceptible universe] is a "single living being which encompasses all the living beings that are within it."[15] It has one soul which extends to all the parts, in so far as each individual thing is a part of it; and each thing in the perceptible All is a part of it, and completely a part of it as regards its body; ... and those things which participate in the soul of the All alone are altogether parts, but all those which also participate in another soul [i.e. individual human soul] are in this way not altogether parts, but the less are affected

by the other parts in so far as they have something of the All, and in a way corresponding to what they have.

(IV.4.32, 4–13)

These lines confirm what we have already noted: the cosmos is animated by one soul which also animates us humans and other living beings; this makes us parts of this cosmos; in so far, however, as we also have another soul, i.e. our individual soul, we are not merely parts of the cosmos but something more. Plotinus then continues:

> This one universe is all sympathetic (*sympathes dē pan touto to hen*) and is like one living creature, and that which is far is really near, just as, in one of the individual living things, a nail or horn or finger or one of the other limbs which is not contiguous: the intermediate part leaves a gap in the affection and is not affected, but that which is not near is affected. For the like parts are not situated next to each other, but are separated by others between, but they are sympathetic (*sympaschonta*) by their likeness, and it is necessary that something which is done by a part not situated beside it should reach the distant part; and it is a living thing and all belongs to a unity, nothing is so distant in space that it is not close enough to the nature of the one living thing to be sympathetic.
>
> (IV.4.32, 13–22)

This passage shows some crucial features of Plotinian sympathy: (a) sympathy is based on the unity of soul; (b) affections resulting from sympathy are typically between non-adjacent parts of the organism, distance being no hindrance; (c) whether part B of an organism becomes sympathetically affected by part A is determined by similarity: if parts A and B are similar, a certain affect in A may give rise to a similar sympathetic affect in B. This explains why there may be no discernible affection in the intervening space. A further point to note about this similarity requirement is that this must primarily be a similarity of disposition or constitution, not of actual properties: in the most clear-cut cases, at least, sympathy involves B's becoming F as a result of A's being or becoming F. This implies that B was not F before A became F. The claim is, however, that A and B are similar, and this must mean that they share some relevant properties. These are evidently not the properties that come to be as a result of sympathy.

In his discussion of the causality of the heavenly bodies, Plotinus' primary objective is to disavow some views on the nature of this causality that were apparently current at the time. One might even say that while admitting the efficacy of occult phenomena, Plotinus' primary concern is to hold their scope and power in check. What he wishes to avoid is the attribution to the heavenly bodies of deliberate actions affecting us. His claim here concerns any action, good or bad, but what he particularly objects to is any view that renders the heavenly bodies deliberate agents of evil. His answer, quite in accordance with his general views on causation and on evil as lack of good, is twofold: (1) the heavenly bodies do not deliberately act so as to have an effect on things on earth; and (2) in so far as there are bad effects of the heavenly bodies on us, these are due to our incapacity to receive what in itself is good, or to a kind of chance. Let us consider these answers a little more closely.

As we have previously noted, the sensible world and its course of life are not the result of anybody's deliberation or planning. In general, the higher principles contemplate only what is above them (except the first principle, the One, of course, which has nothing above it and doesn't contemplate anything). The lower strata in the Plotinian hierarchy of being are in general seen as side effects, a kind of irradiation or emanation, from the higher. Plotinus explicitly applies this to the effects of the heavenly bodies on us. He says:

> If then the sun and the other heavenly bodies act in any way on the things here below, one must think that the sun—it is best to speak of one body only—remains looking above, but just as its warming of things on earth proceeds from it, so do any subsequent actions upon them, by a transmission (*diadosis*) of soul, as far as it is in its power, since there is plenty of the growth soul in it. And in the same way any other heavenly body, without choosing to do so, gives off a kind of irradiation from itself.
>
> (IV.4.35, 37–44)

Sympathy is not explicitly mentioned here but in the context of the same discussion Plotinus has ascribed the effects of the heavenly bodies to sympathy. So we must suppose that what he says here about the "subsequent actions" of the Sun that take place "by a transmission of soul" refers to sympathetic effects. This relates sympathy to the pattern of emanation and double activity that pervades his thought. So sympathetic effects of the heavenly bodies are non-deliberate effects of their internal activity; they are side effects, emanations, of the internal activity of the higher beings.

As regards bad things that occur as a result of sympathetic influence of the heavenly bodies, Plotinus notes that in general these are due to our incapacity of receiving effects, which so far as the agent is concerned are not bad at all, even good (IV.4.38). There is an elaboration of this point in the later treatise "On whether the stars are causes," chapter 11. Here we see that an example of this is when the heavenly bodies inspire fortitude but on account of the recipient's incapacity, he takes this in as violent temper and lack of spirit. The word sympathy (or cognates) is not used here but from the other treatise, IV.4, it is fairly clear that this is the sort of case where sympathy gives bad results: the star intended no evil. On the contrary, its own affection was only such as to inspire a good sympathetic affect in the recipient. The recipient, however, was only able to receive some of this, and on account of his inability it was perverted to something less than good.

Despite the fact that Plotinus goes on about phenomena involving sympathy at considerable length, we do not really get an account of how sympathy works, "the mechanics of sympathy," so to speak. Presumably, the reason is that there are no such mechanics: he takes sympathy as a basic fact, which is evident in the case of ordinary organisms animated by a single soul. Given the unity of soul within the cosmos and such observations as we have seen that similar things are particularly liable to sympathetic affections, sympathy needs no further explanation.

7 Soul and time

The *Enneads* contain a few significant discussions of time: there is a whole treatise devoted to this topic, "On eternity and time" (III.7), where especially chapters 11 and 12 contain Plotinus' positive doctrine.[16] This treatise is number 45 on Porphyry's chronological list and thus is a rather late treatise. Chapters 1 and 15–17 of the earlier "On the problems of soul (II)" (number 28) also have interesting things to say about time (see also VI.5.11, 14–21). There is great convergence between these passages. Plotinus' theory of time can be summarily described as an exegesis—a liberal Plotinian exegesis, of course—of Plato's claim in the *Timaeus* 37d–38b that time is an image of eternity and the accompanying Platonic claim that the World-Soul is responsible for the production of this image. Furthermore, all three treatises referred to above convey the idea that the advent of time is the sign of or rather an instance of increasing plurality, here exemplified by temporal dispersion, as we descend further from the One. Plotinus reasonably takes for granted that this greater dispersion is implied by the fact that Plato describes time as an image. Despite this convergence, questions arise about the consistency of the details of Plotinus' account. As we shall see, it seems that his latest and most focused account reveals a certain change of mind.[17] Let us first consider the passages in IV.4.

Souls are eternal and essentially not in time, only their affections and work are (IV.4.1, 26–28; IV.4.15, 16–17). Time is posterior to them (IV.4.15, 18). It is different, however, with us: the embodied human souls are in time. Because of the contingencies and changeable nature of this world "there is one thing after another related to our needs and the present moment, not definite in itself, but always related to one external thing after another" (IV.4.17, 4–6). As we shall see in the next chapter, there is, however, something of us undescended and timeless. For the undescended souls there is no temporal "before" and "after"; there is something "prior" and "posterior" for souls but this applies to the order of being (as e.g. a genus is prior to species), not with respect to time.

Plotinus sees a problem in his account: how can a soul which is in eternity, i.e. (for Plotinus) in timelessness, make something such as the sensible cosmos, which is in time, without being in time? How can it avoid making one thing after another (IV.4.15, 1 ff.)? Must it not give different orders, so to speak, at different times? His answer is to be found in the following lines:

> But if the arranging principle [the soul] is other than the arrangement, it will be of such a kind as to speak, in a way; but

if that which gives orders is the primary arrangement, it no longer says but only makes this after that. For if it says it, it does so with its eye on the arrangement. How then is it the same? Because the arranging principle is not form and matter, but only form and power, and soul is the second activity after Intellect; but the "this after that" is in the [material] things which cannot all exist at once.

(IV.4.16, 13–20)

So Plotinus thinks the soul does not have to give specific orders based on the blueprint of the world each time it does something in the sensible realm. The blueprint, the arrangement, is the same thing as that which determines each step. We may fruitfully compare this with a computer program that determines a temporal process, e.g. on a computer screen: the program stays the same all the time but the events on the screen happen in a certain temporal order according to the program. This analogy is, however, imperfect if only because in the case of the computer we need energy, which is something other than the abstract program, to get the movement going. This energy is responsible for the movements we see on the screen and it is applied to the program in a temporal order. It seems to me that Plotinus' account here does not do much to solve his initial puzzlement about how eternity can produce temporal events without itself being somehow temporal.

Let us turn to the account in the later treatise, III.7. In the first chapters of this treatise, Plotinus gives an account of eternity, which he describes as the life of Intellect: "the life which belongs to that which exists and is in being, all together and full, completely without extension or interval" (III.7.3, 36–38). This account of eternity influenced e.g. Boethius, who gives the classical medieval definition of eternity as "all-at-once and perfect possession of interminable life" (*On the Consolation of Philosophy* V, prosa 6). In chapters 7–10 Plotinus criticizes previous thinkers' theories of time. He classifies these theories into three main groups: (1) time is movement; (2) time is what is moved; (3) time is something belonging to movement. In general Plotinus' criticisms appeal to our intuitive notion of time which he claims the theories of the others fail to live up to: intuitively, time is none of those things and the theories generally presuppose rather than explain time. The Aristotelian and the Stoic accounts of time fall into the third group and receive the most extensive treatment, especially the Aristotelian one, which is resumed in chapter 13 after Plotinus' own account of time. According to Aristotle time is the measure of movement (*Physics* IV, 223a20 ff.). Plotinus advances several critical remarks about this definition and comes to the conclusion that in truth it is the other way around: motion is measured by time.

Plotinus starts off his positive account of time from the stage of eternity, "before" time came about. This is the state of Intellect and of the hypostasis Soul. But "because soul had an unquiet power, which wanted to keep on transferring what it saw there [in the intelligible realm] to something else, it did not want the whole to be present to it all together" (III.7.11, 20–23). There is no indication that the hypostasis Soul has anything directly to do with time. The way Plotinus phrases this, speaking of an "unquiet power" of soul, suggests that not all soul is unquiet in this way. In chapter 12 we learn that the life which is time "is the activity of an always existing soul, whose activity is not directed to itself or in itself, but lies in making and creation" (III.7.12, 6–8). Clearly, the activity in question is an external act of the soul itself, the hypostasis. The context shows that by this "unquiet power," Plotinus has the World-Soul in mind but the same account presumably also applies to the other individual souls. It is true that he says that all souls have a part in the timeless and this of course holds for the World-Soul. This timeless aspect of every soul is presumably simply the hypostasis, which, as we have seen, all souls contain.

Plotinus then proceeds with the following remarkable passage:

> In the same way Soul, making the world of sense in imitation of that other world, moving with a different sort of motion than the one there,[18] but like it and intending to be an image of it, first of all temporalized itself, letting time replace eternity. Then it handed over that which came into being as a slave to time, by making the whole of it exist in time and encompassing all its ways with time.
>
> (III.7.11, 27–33)

We see here that the soul "temporalized" itself. We get some information about what is involved in this temporalization in the following lines:

> As soul presents one activity after another, and then again another in ordered succession, it produces the succession along with the activity, and goes on with another thought coming after that which it had before, to that which did not previously exist because discursive thought was not in action, and soul's present life is not like that which came before it. So at the same time the life is different and this "different" involves a different time. So the spreading out of life involves time.
> (III.7.11, 35–41)

Time is the life of soul (or at least of the unquiet power of soul), which is contrasted here with the eternity, the life of Intellect. The latter's atemporal activity is degraded into one act after another, its togetherness into continuity, the latter being an imperfect image of the former, and "instead of a whole all together" there is a whole which "will come and always will be coming into being part by part" (III.7.11, 55–56).[19] Clearly, we have here once more an instance of increased dispersion the further down we come in the hierarchy. Time is a case of such increased dispersion. In the case of Intellect (see Chapter 2, p. 112) "difference" or "otherness" (*heterotēs*) plays a key role in generating plurality. Here the dispersion involved in the advent of time is also described in terms of difference. It is another kind of difference, of course, but Plotinus evidently sees some kind of difference involved in any pluralization.

The main difference between the doctrine here and what we saw in IV.4 is that in the latter passages there is no hint that anything of the order of soul "temporalizes itself," whereas, as we have seen, a power of soul indeed does this according to III.7. In an attempt to bring the two treatises into accord, Smith (1996: 211) suggests that "before" and "after" in III.7 are not to be understood as temporal before and after. The idea is that "before" and "after" at the level of the pure soul are not really the temporal before and after that we are familiar with as a relation between events in our sensible world but rather indicate an order of causality and importance as "before" and "after" in Intellect do. According to IV.4.1 this is the case also at the level of the pure soul: "before" and "after" really have this logical or ontological sense, not a temporal one. But this can hardly be the case in III.7, where the indications of a truly temporal understanding of "before" and "after" in III.7.11 are very strong and the differences between this passage and the earlier ones quite striking.

Does Plotinus then hold in III.7 that the unquiet power of soul which we identified with the World-Soul is in time? In a sense he may be said to do so, in another sense he does not. It appears that three phenomena are to be distinguished: eternity (timelessness), time as the life of soul, and being in time. The latter is the lot of the sensible world and the things in it. He even equates this with being "a slave to time" as we saw in the quote from III.7.11, 31 above. He does not and would not describe soul's relation to time like that: soul is not subject to time in the same way as the sensible.

How would he describe this life then? There is not a whole lot to go on with respect to this question. As we saw, it consists in ever new thoughts (*dianoia*) and in chapter 12, 2–4, he says it is "the extent of life of this kind which goes forward in even and uniform changes progressing quietly, and which possesses continuity of activity." Why would such activity not be in time? Well, it is in time in the sense that it contains temporal before and after. But soul is not in time in the sense of being constrained by time as something already present to which it has to adjust its life. Time itself is the life of this kind of soul.

One may wonder whether Plotinus has in this later treatise given a better account of what puzzled him in IV.4.15, namely, how time can come from the timeless. In particular, it may seem that the idea that this unquiet power of soul has one thought after another is suspect: how could the soul really have one thought after another without time being presupposed? The answer must again be that these thoughts that indeed come in a temporal order do not so much presuppose time as create it by the order in which they come: they are the first temporal phenomena and the determinants of the movements by which we measure time and determine what comes before what. Nevertheless, Plotinus does not provide any answer to the question how time comes out of eternity other than the necessary increasing dispersion, which is also his answer in the earlier treatises. Perhaps he thought that no other answer is available.

8 Soul and body

Soul, any soul, is truly a member of the intelligible realm. That means that any soul is substance or a true being. What does that mean? In order to be a substance or a true being an item has to be what it is in virtue of itself alone, i.e. it must not be a composite of form and matter. The soul is not a composite of form and a material substrate; it is merely a form. In the Aristotelian terms that Plotinus adopts this means that a soul and what it is to be soul entirely coincide: there is no remainder in a soul that isn't soul (cf. I.1.2, 6; VI.8.14, 4–5). This understanding of the nature of soul is a different way of expressing what we described above in terms of the soul not being anything of body: the soul's existence is totally independent of the body; the body or bodily properties do not essentially enter into the definition or explanation of the soul. Another claim, which is a corollary of the previous ones, is that soul produces/acts on body but not the reverse. It is true that Plotinus may be forced to modify this claim to some extent for empirical reasons—we shall come back to that question—but clearly this is his default view. This view that the soul is an intelligible substance colors everything Plotinus has to say about the relation between soul and body.

We have seen that the hypostasis Soul does not descend into bodies and that the World-Soul rules the sensible cosmos without descending into it. On the other hand, Plotinus often speaks of the descent of human souls into bodies and the manner in which he talks about the lower part of the World-Soul, nature or rational formulas, suggests that they are in the bodies they make and fashion. However, not everything is as it seems here.

In "On the problems of soul (I)," IV.3, chapters 19–23, Plotinus discusses the mode of the presence of embodied souls in bodies. He considers the various ways something can be said to be *in* something and concludes with reasonable arguments that the soul is not in the body in any of these ways. To take a few examples: the soul is not in the body as in a place, nor as in a receptacle, nor as an affection is in a substrate, nor as a part is in a whole. In all this he closely follows the Aristotelian Alexander of Aphrodisias (see Alexander's *On the Soul* 13–15). Following a tentative suggestion in Aristotle's *On the Soul* II, 413a8, Alexander also discusses the suggestion (it is unclear whether Aristotle endorses this) that the soul is in the body as a pilot is in a ship. Alexander interprets this as meaning that the soul is in the body as the art of navigation is in the ship. Plotinus is unconvinced: the proposal amounts to saying that the soul is in the body like an art is in a natural tool. That is, however, not a very helpful suggestion because we do not have a clear idea of how an art is in a natural tool (cf. IV.3.21, 19–21).

Plotinus then presents his own view: the soul is not in the body at all but the other way around: body is in soul. This view also accords with Plato's, who says in the *Timaeus* 36d–e that the Craftsman placed the body of the cosmos in the soul of the world and that the same account holds for the other souls. Plotinus goes on to illustrate his meaning by an analogy: the body is in the soul like the air is in the light (IV.3.22). We might think that this is not particularly helpful but actually the analogy is better than we may at first suppose. First of all we may note that the light is unaffected by the air. Air may blow through a beam of light, which just stays as it is, whereas the air that comes into the light becomes illuminated. The illumination corresponds to the ensoulment of the body, which by the presence of soul acquires capacities and activities that it did not previously have.[20]

Which capacities it acquires depends on the nature of the body in question, in complex organisms it depends on the various organs. This may be compared with the different colors that appear when bodies are illuminated by light: some turn out red, others blue, depending on the properties of the bodies. The so-called embodied soul does not become a part of or a property of the body by the embodiment any more than the light becomes a property of the illuminated air. But we assign specific soul capacities to specific organs or regions of the body, sight to the eyes and feeling to more or less the whole body. Does this not mean that these powers of soul reside in these organs? No, responds Plotinus. People indeed place "the principle of perception and of impulse and in general of the whole living being in the brain" because the organs of touch are in "the first nerves," which also have the power of setting the organism in motion and have their starting points in the brain. This is, however, not quite accurate because

> it would be better to say that the beginning of the activity of the power is there. For it was necessary that at the point from which

the organ was going to be moved that the power of the workman, as we may call it, which was appropriate to the tool should be fixed: or rather not the power—the power is everywhere—but the beginning of its activity at the point where the organ begins.

(IV.3.23, 15–21)[21]

Thus, the powers of soul are not really located in specific parts of the body but their external activities—or actualizations—are. Plotinus says here that the "power is everywhere." We find such a claim about the embodied soul and its powers in many places in the *Enneads*. It is an even stronger claim than it may seem. For what Plotinus really means is not just that the power is spread over the whole body as we may say that the white paint is spread over the whole wall. He wants to say that the soul (or power) is present *as a whole* everywhere.

Though this pervasive presence apparently holds for any kind of soul-power, the most interesting arguments he gives for this concern the unity of perceptual experience. These are to be found in the early treatises, "On the essence of soul (II)" (IV.2. (4)) and "On the immortality of the soul" (IV.7. (2)). Here, Plotinus argues at length against the claim that the soul is a body. In the former treatise he attacks all positions known to him that are incompatible with his own view, namely that the soul is an intelligible substance. The most interesting of the arguments he gives (and the only ones he restates in the other slightly later treatise) are those from the unity of perceptual experience that are apparently directed to undermining the materialism of the Stoics.[22] These arguments make an appeal to the unity of consciousness in sense-perception, claiming that the evident unity here is incompatible with the view that the soul is a body of any sort. Let us consider these arguments in some detail.

The Stoics held the soul to be a special kind of body, breath, extending throughout the body, which, of course, is also a body. The soul has eight parts: the five senses, utterance, a reproductive part, and a ruling part. The ruling part is located in the heart and the other parts are extensions from it to the respective organs. Apparently, they explained sensation, whether external or internal, as a physical transmission from the sense-organs or the affected part of the body to the ruling part. Plotinus' critique aims at showing that no account in merely physical terms can give a plausible explanation of the unity of sense-perception.

In "On the immortality of the soul" he writes:

> if this thing [the soul, the subject of perception] were extended and the perceptions were, so to speak, projected on each end of a line, then either they must be conjoined in one and the same point as before, say in the middle, or else each point would have a perception of its own, just as if I were perceiving one thing and you another. And if it is a question of a single percept (*aisthēma*), say a face, then either of the following must hold: (a) It is contracted in a point without parts. This appears in fact to be the case, for it is contracted already in the eyeballs: for how could we otherwise see large things through them? But then, still more, what reaches the ruling part will be like objects of thought that are without parts. (b) The percept is a magnitude and, hence, that which apprehends would be divided along with it so that each of its parts would apprehend a different part of the object and nothing in us would have apprehension of it as a whole.
>
> (IV.7.6, 15–26)

In the next chapter (see also IV.2.2) he offers arguments of a similar type from the perception of pain, claiming that either the part of the soul that occupies the affected part of the body would perceive the pain, which would be absurd; or else, if some sort of transmission of affection to the ruling part of the soul is invoked, it cannot be explained how we feel pain in the originally affected part, and in addition the problem about the unity of the perceiving subject arises again with respect to the ruling part, which is itself a body with different parts.

As has been noted and we shall explore further in the next chapter, the defining characteristic of a body according to Plotinus is extension.[23] Bodies and immanent corporeal forms such as qualities and shapes are items in space and have different spatial parts: a body is such that "none of its parts is identical either with any other part or with the whole" (IV.2.1, 12–13). Anything that has features that defy this restriction cannot be a mere body. Given this understanding of what a body is, Plotinus argues both from vision and internal sensation such as pain that the soul cannot be a body (IV.2.2; IV.7.6–7). For the evident unity of consciousness in sense-perception shows that the soul defies the division into different parts characteristic of bodies. Take the sight of a face as an example. I see the forehead, two eyes, the nose, the mouth, etc. I see all these different things. It is evidently not the case that something in me sees the nose and something else sees the mouth. In that case the unity of perceiving subject which we directly experience would be lost. It is the very same thing that sees both. This cannot be accounted for without presuming that the selfsame soul is present as a whole to different spatial points or else is a partless point. But nothing of the nature of body can be such, and hence the soul cannot be a body.

We can generalize Plotinus' anti-materialistic arguments from the unity of sense-perception as follows: it holds for bodies generally that if a body performs distinct acts at the same time with distinct parts of itself, these acts are ascribed to the parts severally. To illustrate this, consider the human body: the body regulates the amount of water in itself and it pumps its own blood. It performs such individual acts at the same time. These acts are ascribed to distinct parts of the body, i.e. to the kidneys and to the heart respectively. Moreover, each individual act a body performs with one of its parts is ascribed only to the part involved, not to the other parts: even if the heart and kidneys are parts of the same body, the fact that an individual pumping of the blood is ascribed to the heart does not make it ascribable to the kidneys. This obvious point is what Plotinus has in mind by his remarks, cited above, about the non-identity of distinct parts of the same body. Thus, since seeing different parts of a face, seeing and hearing, or feeling of pain in the tooth and in the toe, are each distinct acts that may be performed simultaneously by the soul, the foregoing ought to hold for these acts, if the soul is a body. But it would clearly be absurd to hold that a given physical part of the soul perceives A and another part B. For in that case each of the parts would perceive its objects on its own, just as the heart pumps its blood on its own or a given part of the body is blue all on its own. In the perception examples it is not the case that one part of the subject does this and another part that without being involved in what the other does. It is evident that numerically the same entity is the subject of seeing the different parts of the face, of seeing and hearing, and of perceiving the pain in the tooth and in the toe. Individual acts of the soul are not performed by parts of the soul to the exclusion of other parts. Thus, we must conclude that the soul is present as a whole in all the sensitive parts of the body. Since no mere body can be so present, the soul is not a body of any kind.

It must be admitted that Plotinus makes the Stoic account appear unduly crude and he is clearly taking for granted his own understanding of what a body is. Our limited sources give us reason to suppose that all within the bounds of their professed materialism the Stoics had quite sophisticated doctrines about the soul, which aimed among other things at explaining the interconnectedness of its functions (see e.g. Sextus Empiricus, *Adversus mathematicos* [Against the professors] VII, 307). The Stoics might, for example, have denied that individual acts of perception could be ascribed to particular parts of the body or of the ruling part, that in fact the whole body that constitutes the soul is involved in each act. There are good reasons for supposing this to be the Stoic view.[24] Plotinus would have to develop his arguments to meet this objection.

Plotinus' arguments attempt to show that absurdities follow from supposing that the subject of a complex perception is something extended. He does not consider the possibility that an extended thing has non-extensional properties. According to him, the unity of the soul, which he claims to find in considerations of sense-perception, is such that it could not be a property of a mere body. Underlying this is the conviction that any proper property of a body must share in the defining characteristic of body, i.e. it must have extension and be located in physical space, and hence be spatially divisible (IV.2.1, 34–40; VI.4.1, 20–21).

Thus, extension is for Plotinus more than an essential property of bodies in the sense of a property anything must have in order to be a body. He also holds that all other properties of bodies as such are extensional in the sense that they are divisible along with the extension. Using Descartes' terminology we could say that extension is a principal attribute of bodies. Descartes, thinking in a similar manner, did not quite understand the doubt some of his objectors expressed as to whether he in his *Meditations* had excluded the possibility that his soul is a property of his body: he thought that since he had identified two distinct attributes, each of which constitutes a complete thing, it would be quite silly, self-contradictory in fact, to maintain that nonetheless these attributes and the modes that presupposed them might belong to the same substance.[25] Hence, a position according to which the body has non-physical properties is ruled out from the start: if Plotinus can point to something which neither is nor presupposes extension—divisibility into spatially distinct parts is the criterion—he will infer that that entity is neither a body nor a property of a body. Moreover, being present as a whole everywhere marks an ontologically different category from anything bodily. Bodies and corporeal qualities have spatially distinct parts: no part of a body is the same as any other. The same is true of qualities of bodies such as colors: though the same in form, the white of the top of a sheet is a different item from the white of the bottom. This is because the same form "has become something of the body" and hence is subject to the same spatial partition as the body. Souls behave entirely differently in this regard. No soul ever becomes "something of the body." Souls are not divided into distinct parts in the way bodies and their properties are. The only sense in which one can say that a soul is divided is that it is everywhere in its body but "everywhere" here means everywhere as a whole.

This difference is of great importance to Plotinus: it marks the distinction between sensible and intelligible natures. Souls belong to the intelligible realm in virtue of not being subject to spatial partition in the way anything bodily is. Above we briefly discussed Plotinus' claim that the body is in soul, the body of the universe as well as the bodies of particular organisms. From the treatise "On the presence of being, one and the same, everywhere as a whole (I) and (II)" (VI.4–5 (22–23)) we learn that this is really the inverse of the claim the soul is everywhere as a whole (see especially IV.2.2). That is to say, given that the soul is a being that is not subject to spatial partition—it is not in any part of extension, nor are its parts dispersed in extension—to say that a body is *in* the soul is equivalent to saying that the body, in all of its parts, participates in the soul as a whole, which in turn is the same as saying that the soul is, as whole, in every part.

Observations about the unity of the perceiving subject had been made before Plotinus. In the *Theaetetus* 184b–e Plato famously remarks that the senses are not like warriors in a Trojan horse, each with its own sensations not shared by the others. Aristotle and Alexander of Aphrodisias discuss the unity of sensory experience at some length.[26] In advancing the arguments we have been considering, Plotinus is clearly building on these predecessors (see Emilsson 1988: 94–101). The greatest novelty in Plotinus' treatment of this subject is the fact that he explicitly uses what he takes to be evident facts about the unity of sense-perception to refute materialism. Nobody had done that before him. This type of argument has enjoyed great popularity—it was endorsed, for example, by Cudworth, Bayle and Leibniz, and is still appealed to.[27] It is indeed the argument Kant called the "Achilles of all dialectical inferences in the pure doctrine of the soul" (*Critique of Pure Reason* A351)—"Achilles" because it seems so powerful. The full account of Plotinus' influence on early modern philosophy remains to be told but the passages we have been considering appear to have directly influenced Cudworth, for instance, who was very widely read in the seventeenth century.

9 Chapter summary

Even if Plotinus holds along with many other ancient Greek thinkers that soul is the principle of life and is responsible for the natural biological functions of the sensible world, he also holds that soul is essentially a thinker informed by Intellect. It is an intelligible being which admittedly is directly responsible for the sensible sphere but whose existence is totally independent of it. There is nevertheless a distinction to be made between the thought of Intellect and that of the Soul: the former is non-discursive or intuitive, whereas the soul's thought is essentially discursive. It was suggested that this means that the soul's thought is essentially propositional as opposed to Intellect's intuitive thought.

Plotinus consistently maintains a rather surprising doctrine about the unity of all souls: each and every soul contains the whole hypostasis, Soul. Nevertheless, he insists that the souls are distinct also at the intelligible level. The relationship between the souls is supposed to be a weaker mirroring of the relationship between the Forms at the level of Intellect: each is in a sense something distinct but carries the whole in itself. The doctrine of sympathy between souls, which asserts that there is connectedness and interaction that goes beyond physical pushing and pulling, is evidence for this unity of the psychic realm.

Plotinus' world has several kinds of soul. Though there are distinctions to be made, the hypostasis Soul, the World-Soul and individual human souls are, as already noted, in a sense just one: the hypostasis Soul. Sometimes Plotinus also counts the souls of the heavenly bodies and the soul of the earth as individual souls but often they seem to be regarded as parts or aspects of the World-Soul. What he calls nature or vegetative soul is the soul-power that is responsible for the lower biological functions. This power is the immanent phase of the World-Soul.

Even if some aspects of Plotinus' psychology have an Aristotelian air, his doctrine is, expectedly, essentially Platonic. The soul is for instance an independent substance or being—independent in the sense that it does not depend on the body for its existence. It does indeed have activities of its own and the activities it exercises through the body are inessential to it. Strictly speaking the soul is not in the body. Rather the body is in the soul somewhat like, we might say, air in the light. The light is unaffected by the air that is in it and that, as a result, becomes illuminated. Similarly, the soul is unaffected by the body which, as a result of its presence to the soul, becomes alive.

Plotinus takes up a debate with other ancient thinkers about the nature of the soul. Stoics and Epicureans hold that the soul is a body of some sort and the Aristotelians that it is a form in matter. He has various objections to these other views but among them one type of objection is particularly novel. The unity of consciousness in sense-perception cannot be explained in materialistic terms because the facts of such everyday experiences—e.g. seeing something complex like a face—defy the logic that bodies must obey. The soul must be as a whole present at different parts of the body (or the different parts of the body simultaneously present to the soul). No mere body is capable of that. This is presumably the first instance of an attempt to refute materialism by appealing to the alleged non-spatial nature of the soul.

Further reading

Primary sources

Ennead III.7. (45) "On eternity and time," especially chapters 11 and 12.
Ennead IV.2. (4) "On the essence of soul (I)."
Ennead IV.3–4. (27–28) "On the problems of soul (I) and (II)." There is an English translation with a commentary by John Dillon and Henry J. Blumenthal (see "Text, Translations and Commentaries," in the Introduction).
Ennead IV.8. (6) "On the descent of soul into bodies." There is an English translation with a commentary by Lloyd P. Gerson (see "Text, Translations and Commentaries," in the Introduction).
Ennead IV.9. (8) "Whether all souls are one."

Secondary sources

Henry J. Blumenthal, *Plotinus' Psychology: His Doctrine of the Embodied Soul* (The Hague: Martinus Nijhoff, 1971), chapters 1 and 2.
Damian Caluori, *Plotinus on Soul* (Cambridge: Cambridge University Press, 2015), chapters 1–5.
Eyjólfur K. Emilsson, "Plotinus on Soul–Body Dualism," in S. Everson (ed.), *Psychology*, Companions to Ancient Thought 2 (Cambridge: Cambridge University Press, 1991), 148–165.

Notes

1 On the notion of *logos* in Plotinus, see Chapter 2, p. 46.
2 For Platonist interpretations of the divine Craftsman prior to Plotinus, see Caluori 2015: 25–36.
3 See Frede 2011: 70 ff.; cf. Caluori 2015: 105–108.
4 About the history of scholarship about the relation between the World-Soul and the hypostasis Soul, see Helleman-Elgersma 1980: 89–103.
5 The account given here of the making of the sensible world owes much to Caluori's (2015) excellent recent book on Plotinus on the soul, though I do not follow him in every respect.
6 Tornau and Michalewsky (2009) present strong arguments for the individuality of souls and even of "predecessors" of individual souls at the level of Intellect.
7 For a full account of Plotinus' views on memory, see King 2009.
8 For a fuller account of Plotinus on sympathy, see Emilsson 2015, from which the present section is excerpted with modifications, and Gurtler 1988 and 2002.

9 For a good overview, see Lawrence 2005 and Helleman 2010.
10 See Helleman 2010: 242. There is considerable literature—see Merlan 1953, Armstrong 1955 and Helleman 2010 with more references—on the question whether Plotinus practiced magic himself. The main ground for this is an anecdote told by Porphyry in *Life* 10 relating to a certain Olympius of Alexandria, a self-proclaimed philosopher, "who adopted a superior attitude towards Plotinus out of rivalry. This man's attacks on him went to the point of trying to bring a star-stroke upon him by magic. But when he found his attempt recoiling upon himself, he told his intimates that the soul of Plotinus had such great power as to be able to throw back attacks on him on those who were seeking to do him harm. Plotinus was aware of the attempt and said that his limbs on that occasion were squeezed together and his body contracted 'like a money-bag pulled tight'" (*Life* 10, 3–12).
11 See e.g. Pigler 2001 and Ierodiakonou 2006. For the notion of *sympatheia* in Stoicism and more generally, see Sambursky 1959, Struck 2007 and Brouwer 2015.
12 The notion of sympathy was adopted in ethical psychology by David Hume and Adam Smith in the eighteenth century. There is one instance of a use of "sympathy" similar to what we find in Hume and Smith in Plotinus: "we do sympathize (*sympathein*) with one another when we suffer along (*synalgountas*) from seeing them suffer and when we rejoice [in their company] and are naturally drawn to love (*philein*) them" (IV.9.3, 1–3). What makes the passage especially noteworthy is the fact that this is a rare case of sympathy between persons. Moreover, the type of case suggested seems to be of the following kind: person A notes that person B is suffering or that person B is rejoicing and A for that reason suffers or rejoices. This kind of sympathy is not merely a biological function but involves A's judgment: A has to see and note that B suffers or is joyful in order to become similarly affected himself: Plotinus says that the sympathetic affect comes from *seeing* the other suffer.
13 For this aspect of Stoic physics, see Sambursky 1959.
14 For a discussion of most of the passages containing *sympatheia* see Gurtler 1988.
15 See Plato, *Timaeus* 30d–31a.
16 There is a commentary on "On eternity and time" by Beierwaltes (1967) and an annotated translation by McGuire and Strange (1988). For valuable discussions see Strange 1994, Smith 1996, Karfík 2012 and Caluori 2015: 98–101.
17 That Plotinus' views on time developed is well argued by Karfík (2012). Others, e.g. Smith (1996), seek to show that the earlier and the later passages can be reconciled.
18 On intelligible motion, see Chapter 2, p. 110.
19 Since the World-Soul's successive, discursive thought constitutes time, Plotinus is unwilling to say that it is in time, as if time were something prior to it (see III.7.11, 58–63). Being time itself, temporal attributes such as "before" and "after" are not applicable to it or at least not in the same way as they apply to the visible cosmos itself. See also IV.4.16 and Smith 1996.
20 For a careful analysis of the air-in-light analogy, see Caluori 2015: 180–186.
21 On this passage and more generally about the soul's relation to space, see Wilberding 2005: 328 ff.

22 I discuss these arguments more fully in Emilsson 1988: 94–101; 1991.
23 See II.4.12, 1–2; III.6.12, 53–54; III.16, 31–32; IV.7.1, 17–18.
24 See Emilsson 1991: 157–158.
25 See Descartes 1985: *Comments on a Certain Broadsheet*, 297–299.
26 See Aristotle, *On the Soul* II, 436b8–427a17 and Alexander of Aphrodisias, *On the Soul* 59–66.
27 For the history of this argument, see Lennon and Stainton 2008.

Six
The physical world

1 The genesis of bodies and matter

In previous chapters we have seen that Plotinus' universe is alive: surely Intellect and the pure souls are alive and so is the body of the universe and the particular bodies of animals and human beings. Even the One may possess life of some kind. It follows from this that an account of the lifeless is in a way an account of a mere abstraction: except perhaps individual stones, dust and suchlike on the surface of the earth, there is nothing that is void of soul and, hence, life (see Wilberding 2006: 46). Still, the lifeless can be studied as an abstraction. This lifeless aspect of the universe contains matter, bodies and corporeal qualities. As we shall see, these come in a certain structural order of plurality and unity: matter has the least unity, then bare bodies, identified with extended bulk, and then corporeal forms (forms in matter) of which the qualities of bodies are a prime example.

Let us first resume discussion of the issue of the generation of bodies and matter. We touched upon this briefly in the previous chapter and said that both are the products of nature (see p. 157). Let us consider this more fully. There are several places where Plotinus unambiguously ascribes the responsibility of the making of bodies to nature or to what can be assumed to be equivalent in the context, *logoi*. We noted earlier that *logoi* are pervasive in Plotinus' system (see Chapter 2, pp. 46–47). It turns out that there are two kinds of *logoi* involved in the production of the visible features of the cosmos, dead ones and live ones: "This *logos*, then, which operates in the visible shape, is the last, and is dead and no longer able to make another, but that which has life is the brother of that which makes the shape, and has the same power itself, and makes in that which comes into being" (III.8.2, 30–34). The dead *logos* is that which produces the visible, natural qualities and shapes, the red and the roundness of a tomato, for instance. The "brother" is the *logos* that works in the body and makes it a living body. Both kinds of *logos* are, as is clear from the context in III.8.1–4, parts or aspects of the lowest phase of soul, nature.

This lowest phase of soul is also what produces matter. The question has admittedly been debated but as Denis O'Brien has convincingly argued in several publications, there is little doubt that this lowest phase of soul also produces matter.[1] The alternative would be that matter pre-exists independently of the emanation from the One. In that case, Plotinus' system would be radically dualistic, holding both the One and matter to be original irreducible principles. This seems to have been Plato's position in the *Timaeus*, and this is definitely the position of Numenius and other Platonist predecessors of Plotinus. But Plotinus thinks otherwise. In "On our allotted guardian spirit," he writes:

> Does it [nature], then, produce nothing? It produces what is totally different from itself; for after it there is no more life, but what is produced is lifeless. What is it then? Just as everything which was produced before this was produced shapeless, but was formed by turning towards its producer and being, so to speak reared to maturity by it, so there too, that which is produced is not any more a form of soul—for it is not alive—but absolute indefiniteness. For even if there is indefiniteness in the things before it, it is nevertheless indefiniteness within form; the thing is not absolutely indefinite but only in relation to its perfection; but what we are dealing with now is absolutely indefinite. When it is perfected it becomes a body, receiving the form appropriate to its potentiality, a receiver for the principle which produced it and brought it to maturity. And only this form in body is the last representative of the powers above in the last depth of the world below.
>
> (III.4. (15) 1, 5–17)

Matter is not mentioned here by its usual name but there is no doubt that this is what is meant by "absolute indefiniteness." The account here fits what is said of matter elsewhere in the *Enneads* and nothing else is so described. Moreover, the passage indicates that there is a distinction to be made between this absolute indefiniteness and bodies: "When [this absolute indefiniteness] is perfected it becomes body," which shows that the absolute indefiniteness is itself not body, which is posterior to it. (As we shall see, Plotinus holds that it is only in a manner of speaking that matter *becomes* body.) Nothing other than matter is distinct from bodies and yet below them on the scale of differentiation.

It is true that Plotinus very often speaks as if matter and in fact bodies too are there beforehand when soul arrives. In these cases, soul is considered as the life-giving principle, that which turns body into a living body or if it is a question of the individual human soul descending into body and matter. Even if he often speaks in this way, it does not follow that he thinks bodies or matter are there independently of any soul. Indeed, in the passage just quoted Plotinus makes it quite clear that while being a product of soul, matter becomes a receptacle of forms also provided by soul. This compound, body, can in turn be the recipient of an even further dose of soul as a result of which it becomes a living body. So passages that present matter as a given, something already there, when forms enter the scene, actually do not speak in favor of a pre-existent matter.

The question of the origin of matter is of considerable importance: as we have noted, Plotinus identifies matter and evil. Thus, if the soul produces matter, matter is, ultimately, a product of the Good. And now we are told that that matter is evil. So evil comes from the Good! This seems paradoxical and the later Neoplatonists didn't follow Plotinus in this. We shall return to this theme shortly.

2 Matter

It remains to address Plotinus' notion of matter as such. There are three treatises, early, middle and late, that deal extensively with matter: "On matter" (II.4. (12)), "On the impassibility of things without body" (III.6. (26)) and "On what are and whence come evils" (I.8. (51)). While each of these treatises has a different focus, the account of matter is quite uniform and does not indicate any change of mind. Porphyry gave II.4 the alternative title "On the two matters" because the first five chapters also deal with intelligible matter—a term hardly used outside II.4. What he understands by intelligible matter, however, is pretty much the same as what was called "the potential intellect" in Chapter 3 (see p. 106). The remaining eleven chapters of II.4 deal with the matter in the sensible world. Here Plotinus designs his concept of matter by accepting some aspects and rejecting others of the Aristotelian and Stoic concepts. With Aristotle he holds that matter is indeterminate, incorporeal and without dimensions (8–13); against him he argues in chapters 14–16 that it is the same as privation. With the Stoics he holds that matter is without qualities (chapter 13). Finally, he identifies matter with evil (chapter 16), a theme he elaborates in I.8.

Plotinus' term for matter, *hylē*, is Aristotelian and picked up from Aristotle also by the Stoics. Plato does not use the word in this sense. There is, however, something in Plato that has an analogous function, namely the receptacle of forms in the *Timaeus*. This is another main source of Plotinus' concept of matter. This is very clear from the second treatise on matter, III.6. This treatise deals with what its Porphyrian title indicates: the impassibility of things without body. There are two sorts of things discussed with respect to this question: souls and matter, neither of which can be affected in Plotinus' view. The notion of affection (*pathos*) here is roughly equivalent to change: to be affected is to acquire a genuinely new property, to be changed. According to Plotinus neither soul nor matter can be affected in this way. Only bodies can be affected. We shall consider the affectability of bodies in the next section and the impassibility of soul in the next chapter: the hard case for Plotinus' impassibility thesis is the human soul, so the discussion of this belongs there. In the present treatise Plotinus argues forcefully for the impassibility of matter: the forms that enter into matter do not really affect it. His treatment of this topic makes heavy use of the account of the receptacle in *Timaeus* 50b ff. As a result parts of the treatise are almost a commentary on this part of the *Timaeus*.

As its title suggests, the third treatise on matter, "On what are and whence come evils," I.8, deals with the question of evil. Evil exists, without doubt; the question is where to locate it. Plotinus identifies original evil with matter as total privation of form. His main concern in defending this claim is to uphold this view against the alternative that identifies evil with an innate fault in souls.

Let us attempt to get closer to Plotinus' notion of matter, elusive though it is. Here follows a list of the main contentions he makes about it followed by some references. Most of the claims are explicit or implicit in all three above-mentioned treatises and elsewhere.

1 Matter is void of form (II.4.8; II.4.13; III.6.6–19 *passim*; I.8.3).
2 Matter contains all forms (II.4.11; III.6.10; III.6.18).
3 Matter is non-being and privation (II.4.14–16; III.6.7; I.8.6).
4 Matter is incorporeal and without magnitude (II.4.8–12; III.6.7).
5 Matter is unchangeable (II.4.8; III.6.8).
6 Matter is lack and want (I.8.3; III.6.14).
7 Matter is unlimited or indefinite (*apeiria, aoristia*) (II.4.11; II.4.16; III.6.7; I.8.6).
8 The forms that enter into matter do not affect it (III.6.7 and *passim*).
9 Matter is evil and the cause of evil in others (II.4.16; I.8 *passim*).
10 Matter is imperceptible and "known by thoughtlessness," as we see darkness (II.4.10; I.8.9).

It is noteworthy that some of these claims about matter are also made about the One, and mostly about these two extremities alone: like matter the One has no form but somehow contains all forms. In a sense the One too is nothing since it is beyond being. The One is also unlimited. Any similarity between matter and the One is, however, merely apparent. The reason for it is that the One is, so to speak, above form, being and limit, whereas matter is below each of these.

As should be clear from the little that has already been said about matter in Plotinus, it is a strange thing, actually not *a thing* at all. It is surely not what we normally call matter today, sticks and stones, molecules, atoms, quarks or what have you. All these have got forms and energy too. Nor is it the kind of matter Aristotle speaks about, which is essentially what things are made of or from: butter is made from cream which is its immediate matter, cream is made from milk, and milk is made from an animal's food, which in turn is made from the four elements in some combination. Aristotelian matter is relative: cream is matter with respect to butter but with respect to milk it is a substance with form. Plotinus also sometimes employs this notion of relative matter but this is not what he primarily means when speaking of matter. What he has in mind is something that lies deeper, so deep in fact that it cannot be grasped by the senses. Reason can tell that it exists but it cannot fathom it with a clear concept.

Considering most of the items on the list such as (1), (3), (4), (5), (6), (8), (9) and (10) are radically negative claims, one may wonder if there really is any such thing as matter. We might easily come to the conclusion that the affirmation that there is such a thing is a mere pseudo-assertion or even a self-contradictory claim: the item said to exist is really nothing at all, and thus cannot exist! Plotinus has a hypothetical opponent ask rhetorically: "If it [matter] is without magnitude, what would it contribute, if it contributes neither to form and quality nor to extension and magnitude, which appears, wherever it occurs, to come to bodies from their matter? ... So this sizelessness of matter is an empty name" (II.4.11, 4–13; cf. I.8.3).

Plotinus proceeds to respond to this charge. While the details of his account remain somewhat obscure, the following points are reasonably clear: matter itself is without magnitude and extension. Magnitude and extension generally belong to the realm of forms and come to matter through the agency of the *logoi* that belong to nature (III.6.18). Nor is matter to be confused with bulk (*onkos*): "[matter] must receive the rest of its qualities at the same time as it becomes a bulk" (II.4.11, 26–27). It is, however, easily confused with bulk because the soul, trying to imagine matter, is at a loss and ends up with a picture of a bulk (II.4.11).

Nevertheless, there is a special relation between matter, on the one hand, and spatial extension. "Bulk" (*onkos*), "magnitude" (*megethos*) and "extension" (*diastēma*) go together in Plotinus; they are the defining characteristics of bodies and all mean or imply spatial extension.[2] He says that matter's first capacity, so to speak, is the capacity for bulk and further that matter "receives the forms of bodies in magnitude," meaning, I take it, that the forms of bodies are expanded, come in determinate magnitudes. Furthermore, in the same context he notes that "matter receives what it receives in extension because it is itself receptive of extension" (II.4.11, 17–19). Apparently, even if matter receives extension at the same time as it receives other forms, colors, for instance, its reception of extension is somehow more basic. How is it so?

The following answer lacks direct textual basis (see however III.6.17, 10–12) but it strikes me as plausible and in line with Plotinus' general way of thinking. As we have seen, one of the characteristics of matter is indefiniteness. Indefiniteness is the final stage of differentiation, the ultimate plurality that contrasts with the One's unity; it is even beyond or rather "below" being many: that is why Plotinus can say that matter *becomes many* by being carried into every form (II.4.11, 40–42). Though being below the determination and plurality of extension, matter is still a principle of plurality. Its indefiniteness is the reason why corporeal forms are expanded. Spatial extension, which is the most differentiated item in the ontology with the exception of matter itself, is the result of the meeting of the absolute indefiniteness of matter and the definiteness of form: matter receives forms, which prior to this are unextended intelligible entities and these forms take on spatial expanse. Spatial extension is, as it were, a compromise between total indefiniteness and the "all-together" mode of being of intelligibles.

I have been using expressions such as "magnitude," "extension" and "expanse" without making it entirely clear what is being referred to: is it spatial extension in general or the particular magnitudes of particular objects? A passage in III.6.17, 16–17, makes clear that Plotinus has both in mind in his discussions of matter and extension: "and matter as a whole became a magnitude, illumined by absolute magnitude, and each part of it became partial magnitude." Plotinus would not say that matter in itself, prior to any determination by form, is a huge or even an infinitely large something. Quantitative terms first apply to it when it receives magnitude, which it receives together with other forms. It follows from this that talk of matter receiving magnitudes does not merely concern how big particular things become but the generation of extension as such. I pay special attention to spatial extension and the role of matter in it because spatial extension is the primary characteristic of the sensible sphere as opposed to the intelligible. We shall address this again in the next section.

This discussion started with an objector's claim that matter as Plotinus conceives of it contributes nothing and hence can be dispensed with. Plotinus' response is that matter is responsible for extension and the extended character of corporeal forms and thus contributes a lot! (Cf. II.4.12, 1.) Assuming the account of this sketched above, the question can be raised whether this explanation doesn't attribute a causal role to matter. The question is tricky: indeed forms that are in themselves without magnitude come to have spatial magnitude on account of matter. Thus, matter clearly plays a role in an explanation of why things in the sensible world are such as they are. Still, I do not think Plotinus would admit that matter is playing an *active* role in this: it does not change the form that enters into it. Rather, it is the powerlessness of matter that explains why the forms in it appear in extension: this is the best matter can do with respect to receiving form.

Let us turn to contention (3) on the list, that matter is privation and non-being. Aristotle, arguing against Plato and other predecessors, insists that a distinction be made between matter as the substrate that persists through change and the privation that precedes change: an uneducated (privation) man becomes an educated one; after the change the uneducated isn't there anymore. Something survives the change, however, namely the matter or substrate, which in this case is the man: he does not disappear in the change (see *Physics* I, 7–9). So one of Aristotle's fundamental contentions about matter is that it is what survives through a change and is to be sharply distinguished from the privation that disappears.

Plotinus agrees about matter: matter remains the same before and after change. He insists, however, that matter is also privation. That is to say, he wants to unite the notions of a substrate, as that which underlies and endures through change, and privation, the state of lacking a property. Obviously, the Aristotelian notion of privation has to be modified: Plotinian matter isn't anything in particular, neither before nor after the change. It underlies change but it isn't changed. This is because matter is indefinite. It isn't a thing with a given definite nature that has something indefinite in itself: it is a total lack of a fixed form or nature. It is indefiniteness itself. It follows that it is privation in the sense of being the lack of, not one particular property, but all.[3]

In these last statements we have come dangerously close to an aspect of Plotinus' theory of matter that I have so far in this discussion evaded—rather than addressing it directly. On the list of statements about matter at the outset of this section we saw that matter receives all forms. I have used such phrases repeatedly, as does Plotinus himself; cf. the claims above to the effect that matter becomes extended. We have seen, however, that matter isn't changed by receiving form and there are a number of statements claiming that matter doesn't really take on the forms it receives. This actually smacks of a contradiction if the statements saying that matter receives form are taken at face value. For if matter really took on the forms in such a way that it became those things that it receives, Plotinus cannot maintain that it isn't changed when it loses any of them or receives one it didn't previously have.

In his precise statements about this topic Plotinus denies that matter takes on any form. This is in fact the central topic of the chapters on sensible matter in III.6. The forms do not affect matter. He compares this with souls that receive all sorts of representations, which, however, do not change the souls in the least: all sorts of thoughts and memories flow through our mind without changing the substance of it (III.6.15). Another analogy is that of a mirror in which real things are reflected (III.6.13–14). Both analogies have their limitations but the mirror analogy is instructive in that the mirror doesn't have itself the properties reflected in it—the mirror does not become red by reflecting a ripe tomato—but takes on ephemeral reflections of real things—real at least in comparison with the reflections in the mirror. In Plotinus' theory the extended visible forms themselves are mere shadows, "falsity falling upon a falsity," he says (III.6.7, 40–41). The meaning is evidently that matter presents itself as some determinate thing but isn't and likewise the visible form may present itself as the form of something real but is, in fact, a mere shadow.

Related to the conception of matter as privation is the idea of matter as non-being. If matter doesn't have any fixed nature of its own and if it doesn't take on the forms that appear in it, doesn't it follow that matter is nothing at all? No, not quite. After declaring that matter is unlimitedness as opposed to the determination of *logoi* bringing form, Plotinus writes:

> Is matter, then, the same thing as otherness? No, rather it is the same thing as that part of otherness which is opposed to the

things which in the full and proper sense of the word *are*, that is to say *logoi*. Therefore, though it is non-being, it is in this way something and is the same thing as privation, if privation is opposition to what is in *logoi*.

(II.4.16, 1–4)

The phrase, "that part of otherness which is opposed to the things which in the full and proper sense *are*" reflects a passage in Plato's *Sophist* 258d–e.[4] "Otherness," as we may recall from Chapter 4, is one of the five great kinds invoked in this dialogue and which Plotinus puts to a variety of uses (see Chapter 4, Section 2, "Plurality Enters the Scene: The five Highest Ideas"). Plato defines non-being here in terms of otherness: in the text of the *Sophist* we have today it says that non-being is that part of otherness which is opposed to the *being of each thing*, which boils down to non-being being for each F what is other than F. As O'Brien (1996: 173) notes, in antiquity after Plotinus the commentator Simplicius (in *Physics* 238.26) cited the *Sophist* slightly differently, but importantly, and that seems to be the text Plotinus is using: non-being according to him is that which is other than real being, by which he seems to mean other than any kind of form.[5] In that sense matter is non-being but it does not follow that it is nothing at all. If the arguments for there being such an ultimate receptacle of forms hold, such a thing as matter must exist even if there is nothing that it is. Thus, matter is non-being in the same sense, but for opposite reasons, as the One is beyond being: no ordinary predicate holds true of it as such.

Yet another claim on the list is that matter is absolute evil and the reason for evils in others. We may wonder how this could be so. We are familiar with moral evils such as cruelty and greed, natural evils such as earthquakes and plagues, social evils such as poverty and drugs, but how could matter, which isn't really anything, be evil? Surely, matter isn't any of these familiar evils. We never directly meet with it in our experience: it does not hurt us nor is it the subject of our regrets, worries or sins. For this reason Plotinus' notion of matter as evil has been called metaphysical evil to distinguish it from these familiar kinds (cf. O'Meara 1998: 1). Yet, according to Plotinus it is the root of all of these more familiar evils.

Considered abstractly and from within Plotinus' system it should be no surprise that matter is the ultimate evil: matter is at the bottom, the Good is at the top. They are opposites. What could matter be, then, other than evil? Matter is not, by consequence, an independent power opposing the Good, however: Plotinus' whole approach to the question of evil consists in explaining its evil nature as its lack of goodness and being, its powerlessness, indefiniteness— in general as the lack of all the negative characteristics on our list of statements about matter. These taken together do not draw a picture of matter as a mighty opponent to the Good. On the contrary, they emphasize its lack of everything.

Logical as it may at first glance seem to posit matter as evil, the view is not free from problems. One problem has to do with matter and the Good as opposites: "But if the Good is substance, or something beyond substance, how could something be its contrary?" Plotinus' skeptical voice asks (I.8.6, 27–28). The question arises from Aristotle's claim in the *Categories* 3b24 that substances have no opposites: opposites are those things within a genus that stand furthest apart. Thus, within the genus of the quality temperature, hot and cold stand furthest apart; within that of color, white and black. But substances such as Socrates have no contrary (and still less would this be the case, the critical voice assumes, for what is beyond substance). But matter and the Good do not belong to a common genus, so how could they be contraries? Plotinus responds by saying that "all the things included in each nature [the Good and matter] are contrary to those in the other; so that the wholes are contrary, and more contrary to each other than are the other contraries" (I.8.6, 34–36). In other words, he proposes to widen the definition of contraries so as to range not only over opposites within a genus but over opposite principles such as the Good and matter that are in every way responsible for opposite results.

Yet another problem relates to the fact that if matter is evil and matter is generated by soul, soul by Intellect and Intellect by the Good, matter is ultimately the product of the Good; hence, the Good is the cause of evil, which is unacceptable: either the Good isn't really the Good or the evil it causes isn't a real evil. If Plotinus wishes to insist on matter being evil, it may seem that he has to give up his monistic view of matter as the last item of a series starting from the Good, and admit matter to be something independent of this series. Already in antiquity Plotinus was criticized along these lines by a fellow Platonist philosopher, Proclus of Athens, who wrote a treatise on evil in which he attacks several points in Plotinus' theory of evil without, however, ever mentioning him by name.[6]

We cannot go into all the intricacies of this problem but here is a suggestion about a possible line of solution on Plotinus' behalf: even if it is true that the Good is the ultimate cause of matter and even if it is in general true that causation consists in the causes producing images of themselves, it is equally true and inbuilt into the system that the image is an imperfect likeness and always less unified than the cause. Since this is so, it follows that there are stages where the resemblance to the Good is reduced. Matter is indeed exactly the stage where there is no longer any resemblance. In formulaic Plotinian terms this means that matter is just indefiniteness, in no way a unity. And if in no way a unity, it is in no way good either.

I shall raise a few questions concerning this account and briefly answer them on Plotinus' behalf.

Even if matter has no goodness whatsoever, does it follow that it is evil? Well, this may be a matter of definition but this is how Plotinus understands evil and matter fits the description (see I.8.3, 12–16; I.8.3, 30–40).

Why should there be a stage in the series of productions starting from the Good where there is no longer any resemblance to the Good? Might there not be an infinite series in which each item is less good than its predecessor but still has a vestige of goodness? Yes, that is logically possible. But Plotinus (and the other Neoplatonists) were convinced for reasons never fully explained that the stages of the hierarchy come in discrete degrees of unity and that the number of stages is finite. As Plotinus says:

> One can grasp the necessity of evil in this way too. Since there is not only the Good, but by the fact of outgoing beyond it—or if one prefers to put like this, by the incessant descent and distancing—there must be the last after which nothing further can be generated, and this is evil. Now, it is necessary that what comes after the First should exist, and therefore that the Last should exist; and this is matter, which possesses nothing at all of the good.

(I.8.7, 16–22)

We may note, incidentally, that this passage too affirms that matter is a product of the Good, its last product.

But even if there must be a last stage, it still does not follow that this stage is matter, as described by Plotinus, and evil. Well, this would indeed follow, if Plotinus subscribes to a principle claiming that everything that has some goodness generates. Now, Plotinus may not say this explicitly but arguably he takes such a principle for granted.

But wouldn't this amount to a breach of the Principle of Prior Possession (see Chapter 2, Section 2)? Or in other words, should not the last resemble its cause or else the cause fail to produce an image of itself? There may be two ways of tackling this question. One way would be to suggest that the causal powers at the penultimate stage that produces matter exceed its paradigmatic powers. Or simply put: the lowest phase of soul which produces matter produces something but it is not an image of the maker. So if we understand the Principle of Prior Possession as implying that all production is the production of an image of the cause, this final production would constitute an exception to the principle. Alternatively, we might say that matter is indeed a sort of image of its immediate cause, the lowest phase of soul, which, after all, is itself weak in comparison with the higher soul and Intellect. But on this account the loss involved in the production of this final image would still result in the something with all the negative attributes of matter. In other words, it might be consistently held that matter is an image of the lowest phase of soul, which is an image of the higher soul, which is an image of Intellect, which is an image of the Good and yet deny that matter is an image of the Good.

I have suggested here in the preceding paragraphs that Plotinus' position on matter as evil and yet a product of the Good is consistent. One may still wonder why he adopted his view. O'Brien (1971: 146), who in general is a very sympathetic reader of Plotinus, suggests that though consistent "in his account of matter as intrinsically evil, Plotinus has left embedded in his philosophy a remnant of the old Platonic and Aristotelian dualism of two eternal and independently existent principles." This may indeed be so. I think, however, that Plotinus may have considered himself to have good reasons for maintaining his position and would not have jumped on an account such as Proclus', which explains evil as an accidental product in the sensible sphere and toys with the idea that it is uncaused (see Opsomer and Steel 2003: 27 ff.), had he been familiar with it. Plotinus takes very seriously Plato's claim in *Theaetetus* 176a that "evils can never be done away with ... for there must always be something opposed to the good; and they cannot have their place among the gods, but must inevitably hover about mortal nature and this region." He thinks that there has to be a general explanation of evil and he thinks matter does the job.

But how is matter the cause of evil in others? One may wonder in light of all the negative characteristics of matter, said to be without qualities and, in fact, inert, how something without qualities and inert could cause anything whatsoever? My short answer is that matter may be the explanation why certain things are such as they are but never be the active cause of anything.[7] It is a principle of explanation for certain features of the sensible world but not strictly speaking a cause—and here I have all four types of Aristotelian causes in mind. It is responsible, I suppose, in much the same way as laziness is responsible for the mess in my room: laziness explains the state of affairs but when you try to describe this alleged "cause" further only negative characteristics come to mind: laziness is *not* being so and so; it is lacking energy, positive will to keep things in order, and so forth. Similarly with matter: it is generally the lack of any positive characteristics. This explains why things that have matter or have to deal with matter suffer from lack. This may on the surface look like the Principle of Prior Possession working backwards from matter onto things that are in or related to matter. But this would be a misdescription.

In the treatise "On what are and whence come evils" (I.8. (51)), chapter 3, Plotinus establishes that there is no evil in the intelligible realm, among the real beings. So it must belong to the sphere of non-being. But matter isn't absolute non-being (because it exists!). So it must belong to what is other than being as a kind of image of it.[8] This kind of non-being, however, comprises the whole sensible sphere. Clearly, it is within this sphere that evil is to be found though it is not identical with this sphere as a whole. But Plotinus thinks that with this he is in a position to identify evil itself: "it is a kind of unmeasuredness in relation to measure, and unboundedness in relation to limit, and formlessness in relation to *logos*, and perpetual neediness in relation to what is self-sufficient: always undefined, nowhere stable, subject to every sort of influence, insatiate, complete poverty: all this is not accidental to it but in a sort of way its essence" (I.8.3, 13–17). This is the primary and absolute evil. Evidently, this description fits matter, as he makes explicit shortly afterwards.

Bodies are a secondary evil because they have a share in matter: "For bodies have a sort of form which is not true form, and they are deprived of life, and in their disorderly motion they destroy each other, and they hinder soul in its proper activity, and they evade reality in their continual flow, being secondary evil" (I.8.4, 2–5). Even if Plotinus insists that "evils are prior to us" (I.8.5, 27–28) and even if bodies destroy one another, I do not think there is evil for lifeless bodies according to Plotinus: evil is always evil for souls or ensouled bodies though the root of what is evil for them is matter. Thus, as regards living bodies, "illness is defect and excess of material bodies which do not keep order and measure; ugliness is matter not mastered by form; poverty is lack and deprivation of things which we need because of the matter with which we are coupled" (I.8.5, 21–26). Evil has to do with sublunary bodily existence. For the stars, even if they have bodies and matter, there is no evil because they completely master their matter (cf. I.8.5, 30–34).

What about the souls then? Isn't vice the primary evil of souls as many Platonic discourses seem to suggest? Plotinus does not think so. Vice is an evil but a derived one just as virtue is a derived good, each depending on matter and the Good, respectively. (In the *Republic* Plato also holds that the Good is the ultimate source of goodness: virtue is for Plato too a derived good.) But how does it come about that the body and ultimately matter is the cause of evil for the soul? There is a general difficulty about assigning any sort of causal role to matter. As we noted in the introductory Chapter 2, causation is in general from above. So how could matter affect soul? Secondly, and this is another given of the discussion of this topic in I.8, the souls suffer no internal, innate faults which make them bad. Still, they turn out rather badly, many of them. How can this be explained? We shall return to topics such as the fall of the soul and virtue and vice in later chapters. What will be said here is limited to the role of matter.

Plotinus begins chapter 14 of "On what are and whence come evils" thus: "But if someone says that vice is a weakness in soul—

pointing out that the bad soul is easily affected and easily stirred, carried about from one evil to another, easily stirred to lust, easily roused to anger, hasty in its assents, giving way freely to confused representations" (I.8.14, 1–5). He agrees with this description of vice as weakness of the soul but he wishes to inquire into the reasons for it. It turns out that matter is responsible in two ways: (1) "it darkens the illumination, the light from the source with a mixture with itself" (I.8.14, 40–41), and (2) it hinders the powers of soul from acting (l. 46). The darkened illumination is the nature of the body and in particular of the living body. The illumination is darkened because of matter, which is responsible for the volatile nature of bodies, as a result of which living bodies are constantly needy. The vicious soul who identifies itself with the life of such a body sees dimly and is in that sense weak. The other point is related: because of its admixture with matter, the body never leaves the vicious soul in peace: the soul becomes preoccupied and taken in so that its better powers, in particular its unadulterated reason, are hampered and lie idle. In his whole account of this Plotinus is careful not to suggest that the causality of matter on soul is such as to alter the soul: to blur somebody's vision and hinder his activities does not amount to changing that person.

3 Bodies

In the last chapter and in the preceding section we have adumbrated some of the basic facts about bodies in Plotinus' world. The topic is nevertheless not exhausted and on the following pages we shall get a more complete picture.

Plotinus takes over the notion of the four elements, fire, air, earth and water, from his predecessors, Plato's *Timaeus* no doubt being his primary source. He evidently thinks that other bodies are built out of these four. Given his notion of matter, it should not come as a surprise that he believes in elemental change—fire can become air, earth can become water, and so on—but he doesn't say a whole lot about the elements, their physical nature and interaction.[9] We learn that he holds fire in some esteem: it is his chosen example of an element and apparently the noblest of them and bordering on the incorporeal (I.6.3, 19–22). Interestingly, he rejects the fifth element, which according to Aristotle fills the heavens and is endowed with circular natural motion. Instead, Plotinus supposes with Plato that the heavens consist mostly of fire.[10]

There is another, more fundamental and, so to speak, more philosophical division in the realm of bodies than that between the elements and composite bodies. In the short early treatise, "The essence of soul (II)" (IV.2. (4)) he discusses the nature of soul, briefly and quite abstractly. In seeking to pin down the essence of soul, he also says something about the neighboring levels in the hierarchy: below soul Plotinus identifies a level which is

> primarily divisible and by its own nature liable to dispersion: these are the things no part of which is the same as either another part or the whole, and the part of which must necessarily be less than the whole. These are the perceptible magnitudes and bulks, which each have their own place, and it is not possible for the same one to be in several places at once.
> (IV.2.1, 11–17)

Later in the chapter he identifies these magnitudes and bulks with bodies. To be distinguished from the bodies but still below soul is

> a nature which is not primarily divisible, like the bodies, but all the same does become divisible in bodies; so that when bodies are divided, the form in them is divided too, but is a whole in each of the divided parts, becoming many and remaining the same, when each of the parts is completely separated from another part, since it is completely divisible: like colors and all qualities and every shape, which can be at the same time in many separate things, while having no part which is affected in the same way in which another is affected.
> (IV.2.1, 32–40)

We see this same distinction between bare bodies and immanent forms at work in a later treatise, VI.4–5. It is made explicitly in the first chapter, but the account of bodies as that which "by its own nature is liable to dispersion" is used throughout the treatise.[11] Although matter is not mentioned in IV.2 (Plotinus only discusses the levels in proximity with soul), this distinction supports what was said in the previous section about spatial properties being in a sense the primary properties of bodies: it is the basic form matter receives and the condition the other forms have to adapt to.

The distinction between "magnitudes and bulks" and "qualities" is a conceptual distinction: it is not the case that there ever are "mere bulks" without any qualities, nor are there qualities without an underlying bulk. Plotinus identifies the "magnitudes and bulks" with bodies because it is on account of this aspect that bodies acquire their character of spatial divisibility and dispersion, which is their defining characteristic.

When Plotinus speaks of the divisibility of bodies here he does not mean that a body can always be divided with a sharp enough knife or some other such device. What he has in mind is that they are conceptually divisible into distinct spatial parts, which does not imply that each part is actually separable. He in fact thinks that bodies are infinitely divisible in this sense (see IV.2.2, 10 ff.; IV.7. 8^2, 18–20). It follows from this that the mereology of bodies is different from that of soul and Intellect. As we have seen in previous chapters, soul and Intellect cannot be divided into distinct spatial parts in the way bodies can: the whole is undivided in each so-called part. The mereology of bodies that he sketches here is the defining characteristic of the purely sensible realm: bodies have spatially distinct parts and the whole is just the sum of these parts.

But what, more exactly, is he saying about magnitudes and bulks and how do they differ with respect to divisibility from e.g. colors? To say that white is the same in many bodies and body parts makes good sense: there is white on the surface of this egg and also on that other egg; there is also white both on the top and on the bottom of this one. These whites are the same in form or rather the same form is in all these places. As we saw, Plotinus nevertheless thinks that the whites in these different places, even on the same egg, are different individuals. He expands on this later in the chapter saying that the quality or color "in one bulk is totally separate from that in the other, just as much as one bulk is separate from the other; and that even if the magnitude is one, yet what is the same in each part has no community [with any other] leading to a common affection" (IV.2.1, 48–52; cf. VI.4.1, 21–23). These qualities belong to the body and share in its divisibility.

So far so good. But let us say that a given bulk is a cube of 1 meter^3. Two questions spring up about this bulk. First, what is its relation to place? Secondly, why aren't the bulks in just the same position as the qualities? It may seem that there are just as many 1-meter^3 bulks as there are whites. So why not say the same about both cases, namely that we have the same form in many? In one case, it is the form of a 1-meter^3 bulk; in the other, the form of white. The answers to these two questions overlap. Considering the former question first, let us note that there isn't any notion of place independent of bulks and magnitudes: surely matter, having no determinations, is not a place nor does it in and of itself contain places. Plotinus doesn't say much about the notion of place but my best guess is that place is for him a relative notion: the place of X is to be above Y, next to Z on the right, and so forth. Something along these lines. Secondly, Plotinus evidently wishes to understand bulk in such a way that a given bulk shares nothing with another bulk: it is purely an individual. It is true that there may be many 1-meter^3 cubes but a bulk or a magnitude in this context is a total loner. Since our cube cannot be individuated by reference to an independently existing place or space, the idea must be that the cube is individuated by its relation to other bulks each of which is similarly individuated. The different parts of a single bulk would be similarly individuated by their unique relations to the other parts. If this account is right, bulks and magnitudes are truly spatial individuals.[12]

A picture of pure bodies is emerging from the preceding account: they are spatially extended things with equally extended immanent forms. Moreover, these forms tend to be unstable and the bodies that carry them are liable to be affected by the qualities of other bodies. This general picture is developed by and largely in accordance with Plato's account in the *Timaeus*. The forms in matter are reflections on matter of intelligible entities. The ultimate source is the Forms in Intellect but the last intelligible entities that bring about the forms in matter are *logoi* that belong to the order of soul. This general account raises the question whether the sensible object is a mere conglomeration of qualities and matter without any internal ontological structure (see VI.3.8, 19–20) or whether Plotinus allows that some of its features are essential to it. In order to become clearer about what is at issue here, we must take a look at the treatise "On the kinds of being (I), (II) and (III)" (VI.1–3. (42–44)).

4 Sensible substance and the critique of Aristotle's categorial theory

The treatise "On the kinds of being (I), (II) and (III)" (VI.1.1–3) is yet another treatise that Porphyry cut up, this time into three. It contains a very critical assessment of the doctrine of Aristotle's *Categories* and of the Stoic category theory. The whole discussion is carried out on the assumption that so-called categories are genera of being. Thus, Plotinus takes Aristotle's work, the *Categories*, to be about the genera or main kinds of being there are—a work in ontology, in other words. This is a different understanding from that of Porphyry and the subsequent Neoplatonic tradition through Iamblichus to the Aristotelian commentators, which took the work to be about expressions signifying sensible beings. These latter actually continue a tradition of incorporating the doctrine of the *Categories* into a Platonist framework that had started among Platonists before Plotinus (see Chiaradonna 2002: 189 ff. and 2004). A question much debated among scholars is whether Plotinus' treatment of the *Categories* can be regarded as a part of this conciliatory approach towards Aristotle or whether it stands apart as an uncompromising rejection.[13] An aspect of this whole issue is the question whether Plotinus and Porphyry had a debate about the import of the *Categories*. Saffrey (1992: 43) suggests that disagreement on this issue was actually the reason why Porphyry left Rome in 265. Thus, the story about his depression is either made up afterwards or he was depressed because of this very disagreement (see Chapter 1, p. 13). This is highly speculative, however, and I shall not take a stand on this question.

The first part of this treatise, VI.1, contains a critical assessment of the Aristotelian and the Stoic categorial doctrines. In VI.2 Plotinus presents his alternative Platonic theory of intelligible categories that we considered in Chapter 4. In VI.3 he again takes up the Aristotelian theory and presents what may count as a radically revised version of it that is to hold true for sensible objects. This revised account really amounts to a rejection of central features of Aristotle's view. This treatise is unusually difficult, even for Plotinus. It is often hard to discern whether Plotinus is fully speaking his own mind or merely working out the consequences of the views under discussion. In addition the treatise draws heavily on the complicated theories of others. I have for this reason chosen not to try to give anything like a full account of the contents of this treatise (the Platonic categories doctrine of VI.2 is a topic already dealt with in Chapter 4, Section 2, "Plurality Enters the Scene: The Five Highest Ideas," though presented mainly through a different text). Some aspects of Plotinus' criticism of Aristotle must, however, be addressed. In particular Plotinus' criticism of Aristotle's account of substance is of consequence for his views on the nature of sensible objects.

Plotinus notes that the doctrine of the *Categories* only deals with sensible substances and leaves out the intelligible ones—Aristotle himself holds that there are substances of both kinds, God as presented in *Metaphysics* XII, for instance, is a purely intelligible substance. This shows that the account of the ontology in the *Categories* is at best limited and cannot be taken as a general account of the genera of being since intelligible beings are left out. He has several more specific critical points. He laments the lack of a true definition of substance, complaining that there is no general account of all things Aristotle recognizes as substances and that the negative characterization, "not in a substrate," is incomplete and too wide (VI.1.2; VI.1.3; VI.3.5). Plotinus also points out problems that would arise if the theory were to include intelligible substances: the latter are prior in relation to sensible ones (the Aristotle of the *Metaphysics* would agree) and the relation between the two kinds of substance would, hence, be an instance of what Lloyd (1962, 1990: 76 ff.) has called an ordered series, i.e. a series with an order of priority. According to a principle Aristotle himself appeals to in criticizing Plato's theory of Ideas—that the members of an ordered series such as that of the Ideas and their participants cannot be subsumed under one universal or genus— "substance" cannot be synonymously predicated of sensible and intelligible substance (VI.1.1–2). Further, Plotinus raises questions about the very meaning of "sensible substance" in Aristotle, taking into account the view expressed in the *Metaphysics* that form, matter and the composite of the two can all count as substances. Can they all be substances in the same sense? Plotinus does not think so (VI.1.2, 8–9; VI.3.7).

A crucial question in all this is whether Plotinus' pronouncements about sensible substance, especially in VI.3.8 and VI.3.15, amount to a rejection of the Aristotelian distinction between substance, or essence, and accidents in sensible objects. According to Aristotle the substance category contains things, substances, which are the basic constituents of the ontology. Some features pertain to substances essentially: Socrates, for instance, is a substance. He is a human being and that is essential to him and the only thing that is essential. Human beings are essentially animals. That, however, does not distinguish them from the cats and the cows, so we need some differentiating property. Aristotle proposes rationality, which is the so-called *specific difference* of human beings. So the essence of Man, and thus of Socrates or any one of us, is to be a rational animal. Lots of other features are accidental, falling into some of the accidental categories or genera, as Plotinus would have it: some are qualities like Socrates' paleness, others quantities such as his height, yet others times and places that he was in, relations Socrates had to others, and so forth—nine genera in addition to substance.

It is a part of the Aristotelian picture that the specific difference of a sensible substance is something added to the genus: in the case of human beings, the genus is animal and the specific difference is "rational." The specific difference cannot be something that belongs to the genus as such because not all animals are rational. Hence, the specific difference must come from outside the genus as something that qualifies it. In the language of the ancient commentators the specific difference is something that completes the substance. But if this specific difference qualifies the substance, it would seem that it belongs to the category of quality. On the other hand, since it completes the substance and thus is a part of it, one would suppose that it belongs to the category of substance.

Plotinus addresses the question of the status of the so-called completion of substance in the short treatise "On substance, or on quality" (II.6. (17)). Here he proposes that a quality that comes from the rational formula of a thing, such as the heat of a fire, is not to be regarded as a quality but as a form and activity of the substance, whereas heat in other things is a quality, properly speaking. The latter "is no longer the shape of a substance but only a trace, a shadow, an image, abandoning its substance, of which it was an activity, to be a quality" (II.6.3, 17–20).

Thus, in this rather early treatise Plotinus operates with a kind of essence/accident distinction for the sensible object. In the later treatise VI.1–3, however, he seems to abandon this view. In particular, his statements in chapters 8 and 15 of VI.3 suggest this. He says in VI.3.8, 19–20 that "sensible substance is a conglomeration of qualities and matter" and notes that none of its components, qualities and matter, are by themselves substances in their own right "but the whole made up from them all is substance" (l. 30). He adds that it is needless to object that if this is so, sensible substance is made out of non-substances, because this whole of which sensible substance consists is no real substance "but a shadow, and upon what is itself a shadow, a picture and a seeming" (ll. 36–37). And in VI.3.15 we have his final word on sensible substance:

> It was said about the qualitative (to poion) that, mixed together with others, matter and the quantitative, it effects the completion of sensible substance, and that this so-called substance is this compound of many, not an "essence" (ti) but a "such" (poion). And the rational formula of fire, for instance, signifies rather the essence, but the shape it produces is rather a quale (poion). And the rational formula of Man is the essence, what it has produced in the nature of body, being an image of the rational formula, is rather a "such." It is as if, the visible Socrates being a man, his painted picture, being colors and painter's stuff, was called Socrates; in the same way, therefore, since there is a rational formula according to which Socrates is, the perceptible should not rightly be said to be Socrates, but colors and shapes which are imitations of those in the rational formula.
> (VI.3.15, 24–36)

The expressions "such" and "essence" stem from Plato's Seventh Letter 443c; cf. also Timaeus 49d–e. Aristotle also commonly refers to his category of substance by expressions such as the ti esti, the "what it is." Plotinus speaks here of "sensible substance." As we see, he also dubs it "so-called substance," thereby distancing himself from the expression, which really belongs to Aristotle's school of thought. What Plotinus has reservations about is the use of the word "substance" for this compound of matter and qualities. What is meant by "sensible substance" here is just the same as what Plotinus would normally call a body, understood as including all its qualities and quantities (cf. II.7.3).

A few further comments on this are in order. First, the essence and true substance in the case of a sensible object (so-called sensible substance) is a rational formula, *logos*, that produces the qualities and quantities of the object. This formula produces all the qualities that genuinely belong to this object, not just those that serve to differentiate it from other kinds of substances. The rational formula does not count as a sensible substance, however. It belongs to the intelligible realm. The fact that something of the intelligible order, the *logos*, has to enter into the account of the sensible object is significant: it shows that as opposed to what Aristotle seems to presume, the sensible object, the so-called sensible substance, does not stand by itself (see Chiaradonna 2004: 124–126; Wagner 1996: 136).

Secondly, the question whether there may be something accidental to a sensible object is not directly addressed here. The question at issue is only whether the qualities or a subset of them can count as a part of the essence of the object in such a way that without these qualities there would not be a sensible substance there at all. The answer is that it is impossible to single out one quality as substantial: all the qualities of the object that come from its rational formula contribute to making it what it is, yet neither a single one nor a subset of them can count as a part of substance in its own right. Only the whole consisting of all the qualities deriving from the rational formula together with matter can count as a kind of substance; but even that whole is no real substance.

The upshot of this is that what Plotinus says in II.6 (cf. VI.1.10) is doctrinally quite compatible with what he says in VI.2 and VI.3: there is nothing in the latter passages that is incompatible with there being a distinction between those features of a sensible substance that derive from its formative principle and other externally acquired features; my rational formula may for instance make my skin generally pale but because of a wound a part of it is reddish. The latter feature is not due to the rational formula or at least not to it alone. This is not saying that in these latter passages Plotinus makes such a distinction but I cannot see that he rejects it either. Thus, there is no reason to see him as totally rejecting the distinction between essential and non-essential features of a thing, even if that distinction importantly differs from Aristotle's. There is a difference in terminology, however: in VI.3.8 and VI.3.15 Plotinus calls the features that come from the rational formula qualities and denies them any substantial status, whereas in II.6 these features are said to be activities rather than qualities, the term "quality" being restricted to externally acquired features.

If the above account is right, Plotinus is not antithetical to making a distinction between essential and non-essential features for sensible objects, even if he insists that sensible objects as such are not true substances. On account of these objects' lack of substantiality, he may, however, regard this distinction only as pragmatic, something that holds "for everyday purposes" (cf. Lloyd 1990: 86).

5 The physical world at large

In the treatise "On heaven" (II.1. (40)), Plotinus argues for the eternity of the sensible world. The picture that emerges is that in the sublunary world the species of living beings are indeed eternal though not their individual bodies: "man and horse always exist but not the same man and horse" (II.1.1, 27). It is different in the heavens: Plotinus argues in this treatise that numerically the same individual exists there for all eternity. As Wilberding (2006: 48 ff.) notes, in addressing this question about the diachronic identity of the heavens Plotinus goes beyond what we find in Aristotle or Plato, who did not raise exactly this question.[14] He does not think immunity to external blows suffices to secure the identity of the heavens through time. In order to establish diachronic identity, Plotinus has to argue that the heavens are indeed corporeally the same for all times, and explain the difference between them and the sublunary region in this respect.

A crucial premise in his argument for the diachronic identity of the heavens is Plotinus' firm belief that the higher realities, the World-Soul, the hypostasis Soul, Intellect and ultimately the One do not change their minds. Given Plotinus' account of the intelligible world this belief seems to be well founded: everything so far said about the One indicates that a change in it would be unthinkable; and unless the One changes there would not be any change in the activities of the other subordinate intelligible levels. So the immediate cause of the movement of the heavens, the thinking activity of the World-Soul and the star souls, is quite uniform. One may wonder whether this conflicts with what was said about the temporal thinking of a power of the World-Soul in Section 7 of the previous chapter ("Soul and Time"). According to that account the World-Soul thinks successively different thoughts. There is no reason, however, to believe that these different thoughts constitute a genuine change of the World-Soul any more than different human thoughts constitute a change in the human soul.

The bodies of the heavens, which consist of fire, remain because the heavens retain everything, and because fire is unaffected by the other elements in the sublunary region which it does not need as nourishment, and is completely pliable to soul.[15] How is it then that the state of affairs on earth differs from that of the heavens? Plotinus's answer is twofold: on the one hand, the elements predominating in the sublunary region are less pliable than the fire of the heavens and, on the other hand, the lower immanent soul which "so to speak flows down from above and makes the living things on earth" (II.1.5, 6–8) is an image of the World-Soul and less powerful than it (cf. *Timaeus* 41a7–b5). This lower soul is nature, which we described in the previous chapter as a lower, immanent phase of the World-Soul.

Let us raise the question: does anything happen in the physical world that is not caused (and hence in some sense willed) by the higher realities? This and related and subordinate questions will occupy us for the remainder of this chapter. We have seen that so far as the heavens are concerned the answer is clearly that everything there happens from unhindered intelligible causes. The question remains about the sublunary region.

As just noted, the bodies in this region are less pliable than those of the heavens. The earthly bodies are genuinely changeable and perishable: they don't hold on to their forms so well. Two compatible and complementary reasons for this are suggested: on the one hand, there are many passages describing the violent action of sublunary bodies on each other, or as seems to be Plotinus' preferred precise formulation, the action of a quality of a body on the opposite quality in the same or a different body (III.6.9, 24–26);[16] on the other hand, the blame for the volatility of corporeal forms has something to do with matter: it is because of matter's negative nature that the forms don't stick. It is important to note, however, that matter as such cannot have any effect on the forms: it will reflect a form mirrored in it but it does not glue it to itself and it does nothing to hinder it from going away.

We saw in Chapter 2 that everything in the sensible realm is caused by and depends on items in the intelligible world. Everything here in the sensible region has an intelligible counterpart which is its cause. Qualities and corporeal forms generally are immediately produced by nature or *logoi* of soul. Even if some qualities may not be produced by the internal rational formula of a body that has them, e.g. the heat of a heated stone, all corporeal forms are ultimately the products of *logoi*. The difference between the heavens and bodies on earth is that the latter are subject to external blows. They even suffer internal conflicts that can result in their ruin.

How are we then to understand the relation between earthly bodies and their intelligible causes? Is it the case that indeed the earthly bodies have intelligible causes but that these causes have become so weak that they don't master this region as a whole, which so to speak moves on uncontrolled and full of internal conflict or even by chance? That would indeed be very far from the truth. The fullest discussion of such issues is to be found in the treatise "On providence (I) and (II)" (III.2–3. (47–48)); also relevant are "On destiny" (III.1. (3)), "On whether the stars are causes" (II.3. (52)) and part of "On the problems of soul (II)" (IV.4. (28)), especially chapters 35–45. In "On providence (II)" Plotinus says:

> The universe is ordered by the generalship of providence which sees for the actions and affections and what must be available, food and drink, and all the weapons and devices as well; everything that results from their interweaving is foreseen, in order that this result may have room to be well placed, and all things come in a well-planned way from the general—though what his enemies planned to do is out of his control. But if it was

possible for him to command the enemy force as well, if he was really "the great leader" to whom all things are subject, what would be unordered, what would not be fitted into this plan?

(III.3.2, 6–15)

Providence, which in this treatise is also called "the universal *logos*" (III.3.1, 1–4) is likened to a general whose control ranges over both "his own forces" and that of the enemy too. The meaning is no doubt to bring home that conflicts and "fights" often seen in nature are part of providence, which contains and controls each of the opposing forces and determines the outcome of their meeting. Plotinus explains the facts of opposition and war between forces as the result of the ever-increasing diversity and individuation the further from the One we get: the principle of increasing plurality necessitates that there will be opposite qualities, which are liable to clash. Nevertheless, they are parts of a single overarching rational formula. From this it follows that the parts "are in harmony with each other; in harmony in such a way that unity comes from them, even if it is a unity produced by opposites" (III.3.1, 7–8).

The impression one gets from some passages in "On providence" (e.g. the passage cited above invoking the general) is that every detail, and the whole interweaving of forces that determines outcomes in the physical world, is contained in the *logoi*. Towards the end of the treatise, however, we find a passage suggesting that not all things happen by providence but certain things may have gone wrong: "and the things that have gone wrong are changed and corrected, as in a single body, where health is given by the providence of the living thing, when a cut or injury of any kind occurs, the directing rational principle again in turn joins it and closes the wound and heals and sets right the suffering part" (III.3.5, 28–32). The things that have gone wrong may be either the results of human action or of something else. However this may be, clearly providence has the upper hand and will set straight anything that may be less than optimal—"optimal" of course in a sense taking into account the nature of the things in question. There are indeed special questions that arise in connection with human action: for example, is everything we do just a part of the providential arrangement and not our doing in any real sense? Plotinus addresses this question in

"On providence" and the other treatises mentioned above; in fact, this is what he is most interested in. We shall address this in Chapter 10, after dealing with the human soul.

Plotinus sometimes speaks about chance events in the sensible world. Being chance events, they presumably have no cause. In "On autonomy and the will of the One" (VI.8), for instance, he frequently mentions that in its bodily existence the human soul will meet with chance situations (*tychai*) (see also III.1.8, 10–12). We may wonder, however, if he thinks these situations are truly random. He might just mean that lots of things happen in the life of the embodied soul that are unforeseen and over which it has no control: from the soul's point of view such occurrences may appear as mere chance. In "On providence (II)" he writes:

> Chance circumstances (*syntychiai*) are not responsible for the good life, but they, too, follow harmoniously on the causes before them, and proceed woven into the chain of causation by so following. The ruling principle [of the cosmos] weaves all things together, while individual things co-operate on one side or the other according to their nature, as in military command the general gives the lead and his subordinates work in unity with him.
>
> (III.3.2, 1–6)

Are there any real chance occurrences if so-called chance occurrences follow harmoniously on causes before them and these causes are rooted in a single all-comprising rational formula (here "the ruling principle")? Perhaps what Plotinus has in mind is something like the following: What we call chance circumstances, e.g. that I should meet this person at this given place at that given time, is explicable from the *logoi* in the sense that my being there then and that other person's being there then is grounded in the *logoi*. Nevertheless, there was no higher plan that exactly these two individuals should meet there and then and that their meeting should bring something about; the universal rational formula is stated in general, not in particular terms. This would then be a coincidence in the sense Aristotle explains in *Physics* II, 5: two events, each of which has solid causes, coincide, but there is no overarching cause explaining that they should be connected. Hence, surely from the viewpoint of each individual this is a chance occurrence. Nevertheless, the fact that such and such a person should meet with such and such a person, and that their meeting should bring about such and such a result lies in the rational formula. Perhaps Plotinus' view here is similar to the deterministic Marxist theories of history. To put it crudely: the revolution is inevitable; if this person will not lead it because he gets killed in a car accident, historical forces will find someone else. Similarly, the great rational formula will complete its course no matter what; it is a part of its set-up that there will be individuals available to accomplish it: if not this one, then someone else. At any rate, I cannot find any support for the view that chance occurrences play any significant role in how the world and particular parts of it unwind themselves according to Plotinus.

Plotinus sometimes writes as if sensible things are causes. In "On the impassibility of things without body," III.6, he even raises the question whether it isn't absurd to attribute real being and power to things like soul and intellect and deny it to body and matter, mountain and rock. He of course denies this but in the course of doing so he admits that bodies may act violently on one another and that "lifeless things deal the severest blows; they hit hardest and hurt most" (III.6.6, 46–48). Doesn't this contradict the claim that real causation is from above according to Plotinus? Not necessarily: we know that according to Plotinus every corporeal quality is a product of a rational formula. That includes the qualities that result in violent blows; so these too must have *logoi* as their causes.

6 The mental and the physical

Bearing in mind the previous discussion about there being nothing in the sensible world without an intelligible cause, the question may be raised about the ontological status of the lifeless sensible realm. On the one hand, it is clear that there are non-mental items in Plotinus' ontology: matter and forms in matter, which make up bodies, are as such soulless, hence lifeless and, a fortiori, thoughtless. On the one hand, it is evident that the sensible sphere is immediately caused by something of the order of soul, hence by something mental. Not only is the sensible sphere so caused, it does not seem to enjoy any sort of independence: it does not move on its own fuel, so to speak. The new feature that appears at this realm is spatial and temporal dispersion with a corresponding loss of unity. It follows from this that in a sense new facts and truths apply to the sensible sphere, truths having to do with for example the part/whole relationships that hold for this sphere and do not apply to the intelligible realm (see p. 176 ff.). Nevertheless, there are no new laws of nature for this sphere that aren't given from what precedes it together with the principle that whatever is to be produced will be more plural than the intelligible, its cause.

The question arises how we wish to classify Plotinus' view. Does his admission of a non-living, non-mental sphere, the sensible realm as such, make him a dualist with respect to soul (mind) and body (extension)? Or is it perhaps the case that such a categorization into mind/body, more or less in the modern sense of the terms, is too coarse and ultimately highly misleading in his case? One might argue for the latter view on the following grounds: his concept of soul is much wider and in many ways different from ours. Moreover, Plotinus has other important distinctions between different spheres of reality that do not at all correspond to our mind/body distinction. There is the distinction between matter and bodies, for instance, which has totally fallen out in later ontologies. There is also the distinction between Soul and Intellect, which is of considerable importance to Plotinus and also more or less obsolete according to modern lights. Furthermore, there is the crucial distinction between the One and Intellect: the One is notoriously not a thinker. Thus, one might think that imposing a mind/body dualism on Plotinus is really anachronistic and doesn't do justice to the complexity of his picture of reality. I shall come back to these considerations towards the end of this section. For the time being I want to ignore them and focus on the question how Intellect's and Soul's relations to the sensible are to be interpreted.

A common classification divides the main philosophical positions on mind and matter as follows, allowing for varieties of each, naturally: there are idealists (thinking that everything is mind, somehow), materialists (holding that everything is matter), dualists (thinking that there are two spheres of reality, mind and matter, that are irreducible to each other) or the proponents of parallelism, which claims independent but parallel sequences of events for the mental and material spheres. Spinoza is the classical representative for this view, though he also presents himself as a monist, the two parallel attributes of mind and extension being expressions of one and the same substance.

Clearly, Plotinus is not an idealist in the sense Berkeley is: he does not hold that to be is to be perceived and he clearly thinks that there are things in the world that exist independently of any cognition. Whether Plotinus may rightly be called an idealist in a different sense is another matter, which I shall return to.[17]

Is he a Cartesian dualist? There are certain affinities between Plotinus and Descartes. For instance, they share the intuition that the soul (or anything mental) cannot be extended in the way bodies are and that the concepts of part and whole are radically different for souls than for bodies.[18] Nevertheless, there are very significant differences in their conceptions of soul/mind: at least according to common presentations, according to Descartes any soul or mind is essentially aware of its content.[19] Plotinus, by contrast, allows for unconscious mental activities. Very notably, Plotinus asserts that "we are not aware of everything that happens in our soul before it comes to the whole soul" (IV.8.8, 7–9; cf. Caluori 2015: 143). What is more important for our present concerns, however, is that as opposed to the point of view of Descartes, the bodily sphere is not an independent substance according to Plotinus: as we have seen, bodies have no proper action of their own, all their doings are expressions of the *logoi* or other items at the intelligible level. In Descartes, extended substance has its own laws and mode of operation. Extended substance is of course God's creation and God is a mind. The mode of dependence is, however, rather different from the way the sensible sphere depends on intelligible causes in Plotinus. In Descartes extension follows its own laws. Admittedly, these laws are ultimately determined by God, but nevertheless this sphere acquires an independent status and is comprehensible entirely in its own terms. Not so in the case of the sensible sphere in Plotinus: he is not a dualist in the sense of believing in, as it were, two spheres, two kinds of substances, each of which has to be understood independently.

Nor would Plotinus' position be correctly described as a parallelism of the mental and the physical. According to this view, which presumably was Spinoza's view, the mental and the physical have no interaction but they run exactly parallel courses, one object/event in each corresponding to an object/event in the other but without any causal interaction between them. This differs from Plotinus' if only on account of the lack of causal interaction: according to him at least soul acts on bodies.

So is there any reasonable way of relating Plotinus' position to such latter-day classifications? It has occurred to me that there may be a certain resemblance between Plotinus' position and the supervenience theories about the mental that enjoy some popularity among contemporary philosophers. The idea behind such theories is that the mental is not reducible to the physical—in that sense, the mental has an independent status—but it supervenes on it, which means that there is no difference or change in the mental sphere that does not have a corresponding difference or change in the physical sphere. The inverse does not hold: there may well be differences and changes in the physical sphere that have no correspondence in the mental. An older idea in the same vein is that the mental emerges from the physical as a sphere with genuinely new properties but yet totally dependent on the physical. Some contemporary philosophers characterize the view invoking supervenience of the mental on the physical as non-reductive materialism: materialism in the sense that all there is are physical entities but with irreducibly non-material properties.[20]

What struck me was of course not that Plotinus was a non-reductive materialist but the inverse: a non-reductive idealist or "mentalist." That is to say, Plotinus would of course not think that soul or mind supervenes on the sensible but the other way around: the sensible sphere supervenes on the soul and the intelligible. If this was the case, there cannot be any change or difference at the sensible level without a corresponding change or difference at the level of soul. One could further claim that the sensible, even if its properties are not reducible to the mind or its properties, is nevertheless such that there is a total dependence of the sensible on the mental. As I have read more of the contemporary literature, I have also realized that there are a great variety of supervenience and emergence theories. These and the fine distinctions between the different varieties are couched in terms that are quite alien to Plotinus' thought and it would be idle and potentially lead us astray to try to relate his views to a particular contemporary position. The distinction (to my mind, rather too fussy in contemporary literature) between objects and properties of these objects that allows for non-physical properties of physical things would have seemed strange and counter-intuitive to Plotinus. The modern and contemporary discussions of supervenience and emergence may nevertheless be helpful for framing the questions that arise with respect to Plotinus' views. What at any rate seems beyond doubt is that the physical sphere has an entirely dependent existence, parasitical on the intelligible causes and really a kind of epiphenomenon: it does not act on the intelligible causes (see reservations below, however) and despite warlike states of affairs at times, there is no original agency in the sensible realm.

Let me propose the following thesis: matter, bodies and forms in matter, i.e. the sensible sphere, contain new properties in relation to their causes; these are e.g. the properties that have to do with the emergence of space and presumably also time at the sensible level. But these new properties are idle; they are not true causal agents on their own. Moreover, the new properties of the sensible sphere are latent in, and presumably predictable from, features of the mental causes and the logic of the process towards increased plurality. The hypostasis Soul and the other souls presumably know what they are doing. They would know this theoretically somehow, not by means of sense-perception, which they don't have.

While believing that this is essentially right, I feel this thesis obviously needs some elucidation and even modification. It is not even clear that Plotinus consistently endorses it. The main difficulties lie in the possible effects of bodies on souls, effects for which matter is ultimately to blame. In this connection we may note that it would not solve the problem merely to say that since matter and bodies are produced by soul, any upwards impact they may have on souls is ultimately an impact from soul—well, really ultimately an impact from the Good. This would be a wrong-headed response. The impact at issue here—we can call it evil—is an impact from bodies or matter in so far as they fail to be souls, and an impact from them qua something different from souls, Intellect and the Good. So if there is really such impact, we cannot simply account for it as the impact of one soul upon another.

The question about the impact of the body on souls arises primarily in relation to the human soul, and it is in this connection Plotinus addresses it, in a number of places. While his general tendency is to resist upwards causation, certain obvious facts create problems for this position. The ever-present human and animal phenomenon of sense-perception, for instance, involves at least prima facie a causal impact of bodies on souls. The emotions too and physical pain and pleasure, not to mention vice, similarly seem to involve some upward impact. We shall address these phenomena in the following chapters. Let it suffice to say here that not surprisingly Plotinus seeks to account for them without admitting any change in the souls as a result of bodily impact.

Ignoring the concerns of the previous paragraph, can we come to a verdict about how to classify Plotinus? He is not a materialist, of course, nor is he a substance dualist or a champion of parallelism. Is he a non-reductive idealist (analogous to non-reductive materialists) then? I think it is fair to say so but the case is by no means settled yet for reasons we shall now consider.

Somebody might argue against any such classification as follows: "In characterizing Plotinus' allegedly idealistic position you have used the post-Cartesian term 'mental' to cover the activities of soul and intellect indiscriminately and described the activity of both as thought. This is doubly wrong, it might be said, because in Plotinus' or anybody else's ancient Greek language there is no such term as 'mental' and the word 'thought' is a bad cover for what, for Plotinus, would be at least three distinct activities: the activity of Intellect, a special kind of immediate, intuitive grasp of the nature of things; the discursive cognitive activities of soul; and soul's world-making or otherwise productive activities—to subsume all under the term 'mental' is wrong and anachronistic."[21]

A general discussion of the question whether our post-Cartesian notion of the mental or of thought in Descartes' sense of *cogitatio* can be applied to the ancient Greeks would take us too far afield. A few remarks will have to suffice. Some commentators on the history of mind have emphasized that for Plato and Aristotle there is a categorical divide between the cognitive activities of soul and those of intellect, between sense-perception and intellectual grasp (see e.g. Matson 1966 and Rorty 1979: 46–48). It is also pointed out that for many of the ancients the soul has functions—for instance, nutritive and reproductive—that are alien to our notions of mind and the mental. This is of course all quite true. It doesn't follow, however, that Plato and Aristotle didn't see a unity in the different forms of cognition. Despite the emphasis on differences, they both saw a continuum going from sense-perception through opinion and discursive reason to intellection.[22] And it is worth pointing out that in Plato and Aristotle words like *gnōsis* can be equally applied to perceptual and intellectual cognition. For the Epicureans and the Stoics there is no deep divide between sense and intellect. For the latter "impression" (*phantasia*) is a universal term applicable to the impressions of both sense and mind.

As far as Plotinus is concerned, the allegation of anachronism seems to me to be misplaced. In his treatises there is a strong tendency to see acts of intellect, discursive reasoning and sense-perception as phenomena of the same kind. He, for instance, describes acts of sense-perception as "unclear intellections" (VI.7.7, 30–31). And even if in some contexts the distinction between intellection or intuition (*noēsis*) and discursive reason (*dianoia*) is of great importance to him, Plotinus nevertheless always sees the two as varieties of the same phenomenon, the latter being an imperfect form of the former (see, in particular, V.3.2–4). Even in the absence of a label such as "mental," he definitely regards intellection, discursive thought and sense-perception as falling under one kind.[23] That kind may not be exactly identical with our "mental," a notion which itself is without clear and consistently applied boundaries, but it is close enough for an approximate identification.[24]

Now, someone might point out that I have left out the productive activities of soul. Souls make and maintain the physical world and even matter, and they are responsible for the unconscious biological functions in organisms such as growth and healing. In fact, however, according to Plotinus the productive activity of soul too is a form of intellection or contemplation. We see clear assertions of this in the first chapters of "On nature and contemplation and the One," III.8 (see also V.3.7, 30 ff.). Here Plotinus gives a voice to nature, the productive principle. It says (among other things):

> Understand what, then? That what comes into being is what I see in my silence, an object of contemplation which comes to

be naturally, and that I, originating from this sort of contemplation have a contemplative nature. And my act of contemplation makes what it contemplates, as the geometers draw their figures while they contemplate. But I do not draw, but as I contemplate, the lines which bound bodies come to be as if they fell from my contemplation.

(III.8.4, 4–10)

And in V.3.7, 27–34 he says in the same vein:

> In one part, then, [soul] is made like that from which it comes [i.e. Intellect], in the other even in its unlikeness it is made like, even here below in its action and production; for its action is simultaneously contemplation, and in its production it produces forms, which are like intellections carried out in practice, so that all things are traces of intellection and Intellect proceeding according to their archetype, the ones near it representing it closely, and the last and lowest keeping a faint image of it.

How are we to make any sense of this? Well, nature, the productive soul, being a thinking or contemplative thing, contemplates the intelligible level above it, items in a higher soul or Intellect. When the higher soul contemplates Intellect it does not grasp Intellect as it is in itself in its own thought. Instead, soul has as its proper thought, an inferior manifestation of what it sought to grasp in Intellect. Nature, being the external act of the higher soul, behaves similarly: it, being a thinker, seeks to grasp its source but ends up contemplating itself. This contemplation, however, is weak and blurred. The making of the sensible realm is the external act of its contemplation. The psychological explanation suggested in the former passage is that nature makes this external object as some kind of substitute for clarity of vision, as geometers may draw figures in order to see more clearly what they are thinking. Anyway, there is no doubt that in Plotinus' view the creative activity of soul consists in contemplation, which indeed is a mental activity.

Admittedly, this psychological explanation leaves much unexplained. It does, however, point to the reason why something of the mental kind is crucial in the constitution of the sensible world for Plotinus. The reason is that for him, even on the cosmic scale, imitation or what we have called conversion is necessarily a mental activity, a kind of thinking. Thus, if the Platonic thesis that the sensible world is an imitation of an intelligible model is to hold, there must be a mental mediator, something that mentally inspects the model, absorbs it as best it can, and conveys its vision further.

From one point of view what has been maintained here on behalf of Plotinus may sound like no big news: isn't it generally acknowledged that according to Plato and ancient Platonism the sensible world is caused by and entirely dependent on intelligible causes? Well, this is at least half true, and Plotinus' position indeed fits into this pattern. Not every Platonist would have agreed entirely, however. Plutarch and Numenius, and presumably the Plato himself of the *Timaeus*, thought that the sensible sphere is not entirely the making of the intelligible realm: there is a material principle endowed with chaotic movement that pre-exists and is independent of all intelligible, formal causes. More importantly, intelligible causation in the Platonic tradition does not necessarily give us *mental* causation. Plotinus' clear insistence that Platonic imitation and production always take place by means of thought of some sort sets him apart and may qualify him as an idealist. The matter is not settled yet, however.

The One is not a thinker. This may seem like weighty evidence against a classification of Plotinus as an idealist. However, as we noted in Chapter 3, even if Plotinus painstakingly insists that the One is not a thinker, he suggests in an early treatise that it is far from being senseless (*anaisthēton*), that in fact it "is able to discern itself completely" and that its "thinking (*katanoēsis*) of itself is itself in a kind of everlasting, resting consciousness (*hoionei synaisthēsei ousa en stasei aidiōi*)" (V.4.2, 17–18). And in a much later treatise, VI.8.16, 32, he ascribes to the One a kind of "superthought" (*hypernoēsis*) and a kind of will. As explained in Chapter 3, such remarks do not constitute a genuine inconsistency in his thought about the One. The One is ultimately something of the mental kind, even if none of our mental vocabulary is adequate for it.

Whether or not to attach the label "idealist" to Plotinus should not be of any great concern. The term itself is vague, and what some count as idealism may not qualify according to somebody else's definition and the matter may be impossible to adjudicate. It is of some importance, however, to convey the understanding that for Plotinus something of the mental kind permeates all realms of reality from the One down to bodies and matter. The latter, admittedly, aren't mental, strictly speaking but they are, as we saw, "traces" of something mental and reflect it without any sort of independent action.

7 Chapter summary

The physical world, matter, bodies and bodily qualities, are products of soul or *logoi* that belong to the order of soul. As regards matter, this view is not universally accepted by scholars: some hold that matter in Plotinus exists independently of soul and the intelligible realm generally. It was argued that there is strong textual evidence suggesting that matter too is a product of soul.

Plotinus understands matter as the ultimate recipient of determination. As ultimate recipient it is bound to be without determination itself. Since predication is determination, there is nothing positive that matter can be said to be. It is in a sense nothing. Nevertheless, Plotinus thinks matter is indispensable: there must be such a recipient of form and the utter multiplicity of this recipient explains the nature of the forms that appear in it. Thus, matter, though not identical with space, is responsible for spatial dispersion. Matter is also a principle of evil. Since matter is nothing and in a sense inert, this claim raises the question whether matter does not after all have some causal effect on things above it. It was argued that Plotinus wants to answer this question negatively: matter enters into the explanation of evil without being an agent in a positive sense.

Bodies are the products of the *logoi* of soul in matter. A mere body is identified with bulk: a solid extended thing that is the recipient of qualities such as colors. It is not as if soul first makes matter, then extended bulks, and then e.g. colors as separate layers that arrive at different times: the distinction between matter, bulk and qualities is rather a conceptual distinction between different degrees of plurality. However, since the bulk (extension) is a recipient and bearer of qualities, the qualities—otherwise called forms in matter—become dependent on it and share in its extended nature.

Plotinus is critical of Aristotle's doctrine of sensible substances: the so-called sensible substances are in a sense no real substances, even by Aristotelian criteria of substancehood. The sensible object as such is just a conglomeration of qualities in matter. There is nothing substantial about the conglomerate as such, which has no independent existence. What has substantial, true being are the *logoi* of soul which produce the conglomerate. Such considerations lead to the question of how Plotinus' general ontological position is to be classified: it is clearly neither dualistic in Descartes' sense nor a form of parallelism, since the sensible sphere has no independent existence or mode of action. Nor is Plotinus' idealism in Berkeley's sense according to which everything is either a cognizing subject or something cognized belonging to such a subject. For matter, bodies and enmattered forms are not of the order of soul or intellect. Perhaps Plotinus' position is best described as the inverse of non-reductive materialism: the sensible sphere is irreducibly something *sui generis* but it is a totally dependent product of the intelligible sphere.

Further readings

Primary sources

Ennead I.8. (51) "On what are and whence come evils."
Ennead II.1. (40) "On heaven." There is a commentary with an excellent introduction in English by Wilberding (2006).
Ennead II.4. (12) "On matter."
Ennead II.9. (33) "Against the Gnostics."
Ennead III.4. (15) "On our allotted guardian spirit," chapter 1.
Ennead III.6. (26) "On the impassibility of things without body." There is a translation with a commentary in English by Fleet (1995).
Ennead IV.2. (4) "On the essence of soul (II)," chapter 1.

Secondary sources

Denis O'Brien: "Plotinus on Matter and Evil," in L. P. Gerson (ed.), *The Cambridge Companion to Plotinus* (Cambridge: Cambridge University Press, 1996), 171–195.

D. J. O'Meara, "The Metaphysics of Evil in Plotinus: Problems and Solutions," in J. M. Dillon and M. Dixaut (eds.), *Agonistes: Essays in Honour of Denis O'Brien* (Aldershot: Ashgate, 2005), 179–185.

Michael Frank Wagner, "Plotinus on the Nature of Physical Reality," in L. P. Gerson (ed.), *The Cambridge Companion to Plotinus* (Cambridge: Cambridge University Press, 1996), 130–170.

Paul Kalligas, "Logos and the Sensible Object in Plotinus," *Ancient Philosophy* 17, 2 (1997), 397–410.

Lloyd P. Gerson, "Plotinus against Aristotle's Essentialism," in M. F. Wagner (ed.), *Neoplatonism and Nature* (Albany: State University of New York Press, 2002), 57–70.

There are also fine articles on different aspects of Plotinus' views on the sensible world in the following collections:

Michael F. Wagner (ed.), *Neoplatonism and Nature: Studies in Plotinus' Enneads* (Albany: State University of New York Press, 2002).

Riccardo Chiaradonna and Franco Trabattoni (eds.), *Physics and the Philosophy of Nature in Greek Neoplatonism* (Leiden: Brill, 2009).

James Wilberding and Christoph Horn (eds.), *Neoplatonism and the Philosophy of Nature* (Oxford: Oxford University Press, 2012).

Notes

1 See especially O'Brien 1991a, 1991b, 1996 and 1999. O'Brien has, however, not convinced everyone: Carroll (2002) argues that Plotinus remains ambivalent about the origin of matter and Phillips (2009) argues, in my view ultimately unconvincingly, that the key passages O'Brien appeals to, III.4. (15) 1 and III.9. (13) 3, do not support his view that matter is the product of soul. See also Narbonne 2007.

2 On the notion of bulk, its prehistory, and role in Plotinus' thought, see Brisson 2000b.

3 See II.4.14–16. For a commentary, see Bréhier's (1924–38) "Notice" to II.4 and O'Brien 1996: 177–181.

4 On Plotinus' use of Plato's *Sophist* here and the significance of the textual difference, see O'Brien 1996: 172–175 and, more fully, O'Brien 1991a.

5 There is a slight problem here, however: Plotinus' phrase seems to pick out too many things if matter is identified with otherness in the sense of the whole sensible sphere rather than matter alone (I.8.3, 9–11). Unless, that is, he means to include in being "in the full and proper sense" not only the productive *logoi* and higher intelligibles but also the sensible forms they produce in matter.

6 See Proclus, *On the Existence of Evils* 31. There is a fine English translation with extensive notes by Opsomer and Steel (2003). A number of recent articles address the disagreements between Plotinus and Proclus on matter and evil: O'Meara (1998) presents and discusses Proclus' criticisms without taking a firm stance about their soundness; in two later articles (2005 and forthcoming) he offers a defense of Plotinus' position, as does Schäfer (2004), but at the cost of denying that Plotinus holds matter to be evil as such. Opsomer (2001 and 2007) sides with Proclus. My own view is the same as or very close to that of O'Meara from whose work on this issue I have learnt much.
7 On this I disagree with Opsomer (2007: 157).
8 See Plato's *Sophist* 558b ff.
9 On elemental change in Plotinus, see e.g. II.1.3, 8–9 and Wilberding's (2006) commentary *ad loc.* with further references.
10 On the composition of the heavens, see Wilberding 2006: 68–70.
11 See the commentary of Emilsson and Strange 2015: *ad* VI.4.1, 17–24.
12 I suggested this account in Emilsson 1990. It is admittedly speculative and I am not absolutely confident about it but to my knowledge it has not been challenged.
13 For a good overview of the issues and the scholarly literature, see Chiaradonna 2004. My take on this issue follows Chiaradonna (2002 and 2004), Lloyd (1990 and 2002) and a number of scholars who see Plotinus as a radical critic of Aristotle in VI.1 and VI.3. Others, notably Strange (1987), Horn (1995) and de Haas (2001), see him as admittedly critical but basically philo-Aristotelian.
14 Wilberding (2006) provides an excellent survey of Plotinus' cosmology in his introduction, where Plotinus' views are compared and related to those of his predecessors, Plato, Aristotle and the Stoics.
15 For details, see Wilberding 2006: 57–60 and *passim*.
16 That there is constant and often violent action of bodies on one another is dramatically emphasized in the treatises on providence, III.2 and 3. See also III.6.6–19.
17 Kalligas (2011) argues that because the sensible object is entirely caused by soul (*logoi*), Plotinus' position qualifies as a version of idealism. Chiaradonna has also emphasized that a full account of the sensible object inevitably must bring in intelligible causes (cf. p. 208).
18 In Emilsson 1988: 141 ff. and 1991, I speak of Plotinus as a dualist regarding the soul–body relation. I think that is appropriate in the context of a human being and I still stand by the substance of what I said in these early publications about this matter; but I would now add reservations about using the term "dualist" of Plotinus' position when it comes to reality at large. Also, while still acknowledging certain affinities between him and Descartes, I would now have reservations about suggesting that he was a proto-Cartesian.
19 Doubt can be raised whether Descartes believed that everything in the mind is conscious: in particular in *Meditation* 5, but also in many other places, he appeals to innate ideas that were apparently in the mind all along but could be brought to our conscious attention. They were in the mind before this happened, however.
20 Donald Davidson (1970) is generally considered as the instigator of contemporary ideas about non-reductive materialism and the idea that the

mental supervenes on the physical. For recent advocacy of non-reductive materialism and further references, see e.g. Pereboom 2002.
21 This imaginary opponent is actually Myles Burnyeat, who has expressed such views at a conference where I was present and in private conversations.
22 It should suffice to support this to point to Plato's Divided Line in the *Republic* and Aristotle's treatment of sense-perception, imagination and intellection in Books II and III of his *On the Soul*.
23 Certain terms, e.g. *gnōsis*, *antilēpsis* and even *aisthēsis*, and their cognates, may be applied to cognitive activities of both soul and intellect. This is reflected for instance in the title (admittedly Porphyry's) of V.3, *Peri tōn gnōristikōn hypostaseōn kai tou epekeina*, "On the cognitive hypostases and what is beyond," which discusses all forms of cognition from sense-perception to intellection.
24 The notion of what counts as mental as opposed to not mental in the history of philosophy is vague. Descartes connects the mental closely to the conscious (see, however, note 19 in this chapter). Other seventeenth-century thinkers disagree. Leibniz's *petits perceptions* are not conscious (see Chapter 8, Section 2, pp. 276–277) nor is it plausible to suppose that every item of mind for Spinoza, corresponding even to states of affairs on the dark side of the moon, is the object of anyone's consciousness. So consciousness is, historically speaking, hardly a criterion of the mental.

Seven
The human being I
The soul–body compound

Plotinus has a great deal to say about human psychology, phenomena such as the soul's relation to the body, the emotions, sense-perception, reasoning and memory. While his views must count as dualistic in the sense that the soul is a distinct entity with an independent existence, the picture is not simply that of an immaterial soul occupying a lifeless body: it is much more nuanced and complex than that. Let us say from the start that his psychology is broadly speaking Aristotelian in that the main faculties of the embodied soul are vegetative, sensitive and rational. This Aristotelian scheme is, however, applied in the context of a position that is in all essentials Platonic. Plotinus maintains Plato's conception of the human soul in the *Phaedo* and other dialogues as an essentially rational entity, and following leads from Plato's *Alcibiades* I, he distinguishes between the soul itself, the soul using the body, and a compound of body and soul. Some aspects of his psychology also bear a certain Stoic flavor. I have in mind particularly Plotinus' account of a single center of conscious experience, which resembles the Stoic ruling part of the soul. Partly as a result of this mixture of influences, partly no doubt due to Plotinus' genius, we find moves and views regarding human psychology that are genuinely original.

As already hinted, there are several distinctions to be made within the human being and within the human soul. In particular, one must distinguish between the so-called qualified body (this is a body with a trace of soul; this will be explained shortly), the living being (compound of body and a power or image of soul), and the individual soul. Within the individual human soul a distinction is to be made between the higher, pure soul, i.e. reason, and its image, which together with the body makes up the living being. I shall refer to the latter as the middle soul.[1] The items distinguished are not separated and isolated but interact and even mingle in various ways so that at times the distinctions become somewhat blurred.

This chapter and the next one are closely connected. In the first two sections of this chapter I introduce and discuss some basic distinctions in Plotinus' psychology that will continue to be relevant for the remainder of this chapter, the next chapter and indeed for Chapters 9 and 10 as well. In the third and longest section of this chapter ("The Functions of the Living Being") we shall address functions of soul that involve the body. This means that our main topics here are sense-perception, pleasure and pain, and the emotions. In the next chapter the focus is on the pure soul (reason) and its relation to the functions that involve the soul's embodiment.

1 The body, the trace of soul, and nature (vegetative soul)

Several treatises of the *Enneads* contain relevant information about human psychology. The treatises in the fourth *Ennead* are all about the soul or particular psychological phenomena such as sense-perception and memory. The fullest accounts are to be found in "On the problems of soul (I), (II) and (III)" (IV.3–5. (27–29)), even if it is soul in general and not specifically the human soul that is the subject of this long split-up treatise. The very late treatise, "What is the living being and what is man?" (I.1. (53)), has the advantage of giving a fairly short, relatively systematic account Plotinus' philosophical anthropology. I will take that text as our point of departure, filling in from other sources as needed.

In "What is the living being and what is man?" Plotinus sets out by raising questions about what precisely is the subject of affections and sense-perceptions: when there is pain, for instance, who or what exactly is in pain? Is it the body, the soul or some third thing? In the background of this discussion are Platonic dialogues such as the first *Alcibiades* and the *Phaedo*: the former distinguishes between the body, the soul using the body, and the pure soul (129e), whereas the latter seems to attribute all functions other than rational thought to the body. Another highly relevant background text is

Aristotle's On the Soul I, 493a3 ff., where Aristotle discusses whether there are functions proper to the soul alone or whether the so-called affections of the soul—he mentions among others anger, appetite, sense-perception generally, fear, loving and hating in the context—involve the body. Aristotle's conclusion is that with the possible exception of the intellect, all functions of the soul are the common work of soul and body. Plotinus is aware of this position and seeks to take it into account but ultimately he rejects it: he holds that some functions conventionally attributed to the soul indeed necessarily involve the use of bodily organs and must be considered as common to body and soul, but he draws the line at a different place than Aristotle: as we shall see there is considerably more that belongs to the soul alone on Plotinus' account.

Plotinus discusses this question, to whom or what should we attribute what, back and forth in the first six chapters of I.1 and then finally comes to some sort of conclusion in chapter 7:

> Let us say that it is the compound which perceives, and that the soul by its presence does not give itself qualified in a particular way either to the compound or to the other member of it, but makes out of the qualified body and a sort of light which it gives of itself, the nature of the living being, another different entity to which belong sense-perception and everything else which is called affections of the living being.
>
> (I.1.7, 1–6)

All the items mentioned above appear here: the compound, the soul, the living being, the "light" that the soul gives, and the body qualified in a particular way. The compound and the living being are in fact the same thing. As for now, let us first address the notion of a qualified body that is mentioned here and then consider three different interpretations of the passage just cited.

I shall address the trace or shadow of soul more fully below. Let it suffice to say here that it is the organic, purely biological life of the body.[2] Examples of the work of this trace would be the processes of nutrition and growth, the healing of wounds, the boiling of blood in rage, and the like. These are bodily processes in the sense that they are subject to spatial division like other bodily items and do not as such involve any form of cognition. They are, however, activities—more precisely, external activities of nature—that are goal-directed and go beyond any natural activities of mere bodies: only an animated body can perform them.

In light of what was said earlier about the intimate connection between life and soul (see Chapter 2, p. 41), must the qualified body not also already have a soul since it is alive? Actually this is unnecessary, because the trace, the life of the body, is not a soul; hence, by having the trace the body does not *have* a soul. However, just like the tracks of a wolf indicate the presence of a wolf in the vicinity, the trace of soul is a sure sign of a soul (see Caluori 2015: 192). So the intimate connection between soul and life still holds. The trace of soul is produced by the vegetative soul or nature. This is very explicit in "On the problems of soul (II)": "the soul nearby, which we call nature [or vegetative soul], which gives the trace of soul to the body" (IV.4.20, 15–16).

Excellent interpreters have given radically different accounts of the passage cited from I.1.7 above.[3] There seem to be three possibilities:

1 The body in question, the qualified body, is an organic body that is potentially alive (cf. Aristotle, *On the Soul* II, 408b12–13 and I.1.4, 25–26). The "light" that the soul gives to the qualified body animates it so that it becomes alive (which it wasn't before). On this reading the human soul itself gives a trace of soul to the body and thereby makes the living being, which on this view is identical with the living body. Such a reading is straightforward and would make good sense of this passage taken in isolation. It cannot be right, however. Let it suffice to say here that it does not sit well with Plotinus' statements elsewhere, in particular in "On the problems of soul (II)," chapters 18–19, where the qualified body is clearly understood as an already living body and not as a body that can receive life. This interpretation also faces a serious difficulty even a few lines below in the same chapter of I.1. Here Plotinus says that soul's power of perception need not be of sensible objects "but rather it must be apprehensive of the impressions produced by sense-perception *in the living being for these are already intelligible entities*" (I.1.7, 10–12). This, I take it, refutes the simple identification of the

living being with the living body: "the light" together with the qualified body constitutes the living being and intelligible entities pertain to it (see also IV.3.26, 25–33); but nothing that counts as intelligible can pertain to the living body as such.

2 The qualified body is a body that is alive and already has a trace of soul when the soul gives its light to it. This understanding of "the qualified body" can also appeal to Aristotle's *On the Soul*: "Of natural bodies, some have life in them, others not; by life we mean self-nutrition and growth and decay. ... Now given that there is such qualified body, viz. having life ..." (II.1, 412a13–17). On this interpretation the "light" is not that which makes the body alive—it is already alive—but that which unites with the living body to perform functions such as sense-perception that are common to body and soul.

3 A third possibility is that Plotinus takes the "light" that the soul gives to do both: it provides the functions common to body and soul but it also provides the body with the trace of soul so as to make it alive. It is true that in the passage he says "makes out of the qualified body and a sort of light which it gives of itself, the nature of the living being." This may suggest that the qualified body is already there when the "light" comes. But if we take "the qualified body" as meaning merely the organic but lifeless body as in the first interpretation, nothing prevents the "light" from providing the trace of soul that makes the body alive.

Given that we have successfully disposed of the first alternative, we must decide between (2) and (3). Since it is clear from IV.4.18–20 that it is the vegetative soul (nature) that provides the trace of soul, the question becomes whether the vegetative soul is included in our soul, as part of the "light." We shall have more to say about this soon, but by "our soul" I mean the individual human soul, the soul which gives the "light." So the question is whether or not the vegetative soul is included in the light. This question turns out to be very complicated. In a number of passages Plotinus suggests that some of the soul involved in a human being is not a part of or a product of the individual human soul but comes from the World-Soul (see e.g. II.1.5, 18–24; II.2.2, 4–5; IV.3.27, 1–3). And there is a passage that identifies this soul that comes from the World-Soul with the vegetative soul:

But the nutritive[4] power, if it comes from the whole [i.e. the World-Soul], has also something from that soul. But why does not the nutritive power also come from our soul? Because what is nourished is a part of the whole, that which also is passively perceptive, but the perception which judges with intelligence belongs to the individual soul, and there is no need for this to shape that which has its shaping from the all.

(IV.9.3, 23–28)

Strange though it may seem at first sight, such a view makes reasonably good sense: Plotinus elsewhere suggests that the lowest phase of the World-Soul is nature or vegetative soul (Chapter V, see p. 157) and as Blumenthal (1971: 29) notes, "we, seen as bodies, are just parts of the whole of nature, and … our behavior in this capacity is similar to that of the rest of world." Even if nature in the body of the cosmos behaves in some respects differently than nature in humans and ordinary animals because, as opposed to the latter, the body of the cosmos is self-sufficient and not exposed to dangers, they are largely engaged in similar kinds of activities. Plotinus presumably saw nature as the same kind of soul in both cases. The view expressed in the last quote fits alternative (2) above according to which the body is already alive when the "light" comes: it has been made alive by the vegetative soul, which comes from the World-Soul.

Before we proceed any further, more should be said about the qualified body and the trace of soul it has in it.[5] This seems like a rather mysterious entity. Pioneers in Plotinus' psychology such as Blumenthal (1971: 58–9) and Igal (1979: 326–328) took the trace to be some further very low level of soul below nature, but as several recent commentators have noted the trace is not of the order of soul at all.[6] The trace is mortal, but no soul is mortal (IV.4.29). The difference between the soul–body relation of the embodied soul and the trace–body relation is shown by the two different illustrations that Plotinus employs for the two relationships: the soul–body relation is like the light–air relation, a crucial aspect of this being that the light is not affected by the air and is not a property of the air (see p. 181); the trace–body relation, on the other hand, is likened to heated air, in which case the heat is a property of the air and will as such be destructible (see IV.4.29). Thus, the trace is not a type of soul but exactly what its name says: a trace of soul.

But what does the trace do? Caluori plausibly suggests that the trace is the physical activities themselves. This means, for example, that nature, a power of soul and as such not localizable, has external activities that take place through the body and, in a sense, are activities of the living body. A case in hand is the claim that the activities of sensation and of the movement of the body start in the brain. The processes that start from there would be instances of the trace of soul. These activities are perishable. Some of them may linger on for a while but soon enough they will wither in the absence of soul.

There are some unresolved questions concerning the divisions within the embodied soul. Plotinus often fails to mention the external origin of the vegetative soul and one easily gets the impression that it is simply the lowest phase of the image of soul that has descended into the body.[7] There are even passages suggesting that the individual soul itself is responsible for fashioning its body, even at the embryonic stage.[8] Furthermore, there are ample passages suggesting that the parents of a child also play a significant role.[9] This may seem to make the role of the World-Soul redundant.

These are difficult issues. I cannot do better than to cite Wilberding's (2008b: 427, n. 67) sketch of a solution to these problems: "The basic approach to resolving the conflict between the World-Soul's contribution versus that of the parents would involve acknowledging that the parental contribution is made by their lower parts of soul which are ascribed to the World-Soul in the sense that these individual powers belong to that part of the spectrum." Thus, there is no conflict between parental and World-Soul contribution. The World-Soul, however, evidently also has some other influence: through regulating the environment, controlling the stars, and by overseeing the "cosmic matchmakings" which assign a particular soul to a particular body.[10] Wilberding further suggests that the passages assigning the fashioning of the body to the individual soul could be reconciled with those invoking the parents' souls by noting that according to Plotinus the individual soul appears to arrive prior to birth (IV.3.7, 29–30).[11] However this may be, Plotinus shares with Porphyry the view that vegetative souls in general need a higher ranking soul as a leader or "captain" (see Wilberding 2008b). The "captain" of nature in human beings is no doubt the "light" of soul we have frequently referred to: a phase or image of the individual soul that "uses the body as a tool."

There is yet another difficulty about consistency concerning the sort of issue we have been discussing. We have just seen Plotinus holding that nature in us comes from the World-Soul. One passage, which is not to be lightly ignored, seems to portray a different picture. After establishing that memory does not involve the body and is to be attributed to the soul alone, in "On the problems of soul (I)" Plotinus asks: "But to which soul [is memory to be attributed]? That which we call the more divine, by which we are ourselves, or the other which comes from the whole?" (IV.3.27, 1–3). He goes on to explain that these two souls share memories while they are united in the embodied human life but after their separation at death, each soul will begin by retaining some of the memories of the other but these will soon fade and disappear. What is of interest to us for the present issue is that Plotinus attributes memory to the soul that is said to come from the whole, i.e. from the World-Soul. In fact, the discussion in IV.3.27–32 suggests that the memories of this soul are memories of the life in the sensible world in general, for instance memories of one's friends, family and fatherland. This includes much more than what belongs to the vegetative soul, even if the passive part of sense-perception as well as appetite and the irascible element (anger) belong to it. This would suggest that the soul here said to be from the World-Soul simply is the middle soul, which according to our pilot passage is the "light" emanating from the transcendent soul. The claim that the middle soul comes from the World-Soul is indeed odd and in conflict with Plotinus' general line of thought. I do not know how to resolve this mismatch.

2 The pure soul and the middle soul

Our pilot passage in I.1.7 contends that "the soul by its presence does not give itself qualified in a particular way either to the compound or to the other member of it, but makes out of the qualified body and a sort of light which it gives of itself, the nature of the living being." Evidently, a distinction is to be made between the soul itself and its "light." That the soul does not give itself to the compound or the body means that the soul itself does not descend into the body. To say that it does not descend means that it is not directly implicated in the functions involving the body nor is it the subject of what arises from such functions. That means that the higher soul or pure soul, as I have also called it, is not the subject of the emotions and false opinions that arise from embodiment. The higher soul will be the subject of the next chapter. Let us just state now as a preliminary that it is identical with reason in us.

We noted in Chapter 2 (p. 43) that there is something of our individual human soul that never leaves the intelligible realm. A very clear statement of this is found in the early treatise "On the descent of soul into bodies," IV.8 (6), where Plotinus says:

> And if one ought to dare express one's own view more clearly, contradicting the opinion of others, even our soul does not altogether descend, but there is something of it in the intelligible; but if the part which is in the sensible world gets control, and is thrown into confusion [by the body], it prevents us from perceiving the things which the upper part of soul contemplates.
> (IV.8.8, 1–6)

That something of us always remains in the intelligible realm is a very important feature of Plotinus' philosophy of the human being.[12] Being a member of the intelligible world, this undescended soul is always engaged in purely rational thought. We embodied human beings are not ordinarily aware of this. It then goes without saying that Plotinus is undisturbed by the fact that something is going on in our soul, even thinking activity that we are not aware of. He notes that something analogous is the case with desire which can remain in the desiring part of the soul and only become known by us when it is apprehended by our inner sense or discursive reason (IV.8.8, 9–11).

But what is this descent of the soul really? In Chapter 5 we discussed the soul–body relation in general terms and noted that Plotinus denies that that soul is ever in the body as a kind of place that houses it. As we observed there, his preferred way of expressing himself is to say that the body partakes in soul, which, however, remains undivided by this partaking. Nevertheless, he sometimes uses the traditional language of the descent of souls into bodies. He even gives details about how different souls' travel from the "intelligible region" through the heavens and down to earth (IV.3.15, 1–3). Given what he says about the non-spatial nature of the soul, any reference to such travel may seem suspect: doesn't such talk present the soul as a quasi-body that can move about between regions of space? Caluori, following Bréhier, suggests that this is a question of experience rather than literal soul-travel (Caluori 2015: 139–146). I think this is a reasonable suggestion.

So if some souls are said to descend as far as the heavens, i.e. the star souls, this just means there are souls that are engaged in a certain way, having experiences of a certain kind that is characteristic of the star souls. Other souls are engaged with a particular earthly body and have corresponding experiences. It holds for all souls, however, that their essence remains in the intelligible realm. Thus, it is misleading in at least two ways to speak of the descent of the soul into body. First, because something, in fact the pure essential soul, remains in the intelligible realm; secondly, because the presence of the soul to the body is not the local kind of presence according to which bodies are said to be in other bodies.

Nevertheless, even if the soul in its essence may remain in the intelligible realm, evidently some of it descends in some sense so as to come to have a special relation to a particular earthly body and have experiences that are grounded in that relationship. That which so descends is the middle soul, the "light" spoken of in our pilot passage I.1.7. This is the soul-powers that work through the body, "sense-perception and everything else which is called affections of the living being." This, together with the qualified body, is the entity to which sense-perception is to be attributed and this is the subject of our other everyday conscious experiences: sense-perception, emotions, memories of our lives in the sensible world, and our opinions. This entity, the middle soul, together with the body and the vegetative soul, is what Plotinus usually calls the living being or the animal and this is the same as what he refers to as the "common entity" or "the compound"—"common to" and "compound of" body and soul (see I.1.7, 18–20).

The ethical status of the descent is tainted by the same sort of ambivalence as we see elsewhere regarding any sort of process towards greater multiplicity.[13] There are at least two questions relevant in this context: (1) Do the souls descend on their own accord? And (2) Is it good that they descend? As to the former question, Plotinus suggests that the souls become restless in the intelligible, where they are all together in an intellectual communion with the rest of intelligible reality. According to V.1.1 the souls yearn for a more independent existence. Hence, they replace their all-embracing point of view with the much narrower concern for a particular body, which has been prepared for them already by the World-Soul. He suggests that the souls go down into the sensible willingly (IV.8.5, 7; IV.3.13, 18). Yet he also describes the descent as necessary, as a part of a rigid scheme for the world in the intelligible realm (IV.4.12–13). At least a part of the logic behind the descents is to distribute just punishments for wrongdoings in previous lives. Plotinus sees no contradiction between the voluntariness and necessity involved in this: "There is then no contradiction between the sowing to birth and the descent for the perfection of the All, and the judgment and the cave, and necessity and voluntariness, since the necessity contains the voluntariness" (IV.8.5, 1–4). In "On the problems of soul" he says there is a law stating that the souls must go down but the souls also carry this law in themselves, the clear implication being that they are internally motivated. So they go on their own accord.[14] As we shall see more fully in Chapter 10, Plotinus is a compatibilist on the question of determinism and freedom: our actions as well as the souls' descent may be determined, yet free.

The second question, whether it is a good thing that the souls descend, is even trickier. The fact that the descent is fitted into a universal scheme at the intelligible level would seem to indicate that it cannot be any sort of fault. Plotinus also suggests that the souls may draw a positive lesson from the experience of embodiment (IV.8.7), which is somewhat strange given that he thinks they do not remember any of this in the long run (cf. IV.3.32–4.2). He furthermore says that if the souls take care not to sink too deeply into the sensible and escape quickly, they will be unharmed by the embodiment (IV.8.5, 28–29). On the other hand, he also refers to the souls' audacity, which motivates them to descend as the source of their wickedness (V.1.1, 3–4), and numerous other passages suggest that an embodied soul does best by separating itself from the body and that the intelligible realm is a much better "place" for it. He evidently thinks that it is a good thing that a worse thing comes about. We see the extreme instance of this in the case of matter as evil that was discussed in Chapter 6. It is not certain that this is self-contradictory but Plotinus nowhere addresses the general problem in full.

So the soul itself gives an image of itself, the middle soul, to the body. As we have seen, Plotinus describes this entity as a "light" distinct from the soul itself. The soul itself and its "light" are nevertheless quite close. Metaphysically the metaphor of light signifies an external act, as is also implied by calling it an image. Nevertheless, so long as we are dealing with intelligible entities and not a sensible image as in the case of the trace of soul in the body, an external act is not "cut off from" but potentially contains its source as a whole, so there is a sense in which any such image or power of soul is the soul whose power it is: the part contains the whole.

The soul itself and the "light" it gives, the middle soul, can also be said to be closely related because of the simple fact that they intermingle in the human being. There are two difficult questions of demarcation here that I have so far swept over: one question is where exactly the boundary lies between the middle soul and the pure soul and what are the criteria for drawing that boundary; another is about the relationship between the part of our soul which always remains in the intelligible and what Plotinus refers to as reason and frequently identifies with the self (see Chapter 8, Sections 3 and 4): are these one and the same or do they differ? What will be said about this in what follows is preliminary. The issues at stake here will be with us in the remainder of this chapter and indeed in the remaining chapters.

As already noted, the living being is the same as what Plotinus also calls "the compound [of body and soul]" or "the common entity." In chapter 9 of "What is the living being and what is man?" he says: "So we have distinguished what belongs to the common entity and what is proper to the soul in this way: what belongs to the joint entity is bodily or not without body, but what does not require body for its operation is proper to the soul" (I.1.9, 15–18).

The question is where exactly the line between that which requires body for its operation and what does not is to be drawn.

In this connection it should be noted that Plotinus differs from Aristotle as regards which functions directly involve the body: according to the latter, with the possible exception of the intellect, every soul function, including the operations of memory and discursive thinking, requires the use of the body. Plotinus, on the other hand holds that even if necessarily making use of the body, the process of sense-perception terminates in an act of the soul alone and that nothing above the level of sense-perception involves the direct use of the body. Thus, the power of representation and everything that comes with it—memory images, reasoning and opinions—is purely psychic, they do not use the body directly. It does not follow from this, however, that thoughts or memories about states of affairs in the sensible world are possible without bodily involvement: they are directed at the sensible world and would not have arisen in the soul without bodily involvement.

Are such phenomena as do not need bodily organs but still depend on the body in the sense that they arise from it and are directed at it or the sensible world more generally the work of the middle soul, "the light" in I.1.7, or the pure soul? A possible take on this would be to say that whatever psychic activities do not directly involve the use of bodily organs (such as sense-perception does) are the work of the undescended pure soul. This would mean that the final stage of sense-perception, which is a judgment, every memory, opinion and act of reasoning would belong to the pure soul. This interpretation meets serious obstacles, however. As we shall see more fully in the next chapter, Plotinus frequently contrasts and opposes reason to such phenomena as arise in the soul from its relationship with the body. Reason may for instance oppose an opinion that arises from the body. It would seem that such conflicting powers must belong to different parts of the soul. I tentatively conclude that when attributing something to the "soul alone" in the context of perceptual judgments, imaginations and opinions relating to the sensible sphere, Plotinus does not mean the pure rational soul but rather, as it were, the soul part of that which requires body for its operation: this is "the soul using the body" but soul nevertheless. What he means by "the soul" in connection with the human being is indeed ambiguous.

As to the second question, about the demarcation—if there is one—between the undescended part of the soul referred to in IV.8.8 and elsewhere and the reason in us, one might argue that there is no difference, as follows: to say that this part of the soul is undescended just means that it is not the subject of experiences having to do with the body; reason is not the subject of such experiences. Plotinus even makes a point of insisting that it is free from them; so there is nothing in the way of holding the undescended part of the soul to be our reason.[15] This may be so but I am tempted to think that there is a distinction to be drawn. What Plotinus conceives of as the undescended part of the soul is something which is always engaged in purely intellectual thought, and is, so to speak, always upwards-directed. It is the life of this part that the sage identifies himself with (see Chapter 9, Sections 1 and 2). As we shall see in the next chapter, reason in us draws on its intelligible roots but it is not purely upwards directed. It has for instance a power of representation into which intelligible content can be reflected and even if it does not take into itself anything from the embodiment it can act as a judge regarding states of affairs in the sensible realm, and as a ruler over the living being. Plotinus is not thinking of such roles when he speaks of the part of our soul that never leaves the intelligible realm.

3 The functions of the living being

Plotinus' psychology of the embodied soul is shaped by two antithetical concerns. On the one hand, there is his general aversion to upwards causation: nothing lower should affect or change anything higher. This concern is especially strong in the case of the soul, which is the only intelligible entity to be in direct touch with the sensible realm. The prospect of the soul being affected by the body threatens its immortality: if the soul really can be affected at all, it may be affected so much that it no longer exists (cf. III.6.1, 29–30). The impassibility of the soul is a primary concern in all of Plotinus' psychological writings and very explicitly addressed in the treatise "On the impassibility of things without body" (III.6. (26)).

On the other hand, there is Plotinus' firm belief that embodiment is a risky affair, in fact quite dangerous for the soul. Clearly, he thinks that the experience of the body and the sensible realm may mark the soul. It is also difficult to see how some sort of upwards effect from bodies could be avoided: feelings such as hunger, thirst and pain appear to have their beginning in the body but reach up to the soul and external sense-perception starts in an external sensible object and ends in the soul. Thus, the task becomes that of giving a plausible account of sense-perception and the emotions such that the soul is somehow involved in the affections from below without however being changed itself.

Plotinus' general strategy in tackling these issues is to make distinctions. Sense-perceptions, feelings such as hunger and pain, and the emotions belong to the living being, not to the pure soul. But even within the living being distinction must be made between what is done by the living body and what by the soul part of the compound. What can be genuinely affected so as to be changed is the living body. The soul part is not changed in these affections but it may bear their mark in a sense that we shall explore later on. In the two following sections we shall consider how Plotinus seeks to come unscathed out of this predicament. At the same time we shall have occasion to dig deeper into aspects of Plotinus' views on the human soul. Let us first address external perception.

3.1 External sense-perception: Overview

Sense-perception, in particular vision, is mentioned a great number of times in the *Enneads*. Plotinus evidently took a keen interest in it. Part of the reason is no doubt that he found visual metaphors apt to capture the nature of Intellect's intuitive thought. He, however, also shows interest in sense-perception for its own sake. Evidence for this is the fact that he devoted a short treatise, "On sight, or how distant objects appear small," II.8, to a particular question concerning vision and that more than half of "On the problems of soul (III)," IV.5, is devoted to the nature of the transmission from object to eye. Yet, there is only one systematic general account of sense-perception in the *Enneads*, and it is not a particularly long one: essentially one chapter, "On the problems of soul (II)," IV.4.23, only 49 lines.

We shall turn to this account very shortly but let us first briefly address the question why there is sense-perception. The answer lies in the nature of the sublunary sensible region: it is volatile and contains unforeseen events. The animals in it must move about, and they must locate what they need for their sustenance and be able to avoid dangers to their bodies. But souls are not threatened and they do not need food or drink. Sense-perception is a capacity of soul that is there not for the good of the soul but for the good of the body. It is because soul is in charge of a given body in the sublunary world with the needs such bodies have that it is endowed with this capacity (IV.4.24).

Plotinus begins his account in IV.4.23 as follows:

> We must suppose that the perception (*aisthēsis*) of sense objects is for the soul or the living being an act of apprehension (*antilēpsis*), in which the soul grasps the quality (*poiotēs*) attaching to bodies and assimilates their forms (*eidē*).
> (IV.4.23, 1–4)

This may be taken as a rudimentary definition of sense-perception. It is worth noting that he says "the soul or the living being."[16] Now, as Plotinus will argue as this chapter unwinds, sense-perception is evidently a function of soul that involves the body. This makes it by definition a function of the composite or living being: functions that require both soul and body are referred to this entity (cf. I.1.9, 15 ff.). He wishes, however, to maintain that even if sense-perception necessarily involves the body, it is nevertheless the soul that strictly speaking perceives (see below). This may be the reason for the disjunctive statement "the soul or the living being." The passage continues:

> Well, then, the soul will either apprehend alone by itself or in company with something else. But how can it do this when it is alone and by itself? For when it is by itself it apprehends what is in itself, and is pure thought. If it also apprehends other things [i.e. sensibles], it must first have taken possession of them as well, either by becoming assimilated to them, or by keeping company with something which has been assimilated. But it cannot be assimilated while it remains in itself. For how could a point be assimilated to a line? For even the intelligible line would not assimilate to the sensible one, nor would the

intelligible fire or man assimilate to the sense-perceived fire or man. ... But when the soul is alone, even if it is possible for it to direct its attention to the world of sense, it will end with an understanding of the intelligible; what is perceived by sense will escape it, as it has nothing with which to grasp it.

(IV.4.23, 4–15)

This passage shows very clearly that Plotinus sees sense-perception as the crossing of an ontological gap between the sensible and the intelligible realms. There are at least two problems involved here. First, when alone, the soul does not apprehend sensibles. It is an intelligible thing itself and directs its gaze at intelligibles. Yet, through sense-perception the soul comes to be aware of things and states of affair in the sensible realm. How is that possible? Would not that be contrary to the soul's nature? Secondly, assuming that this is possible somehow, sense-perception is evidently a causal process that starts out in an extended body and ends in the incorporeal soul. How is this not an instance of a lower item in the hierarchy affecting a higher one? How is this not an affecting of the soul? Here is Plotinus' answer:

There cannot, therefore, be only these two things, the external object and the soul, for the soul would not be affected. But what is affected must be a third thing, and this is what receives the form. This must be sympathetic with and similarly affected and of one matter with the sense-object, and it must be this which is affected, whereas the other nature [the soul] knows; and its affection must be of such a kind that it retains something of that which produced it, but is not the same as it, but as it is between the producer of the affection and the soul, it must have an affection which lies between the sensible and the intelligible, a proportional mean somehow linking the extremes to each other, with the capacity of at once receiving and transmitting, suitable to be assimilated to each of the extremes. For since it is the organ of awareness (*gnōsis*), it must not be the same either as the knower or what is to be known but suitable to be assimilated to each, to the external object by being affected, and to the internal knower by the fact that its affection becomes forms. If, certainly, what we are saying is sound, sense-perceptions must take place through bodily organs.

(IV.4.23, 19–34)

There are several distinct comments to be made on this passage, which we shall pursue in order.

1   We see here the Aristotelian idea that perception is a matter of the percipient receiving the form of the object (cf. *On the Soul* II, 24a17–19). This is what is involved in the assimilation spoken of here: the organ is affected by the external object, takes on its quality (see IV.4.23, 1–4 quoted above) and passes this on to the soul. The passage strongly suggests, however, that the way the quality is taken on is not simply a matter of ordinary physical affection as when fire heats the stone: Plotinus holds that, though retaining something of the agent, i.e. the quality of the external body, the affection is something intermediate between sensible and intelligible natures. It is not that the eye becomes green in just the same way as the grass that is seen is green. What would such an affection be? As I argue in Emilsson (1988: ch. 4), and still believe, I think it must be something like a sensation, the phenomenal presence of bodily qualities to the sense. This is arguably something one could conceive of as intermediate between the sensible and the intelligible: a visual sensation, the presence of something colored to our eyes is something extended but without mass.

2   Later in "On the problems of soul" Plotinus has interesting things to say about the mode of transmission from external object to eye in the case of the distant senses, vision and hearing. He rejects both accounts that assume a progressive affection of a medium such as air between the seen object and the eye and accounts such as that of the Stoics that invoke a visual cone going from eye to object.[17] In both cases he gives as a reason that these theories fail to account for the directness and immediacy of sense-perception. Instead, he proposes that the transmission from object to eye or ear takes place by means of sympathy (see p. 161 ff.). This is what is alluded to in the passage where Plotinus says that the sense-organ must be "sympathetic with"

the object, and "similarly affected." He also says that the organ and the object must be "of one matter." This is concise and obscure but what he has in mind is presumably the fact that sympathy presupposes a similarity of disposition between the objects that stand in a sympathetic relation. As a matter of fact he thinks, with Plato in *Timaeus* 45b–d, that there is some sort of light in the eyes. It is less obvious what the similarity would be in the case of a sonorous object and the ear, and Plotinus does not tell us.

3 A second assimilation is involved: that of the organ to the intelligible nature of the soul. Plotinus thinks that the gap between the sensible and the intelligible is bridged, somehow, in the organ of sense: this is the subject of an affection that is already of a special kind; this affection then is transformed into a form in the soul. The work of the soul is further described as a judgment: "We say that sense-perceptions are not affections but activities and judgments concerned with affections; affections belong to something else, for instance, to the body qualified in a particular way, but the judgment belongs to the soul, and the judgment is not an affection" (III.6.1, 1–4; see also IV.4.23, 38 ff.; VI.4.6, 8 ff.).[18] There is every reason to identify the form in the soul and the judgment. A paradigmatic case of a sense-perception is a judgment of the type "this is a human being" or "there is a red book." This amounts to the activation of forms in the soul. These forms, sometimes referred to as "impressions" (*typoi*) are something intelligible rather than sensible. As Plotinus says in I.1.7 (quoted on p. 232, see also IV.3.26, 29–32), the impressions produced from sense-perceptions in the living being "are already intelligible entities."[19]

4 As we have seen, Plotinus says that sense-perceptions are activities and judgments of the soul. We also saw that in I.1.7 he says it is the living being that perceives. So is it the soul or the living being that perceives? The answer is both. The soul involved is the counterpart to the qualified body in constituting the living being. This corresponds to "the soul using the body" (see p. 229) as opposed to the soul alone. More precisely, that which perceives and makes perceptual judgments is sense: sight, hearing, touch, senses of smell and taste (cf. VI.4.6, 16–18).

These are powers of soul that make use of the living body to do their work.

5 What would a paradigmatic perceptual judgment be according to Plotinus? We saw that in sense-perception the soul "understands the quality attaching to bodies and is impressed with their forms" (IV.4.23, 2–4). Aristotle and even more prominently Alexander of Aphrodisias have a notable doctrine about the five special senses. While recognizing each of these as attached to a proper type of sensible quality, they see as well a common sense, which senses sensible features not peculiar to any given one of the special senses and is, at least in Alexander's case, a unifying common meeting place for all the other senses.[20] This common sense has dropped out in Plotinus and even if he holds that the sensation of colors and light pertains specifically to vision, of sounds to hearing, and so forth (cf. II.8.1, 12–16), he doesn't operate systematically with a doctrine of the special senses and proper sensibles. For him there is just one power of sense-perception. I shall return to this topic below. As indicated in the opening lines of IV.4.23 cited above, qualities are what sense-perception immediately grasps. It is, however, not restricted to judgments about the quality of things: clearly a judgment such as "this is a human being" (V.3.3, 1) or "here is a face" (IV.7.6, 7) counts for him as a possible judgment of perception. Such judgments would, however, not count as a sense-perception in every context: in order to count as a perception, the judgment must not involve an inference, at least not a conscious inference, and it must be of something currently present to some one of the senses (see further Emilsson 1988: 123–124).

6 Are perceptual judgments necessarily conscious? I used to think so but I am no longer so sure after reading Chiaradonna (2012). I shall postpone the discussion of this until we deal with sense-perception in relation to the faculties above it, the faculty of representation and discursive reason, in the next chapter.

7 In III.6.1 (cited in comment (3)) Plotinus says that sense-perceptions are activities rather than affections, passive undergoings. Many philosophers, both before Plotinus and after, have on the contrary described sense-perception as an

entirely passive affair. A little later he even says that they are not genuine changes or alterations (III.6.1, 12–15). Let us take a closer look at these claims. How is sense-perception an activity rather than something passive? It might be pointed out against attributing this view to him that he does call the items that arise in the soul in sense-perception impressions (*typoi*) and speaks of the soul *receiving* the form of the external body perceived. Even if he assures us that these impressions are something intelligible and not at all like the stamping of wax that philosophers talk about, the very language of impressions and receiving may suggest a rather passive affair.[21] In response to this, we may point out that he also says that sense-perceptions are judgments, and that, intuitively, judging is an activity rather than a merely passive experience. That may be so but two obvious questions immediately crop up: what really is the distinction between activities (or actualizations) and genuine changes on which so much seems to depend here? Why are individual acts of perception not changes or alterations?

Plotinus is of course not denying the obvious, that the soul is in some way different when it arrives at seeing a red tomato from what it was before and after it saw it. He writes:

> Just as sight exists both potentially and actually without changing in essence, and its actualization is not an alteration (since at one and the same time it approaches that to which it is essentially related and is it by knowing, and discerns without being affected), similarly the reasoning part exists and perceives in relation to Intellect—this is its power of understanding. There is no imprint of a seal; rather it possesses what it sees—yet does not possess it in that nothing is stored up from the act of seeing, like some shape in wax.
> (III.6.2, 34–41; Fleet's 1995 trans.)

There are several points to note here. The first sentence expresses the view which Plotinus has stated more explicitly a few lines before, that actualizations are not changes, because in them the agent simply becomes itself, realizes its own nature (cf. Aristotle,

On the Soul II, 416b2). The following phrase, "at one and the same time it approaches that to which it is essentially related," is especially obscure. The meaning is presumably that actualization, as opposed to alteration, is fully completed at every instant: if I now see a red tomato, I have already seen a red tomato.[22] Then there is the view which Plotinus expresses somewhat oddly by saying that that which sees both possesses and does not possess what it sees. Considerations such as the following may explain his meaning here: genuine alterations and changes generally imply that that which has changed now has a property which it didn't have before the change and, more importantly in our context, which it still has when the change is completed (see VI.1.22, 1–2); if something turns red or moves to the left, it follows by virtue of the logic of the verbs that it is red and is on the left when the change is completed (which is not to imply that they stay this way forever). Something has to be done to these things in order to make them not-red and not-on-the-left. On the other hand, to come to see something, and in general to enter into what Aristotle and Plotinus following him call activities, is not to acquire a new property: if I have been seeing something, nothing follows by the logic of the verb "to see" about my state at the moment when I stopped seeing it: the vision hasn't left me with a property that requires some action to get rid of. It hasn't left me with a genuine new property at all, except in the trivial sense that it is true of me now, after having seen the tomato, that I have seen it (see Waterlow 1982: 188 ff.). Of course, the vision may leave me terrified and I may remember it all too clearly, but that is not a part of the logic of seeing as such, but depends on other causal connections within my soul. On the other hand, obviously the seer enters into a new state on seeing new things, and what she currently sees she also currently, in a sense, has.

3.2 What do we perceive?

The account of sense-perception in the important chapter, IV.4.23, strongly suggests some sort of realism about sense-perception: by "realism" I mean the view that the object of sense-perception, what is perceived, is an external object rather than something in the percipient. Plotinus says towards the end of the last long quote from IV.4.23 above that the organ of knowledge,[23] "must not be the same either as the knower or what is to be known but suitable to be assimilated to each, to the external object by being affected, and to the internal knower by the fact that its affection becomes a form," clearly implying that what is known is the external thing. This is confirmed by other passages. In the short treatise "On sense-perception and memory" Plotinus' commitment to direct realism is very explicit indeed. Arguing against the view that in vision we receive impressions (typoi) of the things seen, he says:

> Most important of all: if we received impressions (typoi) of what we see, there will be no possibility of looking at the actual things we see, but we shall look at images (indalmata) and shadows (skias) of the objects of sight, so that the objects themselves will be different from the things we see.
> (IV.6.1, 29–32)

The impressions at stake here are physical impressions "like the mark of a seal-ring on wax" (IV.6.1, 20–21), and not the intelligible impressions Plotinus sometimes refers to in the context of sense-perception, reasoning and the like (cf. p. 246). This passage from "On sense-perception and memory" strongly suggests that the position he wishes to maintain is not only a form of realism but direct realism: we *directly* grasp an external object or properties of such. The passage and its context indicate that he thinks that theories according to which the percipient is physically stamped with some sort of replica of the object utterly fail in this regard. The same sort of concern seems to underlie his views on transmission between object and eye in "On the problems of soul (III)" (IV.5.1–4): he criticizes theories of others that invoke transitive impressions on a medium in between the object and the eye for failing to account for, in his view, the evident directness of vision.

His positive account, which is primarily to be found in chapter 3 of "On the problems of soul (III)" (IV.5), dismisses entirely the notion of transmission through an affected medium in favor of an account in terms of sympathy. The details of this positive account are not spelled out but I think the following points, which are either explicitly or implicitly stated, hold true: (a) The sympathy in vision and hearing too, depends, like sympathy generally, on the unity of all souls and on similarity. Thus, we can see the colors of things because of the unity of our soul with that of the cosmos and a certain similarity of disposition that holds between the organ of sense and the sensed object. (b) The Aristotelian doctrine that sense-perception is a matter of transmitting and receiving the form of the object is incorporated into the sympathy account: the forms (qualities) of the objects are present in the intermediate space by means of sympathy. The kind of sympathy involved in vision is hindered by solid bodies in between the object and the eye; that is why we do not see things behind our head! (c) Considering the contrast between the sympathy account and the doctrines about transmission between the object and the eye Plotinus rejects, it is tempting to see the sympathy account as a theory maintaining a direct contact between the eye and external qualities.

However this may be, one may wonder how well the intermediate stages Plotinus introduces square with direct realism. There is the external object and there is the affection of the sense-organ, which is somehow transformed into an intelligible entity in the soul part of the compound of body and soul. How is it not the affection of the organ rather than the quality of the external object which is the direct object of apprehension? I think Plotinus is helped to his realist position by his general view that the same things may exist at different levels of the hierarchy of being (see Chapter 2, p. 67). Thus, the quality the eye takes on, the phenomenal color, is in a sense the same item as the external bodily color, just in a different ontological mode. That is to say, the color that the sense-organs take on, though different from the color as it exists out there in the mass of the extended object, is nevertheless ontologically speaking the same color as the one in the object. The internalization of the form is not a matter of having a new entity inside one's soul but rather a matter of, as it were, promoting the external form to a more intelligible status. So if the forms the eyes take on are the very form of the external object, though in a different ontological mode, and if the soul is aware of this form as it exists from the point of view of the eye, we do indeed see the very things themselves. Or so Plotinus wishes to have it, if the account given of his doctrine here holds.

I have previously argued at length for a realist position on behalf of Plotinus (Emilsson 1988; cf. also 1995, 1996 and 2007: 124 ff.). Despite receiving some criticisms, I have not significantly changed my views on this or other aspects of his account of sense-perception (see, however, p. 247).[24] Some interpreters, both before and after my book, read Plotinus in such a way that he discards the idea that we have any access to mind-independent external qualities. Such a view has as a consequence that the things we immediately perceive are not objectively such as we perceive them. In her very interesting paper, Magrin (2010) argues that in objective reality there is nothing but the perceiving subject and the rational formulas, the productive *logoi* (cf. p. 214). The sensible qualities are to be identified with the *logoi*, which belong to the intelligible rather than the sensible order: whiteness, for example, is a rational formula but this is not what we see; rather, what we see is an affection made by such a *logos* on us, the appearance it takes for us (see Magrin 2010: 273 ff.).[25] While admitting that such an interpretation has some virtues—it, for instance, seems to sit well with claims to the effect that "what is seen in matter is false" (III.6.7, 38–39), even if I think these claims admit of a different and in my view more satisfactory interpretation—I find it very difficult to square with Plotinus' general treatment of qualities. He says a great deal about qualities as we saw in Chapter 6; he gives the sensible form or quality a certain ontological status, something belonging to the body and partaking in its divisibility though being one in form. In saying things of this sort he is evidently not talking about the rational formulas, but of their products, the sensible qualities. In none of these discussions is there any hint that the quality is something that first arises in the process of sense-perception. If that was really Plotinus' view, one would have expected him to say so or at least unambiguously hint that this was his view.

A passage that has been cited in support of antirealism or at least indirect realism is I.1.7, 9–12, a continuation of the passage we set out from in this chapter.[26] Here Plotinus says that "soul's power of perception need not be of sense-objects but rather it must be apprehensive of impressions produced by sense-perception in the living being: for these are already intelligible entities." In Emilsson (1988: 114 ff.) I argued that by "the soul's power of sense-perception" Plotinus has in mind extra-sensory apprehension such as we see at work in discursive reasoning and memory and not the direct apprehension of states of affairs in the external sensible world. Hence, the statement is not to be seen as being in conflict with a direct realism about sense-perception: the word most often translated as "sense-perception," *aisthēsis*, need not mean that it can be just any sort of apprehension. I have since slightly modified my view on the interpretation of these lines though not in the direction of antirealism. The ground for discussing this is, however, not fully prepared yet: we first have to see more of Plotinus' account of the human soul. I shall resume discussion of this passage in the next chapter.

A passage that is often discussed in connection with the question of perceptual realism in Plotinus is V.5.1, especially lines 15–19. Here Plotinus says that "for even if it is agreed that what sense-perception is to grasp is in the underlying sensible substrates, what is known by sense-perception is an image (*eidōlon*) of the thing, and sense-perception does not apprehend the thing itself: for that remains outside." At first sight this may sound like a clear expression of skepticism about our ability to know external objects through sense-perception. If this is what Plotinus wishes to maintain here, that would be an isolated case of a view that stands in clear conflict with his explicit general message. Luckily, there are other ways of reading these lines: "image" can be taken in its Platonic sense, meaning an "image" in an ontological sense; this is contrasted with the "thing itself," which in this case presumably is the internal rational formula productive of the thing's qualities, which is what sense-perception grasps.[27] This is not an *ad hoc* solution. Not only would this be a well-attested Platonic and Plotinian use of the term for image (*eidōlon*), the beginning of the next chapter of V.5, which summarizes what has been established so far, goes a long way to providing a confirmation of this interpretation: here Plotinus, in all likelihood referring back to the disputed lines in chapter 1, contrasts the knowledge of "what each thing is," with "knowledge of each thing's qualities, since [in that case] we should have an image and a trace and not the things themselves" (V.5.2, 7–8). The Plotinian take on the distinction between the quality and "what each thing is" is founded on a similar distinction in Plato's Seventh Letter 343e–344a, which, of course, has nothing to do with perceptual skepticism.

3.3 Feelings and emotions

Many of Plotinus' predecessors on whom he drew discussed the affections of the soul or emotions extensively in their works.[28] For them the importance of this subject lay not least in its relevance to their doctrines of motivation and, thereby, to ethics. Aristotle for instance defined vice as an excess with respect to passions and actions (*Nicomachean Ethics* II, 1107a4–5); for the Stoics the passions, being irrational and unnatural impulses, are the primary causes of irrational and unnatural actions (see Long and Sedley 1987: 65). Plotinus refers to emotions a number of times, and for him too they are of great moral significance: the emotions and related opinions and imaginations associated with our bodily existence are a major hindrance to autonomous rational life. Nevertheless, like in the case of sense-perception, extensive detailed treatments are few.

Emotions raise the same problem as sense-perception in that they too seem to involve causation from below. The same holds for feelings such as physical pain, which is not normally listed among the affections of the soul, even if it is an affection of something, a *pathos*. The affections of the soul properly so called, emotions such as anger and fear, pose certain additional difficulties, however, that are not present in sense-perception or physical pain. First, while both sense-perception and anger may be passive experiences in the sense that they come about more or less involuntarily, anger and other emotions are, according to common sense, in addition liable to change the soul's dispositions, even to corrupt it morally. Secondly, in maintaining the soul's impassivity in the emotions, Plotinus has to fight views that are deeply ingrained in his language and philosophical tradition. Impassivity is in Greek *apatheia*, and to ascribe *apatheia* to the soul is of course to imply that the soul doesn't *paschein*, isn't affected, and doesn't undergo *pathē*, affections. But the very expression for the emotions in Plotinus' Greek at least since Aristotle, *ta pathē tēs psychēs*, "the affections of the soul," implies that indeed the emotions are affections of the soul. And the tradition concurs: Plato leaves little doubt that fears, desires and the like are affections of the soul (see *Phaedo* 83c–d; cf. *Timaeus* 42a–b, 69c). Aristotle speaks of affections as one of three types of phenomena in the soul (*Nicomachean Ethics* II, 1105b20) and the Stoics define the passions as "an irrational movement or excessive impulse in the soul, contrary to nature" (Stobaeus, 2.88, 8–9 = Long and Sedley 1987: 65A).

So Plotinus' concern with the so-called affections of the soul is largely motivated by his firm belief that despite the appearances and the conventions of language the soul is not genuinely affected at all in the so-called affections of the soul. Much of what he has to say about the subject aims at making this paradoxical claim plausible. In the account that follows I shall mainly be concerned with the various moves Plotinus makes to accomplish this. There are three main passages in the *Enneads*, where the affections are discussed at some length. These are the first five chapters of "On the impassivity of the things without body," III.6. (26), chapters 18 to 21, and (continuing the same discussion) chapter 28 of the "On the problems of Soul (II)," and "What is the living being and what is man?," I.1. (53). There are no serious discrepancies in doctrine between these treatises but the concerns and emphases are somewhat different. In III.6 Plotinus' immediate objective is to argue for the impassivity of the soul. This is also a topic of I.1, but here the main concern is to sort out which functions are to be attributed to the organism and which belong to the individual soul, and to account for the relationship between us, i.e. the self, and the organism and what belongs to it. The passages in IV.4 are more of the nature of descriptive psychology.

We shall proceed as follows. We start with what may be the most difficult case for Plotinus, namely the phenomenon of physical pain. Desires arising from the body such as hunger and thirst follow roughly the same pattern. After this we shall address the emotions properly speaking, including anger, fear and desire.

Plotinus assigns pleasure and pain to the qualified body that has a trace of soul (IV.4.18). A mere lifeless body may of course be affected, e.g. cut or burnt, but its affection would not be a pain or a pleasure. In a living body the physical change as such (as we would say) belongs to the body qua mere body, but the pain belongs to it as a living body. It arises from the fact that the qualified body is one which has entered into a certain union with something else, a type of soul, and strives to maintain it. The union is however always incomplete, since the body can receive only a trace of the soul and not the soul itself, and insecure (IV.4.18, 21–32). Pain occurs when some part of the body is deprived of its trace of soul, and pleasure when this trace is restored. We ourselves, who are different from the living body, perceive its pain or pleasure through our perceptive soul: "The whole soul perceives the affection in the body without being affected itself" (IV.4.19, 12–13). In support of the claim that the soul itself is unaffected Plotinus says that since the (perceptive) soul is present as a whole everywhere in the body but the pain is evidently localized in a particular part, the soul itself cannot be affected, for in that case the pain would be felt everywhere. On the contrary, it is for instance the finger which has the pain and the man has it too because the man's finger does (IV.4.19, 19–20). The soul perceives the pains and pleasures, but the perceptions, which are a form of awareness or knowledge (*gnōsis*), are different from what is perceived. One should not say that perception of pain is pain but awareness of pain (*gnōsis odynēs*) (IV.4.19, 26–27); perceptions and awareness are not affections. What he is saying here is his response to the suggestion that the meaning of the expression "x aches (*algei*)" actually includes the immediately consequent perception, a suggestion he clearly wishes to resist (IV.4.19, 23–24).[29]

Plotinus' main line of thought in IV.4.18–19 is in my view quite interesting, counter-intuitive though it may be according to our so-called Cartesian intuitions. He is clearly allowing for the logical possibility that pain may occur without being perceived, though he also makes a point of noting that as a rule it does not escape notice (IV.4.19, 24–27). He seems thus to be committed to saying that anesthetic drugs or other pain treatments do not really remove the pain, but bring it about that we are no longer aware of it.

In an important sense Plotinus tries to assimilate the perception of pleasure and pain (and, as we shall see, this is carried over to the account of desire and anger) to external sense perception. In a different passage and context he explicitly says that the perception of what goes on within the body is of externals, meaning evidently that the object of this kind of perception is external to the power that perceives (V.3.2, 4–6). Thus, we, our souls, are dissociated from the qualified body so that perception of what goes on within the body is perception of states or occurrences external to the perceiving soul just like the color or figure we see are external to the soul that perceives it.[30] The pain I perceive in my finger is not just a sign of a disruption in the tissue any more than, say, the green I see is a sign of the color green: the pain is the disruption itself as perceived by me.

The account of pain and pleasure in "On the problems of soul" is followed by discussions of desire (chapters 19 and 20) and anger (chapter 28). Nothing is said about other emotions. This is explained by the fact that Plotinus here follows *Timaeus* 69d ff., where Plato talks about "the third form of soul," to which belong appetite and the irascible element (anger). Plotinus presumably identifies this third form of soul with the vegetative.[31] Plato describes the third form as mortal. Plotinus does not follow him in that. As we have seen, the activities of the vegetative soul are the trace of soul, the biological or physiological processes in the body in virtue of which it is alive. This trace is indeed perishable but not the soul that produces it. It is easy enough to see a connection between the vegetative power and impulses such as hunger, thirst, sexual desire, anger and fear: these impulses are all related to the maintenance, protection, defense and reproduction of living bodies. Moreover, in each of these feelings and emotions the living body is moved: the boiling of blood in anger, blushing, trembling and so forth. As we saw in Section 1 above, these are external acts of the vegetative soul in the qualified body.

In discussing desire Plotinus evidently has in mind primarily bodily desires such as hunger and thirst. Bodily desire starts from the living body, presumably some organic state analogous to the disruption which is physical pain. In desire too

> it is sense-perception which acquires knowledge and the soul nearby, which we call nature, which gives the trace of soul to the body; nature knows the explicit desire which is the final stage of that which begins in the body, and sense-perception knows the image, and the soul [i.e. the individual soul] either provides what is desired ... or resists.
>
> (IV.4.20, 14–18)

Though this passage leaves something to be desired with respect to clarity, there seem to be four stages to be distinguished:[32] (1) the state of the organism, which constitutes the bodily origin of desire; (2) nature's awareness of this state, which involves the formation of an image (*phantasia*); (3) sense-perception's awareness of the image; (4) the acceptance or resistance of the desire on the part of the individual soul. As he continues this discussion, Plotinus goes on to assert that there are in fact two desires at work in every case of a fully fledged desire. Since the qualified body and the vegetative soul are two different things,

> it is necessary that nature should not begin desire; but it is the qualified body which is affected in particular ways and suffers in desiring the opposites of what it undergoes, pleasure instead of pain, and sufficiency instead of want; but nature is like a mother, trying to make out the wishes of the sufferer ... and searching for the remedy, [nature] attaches itself by its search to the desire of what is affected, and the consummation of the desire passes from the body to nature. So one might say, perhaps, that the desiring comes from the body itself—one might call it preliminary desiring (*proepithymia*)[33] and urge (*prothymia*)—but that nature desires from and through something else, and it is another soul which provides what is desired or does not.
> (IV.4.20, 25–36)

One question that arises in connection with these passages has to do with the division of labor between the faculties: it seems odd that some kind of cognitive function is attributed to the vegetative soul, as the first passage explicitly says and the second one suggests. Another question is, given that nature is aware of the bodily state, what need is there for sense-perception to know it too? Isn't the role of sense-perception superfluous here? As to the first of these questions, let it suffice to say that there are more passages affirming that the lower soul operates with images of some sort.[34] In III.6.4, 18–23, he describes such images as "indistinct" and "unjudged" (*anepikritos*). In general Plotinus doesn't have any difficulty with cognitive or quasi-cognitive states that are not distinctively conscious.[35] Thus, we may suppose that the images in question are not images that we must be conscious of. This may provide us with an answer to the second question: we certainly *may* become aware of our bodily desires; when we do, it is through our sensitive faculty, which apprehends the psycho-somatic states of the organism.

But why two desires? The living body has needs, desires, aversions and so forth. This does not mean, however, that the living body as such has what we would call conscious mental life. Its life consists in its goal-directed behavior and biological processes (cf. p. 231). We see from the end of the latter quote above that he qualifies the attribution of desire to the body by calling it "preliminary desire"[36] and "urge." A desire such as hunger starts as an urge in the body. As Plotinus sees it, it is the body that craves to be replenished, not the soul (nature) that desires to replenish the body. As the passage makes clear, there is such desire in the soul too, but this latter desire is based on a prior urge of the body itself. The soul doesn't desire or need food for itself (IV.4.21, 19–21). It wouldn't desire or need food for the body unless the body itself craved it. He further points out in support of separating the bodily and psychic form of desire that a bodily urge may be present without a corresponding desire in the soul: "The desire reaches a certain point, as far as it is in the qualified body, but nature does not attach itself to the desire" (IV.4.21, 10–12). Thus, the physiological affection and urge of hunger may be present and, I presume, even sensory awareness of this affection, without the emergence of a desire for food in the soul.

It is still unclear, however, what the image spoken of in IV.4.20, 17 is actually supposed to be, and in general what the stages Plotinus distinguishes correspond to in our experience. Is the image for instance what corresponds in the soul to the apprehension of the physiological affection so that in the case of hunger, for example, it is what we feel in the region of the stomach when we are hungry? Or is the image a propositional or at least a conceptualized item corresponding to expressions such as "I am hungry!," "Some food by all means!"? The evidence is not clear at all. The first lines of the passage quoted from IV.4.20 above may suggest that the physiological affection is apprehended both by sense-perception and the vegetative soul, in which case it is natural to take the apprehension of the affection in the stomach associated with hunger to be the work of sense-perception, whereas the initial apprehension of the same physiological affection as a craving for food would be the work of the vegetative soul. If this is so, sense-perception would have a double role in the process because, as the end of the passage shows, it is sense-perception that takes over an image presented by the vegetative soul. This image is something the rational soul can either go along with or reject. Alternatively, we may suppose that sense-perception has just a single role. Its apprehension of the image which has arisen in the vegetative soul would include the apprehension of the affection, and the perceptive soul somehow translates this into an articulate demand for food. In any case, at this final stage, at which reason may step in and grant or deny, there is an image with a conceptual if not propositional content.

Plotinus turns to the irascible element in IV.4.28. He suggests that there are two types of anger. One type arises from above, from a rational judgment that some wrong has been done, and as a result the bile and blood are aroused. (He does not say so but presumably bodily desire may start from above too: it is common enough experience that the sight or smell of delicious food wakens hunger in the body.) On the other hand, there is anger that has its origin in a non-rational boiling of blood or bile, which gives rise to an image which may drag reason along (IV.4.28, 47–48). What sort of case does he have in mind here?

Plotinus is not thinking of a case where the physiological condition of the organism simply is such that the blood is seething. That would not be true anger, which includes an impulse to attack the presumed cause of the presumed evil. He recognizes this point in this very context: he argues that even if trees have a vegetative soul, they do not have the irascible element; firstly, they lack blood and bile but even if they had this but lacked sense-perception, they would only be capable of "seething and a kind of irritation." If they had sense perception as well, there would be a drive against the cause (see IV.4.28, 59–64). As the subsequent discussion suggests, he is thinking of cases where blood boils not as a result of a rationally formed judgment, but as an instinctive reaction to pain or irritation. Still some sort of judgment seems to be involved: that a given person or thing caused the pain and that this cause should be attacked.

In III.6 Plotinus generalizes the point about the different origins of the emotions:

> Some of the affections [i.e. affections of the soul, emotions] arise as the result of opinions, as when someone being of the opinion that he is going to die, feels fear, or, thinking that some

good is going to come to him, is pleased; the opinion is in one part, and the affection is stirred up in another; but some of them are of a sort to take the lead without our volition[37] to produce the opinion in the part of the soul whose natural function it is to have opinions. Now it has been said that the opinion leaves the opining [power] unmoved; but the fear which originates from the opinion, coming down from above, in its turn, from the opinion, in a way gives a kind of understanding to the part of the soul which is said to fear. What does this fear produce? Disturbance and shock, they say,[38] over the evil that is expected.
(III.6.4, 8–18)

By the second type of case Plotinus considers here, where the emotion is said to take the lead, he presumably has primarily in mind bodily desires such as hunger and thirst, which start in the body and end in the opinion of the soul that one must eat or drink.

It is evident from the discussion of the elimination of affections in chapter 5 of "On virtues" (I.2. (19) 5) that even persons with a purified virtuous soul may have an element of spontaneous affection: anger, fear and desires for food, drink and sex are mentioned. For such persons it is primarily the physiological affections in the organism that are spontaneous, but the subsequent image in the vegetative soul or even the individual soul's assessment may on occasion also be. The implication is that this happens frequently in unpurified souls. That is to say, the physiological disturbance produces an opinion in the soul without our volition, as Plotinus puts it here in the passage just cited. This is presumably an opinion about what to do in the circumstances: "I should eat that chocolate!" or "that chocolate would be really good to have right now!" for instance. The fact that he says that these opinions are produced "without our volition" indicates that Plotinus does not think of the former kind mentioned, e.g. the fear arising from the opinion that one is going to die, as spontaneous. Such affections depend on opinions that we form and endorse and should be amenable to rational persuasion.

We can summarize Plotinus' account of feelings and emotions as follows: (1) Feelings of physical pleasures and pains have their origin in the qualified body which is either being restored or deprived of its natural form. The perception of this, which is the work of the soul element in the soul–body compound, is not an affection but an activity which leaves the soul unchanged. (2) Desires such as hunger and thirst typically have their origin in the qualified body, though nothing speaks against their being aroused by an opinion or mental image. The same holds for anger, though this will typically be aroused by a perception and thought. (3) Many emotions start in the soul, in an opinion, which gives rise to bodily changes that in turn are perceived by the soul.

So Plotinus maintains that the soul is not affected in the so-called affections of the soul and we have seen his reasons for this claim. How plausible is his view? After arguing forcefully in the first four chapters of III.6 for the impassivity of the soul in the emotions—the soul in question being the soul that makes up the compound with the body—in chapter 5 he asks: "What need is there to seek to make the soul free from affections (*apathē poiein*) through philosophy, if it doesn't suffer (*paschein*) them in the first place?" (III.6.5, 1–2). Kristeller (1929: 40) saw in this sentence a genuine paradox. Actually, there is no real paradox here.[39] The words "free from affections" and "doesn't suffer them" do not describe the same phenomenon. Plotinus has not argued that the phenomena that are called affections of the soul do not occur. They do, and the soul is involved in them, but it is not affected by them. This is what he has argued and this is what "doesn't suffer them in the first place" refers to. The task of making the soul free from affection through philosophy is the task of eliminating this involvement, i.e. purifying the soul. Since the soul's involvement is essential to the affections, this is tantamount to eliminating the affections. So this becomes the task of making the soul such that it doesn't have thoughts, opinions and concerns that give rise to the emotions. I shall have more to say about this elimination of the affections in Chapters 9 and 10.

There is, however, yet another sense in which the soul is free from affection. To explain this we must first address a persistent ambiguity of the word "soul" in Plotinus: in the passages we have been considering, where he argues for the impassivity of the soul, the soul in question is the one which is a partner of the soul–body compound or the living being. Some functions or aspects of functions of this compound do not involve the body or sensible nature directly. We saw this in the case of sense-perception where in the final stage, activities Plotinus identifies with sense-perception itself are acts of the soul only. A fortiori opinions and images arising from or giving rise to the emotions do not directly involve the body. These belong to the middle soul and the living being all the same and involve the body and the sensible realm indirectly, even if they are sometimes said to be the work of the soul alone, which may cause misunderstanding: we may easily think that Plotinus is talking about the pure, individual soul. The following passage from I.1.9 shows that this is not what he is talking about:

> The nature of that higher soul of ours will be free from all responsibility for the evils that man does and suffers; these concern the living being, the joint entity, as has been said. But if opinion and reasoning belong to the soul, how can it be free of fault? For opinion is a cheat and the cause of much evil-doing. Evil is done when we are mastered by what is worse in us—for we are many—by desire and passion or an evil image. What we call thinking falsities is a making of mind-pictures which has not waited for the judgment of the reasoning faculty—we have acted under the influence of our worse parts, just as in sense-perception the perception of the joint entity may see falsely before the reasoning faculty has passed judgment on it.
>
> (I.1.9, 1–12)

As this passage makes clear, the pure soul isn't even involved in the emotions except as a kind of stopper: the dreadful opinions Plotinus mentions here do not pertain to it but it has a role in dispelling them and enabling us to avoid them. We shall consider the relationship between the pure soul and the middle soul more closely in the next chapter. In any case, the upshot is that there are two sorts of impassivity: that of the pure soul, which is pure reason and does not admit of any emotions whatsoever; and secondly, that of the middle soul, whose involvement in the emotions does not constitute a change in it, because it is of the nature of activity, although it is liable to endorse false and harmful opinions—as a result of which it remains in its fallen state.

4 Chapter summary

Plotinus' human psychology is in several respects rather complex. The following list presents the principal items to be distinguished:

1. A part of the human soul that stays in the intelligible realm.
2. "Our soul." This is the center of our ordinary conscious life, an image of the previous one. It is often identified with reason. This soul has often been referred to above as the middle soul.
3. Nature or the vegetative soul. This is responsible for biological functions in the body. It is involved in sense-perceptions, feelings and emotions, though these typically also involve our soul.
4. The trace of soul. This is not a type of soul but the external activity of nature expressed in the body so as to make it alive.

In addition to the items on this list we have the notion of the living being (the organism). This is the compound of soul and body. Many psychological functions—those that involve the use of bodily organs—are attributed to it. There is often a certain ambiguity surrounding Plotinus' attribution of psychological functions: sense-perception, for instance, is attributed to the living being because it involves the use of bodily sense-organs. It is also attributed to the soul alone because strictly speaking Plotinus identifies sense-perception with a judgment that is the work of the soul part of the compound alone.

Plotinus' account of sense-perception, the emotions and bodily pleasures and pains is marked by the fact that he is concerned to keep the soul unaffected in these functions. His basic strategy for this purpose is to relegate the passive affection involved in these functions to the living body (the trace of soul) while maintaining that the soul's part in the affair is an act of cognition, which is in its nature an activity.

Further readings

Primary sources

Ennead I.1. (53) "What is the living being and what is man?"
Ennead IV.4. (28) "On the problems of soul (II)," especially chapters 18–23.

Secondary sources

Henry J. Blumenthal, *Plotinus' Psychology: His Doctrine of the Embodied Soul* (The Hague: Martinus Nijhoff, 1971).
Eyjólfur K. Emilsson, *Plotinus on Sense-Perception: A Philosophical Study* (Cambridge: Cambridge University Press, 1988).
Sara Magrin, "Sensation and Scepticism in Plotinus," *Oxford Studies in Ancient Philosophy* 39 (2010), 249–297.
Damian Caluori, *Plotinus on Soul* (Cambridge: Cambridge University Press, 2015), chapters 6–8.

Notes

1 In "Against the Gnostics" (II.9.2, 4–6) Plotinus says that "[o]ne part of our soul is always directed to the intelligibles, one to the things of this world, and one is in the middle between these." I take it that the part in the middle is our power of representation, which can be directed either way, see p. 237. I, thus, call this part the middle soul. By contrast, in his recent book Caluori (2015) calls the power of representation "the lower soul" (in contradistinction to the undescended individual soul). Perfect agreement about terminology seems to be out of reach in this area.
2 For fuller discussions of the trace of soul and the qualified body, see Noble 2013 and Caluori 2015: 86 ff.
3 See e.g. the very different interpretations of Aubry 2004 *ad loc.* and Chiaradonna 2009: 90–91.
4 Nutritive power (*to threptikon*) is here and elsewhere used as synonymous with *to phytikon*, the vegetative power, cf. Blumenthal 1971: 26–27.
5 Plotinus uses several words with kindred meanings for this trace of soul: *ichnos* ("trace," "vestige"): II.3.9, 22; IV.4.28, 52 ff.; VI.4.15, 15; *indalma* ("appearance"): IV.4.19, 3; *skia* ("shadow"): IV.4.18, 7.
6 The most elaborate interpretations of the notion of the trace of soul are those of Noble (2013) and Caluori (2015: 186–192).
7 In our treatise, I.1.8, 15–21, Plotinus says that the soul shines into bodies and "makes living creatures, not of itself and body, but abiding itself and giving images (*eidōla*) of itself, like a face seen in many mirrors. The first image is the faculty of sense-perception in the joint entity, and after this comes everything else which is called a form of soul, each in turn proceeding from the other; the series ends in the powers of generation and growth." So we might think that he is affirming here that the undescended individual soul produces every other form of soul down to "the powers of generation and growth." Plotinus is, however, speaking about soul generally here and not specifically about the human soul (cf. Aubry 2004: 248–249, who takes the soul in question here to be the World-Soul; I would rather suggest soul in general).

8 Wilberding 2008b: 427, n. 66 refers to III.3. (48) 4, 27–44; VI.7. (38) 7, 8–16 as asserting that the individual soul is responsible for even basic biological functions at the embryo stage. This may be so but I find these passages rather vague in this regard.
9 II.3. (52) 12, 1–11 and 14, 4–7; III.1. (3) 5, 26–8 and 6, 4–5; III.3. (48) 7, 26–28; V.7. (18), 2–3.
10 The phrase "cosmic matchmaking" is borrowed from Wilberding's (n.d.) so far unpublished paper, "The World-Soul in the Embryological Theories of Porphyry and Plotinus."
11 Wilberding (2008b) sees Plotinus as adumbrating the views on the nature of the embryo that are expressed in much greater detail by Porphyry in *To Gaurus: On How the Embryo Receives the Soul* (English translation by Wilberding 2011). The father's seed transmits vegetative power to the mother's womb, where it mixes with the mother's vegetative soul. The embryo itself has only a vegetative soul. The mother's vegetative soul (and any other vegetative soul), however, needs a soul of a higher rank as a leader. This is the mother's individual soul. Thus, the embryo's vegetative power is mixed with the mother's vegetative soul, which in turn is ruled by the mother's individual soul. This cohabitation with and subjugation under the soul of the mother sets its marks on the fetus, which explains inheritance on the mother's side. When the individual soul of the new human being arrives just before birth, it takes over this rule over the vegetative soul of the newborn. This need for a ruler of higher rank explains why the vegetative soul and the individual soul form a unity and are often spoken of as such by Plotinus.
12 That human souls have an individual existence in the intelligible realm is clearly asserted also e.g. in VI.4.4, 1 ff. and IV.3.12–15.
13 On the descent of the individual souls, see especially IV.8. (6) 3–4; V.1. (10) 1, 3 ff.; IV.3. (27) 12–13. On this topic, see O'Brien 1977, who convincingly argues for the consistency of Plotinus' various accounts of this descent.
14 With Theiler I read *akousiai* ("unwilling"), not *hekousiai* ("willing") in line 17 of IV.3.13. This reading seems necessary to make sense of what follows.
15 If I understand Caluori (2015) right he interprets Plotinus along these lines.
16 See Blumenthal 1971: 61–63, and Emilsson 1988: 31–32, 76.
17 On visual transmission in Plotinus, see Emilsson 1988: ch. 3.
18 Magrin (2010: 281, n. 73) seems to question this distinction between the affection of the organ and the work of the soul in sense-perception. I think it is evident, e.g. in these opening lines of III.6.1 as well as in IV.4.23 and VI.4.6, that Plotinus insists on such a distinction.
19 In using the word *typos*, "impression" for intelligible entities in the soul Plotinus of course deviates from the Peripatetic and Stoic traditions, which also make use of this term in similar contexts. Though Plotinus is aware of these traditions, his model here is, as usually, Plato: see *Theaetetus* 191d.
20 For a discussion of Aristotle and Alexander in relation to Plotinus and references, see Emilsson 1988: 94–101.
21 Plotinus' adoption of the language of impressions (*typoi*) is presumably based on the wax-tablet passage in Plato *Theaetetus* 191c ff. When Plotinus criticizes

doctrines that explain perception or memory in terms of impressions, he has the Stoics and Aristotle and his followers in mind.
22 See the illuminating commentary by Fleet (1995: 94–95, 97).
23 The word translated as "knowledge" here, for want of a better single word, is *gnōsis*, which is the sort of knowledge or awareness that depends on intimacy, a direct exposure to the object known.
24 For a different take than what I have given of the two most significant passages that may seem to endorse non-realism about sense-perception, V.5.1 and I.1.7, see Smith 2006 and, on V.5.1, O'Meara 2000. See also Ganson 2005.
25 Magrin's interpretation constitutes a refined alternative to and criticism of my view in Emilsson 1988. For a thorough criticism of Magrin's position, for the most part in favor of my interpretation, see Chiaradonna 2012.
26 Cf. Blumenthal 1971: 71–72, and Smith 2006.
27 I argue for this interpretation at some length in Emilsson 1988: 117 ff.; it is further developed and supported in Emilsson 1995, 1996 and 2007: 129–141. Chiaradonna (2012) accepts it. O'Meara (2000) provides an alternative interpretation, which claims that Plotinus accepts skeptical arguments as valid against any dogmatic position founded on sense-perception; it is not clear to me whether he regards the actual lines as merely ad hominem and, thus, not representing Plotinus' actual views. Smith (2006) rejects my interpretation of V.5.1.
28 The account of feelings and emotions here is partly excerpted from Emilsson 1998.
29 In light of this the opening lines of this same chapter are surprising: "This is what is called pleasure and pain: pain is awareness of withdrawal of a body which is being deprived of an image of soul" (IV.4.19, 1–3). Thus, here pain is said to be a kind of awareness, which is exactly what he goes on to deny. Perhaps the phrase "what is called" (*to legomenon*) is significant here and indicates that Plotinus is not yet expressing his considered view. The shift from *algēdōn*, which is the word for pain here, to *odynē* later in the chapter is hardly significant, and in any case Plotinus also uses the verb *algein* to make his point about the separation of pain and the awareness of it.
30 Interestingly, Plotinus also pushes for such an assimilation of the external and the internal senses from the other direction, as it were: the external distance senses, sight and hearing, depend in his view on the unity of our organism and that of the world, and of our soul and that of the world. Thus, vision, for instance, becomes like an internal sensation within a large organism, i.e. the cosmos. See especially IV.5 and Emilsson 1988: ch. 3.
31 A word of caution about terminology: Plotinus' usual terms for the vegetative soul is *to phytikon* or simply *physis*. The latter is the same term as he uses for the lowest phase of the World-Soul which produces and informs the inanimate world. In the context of psychology, however, *physis* is a specifically animating principle, not that which makes body, but that which makes it alive. Presumably, Plotinus conceives of these as parallel functions and that at bottom there is only one kind of *physis*. He certainly draws parallels between *physis* in the world at large and *physis* in organisms (cf. III.6.4, 22 and pp. 185–186) and in IV.4.13 he seems to assume

that they are one and the same. It is nevertheless important in our context to be clear about the difference between the kinds of function.
32 See Blumenthal 1971: 38–39 and Fleet 1995: 127.
33 The word *proepithymia* is a conjecture, which if correct is a *hapax legomenon*.
34 See IV.4.17, 12 and IV.4.28, 41 and Blumenthal 1971: 91–94. Cf. also III.6.4, 19–23 and the dim consciousness ascribed to nature in III.8.4, 22 ff. Admittedly, in IV.4.13, Plotinus denies knowledge, consciousness and images to nature (the world-making principle, cf. Chapter 5, p. 158), affirming that it produces without knowing. He does however ascribe some kind of *typos* (impression) to it (IV.4.13, 6), which may correspond to the indistinct and unjudged image in III.6.4, 19–23; cf. Fleet 1995: 126–128. I don't think it is significant that in IV.4.13, Plotinus is discussing nature at large, rather than nature as an animating principle. For in III.8.4, where nature in the former sense is also at stake, he does ascribe a kind of consciousness to it. The philosophical point at issue here is that in order to perform the functions ascribed to it, nature has to receive information and carry it out in physical activity or pass it on to higher faculties. Plotinus wishes to avoid describing this activity in merely human terms. He nevertheless finds it appropriate, at least at times, to describe it in some minimally cognitive or quasi-cognitive terms: rational making presupposes a formative principle (*logos*), the possession of which in turn presupposes some form of thinking (cf. III.8.3, 1–3).
35 See several examples of this in I.4.10; see also the account of how the lower soul retains a trace of past events in the form of a disposition in IV.3.28.
36 I am accepting the emendation of *pros epithymian* in the manuscripts to *proepithymia*.
37 See Fleet's (1995) translation and commentary *ad loc*.
38 The reference here, "they say," is presumably to the Stoics, although the terminology is a mixture of Stoic and Aristotelian terms; see Fleet (1995) commentary *ad loc*. The main Stoic theoretician, Chrysippus, identified the emotions with irrational, fresh opinions of good and evil; cf. Galen in Long and Sedley 1987: 65D. Plotinus' emphasis on the role of opinion in the emotions reflects Stoic influence. Galen criticizes Chrysippus, for identifying emotion with opinion and, thus, ignoring the physiological aspect of emotion. Plotinus takes the physiological aspect to be essential to emotion, as is evidenced by his remark that "the [mere] opinion about someone's evil does not contain the affection of grief" (I.1.5, 17–18).
39 Cf. Blumenthal 1971: 54 ff. and Fleet 1995: 133.

Eight

The human being II
The higher soul and we ourselves

In this chapter we shall consider various issues relating to the conscious life of human beings. For reasons that will soon emerge the faculty of representation (*phantasia; to phantasticon*) and its relation to both what is below it (sense-perception; the compound) and above it (Intellect; the undescended soul) will be center stage. In so far as the relation to the what is below is concerned, this will involve resuming and exploring further themes adumbrated in the previous chapter.

Details will be presented below but here is a short summary and presentation of the issues in store for us: Plotinus posits a power of soul, the power of representation (*to phantastikon; phantasia*), which serves as an intermediate level and in a sense as an intermediary between Intellect, on the one hand, and sense-perception, the living being and the external world, on the other. Sense-perceptions, whether external or those that arise from internal states of the living being, terminate in the faculty of representation or, as Plotinus also sometimes suggests, in reason (*hē dianoia*).[1] (Reason is often closely linked to the power of representation—but the two are not the same; their relationship will be addressed shortly.) Both these faculties are not only informed from below but also from above by the transcendent soul and even Intellect. The picture that emerges is that of the faculty of representation as a meeting place for sensibles and intelligibles, each translated into the same kind of currency in this faculty, namely mental images or intelligible impressions. As such this faculty is involved in memories, opinions and reasoning. It may be said to be the main locus of our conscious life.

1 The power of representation: General remarks

In the context of discussing whether one can be happy (*eudaimōn*) without being aware of it in the treatise "On happiness" (I.4), chapter 10, we find the following striking passage:

> It seems as if awareness (*antilēpsis*) exists and is produced when intellectual activity is reflexive and when that in the life of the soul which is active in thinking is in a way projected back, as happens with mirror reflections when there is a smooth, bright, untroubled surface. In these circumstances, when the mirror is there the mirror-image is produced, but when it is not there or when it is not in the right state, the object of which would have been is [all the same] actually there. In the same way as regards the soul, when that kind of thing in us which mirrors the images of reason (*dianoia*) and Intellect is undisturbed, we see them and know them in a way parallel to sense-perception, along with the prior recognition that it is Intellect and reason that are active. But when this is broken because harmony of the body is upset, reason and Intellect operate without an image (*eidōlon*), and intellectual activity takes place without a representation (*phantasia*).
> (I.4.10, 6–19)

Plotinus does not speak of the power of representation here but refers to representations, the images dealt with by this power, and he explicitly mentions the power in another, similar passage in "On the problems of soul (I)," IV.3.29–30. Here he says that the power of representation is "that in which sense-perception terminates" (IV.3.29, 25). There is little doubt that it is indeed this power that receives images or representations from reason and Intellect as well as from the senses. Thus, this power is a kind of meeting place where intellectualized impressions from the outside and pure thoughts, which have been transformed into representations, meet and can interact. It is here that our conscious life takes place for the most part and here where the empirical "we," is located. This is the locus of our embodied human soul.

The images in the power of representation can come from below, from the senses, or above, from the transcendent soul or Intellect.

Interestingly, Plotinus takes awareness to depend on the projection of images into the power of representation: if no image arrives in this power, we are not aware of anything but the transcendent thoughts that are the source of such images are there all the same. Something analogous can apparently happen with things from below: for various reasons, images of sensible things may fail to come into the power of representation in which case we are not aware of them; cf. p. 216.

The question arises, of course, what these images or representations exactly are. It seems clear that Plotinus' notion of the power of representation owes a great deal to Aristotle's power of the same name as well as to the Stoic notion of the ruling part of the soul, to *hēgemonikon*. There is, however, a very important difference. As opposed to these powers in these predecessors, Plotinus' power does not depend on the body for its operation and the images it contains do not have a material basis. This holds also for images of sensibles: as we have seen, they are already intelligible at the final stage of sense-perception (cf. IV.3.23, 29–34; I.1.7, 9–12).

But what does Plotinus mean by saying that the impressions (representations, forms) that derive from sense-perception are intelligible? Are not such impressions of sensible things entertained by the soul as information about things or states of affairs in the sensible world? They are certainly rather far removed from Intellect's non-discursive intuition of the Forms. In IV.3.26, 29 ff., in explaining that the impressions in sense-perception and memory are not at all like stamps on wax, he also makes the point that these impressions are not magnitudes. As explained in Chapter 6, spatial magnitude is the essential characteristic of what is sensible as opposed to intelligible. In claiming that these impressions are not magnitudes Plotinus is saying that they have no length or breadth (nor indeed weight). They exist in the soul, nevertheless, but their mode of existence is not of the sensible sort.

Another question it is natural to ask concerning these images is whether they are mental pictures like the pictures we produce in our minds when asked to imagine, say, a triangle or a cat. Or are they rather primarily linguistic representations, mental words and sentences accompanied by some sort of understanding of their meaning? In "On the problems of soul (I)" Plotinus says that "the *logos* unfolds and brings out the intuitive thought into the faculty of representation, and so shows the intuitive thought as if in a mirror, and this is how there is awareness and persistence and memory of it" (IV.3.30, 9–11). Shortly before he has called that which is remembered a "representation" (*phantasia*). These representations are the same items as what he in chapter 7 of "What is the living being and what is man?" (I.1) calls "impressions" and "forms": my bet is that Plotinus may mean both mental pictures and linguistic or otherwise intellectual apprehension of the content of the pictures. In so far as he may have mental pictures in mind, it is clear that these would be mental pictures accompanied by a conceptual understanding of their content: a mere picture of a triangle in my faculty of representation is cognitively useless unless I know it for what it is: a picture of a triangle.

It was said above that sometimes Plotinus speaks as if reason (*dianoia*) is the mental power immediately above sense-perception rather than the power of representation. In a passage that we shall examine more closely later in this chapter, V.3.3, 1 ff., Plotinus says that sense-perception sees a human being and gives the impression to discursive reason. The same account is suggested by I.1.7. In neither of these passages is there any mention of the power of representation. Given what we have just seen, that the power of representation is that in which sense-perception terminates, this may seem confusing: are the power of representation and reason the same thing? The answer is that the power of representation is a power involved in discursive reasoning, opinions and memories but is not to be identified with any of these. It is the general power to form mental images or representations. Thus, if Plotinus sometimes speaks as if the power of reasoning is the power immediately above sense-perception this is not to deny that sense-perceptions are taken over by the power of representation: the latter is involved in whatever the power of reasoning does. The reason why he picks out reason in such contexts is that reason is judgmental, a power that seeks the right and the true. Hence, it is this power that evaluates sense-perceptions (cf. I.1.9, 18–19; V.3.2, 7–8) and is in general responsible for taking a cognitive stance. That explains why Plotinus often specifically names it in such contexts rather than the broader power of representation.

2 The power of representation and sense-perception

In the passage from chapter 7 of I.7 that was quoted and partly discussed in the previous chapter (p. 252), Plotinus says that the soul is "apprehensive of impressions produced by sense-perception in the living being: for these are already intelligible entities." He goes on to describe the soul's perception—*aisthēsis*, the same word as he uses primarily for sense-perception—as "a contemplation of forms alone," noting that from these forms, which give the soul leadership over the living being, "come reasonings, opinions and intuitions." The faculty of representation is not mentioned by name in this passage but it is there implicitly. It is this faculty and more specifically reason that operates with the intelligible forms. As this passage indeed states, the forms that arise in the living being through sense-perception are "already intelligible entities." It emerges from this account that what Plotinus in contexts like these calls form (*eidos, morphē*), (intelligible) impression (*typos*) and representation or image (*phantasia, phantasma*) may all refer to the same items, though perhaps with different connotations.

In the previous chapter we noted that sense-perception is a cognitive faculty in its own right and that it ranges over a variety of states in the sensible world. In particular, the view held by some that it is limited to the grasp of proper sensibles was rejected: sense-perception may equally grasp that there is something green out there, that the grass is green, that what I see is a human being, that my toe aches, and that a dog is barking.[2] But what exactly is the relationship between sense-perception and the power of representation? Chiaradonna (2012: 201–202) suggests that we first become conscious of our perceptions when they enter the power of representation. This strikes me as correct: Plotinus refers to sense-perceptions that we are not aware of (IV.4.8). The borderline between sense-perception and the power of representation is, however, vague. Consider the following passage from the long discussion of memory in "On the problems of soul (I)":

> Now nothing will prevent a percept (*aisthēma*) from being a mental image (*phantasma*), and the memory and the retention of the object from belonging to the faculty of representation,

which is something different [from the power of sense-perception]: for it is in this that sense-perception terminates, and what was seen is present in this when the perception is no longer there.

(IV.3.29, 22–26)

This passage says that sense-perceptions terminate in the faculty of representation. That is to say that the "intelligible impressions that have arisen in the living being" that we discussed earlier end up there. When we see, i.e. perceive through the senses, a red tomato, for example, the intelligible impression is already in the faculty of representation. When the tomato is removed from our field of vision, this impression remains as a memory. It could not remain unless it had arrived there in the first place while the tomato was present. There is little doubt that this describes the standard case of sense-perception (see further Emilsson 1988: 110–111).

Sense-perceptions do not, however, always reach the level of representation. In a discussion of the question whether the fact of unity of all souls implies that we should share each other's affections, Plotinus notes that "the soul having made the judgment does not say 'I have judged': it merely judged. Our sense of sight does not say this to our sense of hearing either, even though both have made judgments, but rather it is our reasoning power, which is something different from each, that says this in both cases" (VI.4.6, 15–18). According to this passage, both sight and hearing judge their objects but neither is aware of the other's judgment. It is only the faculty of reasoning (*logismos*) that is aware of both.

Another very interesting passage from the discussion of memory in "On the problems of soul (II)" seems to imply that there may be unconscious sense-perceptions:

> Now it is not necessary to deposit in one's memory whatever one observes, or that altogether incidental consequences should come to be present in the power of representation. ... What I mean by each of these statements is as follows: First point: that it is not necessary to keep stored up in oneself what one sees. When what is perceived makes no difference, or the perception is not at all personally relevant, but is provoked involuntarily by

the difference in the things seen, it is only sense-perception which experiences this and the soul does not receive it into its interior, since the difference is not of concern to it either because it meets a need or is of benefit in some other way. And when the soul's activity is directed to other things, and completely directed to them, it would not keep the memory of things like these when they have passed away since it is not even aware of the perception of them when they are present.

(IV.4.8, 1–16)

The last sentence suggests that a perception may take place without our being aware of it. This is confirmed a little later in the chapter where Plotinus says that "an impression of such a thing does not yield a conscious perception (*synaisthēsis*)" (ll. 19–20). It is of course possible that by "perception" in the last sentence of the long quotation Plotinus means what he normally would call affection, the idea being that the sense-organs are indeed affected in these cases but the perceptive soul takes no note of this.[3] Calling the affection a perception would, however, be in conflict with his strong insistence on keeping the affections and the perceptions apart and reserving the word "perception" for a cognitive act (cf. p. 246). Moreover, the passage quoted from VI.4.6 above indicates that perceptual judgments can occur prior to the involvement of the power of reasoning or representation.

Clearly, attention is at the heart of the matter in the long passage just quoted. Plotinus is saying that we may attend to what we perceive through the senses or we may not. Whether we do or not depends on interest and whether we have a focus on something else. A typical case would be that of the lamp-posts we pass when driving: we register them, recognize them for what they are, enough to avoid colliding with them, but we take no note of the particular features of any one of them. Should we for some reason become interested in the lamp-posts, we could with a turn of attention take note of each of them—even if this would no doubt soon become tiresome and dangerous: better that a passenger does this than the driver! Even if Plotinus says that sense-perceptions terminate in the power of representation, this seems to describe only the standard case: as a rule we are conscious of what we perceive or at least of some aspects of it. But we need not be conscious of all of it or, in fact, any of it.

The position I have been attributing to Plotinus is in line with what has been mentioned earlier about his willingness to accept unconscious mental phenomena. The great scholars of Plotinus and Neoplatonism, Hans-Rudolph Schwyzer (1960) and Eric Robert Dodds (1965: 88, n. 4), actually went so far as to suggest that Plotinus was the one who discovered the unconscious. According to Dodds, at least, this makes Plotinus a precursor of Freud. This is in my view misleading and partly wrong: the ancients generally had no problems with unconscious mental phenomena, and Plotinus' unconscious has little to do with that of Freud. A much more appropriate comparison would be with Leibniz. He too claims that there are unconscious perceptions. Both thinkers explain this fact by means of similar considerations: when there is no difference in what we perceive, says Plotinus, "when the perceptions are too minute or too many," says Leibniz in the preface to his *New Essays on Human Understanding* (Leibniz 1981 [1765]: 53). Then there is the effect of habituation: we "become so accustomed to the motion of a mill or a waterfall, after living beside it for a while, that we pay no heed to it" (Leibniz 1981 [1765]: 53). And Plotinus: "Again, when someone is always doing the same thing, there would be no point in his observing the details of this same operation" (IV.4.8, 33–34). Yet again, about being preoccupied with something else Plotinus says that when the soul's activity is completely directed towards other things, it will not remember what has passed by, "since it was not aware of the perception of them when they were present" (IV.4.8, 14–16). And again Leibniz: "but these impressions in the soul and the body, lacking the appeal of novelty, are not forceful enough to attract our attention and our memory, which are applied only to more compelling objects" (Leibniz 1981 [1765]: 53).

For both philosophers there is no denying that these unconscious perceptions are genuine perceptions: it is not only the organs that are affected; the senses really perceive these things that we are unaware of. Both philosophers maintain that we can become aware of these unconscious perceptions and each of them has a similar technical or quasi-technical term for this. Plotinus says that these sense-perceptions do not yield conscious apprehension (*synaisthēsis*);

Leibniz speaks about *apperception* of our perceptions. Leibniz does not refer to this passage but there is good evidence that he read Plotinus. One wonders whether there is a historical connection here.[4]

The upshot of this is that while sense-perceptions are judgments of the perceptive soul that commonly are conscious, they need not be. Such sense-perceptions that do not reach the faculty of representation will nevertheless serve us in daily life: with their aid we can avoid going off bridges, stumbling into sharp corners and the like. Avoiding things of this sort involves making perceptual judgments but these are in the perceptive soul. They are available for our attention but they need not be fully conscious.

3 Discursive reason and Intellect

In Chapter 4 we saw how Plotinus emphasizes Intellect's infallible non-discursive knowledge. The identity of subject and object as well as what we called the holism of Intellect were crucial features in establishing this totally secure grasp. A question that seems natural to ask is what relevance Intellect's impeccable cognitive abilities have for our less perfect discursive knowledge. Plotinus says or implies that what there is is grounded in Intellect's thought and he clearly also thinks that other, lower modes of cognition are inferior reflections of Intellect's supreme kind of thinking. But the question can be raised why I should be better off with respect to cognition because Intellect, which is not me, knows its objects perfectly? We can distinguish at least two relevant questions here: (1) What difference does the fact of Intellect make for the reliability and confidence of discursive reason, or, for that matter, sense-perception? (2) What role do the forms (concepts) derived from Intellect that we possess in our souls play in discursive reason and sense-perception?

To address the former question let us see what Plotinus has to say about our relation to Intellect. He says that we have Intellect itself as something which transcends us "either as common to all or particular to ourselves, or both common and particular; common because it is without parts and one and everywhere the same, particular to ourselves because each has the whole of it in the primary part of his soul" (I.1.8, 3–6).[5] From this he concludes that "we possess the forms in two ways, in our soul, in a manner of speaking unfolded and separated, in Intellect all together." We find the same distinction between two ways of possessing the forms in the treatise "On the cognitive hypostases and what is beyond" (V.3. (49)):

> But we too are kings, when we are in accord with [Intellect]; we can be in accord with it in two ways, either by having something like its writing written in us like laws, or by being as if filled with it and able to see it and perceive it as present.
> (V.3.4, 1–4)

In the context he makes clear that both ways of being in accord with Intellect are possible for us but the one who has the forms in the manner of the lawgiver is no longer a human being, i.e. no longer a soul or reason, but has become Intellect (V.3.4, 10).

Such an ascent is clearly of utmost importance to Plotinus. Indeed, as we shall see more clearly in the next chapter, the life of Intellect is the good life, the happy life and as such the life anyone at all capable of it should aim at. It is not so clear, however, that an ascent to Intellect makes us better able to deal cognitively with things of the sensible world as such. The question how Intellect bears on reason's ability to judge sensibles is not Plotinus' main concern here in the first chapters of "On the cognitive hypostases and what is beyond." Nevertheless, his discussion here gives us some indication of how he thinks our relation to Intellect is relevant to our everyday cognitive capacity.

First, the comparison with written laws and someone, a lawgiver, who writes the laws, suggests that reason is in a passive position in relation to Intellect: it doesn't decide about the laws, this is determined by the lawgiver. So there is at least this evident difference between reason and Intellect. Second, the written laws and the lawgiver's act of writing them in the reason of human beings correspond to archetype and image. In fact, Plotinus implies as much in the context.

One way in which the truthfulness of reason is guaranteed for us is by its being illuminated by and being an image of Intellect, whose truthfulness is beyond question. In so far as reason is illuminated by Intellect it does not go wrong. All error is due to the soul's association with body and the compound (I.1.9, 24–26). But do Plotinus' analogies with a lawgiver and his subjects imply that reason, being in the place of a subject, is a mere passive recipient following orders from above, without the slightest understanding of their point or why it should follow them? That is actually not the message conveyed by these passages. It is true that reason lacks the internal point of view of the lawgiver but it knows something. He notes that reason knows that it "is from Intellect and second after Intellect and an image of Intellect" (V.3.4, 21). He further suggests that reason knows that "it judges what it judges, and that it does so by rules in itself that it has from Intellect, and that there is something better than itself, which does not seek but totally possesses" (V.3.4, 16–18). All this indicates that the soul in its capacity of reason is not at all an alienated, passive subject: it knows where it comes from, it has a notion of what Intellect is like (see V.3.4, 15 ff.), it realizes its own inferiority and totally accepts Intellect's authority, seeing that this is how things should be. Hence, it confidently applies what it has from Intellect with some understanding of the fact that this must be right.

Still the knowledge and understanding embedded in reason is far from being as complete as that of Intellect. The passages just quoted from "On the cognitive hypostases and what is beyond" suggest that there is a crucial epistemic difference between the two ways in which we can be said to be in accord with Intellect: the way described as "being as if filled with [the law] and able to see it and perceive it as present" corresponds to Intellect's own way of grasping the law, the kind of understanding the lawgiver enjoys in the act of writing it. It is clearly implied by the context here that in the discursive case we do not see it and are not aware of it as present in this way.

Let us now turn to the second question: What role do the forms (concepts) derived from Intellect that we possess in our souls play in discursive reasoning and sense-perception? Plotinus clearly holds that our ability to reason discursively depends on our accessing the realm of transcendent Forms. In "What is the living being and what is man?" (I.1. (53)) he says that

> [r]easoning when it passes judgment on the impressions produced by sense-perception is at the same time contemplating forms and contemplating them by a kind of sympathy—I mean the reasoning which really belongs to the true soul: for true

reasoning is an act of intellection, and there is often a resemblance and community between what is outside and what is within.

(I.1.9, 18–23)

He does not explain what he means here by "contemplating them by a kind of sympathy" but the expression suggests he is not thinking that the soul must rise to the Intellect's internal, non-discursive point of view in order to evaluate the evidence from the senses. Such a view would in any case be a counter-intuitive position at odds with our experience—only a few people do or even can adopt Intellect's internal point of view, all of us can see tomatoes, tables and chairs. Rather, what he is referring to is the projections from Intellect into the faculty of representation that we discussed in the previous section: in having intellectual content projected into this power we are making use of Intellect without necessarily rising to that level.

There is an interesting passage bearing on this issue in "On the three primary hypostases." Here Plotinus says that

Since, then, there exists soul which reasons (*psychēs logizomenēs*) about what is right and good, and reasoning (*logismos*), which enquires about the rightness and goodness of this or that particular thing, there must be some further permanent rightness from which arises the discursive reasoning in the realm of soul.

(V.1.11, 1–4)

Again, I do not think that Plotinus here intends to suggest that the soul must rise up to this permanent goodness and rightness in order to reason about what is good and right; but the permanent goodness and rightness must be there for it to draw on.

This was rightness (or justice) and goodness, concepts that arguably could not be empirically acquired. But what about other concepts, that of the cat or the tomato? The mobile phone? Do we have to draw on Intellect in order to judge that something is a cat or a tomato or a mobile phone? Or that the mobile phone is ringing? It may seem that the former passage just cited, the one from I.1.9, suggests this, and other passages that emphasize our possession of all forms in our souls may be taken as at least indirect support. It is widely claimed by interpreters, including my former self (cf. Emilsson 1988: 137) that even perceptual judgments depend on the prior possession of the forms (or Forms) in the soul, if not access to Intellect itself. The general idea is that when for instance vision recognizes something it sees as a tomato, the soul unfolds the intelligible form of the tomato into the power of representation and notes that the image that has arisen through the senses fits the image derived from the intelligible tomato.

While I do not question that Plotinus generally considers perceptual judgments to consist in some sort of fitting of the forms taken in to forms possessed by the soul, even if direct evidence for this is not abundant, I am not convinced that perceptual judgments generally depend on the unfolding of purely intelligible Forms (or forms in the transcendent soul) into the power of representation. In order to come to better grips with what is at issue here, let us consider a well-known passage from "On the cognitive hypostases and what is beyond." This is in fact the fullest passage to be found in the *Enneads* about the issues presently occupying us. Here Plotinus says:

> Well, sense-perception sees a human being and gives its impression to reason (*dianoia*). What does reason say? It will not say anything yet, but only knows, and stops at that; unless perhaps it asks itself "Who is that?" if it has met the person before, and says, using memory to help it, that it is Socrates. And if it makes the details of this form explicit, it is taking to pieces what the power of representation gave it. And if it [the soul] says whether he is good, its remark originates in what it knows through sense-perception, but what it says about this it has already from itself, since it has a norm of the good in itself. How does it have the good in itself? Because it is like the good, and is strengthened for the perception of this kind of thing by Intellect illuminating it; for this is the pure part of the soul and receives the reflection of Intellect coming down upon it.
> (V.3.3, 1–12)

Clearly, the question whether the object is a human being is settled at the level of sense-perception, which recognizes what it sees as a human being.[6] If that were not the case, we would have expected reason to raise the question, "what is this?," and answer that this is a human being. But this is not what happens: reason asks "who is this?," it already being settled by sense-perception that it is a human being. Thus, "sense-perception sees a human being" expresses a perceptual judgment accomplished by sense-perception. There is no mention of a need for sense-perception to fit its impression to the concept of a human being. Plotinus is taking such a process for granted. In any case, sense-perception gives its impression to reason. The latter may simply stay content with knowing that there is a human being there or it may become curious about who this is, whether it is Socrates, for instance, this not being immediately evident to it from the impression. This latter question is settled with the help of memory: it is Socrates because the impression fits the memory the subject has of Socrates. Another question that reason may raise is whether Socrates is good. This question is decided by applying something the soul has from itself, namely the rule or norm of the good, to the impression it has from the senses. The soul's ability to apprehend such things as goodness is strengthened by its pure part having reflections of Intellect.

All this is in good harmony with what has been proposed above. It is noteworthy that no unfolding of Forms in Intellect is invoked here except for the judgment of goodness: sense-perception recognizes a human being without such recourse and reason relies on a sensible memory representation for the judgment that this is Socrates.[7] As we have seen, it is true that Plotinus holds that we innately possess the forms of all things in our souls (it is, however, a question how strictly this is to be understood; cf. Chapter 3, p. 113 ff.) and that at least potentially we can ascend to Intellect. It does not follow that he thinks we draw on Intellect directly in making any perceptual judgment or in reasoning about sensible affairs. First of all, not everything that exists in the sensible world has a specific form; e.g. there are no specific forms of artifacts such as mobile phones (cf. Chapter 3, p. 115). Even if there is no doubt that Plotinus thought that basic conceptual knowledge is innate, nothing prevents its being the case that many concepts are empirically acquired or, rather, are the result of combining and applying innate notions to empirically acquired content so as to give rise to a new concept. How else could we make the perceptual judgment that the mobile phone is ringing or, to take an example nearer to Plotinus, that the horses are pulling a catapult?

There is not much textual evidence that bears directly on the question we have been discussing. My main aim is not so much to refute the common view that sense-perception directly relies on access to Intellect and that all forms/concepts are innate as to suggest that the evidence for such an account is rather poor. That sense-perception involves some sort of use of concepts is clear. It is also clear that a great deal of conceptual knowledge is innately given and it would be in line with Plotinus' thought to suppose that the generation of new concepts depends on the possession and application of those already in the soul, crucially the concepts of the same and the different and the other primary kinds. Nothing, however, would stand in the way of some concepts, e.g. that of the mobile phone or the catapult, being partly empirically acquired. That would, moreover, result in a more plausible account.[8]

Yet another question that naturally arises in connection with sense-perception and the employment of concepts is whether animals, when they perceive, use concepts. As has been frequently noted, according to Plotinus sense-perceptions are judgments. Judgments, one presumes, involve some kind of use of concepts and can be true or false. Animals are endowed with senses and can perceive through them. Does this entail that animals make judgments that involve the use of concepts and can be true or false? Now, unfortunately, Plotinus does not say much about animals in this regard. We could take two different lines on this question. Here is one line: human sense-perception is radically different from animal sense-perception. This was apparently the line the Stoics took: the impressions animals have are not rational, i.e. conceptualized, and in their case there is no question of an assent to the propositional content of an impression.[9] Skeptics would question this and Platonists such as Plutarch and Porphyry disagreed (see Caluori 2015: 192–193).

The closest Plotinus comes to saying anything relevant to this issue is in I.1.11, 8–15, where we find the following passage:

> And how does the living being include brute beasts? If, as is said, there are sinful human souls in them, the separable part of the soul does not come to belong to the beasts but is there without

being there for them; their consciousness (*synaisthēsis*) includes the image of soul and the body: a beast is then a qualified body made, so to say, by an image of soul. But if a human soul has not entered the beast, it becomes a living being of such and such a kind by an illumination from the universal soul.

There is a lot in this passage that needs elucidation. I shall, however, be brief and at the risk of sounding dogmatic state what I make of it. First of all, clearly there is a reference here to the Platonic doctrine of transmigration of souls into animal bodies. This is a debated issue among scholars.[10] Plotinus here qualifies his phrase by saying "as is said," which may suggest that he does not fully commit himself to such transmigration as an objective fact. However that may be, he seems to me to be committed to the rebirth of souls: such a doctrine is an integral aspect of his views about divine justice (cf. Chapter 5, p. 238 and Chapter 10, Section 2). He may for all that still be skeptical about the transmigration of human souls into animals. Secondly, I take it that the "image (*eidōlon*) of soul" here is the middle soul, the "light" spoken of in chapter 7 of this same treatise (see Chapter 7, p. 239), not the trace of soul in virtue of which the body is alive.[11] In any case, Plotinus is here willing to entertain the hypothesis that animals have sinful human souls in them. But if this is the case, he insists, "the separable part of the soul does not come to belong to the beasts but is there without being there for them," which means that the beasts don't have an active power of reason but this power lies there idle in them. Yet, these beasts have the part of the human soul which gives them some sort of consciousness. What would be involved in that? None of the functions of reason in humans, nothing at all which requires drawing on Intellect but presumably most of the functions of the middle soul, including perceptual judgments. If these beasts are not animated by sinful human souls, the World-Soul does the same job for them.

It is true that there is no explicit mention of sense-perception here, still less of judgments involved in sense-perception. I take it, however, that since the animals are endowed with psychic capacities comparable with those that the middle soul is endowed with in human beings, they have the capacity to judge, for instance: "This is sweet!" or (for a dog) "Here is another dog." Every dog owner knows that dogs have expert knowledge about such matters. Does this involve the use of concepts? Yes, but minimally. The animal is incapable of human reason's use of the resources of the higher realms.

4 The soul and we ourselves

In passages quoted above we have seen Plotinus referring to *us* or *we ourselves*: "we are in accord with Intellect" or "Intellect too is a part of *ourselves* and to it *we* ascend." Much of the treatise "What is the living being and what is man?" is concerned with distinguishing what is merely "ours," i.e. the living being, from what is "we ourselves." We find Plotinus discussing not merely what human psychological faculties are but what *we* are.

This aspect of his thought has prompted scholars to attribute to him a more advanced notion of the self than any previous thinker (see O'Daly 1973: 6–7). But what do we mean when we talk about the self? The self is indeed a notoriously many-faceted and elusive notion. Scholars have distinguished different conceptions and correspondingly different approaches: Seigel (2005: introd.) names selfhood seen from a social or cultural perspective, the self as the body with its biological needs, urges and emotions, and the self as an entity capable of reflection: the general idea is that the self is an entity able to reflect on what it itself is and what is happening as happening to it. To this we must add the self seen as an entity—in the philosophical tradition often an immaterial entity—that unifies mental phenomena and is so to speak their locus. This conception is common to, for instance, Descartes, Leibniz and Kant, who, however, differ widely in their views on the self. Plotinus' take on the self falls under the latter two. He is, however, also keenly aware of the relevance of the organic functions for our notion of self: while it is strictly false we are identical with the living being, many people, most people in fact, identify themselves with it and in any case it is *ours*. As we shall see, he even admits that there is a sense of self which includes the beast.

Plotinus' relevant word for self is "we" (*hēmeis*). The plural is significant: in discussing the self he is mostly not referring to his own or any particular individual's experiences but describing something he takes to apply to human beings generally (cf. Remes 2007: 4–5). Thus, his inquiries into the self are at the same time an attempt to answer the question: what is the human being? They are a contribution to philosophical anthropology in other words. Plotinus repeatedly says or implies that "we," the selves, are our souls. He definitely does not think that there is some kind of independent entity, the self, in addition to the individual human soul. Yet, his statement, "we are our soul" (which applies to each of us) is informative and not a mere tautology. It serves to remind us about what we are not but may come to think we are: the body and the living being. We might think it also serves to remind us that we are not the One or Intellect or generally the gods. As Plotinus sees it, this is, however, more complicated. Even if he would not recommend to anyone to suppose, just like that, that he or she is a god, Intellect or the One—this identity is merely potential and needs to be worked on—there is a sense in which each of us can become these things. In any case, the soul which we are is a precious divine thing. As we saw in Chapter 2 (p. 40), Plotinus thinks it is of crucial importance to realize this.

Plotinus distinguishes between two senses of self: "So 'we' is used in two senses, either including the beast or referring to that which even in our present life transcends it. The beast is the body which has been given life. But the true man[12] is different, clear of these affections [of the beast]" (I.1.10, 5–7). As for Plato, whom he alludes to here, the true man for Plotinus is reason, and this is also what we really are. The distinction between these two senses of self is in the continuation explicated by reference to the story of the sea-god, Glaucus, in Plato's *Republic* X, 611d ff.: just as we should not judge the true nature of the sea-dwelling Glaucus from the encrustations he has acquired by his sojourn in the ocean, we should not judge the nature of the soul by the additions caused by its embodiment: "This is why [Plato] says, 'We have seen the soul like the people who see the sea-god Glaucus.' But, he says, if anyone wants to see its real nature, they must 'knock off its encrustations' and 'look at its philosophy,' and 'see with what principles it is in contact' and 'by kinship with what realities it is what it is'" (I.1.12, 12–17). It is this sense of self, the higher soul, which is the primary sense of "we ourselves" for Plotinus. As the last quote shows, however, he also allows for a wider sense of self according to which we are not merely the higher soul but also the living being, the compound of the lower soul and the qualified body.

There is a third kind of thing that may be called "we ourselves," namely, the source of our soul in Intellect. Admittedly, Plotinus says explicitly in "On the cognitive hypostases and what is beyond" that "we are not Intellect" (V.3.3, 31), no doubt meaning that the life of Intellect is not our everyday life. He, however, also says in the same discussion that "Intellect belongs to us and we belong to it" (V.3.4, 26) and that we may become it, which are claims he makes also in several other places. The reason why this is at all possible is that even before we ascended to this level "[we] were the whole [of intelligible reality]" (VI.5.12, 19).

Some of Plotinus's statements about the self reveal a special kind of reflexive stance. In the first chapter of "What is the living being and what is man?," for instance, after raising such questions as to what feelings and opinions belong, he says that we "must observe what sort of thing it is that acts as overseer and carries out the investigation and comes to a decision about these matters" (I.1.1, 9–11). The investigation he is starting is about the soul and the living being but the reference to that which "carries out the investigation and comes to a decision about these matters" shows an additional concern: not only must we investigate psychological phenomena, we must reflect on who is asking and answering these questions. In the final chapter of the treatise he resumes this reflexive stance:

> What is it that has carried out this investigation? Is it "we" or the soul? It is we, but by the soul. And what do we mean by "by the soul"? Did we investigate by having soul? No, but in so far as we are soul. ... And intellectual activity is ours because the soul is intellectual and intellectual activity is its superior life, both when the soul operates intellectually and when Intellect acts upon us. For Intellect too is a part of ourselves and to it we ascend.
> (I.1.13, 1–8)

We investigated, not by means of having a soul that we used for this purpose but in so far as we are soul. So the inquiry which has established the separation of the soul from the body and the living being, and its grounding in the intelligible world was an inquiry into what we, the investigators, are. This means that the investigator has not merely become clearer about the nature of the soul but at the same time gained self-understanding. This sort of self-understanding is the first step in what Plotinus describes as "the separation of the soul by philosophy" (I.1.3, 17–18).

In a passage in chapter 7 of this same treatise, Plotinus asks how it is we who perceive given that sense-perception belongs to the living being. Let us consider this passage again. That we should perceive is indeed not evident from the fact that the living being is the subject of sense-perception, unless, of course, "we" is taken to be identical with the living being, a view Plotinus does not endorse. He answers:

> It is because we are not separated from the living being so qualified even if other elements of greater value enter for us into the composition of the whole essence of man, which is composed of many elements. And soul's power of perception need not be of sense-objects but rather it must be apprehensive of impressions produced by sense-perception in the living being: for these are already intelligible entities. So external perception is an image of this perception of the soul, which is a contemplation of forms alone free from affection. From these forms, from which the soul alone receives the hegemony over the living being, come reasonings, opinions and intuitions; and this is where we primarily are. That which comes before this is ours but we, in our presidency over the living being, are what extends from this point upwards.
>
> (I.1.7, 7–18)

So Plotinus identifies the self, what he refers to as "we ourselves," with the pure soul. Elsewhere he explicitly identifies the self with reason (cf. V.3.3, 35–36), a view which is implied here. The soul has the power to entertain intelligible forms. These forms are not the Platonic Forms in Intellect but lower level descendants of these in the soul: "We then possess the forms in two ways, in our soul, in a manner of speaking unfolded and separated, in Intellect all together" (I.1.8, 6–8). It is tempting to identify the forms in the soul with concepts. Entertaining these forms is the act of reason employing the power of representation. This is where our conscious life takes place, this is where we are. The body and the functions attributed to the organism belongs to us but they are not we ourselves. The most plausible way of understanding his point here about the relation between us and sense-perception is by supposing that *we*, i.e. our power of reasoning or, more generally, of representation, can share in the already intelligible perceptual judgments of the sensory powers.

Would this account not imply that so far as "we" are concerned, "we" perceive external things in the sensible world only indirectly? The sensory judgment is of the external object but *we* only grasp this judgment (or, which I take to be the same thing, the intelligible impression that has arisen in the living being), not the external object. While we may feel that Plotinus owes us a fuller explanation of how he thinks this works, I do not think that he sees what he says here as in any way in conflict with his direct realism about sense-perception. He is not supposing that reason is observing the perceptual impressions made by the living being as if from the outside, making a second-order judgment about the judgments or impressions of the sensory power. Rather, as the passage from IV.3.29 quoted on pp. 273–274 in fact suggests, the idea must be that the power of representation can literally share in the judgments made by the senses: thus, when the power of representation attends to the senses, it really participates, shares, in the judgments of the senses.

Another question that arises in this connection is whether the soul that entertains these forms is the higher soul or, so to speak, the top part of the middle soul. Plotinus speaks simply about "the soul" and there is no indication that there may be any ambiguity. On the contrary, the whole tone of these lines and especially his remark that his soul has "the hegemony over the whole living being" suggest that he is simply referring to the higher soul. On the other hand, it is also clear that there are activities of the lower soul that do not directly involve the use of the body and hence are the work of soul alone: as we saw in connection with sense-perception and the two memories and twofold power of representation in IV.3.27–32 ff. in the previous chapter, the lower soul has its own power of representation in charge of its proper memories. Furthermore, Plotinus at least sometimes wishes to keep the higher soul itself quite elevated, especially in contexts where he claims its freedom from affection and sinfulness. Consider the following passage:

> The nature of that higher soul of ours will be free from all responsibility for the evils that man does and suffers; these concern the living being, the joint entity, as has been said. But if opinion and reasoning (*dianoia*) belong to the soul, how is it free from sin? For opinion is a cheat and the cause of much evil-doing. Evil is done when we are mastered by what is worse in us—for we are many—by desire or passion (*thymos*) or an evil image. So-called false thinking (*hē tōn pseudōn legomenē dianoia*) is representation which has not waited for the judgment of the reasoning faculty—we have acted under the influence of our worse parts, just as in sense-perception the perception of the common entity may see falsely before reason has given its overarching judgment of it.
>
> (I.1.9, 1–12)

Plotinus does not deny here that opinion and false reasoning belong to the soul, even if they are rooted in the living being. The thrust of his argument is to establish that our higher soul is free from these sorts of opinion and reasoning. They must then belong to the middle soul, the power of representation of the middle soul. It also emerges that "reason" (*dianoia*) is ambiguous: there is the "so-called reason" which may think falsities and there is true reason. This is made quite explicit in the next chapter where he distinguishes "the reason which really belongs to the true soul" from this "so-called reason." He evidently means that only the former is the pure soul and "we ourselves" in the second sense of self he identifies in I.1.10, "that which even in our present life transcends [the beast]" (see p. 286).

We may suspect that there is something unresolved in Plotinus' thought about the lower limit of the higher soul, which is also our true self: sometimes it may sound as if it can have no part in what is going on in our embodied life, sometimes it seems as if the higher soul is the ultimate subject of our sense-perceptions and hence highly involved. The following considerations may help to resolve the conflict, even if some issues doubtless remain obscure.

The higher soul must to some extent be involved in the living being, otherwise Plotinus could not maintain that the soul has "the leadership over the whole living being" (see p. 273). The soul's involvement is also clearly confirmed by passages such as this one:

But is it really the best part of us that has different opinions? No, being unresolved and having vacillating opinions belongs to the compound. The right reason (*orthos logos*) from the best part when given to the compound is weakened because it is in the mixture: it is not so by its own nature, but it is as when the best of counselors speaks in the great clamor of an assembly but does not prevail, but rather the worst of those who make a commotion and shout, while he sits in silence, able to do nothing, overcome by the commotion of the worse.

(IV.4.17, 19–27)[13]

The "best part of us" referred to here is the pure soul. The pure soul clearly knows the state of affairs in the compound and seeks to do something about it—sometimes with limited success according to this passage. Its role in this is exclusively cognitive and directive. In both these functions it may draw on its access to Intellect—unfolding contents of Intellect into the discursive capacity. None of this involves any affection of the higher soul by what is going on in the living being. It further follows from this that the lower and the higher souls share consciousness: each of them has a faculty of representation but in our embodied life they mingle. Plotinus indeed explicitly says so (see IV.3.31).

Why does Plotinus call both the pure soul and the whole consisting of the pure soul and the living being self as we saw him doing in I.1.10 (cf. p. 286)? I believe it is because he is operating with two different concerns that often coincide but not always or necessarily. On the one hand, he sees the self as that which we in fact refer to when we say "I" or "we." The self in this sense is our consciousness and its contents. This may and usually does include the states of our bodies, our sensations, emotions, opinions and whatever else pertains to the soul's embodied existence. Thus, the self in this sense includes the beast but it also includes our consciousness of the higher realms in so far as we project their contents into the faculty of representation. On the other hand, the self is reason, the pure soul without the "encrustations." As we have seen, reason may be involved in the affairs of the living being: it evaluates input from the senses, makes inferences, and judges about goodness and rightness. In performing acts of this sort reason draws on Intellect with which it is in touch.

Reason in this sense is not to be strictly identified with consciousness: our consciousness may be focused on other things and not involve reason; "while we are children the powers of the compound are active, and only a few gleams come to it from what is above" (I.1.11, 1–2). Reason is, nevertheless, there and is still our true self. Thus, reason is we ourselves in the sense of our substance or essence.

Even if contemporary philosophers under the influence of Hume and Kant tend to be very suspicious of the self as some sort of entity, I believe Plotinus' understanding of the self in both the senses just distinguished resonates with common intuitions of many ordinary people. Many of us do think with Plotinus that we ourselves are there where our consciousness is. At the same time we may fancy the idea that there is more to us than this: behind and often silenced and obscured by the tumult of sensible phenomena there is "the real me." If we believe in addition that this higher self is the best in us and that it is akin to and in touch with higher realms of being, we are closely approaching Plotinus' conception.

5 Chapter summary

The powers of representation and reason have been center stage in this chapter. These powers are involved in our everyday consciousness. Of these two, reason is the narrower notion in the sense that reason makes use of images that belong to the faculty of representation but not every such image belongs to reason. Thus, the faculty of representation is our faculty of consciousness but strictly speaking we ourselves are the reason in the affair.

The power of representation receives forms from sense-perception. These forms are already intelligible when they arrive there. The information provided by the senses or the body can be subjected to evaluation by reason. When this occurs, reason may make use of its innate ties to the higher soul and Intellect and project intellectual content "from above" into the faculty of representation. We may describe the matter by saying that the faculty of representation functions as a mediator to translate both information "from below" and "from above."

This general picture, which without doubt correctly represents Plotinus' view, however leaves some details unsettled. Is it, for instance, the case that every perceptual judgment involves the use of our innate knowledge of Forms as is sometimes maintained? I question this both on the basis of textual evidence and the internal implausibility of such a view. Instead it is suggested that even if all cognitive activity depends on the possession of concepts, of which at least some basic ones are innate, Plotinus' thought can accommodate empirically acquired concepts.

Finally, we considered Plotinus' conception of the self. There is indeed a distinction between the mundane self that is conscious of and involved in the affairs of the body and the sensible realm and a higher intelligible self, which is either the soul that never leaves the intelligible realm or an entity in Intellect itself from which our everyday soul descends. The texts are not very clear on this. Clearly, despite various differences in their respective philosophies, this distinction parallels the Kantian one between an empirical and a noetic self.

Further readings

Primary sources

Ennead I.1. (53) "What is the living being and what is man?," especially chapters 7–13.
Ennead IV.3–4. (27–28) "On the problems of soul (I) and (II)," especially chapters 26–32 of IV.3 and chapters 1–2 and 23 of IV.4.
Ennead V.3. (49) "On the cognitive hypostases and what is beyond," chapters 1–4.

Secondary sources

Gerard J. P. O'Daly, *Plotinus' Philosophy of the Self* (Dublin: Irish University Press, 1973).
Eyjólfur K. Emilsson, *Plotinus on Sense-Perception: A Philosophical Study* (Cambridge: Cambridge University Press, 1988), chapters 6 and 7.
Pauliina Remes, *Plotinus on Self: The Philosophy of the "We"* (Cambridge: Cambridge University Press, 2007).
Damian Caluori, *Plotinus on Soul* (Cambridge: Cambridge University Press, 2015), chapters 6 and 7.

Richard A. H. King, *Aristotle and Plotinus on Memory* (Berlin: Walter de Gruyter, 2009).

Sara Magrin, "Sensation and Scepticism in Plotinus," *Oxford Studies in Ancient Philosophy* 39 (2010), 249–297.

Riccardo Chiaradonna, "Plotinus's Account of the Cognitive Powers of the Soul: Sense Perception and Discursive Thought," *Topoi* 31, 2 (2012), 191–207.

Notes

1 Plotinus' words for this power are *hē dianoia, to dianoētikon, logos, to logikon* or *to logistikon*. In translations of Plotinus and in the secondary literature this power is often referred to as "discursive reason," to distinguish it from non-discursive reason, i.e. the intellect. In most contexts "reason" alone will do just as well as a translation.

2 In this regard my interpretation differs radically from those of Lavaud 2006 and Magrin 2010.

3 The interpretation of "On the problems of soul (II)," chapter 8, offered here differs from that given in Emilsson 1988: 87.

4 The verb *apercevoir* had existed in French since the twelfth century and it could mean "to notice," "become aware of." But Leibniz uses it technically for this special case of noticing what already is internal to the soul, and invents the corresponding noun and adjective, "aperception" and "aperceptive," in French. The first public occurrence of the substantive "aperception" is in Leibniz *Monadology* 14 from 1714. See *Le Robert Dictionnaire historique de la langue française*, s.v. "percevoir." Plotinus uses the word *synaisthēsis* in a corresponding context. He says about the unnoticed perceptions that "the impression of such a thing does not yield *synaisthēsis*" (IV.4.8, 19–20). *Synaisthēsis* too is a semi-technical term in Plotinus, which he often uses to refer to awareness of inner states. Even if the prefix "ad" hidden in "aperception" does not correspond exactly to *syn* in *synaisthēsis*, the "perception" part of course corresponds to *synaisthēsis*. Is it possible that "aperception" is intended as a translation of *synaisthēsis* as Plotinus uses it here?

5 What is called here "the primary part of the soul" must I think refer to the individual undescended soul. Blumenthal (1996) suggests that this refers to the hypostasis Soul. This interpretation is convincingly rejected by Aubry 2004: 230, n. 20.

6 Several interpreters, including Lavaud (2006: 40–42), Remes (2007: 144), Magrin (2010: 286–287) and Chiaradonna (2012: 201–202), read this passage differently and in my view unnaturally and, hence, wrongly: they seem to suppose that (discursive) reason must be involved in recognizing what is seen as a human being.

7 There is yet another passage in the same vein in V.1.11, 1–7. Here it is said that since soul reasons about what is right and good in relation to particular things,

there must be some "further permanent rightness from which arises the discursive reasoning in the realm of soul. Or how else would it manage to reason?"
8 In this respect I am in agreement with the account in Magrin 2010: 285–286.
9 For the Stoic view, see Frede 1983 and Sorabji 1990 with ample references. Sorabji opposes what he sees as the orthodox view represented by Frede that the Stoic doctrine denies that animal perception involves propositional attitudes.
10 For a recent account with abundant references to the scholarship, see Stamatellos 2013.
11 Cf. the chapter after this one, I.1.8, 18, where Plotinus uses the same word, *eidolon*, for images of soul that clearly are not to be identified with the trace of soul; see also Noble 2013: 252, n. 6.
12 Here is a clear allusion to Book IX of Plato's *Republic*, 589b. Plato has in the context divided the human being into two sorts of beasts and a human being within them.
13 Dillon and Blumenthal's (2015) translation modified.

Nine

Ethics I

Virtue, happiness and the ethics of everyday life

In a sense there is hardly any ethics in the *Enneads*, in another sense Plotinus is primarily an ethical thinker. That is to say: if we take ethics first and foremost to be a doctrine about the ethical rightness and wrongness of actions or a theory about the nature of morality, we find little in Plotinus that directly addresses these issues. There is no systematic discussion of the rightness or appropriateness of particular acts or practices and very little in terms of theory. On the other hand a philosophy such as Plotinus', which takes the Good to be the first principle of everything and which puts a value on everything according to its proximity to this first principle, must count as ethics widely understood. Differently put, we are faced with a metaphysical doctrine, according to which values are an integral part of reality. The more one anything is, the better it is. In fact, as we noted in Chapter 3, unity and goodness are according to Plotinus ultimately one and the same. Human beings have an existence somewhere near the middle of this scale of goodness but we enjoy a unique mobility on it. Plotinus' metaphysics, and the placement of human beings within it, has evident normative implications for us. The first command of his ethics for humans may be succinctly summarized as: "Don't let the worse element in you rule; ascend to your own intelligible source!" As the second command, I suggest: "You are here in this body in this setting for a reason and you are to take proper care of the body and everything else that relates to its life." We might think that these commands are incompatible: it may seem as if the former asks us to look and even "go" "upwards," whereas the latter asks us to look "downwards."

As we shall see, Plotinus does not think they are in conflict at all. Nevertheless, how these two principles relate is perhaps the most pressing question in Plotinian ethics. With something like these commands as his guiding principles, he addresses such conventional ancient ethical topics as the virtues and happiness. It almost goes without saying that Plato's *Phaedo*, the *Republic* and a crucial passage in the *Theaetetus* set the scene.

We have seen in the two previous chapters that the attitude expressed by the first command permeates Plotinus' account of human psychology and anthropology, including his views on the end for human beings. However, he also wrote treatises that deal more directly with ethical matters: there is the treatise "On virtues" (I.2. (19)) and two treatises on happiness, "On happiness" (I.4. (46)) and "On whether happiness increases with time" (I.5. (36)). The first six chapters of "On autonomy and the will of the One" (VI.8) are also a very relevant source of Plotinus' views. In addition, there is the topic of freedom and related notions most fully treated in VI.8, which is closely connected to his views on the virtues and happiness.

In Sections 1 and 2, Plotinus' views on the virtues and happiness will be presented. I am mostly concerned with paraphrasing and citing what he says without providing much comment or seeking to penetrate into controversial points. In the third section, however, I address some debated issues about Plotinus' ethics. It is mainly for esthetic reasons that the material presented in this chapter and the next one is split between two chapters: the two chapters are very closely connected and present different aspects of Plotinus' views on values.

1 Plotinus' doctrine of grades of virtue

In the treatise "On virtues" Plotinus deals with problems Plato's accounts of virtue give rise to. He begins the treatise by citing Plato's *Theaetetus* 176a–b: "Since it is here that evils are, and 'they must necessarily haunt this region,' and the soul wants to escape from evils, we must escape from here. What then is this escape? 'Being made like god,' Plato says" (I.2.1, 1–4). The treatise may be said to be an interpretation of this pregnant statement that virtue is assimilation to god. But how are we to bring this into harmony with other Platonic statements about the virtues? The *Republic* famously presents an account of the four cardinal virtues, which Plotinus calls "the civic virtues" (politikai aretai), wisdom, courage, self-restraint and justice. The Phaedo describes the virtues as purifications, meaning dissociation of the soul from the body. Are these purifications the same sort of virtue as the cardinal virtues, and how can either be seen as an assimilation to god? The gist of Plotinus' answer is that there are grades of virtue. Thus, we have justice, for instance, as a civic virtue, as a purification and, finally, as the paradigm, the Platonic Idea of Justice. We shall explore this doctrine in the following pages.

A doctrine of different grades of virtue can, I think, be seen to be latent in Plato: Plato distinguishes between "vulgar and political virtues" and the kind of virtue possessed by the philosopher (Republic IV, 442). Aristotle's ethics too, which is notoriously unclear about the exact relationship of the contemplative (theoretical) virtues and the contemplative life, on the one hand, to the practical virtues and life on the other, seems to advocate two kinds good life, the contemplative one being higher and better (Nicomachean Ethics X, 8). There is, however, no doctrine of grades of virtue as we see in Plotinus accompanying this picture. The virtue of practical wisdom, crucial in practical life, is, for instance, an intellectual virtue, a virtue of reason as such. Nevertheless, clearly the person of the practical life and the one leading the contemplative life will draw on different sets of virtues in what they do. It was left to Plotinus to make these grades more explicit. In this he was followed by Porphyry, who in his Sententiae 32, takes up Plotinus' doctrine and develops it.[1] Later Neoplatonists and Augustine too followed suit and made even more distinctions between different grades of virtue.

One specific problem arises from the fact that the civic virtues presuppose beings with emotions and other imperfections pertaining to life in the sensible world. Actually, Plotinus seems to understand the civic virtues to consist in the proper measure of the emotions. They belong to the living being. The gods do not have to temper their emotions—they don't have any—or employ practical reasoning in new circumstances: their thought is intuitive and they do not meet new circumstances (cf. Aristotle, Nicomachean Ethics X, 10, 1178b9 ff.). Hence, they cannot have virtues that specifically apply to a context that is totally alien to them. So how could the civic virtues assimilate us to the divine? On the other hand, Plotinus notes that "tradition calls men of civic virtue godlike" (I.2.1, 24–25). He responds to this dilemma by saying that there are two kinds of similarity only one of which presupposes that the things said to be similar share the same attribute.

> But in the case of two things of which one is assimilated to the other, but the other is primary, not reciprocally related to the other thing and not said to be like it, assimilation must be understood in a different sense; we must not require the same form in both but rather a different one, since the assimilation takes place in this different way.
>
> (I.2.2, 6–10)[2]

Thus, it is possible to say that assimilation to something divine is taking place in the case of the civic virtues without assuming that the divine possesses the very civic virtues themselves. The civic virtues do "set us in order and make us better by giving limit and measure to our desires … and rid us of false opinions" (I.2.2, 13–17). None of this presupposes that there is the same kind of limit and measure in the cause. In fact there cannot be because such material as needs to be ordered and limited is not there in the intelligible divine cause in the first place.

He also expresses this role of the civic virtues in a more metaphysical language connecting his doctrine of measure to his views on the body as sharing in the indefiniteness of matter (see Chapter 6, p. 196). The soul which is set over the body is of course closer to the Good than the body is; but a well-ordered soul of this kind is still not particularly close, even if we may be "deceived into imagining that it is a god, and that all divinity is comprised in this likeness" (I.2.2, 25–26). Thus, Plotinus seems to admit that a kind of assimilation to the divine takes place in a person who merely possesses the civic virtues but it is a low kind of assimilation that should not be overrated.[3]

Plotinus holds that Plato himself draws a distinction between a higher and a lower form of virtue (I.2.3, 5–8). He is right about that: in *Republic* VII, 518d–e, for instance, Plato refers to "other so-called virtues of the soul" which are "akin to those of the body" because they result from "habit and training (*askēsis*)" (cf. *Republic* X, 619c–d). Plotinus alludes to this passage in I.1.10, 11–13, where he speaks about "virtues that result not from practical wisdom but from 'habit and training.'" In the *Phaedo* too (67e–69d) Plato contrasts illusory appearances of the virtues with the virtue of practical wisdom (*phronēsis*), which consists in a cleansing of the soul. Plotinus identifies these appearances of virtue with the lower form of the virtues Plato refers to in the *Republic*.[4] These are the virtues he calls civic in the treatise "On virtues," and they constitute the lowest grade of virtue.

The civic virtues are to be distinguished from the virtues that are purifications (*katharseis*), and these in turn from the intelligible paradigms of the virtues. In the *Phaedo* Socrates says that "in truth, self-restraint and courage and justice are a purging away of all such things [pleasures, pains, fears, etc.], and practical wisdom itself is a kind of cleansing or purification" (69b–c). Plotinus devotes several lines in chapter 4 of "On virtues" to discussing what Plato exactly means by calling virtues purifications. Is the virtue the process of purification or is it the state achieved by it? In chapter 3 he focuses on the process, in chapters 4–6 on the achieved state. This distinction is the basis of Porphyry's three grades of virtue as opposed to Plotinus' two. The relevant text (I.2.4, 1–8) is obscure and probably corrupt, but Plotinus seems to say that purification and the achieved state should be distinguished and that the latter is more complete. It is this distinction which gives rise to Porphyry's third grade of wisdom in *Sententiae* 32.

But what is this which is left after the purification? The answer he comes to is that it is the soul turned to Intellect, "gazing" at it and absorbing what it "sees." It is "a sight and the impression of what is seen implanted and working in it" (I.2.4, 19). Thus, Intellect is the divinity the assimilation to which is virtue. This sort of answer, that true virtue consists in a kind of turning of the soul, is also suggested by the passage in Plato's *Republic* cited above. It is to be emphasized that even the virtues of the purified soul are *virtues of soul*, not of Intellect, which contains the paradigms that are not virtues themselves. The language of the whole passage discussing this (I.2.4, 18–29) clearly suggests that Intellect is an external object of sight for the virtuous soul. This is of considerable importance: it follows that the thought of the fully virtuous person is not the non-discursive kind of thought of Intellect, which is identical with its object: "[the soul] did not have the realities themselves but impressions of them" (I.2.4, 23). This is not to say that it is impossible for the virtuous sage to transcend beyond this stage and move on to the level of Intellect itself (see Chapter 10, Section 1, "Mystical Experience"). Virtuous intellectual activity, however, does not essentially require this.

The four cardinal virtues of the *Republic*, wisdom, courage, self-restraint and justice, are the basis of Plotinus' theory of virtue in this treatise.[5] It is a feature of the doctrine of the grades of virtue that the same virtues exist at different levels, i.e. they have the same names but different definitions that, however, are meant to be analogous. It is interesting to compare the definitions of the cathartic virtues with the civic ones. Civic practical wisdom "has to do with discursive reasoning," whereas cathartic practical wisdom (*phronēsis*) and wisdom (*sophia*) is "the contemplation of what Intellect contains"; civic courage "has to do with the emotions," cathartic courage is "freedom from affections"; civic self-restraint "consists in a sort of agreement and harmony of appetite and reason" and its cathartic counterpart is the "inward turning to Intellect"; finally, civic justice is "each [part of the soul] minding its business with respect to ruling and being ruled," while cathartic justice is "minding one's business even if it is the business of a unity." The paradigms of the virtues, in turn, are accounted for as follows: knowledge and wisdom at that level is intuitive thought (*noēsis*), self-restraint is self-concentration, "minding one's business" is Intellect's proper activity; and courage is "immateriality and abiding pure by itself."

The cathartic virtues are informed by and imitate the very paradigms of the virtues. Interestingly, Plotinus makes a point of insisting that these paradigms are not the virtues themselves: "Wisdom, both practical and theoretical [the cathartic ones], consists in the contemplation of what Intellect contains; but Intellect has it by immediate contact. There are two kinds of wisdom, one in Intellect and one in soul. That which is there [in Intellect] is not virtue, that in soul is virtue" (I.2.6, 12–15). The reason for this is that he considers virtue as necessarily an imposed feature: it is always someone's virtue, a state of something else, whereas "the paradigm of each virtue in Intellect belongs to itself, not to someone else" (I.2.6, 18–19). Thus, there are three (possibly four) grades of justice, for instance, including the paradigm, but only two (or possibly three) grades of justice as a virtue.

In chapter 3 of the treatise, where the cathartic virtues are introduced, they are described mostly negatively, as freedom from the influence of the body. For instance: "Since the soul is evil when it is thoroughly mixed with body and shares its emotions and has all the same opinions, it will be good when it no longer has the same opinions but acts alone" (I.2.3, 11–15). In chapter 4 there is a more positive description of the intellectual activity the soul is engaged in after the purification and this is identified with virtue: "[virtue] is what results for it after the purification" (I.2.4, 18). This distinction gave Porphyry reason to introduce the third grade of virtue mentioned above and he does this apparently supposing that this was Plotinus' meaning. While not doubting that Plotinus makes a relevant distinction here between virtues that purify the soul and those pertaining to the purified soul, I am less sure he intends the two to be different grades: surely, he calls both purifications and he does not give separate definitions of the four virtues for these two aspects.

A crucial difference between the civic and the cathartic virtues is the fact that the former involve the lower soul and the body, whereas the latter do not. At least civic courage and self-restraint simply consist in measures and limits put on the emotions and passions arising in the living being (cf. I.2.2, 13–18). Justice, understood as each part's minding its own business, will at least partly also consist in such measure and limit of the lower element. But what about civic practical wisdom? It cannot be a property of the soul that operates through the body. In a person who has merely the civic virtues this practical wisdom is, however, not illuminated from above. But if it is not, how can it still be called practical wisdom? Plotinus does not expand on civic practical wisdom. Allowing myself to speculate, I suggest that it is a feature of the reasoning power of a soul still "mixed with body". It is primarily directed at the body and states of affairs in the sensible world. Thus, civic practical wisdom may correctly judge that this much wine would be too much, that running into the burning house would be foolhardiness and not virtue, or that it is right to help my old neighbor clearing the snow. Such a person has emotions and is moved by them. His or her practical wisdom calculates discursively what is within and what exceeds the right measure in the non-rational part. While perfectly able to calculate and compare different courses of action with a view to the best result, this person is untouched by true philosophy.

What does the purification consist in? How "does it deal with passion and desire and all the rest, pain and its kindred, and how far is separation from the body possible?" (I.2.5, 3–5). In the texts we see more about what the result of purification is supposed to be than about how it is actually achieved. Let us consider the results first. They take place at two levels, in the higher soul and in the middle. The higher soul "collects itself in a sort of place of its own away from the body" (I.2.5, 5–6). This means that the higher soul distances itself from the emotions, pains and pleasures that originate in the body and the life of the living being. Plotinus evidently thinks it may not be realistic to entirely escape these disturbances: "the soul gets rid of passion as completely as possible, altogether if it can, but if it cannot, at least it does not share in the excitement" (I.2.5, 11–13). Fear will be abolished entirely, because there is nothing to fear.

This is not to deny that there may be involuntary impulses. These, however, do not belong to the higher soul but to the living being. The involuntary impulses, which Plotinus actually refers to only as "the involuntary," are no doubt the same phenomena as what the later Stoics called pre-emotions (*propatheia*, Latin: "propassio")—these are impulses that arise involuntarily in the soul and have not been assented to. Even the wise may be subject to such impulses, which do not count as emotions because there is no assent and no action follows.[6] An example could be the immediate urge to run away when one feels an earthquake. But in the virtuous person "the involuntary impulse is small and weak" (I.2.5, 14). As to desire, the higher soul itself will not "have the desire of food and drink for the relief of the body, and certainly not of sexual pleasures either" (I.2.5, 17–19). It is as if Plotinus immediately retracts this, however, at least in part: "If it does have any of these desires, they will, I think, be natural ones with no element of involuntary impulse in them" (I.2.5, 19–20). The point is presumably that the purified person does not eat, drink or have sex because he or she has given in to involuntary impulses, but may engage in such activities for "for natural reasons."

This was the effect of purification on the higher soul. The purification also affects the lower soul. The higher soul will "want to make the irrational part, too, pure so that this part may not be disturbed; or, if it is, not much" (I.2.5, 21–23). Somewhat optimistically, perhaps, Plotinus goes on to describe how the middle soul will be calmed down by living in the neighborhood of the purified higher soul "just as a man living next door to a sage would profit by the sage's neighborhood, either by becoming like him or by regarding him with such respect as not to dare to do anything of which the good man would not approve" (I.2.5, 25–27). He presents this calming as a part of the purification. As we saw, however, the civic virtues are essentially measures and limits of the lower and middle soul's emotional states. It is possible to have the civic virtues without the cathartic ones but not vice versa (I.2.7, 10–12), so this calming down must be something in addition to the mere possession of the civic virtues, something that first comes with the cathartic virtues.

The crucial part of Plotinus' account of purification is the separation of the higher soul, which enables it to live its own life more or less undisturbed. Apparently, this goal cannot be reached unless the middle and lower soul has been tamed by the civic virtues. It is not as if the middle and lower soul can have a wild life of sex, and drugs and rock and roll while the higher soul enjoys the peacefulness of a fully intellectual life.[7] The separation of the higher soul from the living being means that the higher soul ceases to regard the affections of the living being as its own, it no longer appropriates them. This does not mean that it is not aware of them but its awareness is as of the affections of someone else, indeed something it is concerned with and more attached to than to anything else in the realm below, but nevertheless another.

There is surprisingly little in the *Enneads* about how this separation is achieved in practical terms. How does one go about alienating one's soul sufficiently from the lower soul and the body? Plotinus' standard answer is: "through philosophy" (I.1.3, 16 ff.; III.6.5, 1; VI.4.16, 41). But how does one achieve this through philosophy? I think the answer here is simply that if we understand, fully appreciate and accept the Platonic view of the world we will achieve this: we will then have understood that though not worthless, the things of the sensible world are not what is ultimately real and that their value pales when compared with that of the intelligible realm. We shall also have realized that we ourselves are our soul and this soul belongs to the intelligible realm and is something quite different from the body and the living being. We shall discover the hypostasis Soul and Intellect and, perhaps, at last get a glimpse of the Good itself—at least we shall become aware of its existence even if we cannot fathom it as it is in itself. If we have fully realized all this, we will have separated our soul. No doubt it doesn't suffice to read through Plato or the *Enneads*, even with some understanding of what is being said; one must really see this fully and clearly so that the understanding is accompanied by deep and lasting conviction. In that case, we will not be so stupid as to think that a bodily pain really affects us.

In the last chapter of "On virtues" Plotinus addresses the question of the relation between the cathartic and the civic virtues. He holds that "whoever has the greater virtues must necessarily have the lesser ones potentially, but it is not necessary for the possessor of the lesser virtues to have the greater ones" (I.2.7, 10–12; cf. I.3.6, 14–20). Given that the civic virtues are essentially the tempering of the emotions, one may wonder whether there is any room for the civic virtues, so understood, when the emotions have been largely purged away. He concludes the discussion by saying that the man of cathartic virtue "will altogether separate himself, as far as possible, from his lower nature and will not live the life of the good man, the good citizen, which civic virtue requires [cf. I.4.16]. He will leave that behind, and choose another, the life of the gods: it is to them, not to good men, that we are to be assimilated" (I.2.7, 23–28). This may suggest that the sage is totally unconcerned with anything other than his contemplation. I do not think, however, that this is what these lines imply; and that would in any case not square well with other evidence. First, Plotinus is noting that the civic virtues, understood as measured emotions, are no longer the ruling principles of the sage. Second, he is presumably pointing out that the sage has a different set of values than the merely "good man": the latter is primarily concerned with ruling and managing affairs in this world in a virtuous way; the sage is much more detached, and would, for instance, avoid politics and offices of worldly power (see, however, p. 228). Yet, this does not mean that he seeks to ignore everything of this world entirely. We shall return to this topic when we have considered the sage more fully.

In other treatises, Plotinus gives a somewhat different picture of the virtues. In chapter 6 of the treatise "On dialectic" (I.3. (20)), which is next after "On virtues" on Porphyry's chronological list, Plotinus addresses the role of dialectics in the virtues. Here dialectic is described as the crown of philosophy concerned with Platonic Ideas (I.3.4–5). Other parts of philosophy such as physics and ethics are aided by dialectic. The ethical part of philosophy derives its contemplative aspect from it and adds the dispositions and the training that produces them. The other virtues apply reasoning to particular cases, whereas

> practical wisdom is a kind of superior reasoning concerned more with the universal; it considers questions of mutual implication, and whether to refrain from action, now or later, or whether an entirely different course of action would be better; dialectic and theoretical wisdom (sophia), which here have the role of the higher virtues, provide everything for practical wisdom to use in a universal and immaterial form.
> (I.3.6, 10–14)

The role given here to practical wisdom (phronēsis) is different from that of civic practical wisdom in "On virtues": it is informed by wisdom and dialectic. The other virtues too are no mere attunement of the non-rational part of the soul but principles that apply reasoning to particular cases. This suggests that these virtues are not to be identified with the civic virtues of the earlier treatise, but with virtues of an already purified soul.

Finally, Plotinus asks whether the lower kinds of virtue can exist without dialectic and theoretical wisdom (sophia) and vice versa. By "the lower kinds of virtue" he means practical wisdom and other virtues directed at the body and the sensible realm. The answer is that the higher cannot exist without the lower and the lower only incompletely and defectively without the higher. Admittedly, natural virtues—these are doubtless innate character traits[8]—can precede wisdom but without wisdom the natural virtues are imperfect with respect to both insight and character.

In the slightly later treatise "On the impassibility of things without body" (III.6. (26)) there is a discussion of the question whether acquiring virtue should count as affecting the soul. The answer is that it shouldn't. Here the parts of the soul from Plato's *Republic* and the *Timaeus* are introduced as the recipients of virtue. The account here is more in harmony with "On dialectic" than with "On virtues." In general virtue consists in "listening to reason (*logos*)." In the case of the reasoning part of the soul (*to logizomenon*) this consists in receiving reason from the intellect (or Intellect) and the other parts, the irascible and the appetitive receive it from the reasoning part. There is no explicit mention of practical wisdom here but the perfection of the reasoning part referred to is no doubt the same as practical wisdom. Like practical wisdom in "On dialectic" the virtue of the reasoning part is informed from above and plays an overarching role with respect to the other virtues (cf. *Phaedo* 69b–d). Similarly, in "On autonomy and the will of the One" (VI.8.5–6), Plotinus says that virtue intellectualizes the soul and thereby makes it free. The context shows that this applies also to virtues that are expressed in external actions.

Common to the accounts of virtue in all these treatises is some sort of distinction between intellectual capacities or virtues and the civic virtues, and in all the necessity of influence from above is emphasized at least for perfect virtue. The differences are, however, notable: the full doctrine of grades of virtue, where virtues bearing the same names exist in different grades at different levels, is absent in the chronologically later treatises. This does not necessarily mean that Plotinus abandoned this doctrine, after all these accounts are much shorter than what we have in "On virtues" and he may be leaving out details of his account. I still find it somewhat surprising that we do not see explicit echoes of this doctrine in other treatises. The different status and role of practical wisdom is also noteworthy. In the later treatises practical wisdom (I am assuming it is implicit in III.6) is a kind of intermediary between the higher intellectual virtues and the ones relating to the non-rational parts of the soul. By contrast, in "On virtues" the lowest grade of practical wisdom (the civic practical wisdom) seems to be able to operate without the involvement of the intellect.

In "On happiness" (I.4) there is a detailed account of the sage. The sage (ho spoudaios) is the same as the cathartically virtuous person, and is also the truly happy (see I.2.7, 11–13).[9] The focus in this treatise is indeed on the sage's happiness but this is intimately connected to the sage's virtues. We shall first consider Plotinus' general view of happiness, and then address questions about the sage's attitudes and behavior in everyday life. As will emerge, some questions arise for his account that are at best only tentatively resolved. This will give us reason to revisit the passages just recounted from "On virtues" and "On dialectic."

2 Happiness

As already noted, Plotinus wrote two treatises on happiness, "On happiness" (I.4. (46)) and "On whether happiness increases with time" (I.5. (36)). The latter but earlier treatise is short and it deals with just one question: whether happiness increases with time. We shall consider shortly what is at stake here. The other treatise is much longer and more complex. We shall come to it in due course.

The Greek words at issue here are *eudaimōn*, "happy," and its derivatives, *eudaimonia* ("happiness") and *eudaimonein* ("to be happy," "to fare well"). Other scholars and translators have thought that the word "happy" and its derivatives have some wrong connotations and prefer e.g. "human flourishing" or, as Plotinus' translator A. H. Armstrong does, "well-being." The ancient Greek philosophers since Socrates had discussed and debated about *eudaimonia*. Though disagreeing, sometimes strongly, there was general agreement that *eudaimonia*, whatever it exactly consists in, is what we are all always after, it is our *telos*, our final end. It is something such that if we have it we are not missing anything essential; and if we don't have it, we do miss something essential. Arguably, we are all always after well-being, but if we ask people generally they would doubtless say that it is happiness. "Well-being" strikes me as too remote from everyday discourse to serve as an ideal rendering of *eudaimonia*. This is not to deny that "well-being" and "being well off" suit Plotinus' particular views on happiness rather well.

Let us first consider the shorter and earlier treatise, "On whether happiness increases with time" (I.5).[10] The question here is whether past and future happiness can be at all relevant to present happiness in such a way that the former counts as a current asset contributing to a person's present happiness. If I have been happy for a long time and you have been happy only for a short period and our present state is equal in happiness, am I happier than you just because I have been happy longer? Plotinus answers "no." He considers the doubts someone may have about his position: suppose one person has been happy her whole life, and another in the latter part of life, and yet another has been well off at first and then changed his state, do they have equal shares (see I.5.5, 1–3)? The skeptic is obviously suggesting that the person who has been happy throughout has a larger share of happiness than do the two others because he has been happy longer. I do not know why Plotinus has his skeptic bring in two others who differ in their allotted periods of happiness. It seems that one such person would suffice. Perhaps he is inviting the reader to think of both late losers and early bloomers, and early losers and late bloomers, assuming we would reach the same conclusion in both cases, even if there may be a certain presumption in favor of the late bloomer when compared with the early bloomer, when we compare such persons with someone happy throughout his or her life. He does not follow up this possibility. In any case, Plotinus responds:

> Here the comparison is being made between people who are not happy, with a man who is happy. So if this latter has anything more, he has just what the man in a state of happiness has in comparison with those who are not; and that means that his advantage is by something that is present.
> (I.5.5, 3–8)

I take it that with this response Plotinus is saying: You may think that the person who has been happy his or her entire life has a larger share in happiness and, hence, is happier than those who have been happy only for a part of their lives. But note that when you compare the one who is always happy with the one who was happy only in, say, the first part of life but not in the latter half and come to the conclusion that the former is happier, you will agree that in the first part of their lives there was no difference between the two: they are both happy. When comparing the latter halves of their lives, you see that the one is happy, the other not happy, and of course you judge that the happy one is happier than one who is not happy at all. In any case, in so judging we are not comparing accumulated happiness over time but only judging on the basis of something present.

Plotinus' imaginary objector doesn't surrender. Obviously, we can count things in the past, for instance, dead people. Why can't we count past happy times in the same way and judge the person who has the most of them the happiest? That cannot be because "it would be absurd to say that happiness that no longer is present is greater than the happiness that is present" (I.5.7, 10–12). The thought is that past or future happiness isn't ours, it is gone or not yet here; whether we are happy or not must be evaluated by what we presently have. Those who think otherwise are assuming that the judgment of happiness is about the achievement of a lifetime, on par with "Pelé is the greatest soccer player ever." He may well be, but that is irrelevant to the question whether he is a great soccer player in terms of his present abilities: the same with happiness, happiness does not accumulate.

The question at issue here is not new with Plotinus: Hellenistic philosophers, both Epicureans and Stoics, had essentially the same view, which was questioned, for instance, by Cicero.[11] As Linguiti (2007: 79) notes, Aristotle seems to be Plotinus' adversary. Admittedly, Aristotle nowhere says or implies that happiness can accumulate over time like money or a collection of stamps, but he does indicate that the judgment of someone's happiness contains an evaluation of a considerable period of time, even of a whole lifetime. So in that way at least Plotinus and the Hellenistic philosophers dissent from his view.

One might get the impression from the preceding account that Plotinus thinks that happiness is a matter of momentary bliss, an episode of ecstasy or something of that sort. This is, however, not at all his view or that of his Hellenistic predecessors. To repeat: the point is just that happiness does not accumulate over time; the judgment about happiness can only be based on something present, something the person presently has; the past and the future are not like that. In chapter 7 of I.5, Plotinus, however, takes a leap that sets his view apart from that of the Stoics and the Epicureans:

> In general, extension of time means the dispersal of a single present. That is why it is properly called "the image of eternity," since it intends to bring about the disappearance of what is permanent in eternity by its own dispersion. So if it takes from eternity what would be permanent in it and makes it its own, it destroys it—it is preserved, up to a point, by eternity, in one way, but destroyed if it passes altogether into temporal dispersion. So if happiness is a matter of good life, obviously the life concerned must be that of real being; for this is the best. So it must not be counted by time but by eternity; and this is neither more nor less nor of any extension, but is a 'this here,' unextended and timeless[12] ... one must take it all as a whole, if one takes it at all, and apprehend not the undividedness of time,[13] but the life of eternity, which is not made up of many times, but is all together from the whole of time.
> (I.5.7, 14–30)

We see here in the first part some of the ideas about time that we considered in Chapter 5, Section 7 ("Soul and Time"). Time disperses the beings that exist as whole all together in Intellect. So features that are "all together" in a timeless repose in the intelligible realm are spread out in time in the sensible realm. Intellect is intuitive thought and thought is alive (see Chapter 4, p. 112 ff.). Being the most self-contained and unified life there is, it is life par excellence. Hence, it is the best life. Since, being happy—on this Aristotle and most philosophers would agree—is living well and Intellect's life is the best life, happiness must be identified with the life of Intellect.

Plotinus argues for this last claim in greater detail in the other later and longer treatise, "On happiness," I.4. (46), to which we shall now turn. It is an assumption of his discussion here that being happy consists in living well (*eu zēn*), an assumption he shares with Aristotle's account of happiness in Book I of the *Nicomachean Ethics*. Despite this juxtaposition of happiness and living well by both philosophers, they both wish to deny happiness to the lower kinds of living beings, even if they admit that they can live well or not so well. Plotinus, however, has a different take on this than Aristotle. In chapter 3 of I.4 we see him arguing as follows: (1) If "life" applies to all living beings exactly in the same sense, there would be no reason to deny happiness to plants and non-rational animals: they all live in the same sense and may do so well or badly. (2) Those (presumably Aristotelians and/or Stoics) who place happiness in rational life rather than life as such are unknowingly assuming that happiness depends on a quality of life, i.e. its being rational. (3) As it is, however, happiness consists in "the totality of this [life], that is, in another form of life," i.e. not in life qualified in a particular way or in a particular quality of it but in the totality of life. (4) To say that happiness consists in the totality of life is just to say that happiness is life at its best, life in the fullest sense of the word. What he means emerges from the following passage:

> Since life is spoken of in various ways, differentiated in terms of first and second and so on in order, and living is spoken of homonymously, in one way of plants, in another way of non-rational animals, differentiated according to clarity and dimness [of their lives], clearly living well is analogous. And if one thing is an image of another, clearly its living well is an image of another's living well. If then happiness belongs to that which has a superabundance of life—this means that which in no way is deficient in life—it will belong only to the being which lives superabundantly: to this the best will belong, if what is truly the best in life and the perfect life is to be found among real beings.
> (I.4.3, 18–28)

A few comments on this are in order.

1 Plotinus alludes to Aristotle's idea of an ordered series.[14] Such a series contains two or more items that come in an order of prior and posterior. Examples of ordered series according to Aristotle are the number series, Platonic Ideas and things that depend on them, and life and souls. They are characterized by a progression from a first from which the subsequent items in the series are built. Aristotle holds that there can be no common definition

2. Plotinus says that "living is spoken of homonymously," which means that we do not always mean the same thing when we say that something is alive. Things are homonymous according to Aristotle, the inventor of this technical term, which have only the name in common and not the definition (see *Categories* 1a1). He does not, thereby, exclude the possibility that homonymous things can be connected and that their connection explains their common name: such are, for instance, things that are said "in relation to one thing" or "from one thing," such as the various things that are called "healthy," all so called in relation to one thing, namely health.[15] Some are said to be healthy because they produce or preserve health (e.g. healthy apples), others because they are a sign of it (e.g. a healthy complexion). It is the latter kind of homonymy that Plotinus has in mind here: life is something different for each: an oak, a horse and Intellect have life in different ways that do not permit a common definition but the senses in which they are said to be alive are not unconnected.

3. The way the different forms of life are connected is as prior and posterior. That is to say: there is a first "superabundant life," which must be what Plotinus has in mind by "the totality of life." This is the life of Intellect, which is the best life because it is the perfect life, in no way deficient in life's actuality. Other forms of life are images of this one. Thus, happiness and living well apply primarily to this life.

4. We might think that the Good (the One) itself rather than Intellect must be at the top of the series of lives. Plotinus actually mentions this possibility in the context: "For what could be added to the perfect life to make it into the best life? If anyone says 'the nature of the Good,' that would be appropriate to our account, but we are not looking for the cause, but for that in which it [happiness; the good] exists" (I.4.3, 30–33). This confirms that indeed he regards the Good as the cause of the good life. He does not say here, however, whether the Good is itself alive or not. If it is, it would be the first life and first in the series of lives. The *Enneads* do not speak with one voice on that question.[16] The impression one gets from "On happiness" is

that the life of Intellect is the first life, which is not to deny that this life with its inherent Goodness flows from the Good.

5   A question arises: it may seem from the foregoing that the activity with which happiness is identified is that of Intellect rather than of soul; yet, Plotinus indicates elsewhere in I.4 that the activity by virtue of which the sage is happy is one of soul (I.4. 14, 4–6). Furthermore, as we saw when considering "On virtues" (p. 301), the activity of the highest stage of cathartic virtue is said to be an activity of soul and of the sort that looks to and is informed by Intellect rather than being an activity of Intellect itself. So it may seem that happiness is both said to be the original superabundant life of Intellect and a lower form of activity of a soul imitating it. I do not know for sure how to resolve this. We may note, however, that the life of a soul that looks to and conforms to Intellect in every respect is an intellectual life and belongs to the intelligible realm. Presumably, Plotinus thinks that this suffices to render this sort of life a truly happy one.

Plotinus' conception of the happy life as the life of Intellect owes a lot to Aristotle's conception of the contemplative life in the *Nicomachean Ethics* X, chapters 7–8. Aristotle claims here that this life is divine and that when humans engage in contemplation their life is as divine as humanly possible. Plotinus agrees, but unless one reads quite a bit into Aristotle, Plotinus' argument for the superiority of this life is different from Aristotle's. Aristotle adduces several reasons for the superiority of the contemplative life: it is the most purely pleasant life, it is the most self-sufficient, and it is the most lovable for its own sake. Plotinus too points out that this kind of life is pleasant and that it is self-sufficient, but for him this is something that flows from its being the Platonically paradigmatic life, lacking in nothing so far as life is concerned.

In the preceding paragraphs we have been taken back to metaphysical issues. Indeed Plotinus' views on the virtues and happiness are inseparable from his general metaphysics. We shall now turn to the human being and consider the life, attitudes and acts of the happy person.

After he has established that true happiness consists in living the perfect life of Intellect in chapter 3, Plotinus raises the question whether this kind of life is possible for human beings (I.4.4, 1 ff.). He asserts that "it is clear from other considerations that man has perfect life through having not only sense-perception, but also reasoning, and true intellect (noun alēthinon)" (I.4.4, 6–8). Moreover, this is something every human being has: "He is not really a man if he does not have this either potentially or actually, the one we indeed call happy" (I.4.4, 9–11). The difference between those who are potentially happy and those who are actually so consists in the former having this kind of life as a part of themselves, whereas the latter are totally identified with it: the person who is actually happy "has passed into [this kind of life] and is it" (I.4.4, 14–15). The context makes clear that "the one we indeed call happy" (in ll. 10–11) refers to the one who actually, and not merely potentially, lives the intellectual life, the sage. Those who do so merely potentially are all human beings deserving of the name, which presumably means: any normal human being. As noted in the previous section, the sage is the same as the cathartically virtuous person: the latter is called a sage in the treatise on the virtues (I.2.7, 13).

There is notoriously little said in either "On virtues" or "On happiness" about what the sage is actually thinking when he is engaged in intellection. No doubt the sage may be one with Intellect, immersed in thought of the timeless realm of Platonic Ideas. There is reason to suppose, however, that what counts as the intellectual life is wider than this but let us leave that question for the time being and consider Plotinus' portrayal of the sage as he appears in daily life. The treatise itself mentions quite a few characteristics of the happy sage that we can safely assume stand in contrast to the non-sage and non-happy person. Indeed, the bulk of the treatise actually is more or less an essay on the characteristics of the sage. We shall let a few examples suffice, which, however, will give us the general picture.

The happy sage wishes necessities such as health and freedom from pain to be present and rejects their opposites. "We will say that it is not because they bring any addition to happiness, but rather to his existence. He avoids the opposites of these either because [they contribute] towards non-existence or because being present they disturb the end" (I.4.7, 2–5). And a few lines further on: "if something the happy person doesn't want is present, it doesn't take away, as a result, anything of this happiness" (8–10). He thinks nothing of "kingships and rule of cities and nations, and founding of colonies and cities. So why should the expulsion from power or destruction of his city be a momentous matter for him either?" (18–22). He would no longer be a sage if he thought that "wood or stones, or, by Zeus, the death of mortals is a very serious matter" (23–24). The possibility and, in fact, the actuality that his daughters and daughters-in-law are dragged off into slavery does not reduce his happiness (33–40). This last statement is said with a clear reference to King Priam of Troy, who was in antiquity a stock example of a man who suffered great misfortunes in old age (cf. Aristotle, *Nicomachean Ethics* I, 1100a8).

Such so-called goods as health and freedom from pain "contribute nothing to our happiness" and should be called necessities rather than goods (I.4.6, 26–30). They seem to have a similar status to the "preferred indifferents" in Stoic theory (cf. Brittain 2003: 245). Thus, the sage does not want such things because he thinks they make him happy: they are purely instrumental either for sustaining his life or for avoiding what distresses him and interferes with his intellectual activity. In so far as the sage's actions are directed at other people, he no doubt has the same attitude as towards himself: even when saving their lives, he is not contributing to their happiness, at best providing for their "necessities." It follows from this that the close ties between the lower kind of virtuous life and happiness are severed in Plotinus (cf. Cooper 2012: 343 ff.).

The sage will endure extreme pain and need not be pitied because "his own internal light burns, like the light in a lantern when it is blowing hard outside with a great fury of wind and storm" (I.4.8, 3–5). Clearly, such a sage has firmly separated his soul from his body. And if he should suffer unbearable pain that, however, fails to kill him, the sage "will consider what he must do, for it has not deprived him of his power of self-determination in this situation. It is necessary to understand that such things do appear to the sage not as they appear to other human beings, neither the other things, nor pains nor sorrows, reach the inner man" (I.4.8, 8–12). As McGroarty (2006: *ad loc.*) notes, Plotinus seems here to be willing to consider suicide as a valid option.[17]

As to the fortune of others, the sage "would want all men to do well and no-one to be involved in evils; if this does not happen, he is nevertheless happy" (I.4.11, 12–14). Nevertheless, the sage does not pity other people in pain any more than he pities himself: "To pity them would be a weakness in our soul" (I.4.8, 13). He responds to the objection that it is in our nature to feel pain at the misfortunes of others by saying that "this does not apply to everybody, and that it is the business of virtue to raise common nature to a higher level. ... One must not behave like someone untrained, but stand up to the blows of fortune, and know that though some natures may dislike them, one's own can bear them, not as terrors but as children's bogeys" (I.4.8, 20–27).

What can be pleasant in such a life? Those who raise this issue "will not be demanding the presence of the pleasures of the licentious or the pleasures of the body—these could not be there and would do away with happiness" (I.4.12, 1–4). As opposed to such pleasures, the sage will enjoy those "accompanying the presence of goods, and not such as consist in movements or generation; for the goods are already there and he is present to himself; and this pleasure and contentment are stable: for the sage is always content (hileōs)[18] and his constitution peaceful and his disposition satisfied, undisturbed by any of the so-called evils, if he [truly is] a sage" (I.4.12, 5–10).

Plotinus' views on the irrelevance of conventional goods such as health, wealth, power and physical pleasure, and evils such as physical pain, for happiness are in accord with those expressed by Socrates and Plato.[19] The Stoics too maintained similar views.[20] Plotinus' discussion in "On happiness" is clearly influenced by the Stoics and Hellenistic debates on the matter. The Stoics held that nothing is good or bad except the perfection or corruption of reason. To put it succinctly, evil and misery consist in judging indifferent things such as the conventional goods and evils to be truly good or evil. The failure is a failure of reason and is equivalent to succumbing to emotions: distress, for instance, "is the irrational fresh opinion that something bad is present" (Andronicus, *On Passions* I = Long and Sedley 1987: 65B). There is something analogous to this in Plotinus: an error that is bound to lead to misery is to become preoccupied with sensible apparent goods and evils and regard them as that on which one's happiness depends. This is, however, also entirely Platonic. The crucial difference between Plotinus and the Stoics lies in the fact that Plotinus has a strategy of alienating the body in a way the Stoic unitary conception of the human being does not allow: we are to realize that we ourselves are not the subjects of whatever goes on in the body or originates in it; its needs, desires and affections are not our needs, desires or affections.

We have sketched the sage's emotional life (or rather the lack thereof) and his attitudes towards things in this world. But what about his intellectual life? What does this consist in and how does it relate to his life in the sensible world? Is the sage engaged in intellectual activity also when he is attending to the needs of his body or acting on civic virtues, which we saw in the previous section that he sometimes may do?

> [activity constituting happiness] is sleepless, and then the sage, in that he is a sage, would be active even then. This activity would not escape the attention of all of him, but only a part of him; as is the case when our vegetative soul is active, the conscious apprehension of such activity through sense-perception does not go to the other man, and, if we were our vegetative soul, we ourselves would be active [irrespective of the fact that we are conscious of it]. But as a matter of fact, we are not this but the activity (*energeia*) of the thinking (*tou noountos*) part.
>
> (I.4.9, 22–29)

The view expressed here raises several problems and questions: (1) Every human being is potentially engaged in intellection; as we have seen, the majority of people have this as a part of themselves but the sage is this.[21] This presumably means that everyone's intelligible self is always engaged in intellection (cf. Chapter 2, p. 43) but most people are not aware of this and are, hence, only potentially happy. Thus, Plotinus appears to make the following claims: (a) every human being has, and in some sense really is, a higher soul or intellect, the noetic self, which is constantly, in fact, timelessly, engaged in intellectual activity; (b) happiness for human beings consists in this activity; (c) the mundane self's consciousness of this activity is irrelevant to happiness; the possessor of the higher soul is happy all the same. From (a), (b) and (c) it follows that every human being is always happy. But that would be in clear conflict with his general message in "On happiness," which is that only the sage is happy. The question then becomes: what is the difference between the sleeping or drugged sage and ordinary people? Aren't both equally actively and equally potentially engaged in intellection and hence equally happy?

We have seen that Plotinus thinks that the person he calls a sage and happy has undergone a kind of change, "has passed into [the intellectual life] and is it" (I.4.4, 14–15).[22] It is this change which enables the sage to face such so-called disasters with equanimity. Plotinus is clearly presuming that this change has made the sage different from other people for good. I propose as a solution to our puzzle about the sleeping sage that he is differently related to intellectual thought than other people, even when he is not conscious of this thought. When he wakes up from his sleep or his drug wears off, he can immediately resume his intellection. Ordinary people cannot. It follows from this that even if the sage, considered from the viewpoint of his mundane self, may be said to be only potentially engaged in intellection when he is asleep, this potentiality is of a higher degree than that of the ordinary person. This is comparable with the two senses of potentiality suggested in Aristotle *De anima* II, 417b30 ff.: a grown-up military man is a potential general in a different (and fuller) sense than a boy. And as Aristotle would say, a builder who is resting at home is even then in a sense an actual builder although he is also a potential builder in the sense that he can actually build (cf. *On the Soul* II, 5).

It is to be admitted that Plotinus does not argue for his view concerning the sleeping sage in these terms and that there is an element in his account that goes beyond these Aristotelian considerations: Plotinus holds that even when asleep the sage is actually engaged in intellection in a way ordinary people are not. However, Plotinus may well think that the difference between the sage and ordinary people is shown by the sage's readiness to resume conscious intellection and that this is evidence that something in him must have been so engaged the whole time and closer to his consciousness than in the ordinary person—how else are we to explain the relation of the availability of intellection to the sage?

This response to the question above suggests that the sage is much engaged in conscious intellection when awake. This is not uncontroversial. It has been suggested, primarily on the basis of "On happiness," chapters 9 and 10, that the sage's lower self, his mundane consciousness, is in general unaware of his contemplative side.[23] So in his everyday mundane life the sage may be thinking and doing all sorts of things but still engaged in contemplation at a higher level of which he is conscious at that level but not at the level of his mundane self. This has been dubbed the multi-operation view as opposed to the single-operation alternative, which holds that there is just one sort of activity the sage is conscious of at any given time (Brittain 2003: 225).

I shall not discuss the various pros and cons of these interpretations in detail. Let me, however, make two observations, which seem to me to suggest that the sage is in fact consciously engaged in contemplation a lot of the time. In "On happiness," chapter 13, we find the following passage:

> As for [the sage's] contemplative activities, some of them which are concerned with particular points are perhaps hindered by circumstances, for instance those which require search and investigation. But "the greatest study"[24] is always ready to hand and with him, all the more if he is in the so-called bull of Phalaris[25]—which is silly to call pleasant, though people keep on saying that it is.
>
> (I.4.13, 3–8)

This could be taken to mean that the sage is undisturbed and, it is implied, remains happy simply because his noetic self is still contemplating, even if his mundane self is not aware of this. That would, however, not only be a highly implausible view in itself—who in bodily agony would be consoled by the fact that he is thinking splendid thoughts of which he is not aware?—I think it is also refuted by the context: Plotinus admits that great pain may hinder the kind of contemplative activity that requires search and investigation. When he says that "the greatest study" would not be hindered, it is most natural to take him to mean the contemplative activity which does *not* require search or investigation but of which the sage is mundanely conscious. He notes that "the greatest study" is always at hand (*procheiron*), which would not make good sense if the subject to whom "the greatest study" is always available was the noetic self which is by nature always engaged in intellection: the subject to whom this is "at hand" must be one not necessarily always applying what is "at hand," i.e. the ordinary mundane consciousness of the sage. Though we may remain skeptical that concentration on the intelligible realm always works as an anesthetic against pain, it does make sense to suppose that it helps.

Another passage which has been taken as evidence for the multi-operation view is Porphyry's description of Plotinus himself in the *Life*. Here Porphyry says:

> Even if he was talking to someone, engaged in continuous conversation, he kept his train of thought. He could take his necessary part in the conversation to the full, and at the same time keep his mind fixed without a break on what he was considering. (When the person he had been talking to was gone, he did not go over what he had written, because his sight, as I have said, did not suffice for revision.) He went straight on with what came next, keeping the connection, just as if there had been no interval of conversation between. In this way he was present at once to himself and to others, and he never relaxed his self-turned attention except in sleep.
> (*Life of Plotinus* 8, 11–21)

Now this and other passages about Plotinus in the *Life* can only be taken as evidence about the Plotinian sage if we make the two following assumptions: first, that Porphyry wishes to present Plotinus as a sage of the sort Plotinus himself holds up as an ideal human being; secondly, that Porphyry has an accurate understanding of the Plotinian sage. (We need not assume that Porphyry's portrayal is accurate in every detail: he may well be exaggerating Plotinus' sage-like qualities on purpose or succumb to wishful thinking about them to some extent.) The first assumption strikes me as positively certain. In the *Life* Porphyry idolizes Plotinus both as a philosopher and as human being. He would not wish to suggest that Plotinus fell short of his own philosophical ideal. Moreover, Porphyry reports in *Life* 23 that Plotinus reached a union with the One on four occasions during the time he was with him. He would not say this of anyone whom he doesn't regard as a sage. The second assumption is less certain but plausible. Porphyry certainly knew what Plotinus says about the sage in his writings and, moreover, he would likely have had additional clues about Plotinus' conception of the sage that we do not possess. And he was a highly trained philosopher and no fool. Although we cannot exclude the possibility that he misunderstands something, I find the second assumption quite plausible and shall take it for granted in what follows. Some interpreters see the account of the sage in "On happiness" and that of Plotinus in the *Life* as plainly incompatible: a cold, distant (to his fellow human beings) sage is contrasted with a compassionate and friendly Plotinus. I do not see it this way. Let us recall that the sage "would want all men to do well and no-one to be involved in evils" (I.4.11, 12–13) and that he "will not be unfriendly or unsympathetic; he will be like this to himself and in dealing with his own affairs; but he will render to his friends all that he renders to himself, and so will be the best of friends as well as remaining intelligent" (I.4.15, 21–25). In "On happiness" Plotinus' primary concern is the features of the sage in virtue of which he is truly happy. He is not happy in virtue of his interpersonal relationships or external actions generally; hence, these are not focused on here. The remarks just quoted, however, summarize his attitude towards others and from it, it is natural to presume, kind acts follow. This suffices to show that the account of the sage in "On happiness" and that of the *Life* are fully compatible.

The question is whether this passage provides evidence for the multi-operation view. I do not think it does. A very notable difference between the sleeping sage, who is still said to be engaged in contemplation, and Plotinus as described here is that Plotinus' concentration is relaxed when he sleeps. This strongly suggests that whatever of the intellectual kind Plotinus keeps concentrating on even while engaged in conversation, this mental activity assumes and depends on his ordinary waking consciousness. What Porphyry is describing here is nothing very mysterious or even so unusual: he is saying that Plotinus' mind was very fixed on his philosophical thought and that he would not lose his thread even if he was conversing. This is an ability that good teachers and lecturers have: they can take questions from the audience and pick up the thread exactly where they were interrupted. Perhaps he wishes to imply an even greater concentration than that of the typical good lecturer: we might compare his concentration with that of someone preoccupied with a specific puzzle or someone in deep remorse: it is tempting to say of such people that their minds are constantly fixed on the puzzle or the ground of remorse, even if they are perfectly able to converse about other matters, watch movies and so forth. Still the puzzle or the remorse looms over them. There is a constant inarticulate sort of awareness of it while their attention is directed at other things, and when nothing interferes the puzzle or the remorse preoccupies their thought. Given what philosophy was for Plotinus and Porphyry it is reasonable to suppose that Porphyry means to imply that Plotinus was concentrating on it in the way suggested and that means primarily the intelligible world. Given what he says in particular in I.2.6 and in VI.8.5–6 (see p. 307), we may surmise that this concentration on the intelligible has repercussions relevant to the sage's mundane life.

I do not wish to suggest that there is nothing to the multi-operation view. As we have seen, each of us has an intelligible counterpart, whose activity consists in contemplating the intelligible realm. We ordinary people are not aware of this. This is undeniably Plotinus' view. What I wish to question is the view that cathartic virtue, and hence the intellectual life of the sage, consists primarily in such unconscious intellection. In fact, there is much that speaks in favor of his being aware of his intellectual activities, even if he will also attend to other things.

So, if this is right, the sage is consciously engaged in contemplation at least a lot of the time. This raises two related questions: (1) Assuming, as Plotinus' texts as well as Porphyry's *Life* actually suggest, that the sage sometimes attends to and acts towards sensible things in accordance with the virtues that apply to such things, there is still the question of how he manages to do so: being preoccupied in contemplation, how does he take notice (cf. Brittain 2003)? (2) Why should the sage care about anything other than the life of pure intellection? Isn't the life of contemplation the best life? Why should the sage not just stick to it? I shall take up the former question now. The latter I shall postpone until the next section on the ethics of everyday life.[26]

In the context of Plotinus' metaphysics, bodily action in the sensible world can be seen as a case of an external activity of the soul along the lines of the double activity scheme described in Chapter 2.[27] As such the external action is an image or even a by-product of the internal activity of the soul (see III.8.4–5; VI.8.6, 19–22). In the same vein Smith (1999: 236) suggests that "the norms of ethical conduct would flow automatically and without difficulty from the higher life of intellect, when we conduct ourselves like the World-Soul." While I believe this is right and insightful (Plotinus indeed suggests as much, cf. p. 306 and I.3.6, 5 ff.), receiving the right norms is not enough: even if the norms of ethical conduct flow automatically and without difficulty from the higher realms, the question still remains how the sage takes notice of ethically or prudentially relevant facts in his surroundings and reasons about them (see Brittain 2003: 34 ff.). Some prompting from below seems to be needed as well and some tasks will require deliberation. And some, perhaps many or even most, of the sage's tasks will require deliberation, as Plotinus indeed admits (I.4.13, 3–5, quoted on p. 320). Thus, even if I am sympathetic to Wilberding's drawing attention to the immediacy of virtuous action inherent in virtue ethics as opposed to contemporary ethical views, and even admitting that Plotinus may have conceived of automatic action as the ideal, it strikes me that neither is there strong textual support for supposing that this is the normal case nor would the result of supposing that be a plausible theory. After all we live in a world full of contingencies and coincidences, even from the sage's point of view.[28] Thus, even if the sage's ethical norms may come to him from above and even if we may assume that he acts more effortlessly than others, often at least his action would not be automatic. Plotinus could not, I think, have contemplated the intelligible realm while checking the accounts of the finances of the children in his custody (see Life 9).

The answer must be that the sage's soul is simply tuned to note the relevant facts, even while he is contemplating. Internally, he will be prompted by hunger, thirst, pain, fatigue and other such bodily affections. Through his external senses, aided by discursive reason, he will notice ethically relevant facts in his environment. Perhaps the residual emotions he is liable to also play a role in alerting him (cf. Brittain 2003: 34 ff.). There is surely no hint that the sage's senses are inactive while he is contemplating, even if his sensual experience is not what he is focusing on. Plotinus may well have believed, however, that the sage's wisdom, contemplative and practical, makes him especially sensitive to facts that ethically require his attention. Although there is no direct evidence for this in the treatises, this is compatible with them and is suggested by Porphyry's account of Plotinus himself in the *Life*. If the facts require full attention and deliberation, he will stop actively contemplating and focus on them.

3 The ethics of everyday life

In approaching the topic of Plotinus' views on the ethics of everyday life it is useful to remember that Plotinus never wrote anything corresponding to the nine first books of Aristotle's *Nicomachean Ethics*: he had, as we have seen, a notion analogous to that of Aristotle's "wise man," that of the decent, active person. But what he says about that person's ways of life and modes of thought is very limited. We do learn, though, that this person also imitates god, though to a very modest degree (see p. 299). Plotinus puts all his efforts into describing and praising the sage. He is much less interested in the merely civically virtuous person because he sees that person as falling quite short of the human ideal: he isn't even granted a lower kind of happiness. Aristotle, by contrast, is very brief about the character and ways of life of the one of contemplative virtue, who corresponds to the Plotinian sage, even if he regards his as the best human life. I do not wish to suggest that Aristotle's ethically virtuous person is in every respect comparable to Plotinus' civically virtuous one: the latter, lacking in pure intellectual activity, doesn't merit being called happy according to Plotinus, whereas the Aristotelian counterpart is happy, though this happiness is perhaps not of the supreme kind. Nevertheless, if one wished to compare Plotinus' and Aristotle's ethics it is these two, the contemplatively virtuous philosopher and the Plotinian sage, that ought to be compared rather than the sage and Aristotle's ethically virtuous person.

Discussing Plotinus' ethics through the lenses of contemporary ethical theory or ethical beliefs can easily lead one astray and block understanding. It is commonly assumed that ethics is essentially about preserving and promoting the good of others and hence about holding partiality and egoism in check. Though incorporating other-regarding norms in various ways, ancient ethics does not generally make these assumptions about the nature of ethics. It is even more important to note this in Plotinus' case than in most others. Yet, it is perfectly fair to ask if we find the Plotinian sage ethically palatable. Is he, for instance, an egoist? Is the sage notably and culpably lacking in compassion and interest in the needs and fate of other people.[29] The sage as described in "On happiness" is even contrasted with the "compassionate" Plotinus of Porphyry's Life.[30] As indicated above, I do not think that there is a discrepancy between the sage and Plotinus as described; the latter can indeed complete the picture of the former. Still, we can raise the question about that person, the sage, which emerges from "On happiness" and other parts of Plotinus' writings along with Porphyry's Life, whether there is an ethics of action to be found here and, if so, how that ethics fares in comparison with contemporary ethical intuitions.

In a fine recent overview article on Plotinus' ethics, Stern-Gillet (2014) notes that much of recent research on Plotinus' ethical views goes against the previously common trend to dismiss him as an ethical thinker on account of the alleged self-centeredness and other-worldliness of his views. In this recent work we see arguments and claims to the effect that Plotinus' philosophy makes room for a "return to the cave," though perhaps not necessarily or typically a return involving political involvement. A picture along the following lines emerges from a great number of the recent works.[31]

The sage is imbued with the contents of the intelligible world. According to the normal pattern in Plotinus this content will find expression at a lower level, i.e. in the sage's discursive thoughts and finally external actions. It is to be noted, however, that the sage's action must not in any way be conditioned on particular results in the sensible sphere: "if one carries out the so-called noble actions as necessities, and grasps that what is really noble is something else, one has not been enchanted" (IV.4.44, 18–20). In the context he argues that actions motivated by values pertaining to the irrational parts of the soul—love of sex, wealth and power—are done under a kind of spell and that their agent is unfree. As Bene (2013: 158) and Remes (2006: 10, n. 25) have noted, this is, however, not a depreciation of external action as such but of the actions of agents who have no higher end than the images of nobility brought about by the action. In other words, Plotinus is here expressing agreement with the view which is most explicit in the Stoics that the real value pertaining to virtuous action lies in the state of the soul that causes it, not in the result. Clearly, the sage will not be motivated by the desired results as such.

But why, really, does the sage act externally at all? One answer is that he is at once a citizen of the intelligible world and of the sensible one. The former membership will color, actually transform, the latter: whatever he does in the sensible world is done from goodness and is good, in so far as external action can be, because his soul is imbued with Intellect if not with the Good itself.

This, however, does not fully explain what would motivate the sage to act. The best answer to this, I think, lies in the fact that individual human souls "contribute to the creation of the complete sensible world" (Remes 2006: 20). In general, Plotinus adopts and frequently cites Plato's statement in *Phaedrus* 46b where it is said that "all soul cares for what is soulless." This holds for the human soul as well as the World-Soul. The human being has come into body in order to care for it and the particular region with which it interacts. The problem is that as opposed to the World-Soul the human soul— the image which descends into the body—is liable to fail in its tasks: instead of ruling what it is set over, it comes to be ruled by it. But the purification of the soul, its emancipation even in its embodied life, does not release it from its tasks. Far from it; it enables the soul to perform them properly. The sage sees these tasks in light of his understanding of the whole and accepts the obligation to perform these tasks gladly.

So the sage will act. Exactly how much or how often our texts are vague about. The impression given is that the application of the virtues in the sensible sphere is primarily reactive and rectificatory: the actions that issue from them are aimed at responding to and correcting some given state of affairs. The virtuous person does not seek out situations in which he might exercise his virtues. Plotinus remarks that

> certainly, if virtue itself were given the choice whether it would like in order to be active there should be wars, that it might be brave, and that there should be injustice that it might define

what is just and set things in order, and poverty, that it might display its liberality, or to stay quiet because everything was well, it would choose to rest from its practical activities.
(VI.8.5, 13–18; cf. Aristotle, *Nicomachean Ethics* X, 8 1178a26–34)

Thus, the virtuous would prefer not to have to do anything. Should the situation demand it, however, there is no doubt that they would act.

Is this compatible with undertaking political rule? O'Meara (2003) has recently made a strong case for a Neoplatonic political philosophy. The general idea is that Platonism is open to a return to the cave along the lines sketched above and that this return may take the form of political leadership. While admitting that not much points in this direction in Plotinus, O'Meara can nonetheless cite a passage to show that the idea of the philosopher's return is at least not alien to Plotinus. After describing how the philosopher must share his experience of the Good with others, Plotinus mentions the legendary lawgiver, Minos, who "attained this kind of union" and, according to the story, "'was the familiar friend of Zeus,' and it was in remembering of this that he laid down laws in its image, being filled full with lawgiving by divine touch" (VI.9.7, 23–26). Clearly, it is suggested here that ascent to the intelligible world may result in a fecundity which finds its expression in the political sphere.[32] This allowance of political expression of divine wisdom may seem somewhat cut back by the continuation of the passage, where Plotinus adds that the one who has seen much may wish to remain always above and think political matters unworthy of himself (cf. Stern-Gillet 2014: 414). Is Plotinus suggesting then that, after all, the philosopher should remain in the heights and leave politics alone? This does not really follow as a general rule: we must remember that in Plato's *Republic* a philosopher does not go into politics under any conditions and that actually in the present state of affairs he won't (*Republic* VI, 496a). Plotinus will no doubt follow suit in this regard: a philosopher has no obligation to meddle in politics unless he thinks he can accomplish something worthwhile thereby.[33]

One might also suppose that the account of Plotinus' associate, the senator Rogatianus, in the *Life* shows that Plotinus disapproved of philosophers' political involvement. Rogatianus gave up his political career and possessions in order to devote himself entirely to philosophy. Plotinus praised him and held him up as an example (Life 7). We are not told what advancement Rogatianus made in higher wisdom but at least he lost a lot of weight and regained physical proficiency. I am not so sure that we should draw any specific inferences about Plotinus' attitudes to political involvement from what is said about Rogatianus. It is at any rate clear that before committing himself fully to philosophy Rogatianus was no Minos: he was not ready to enter the political sphere as a philosopher and have beneficial effects there. Thus, his abandonment of politics and Plotinus' praise of his turn shows nothing in particular about Plotinus' attitude to philosophers entering public service.

Is the sage a self-centered egoist? It seems to me not at all. By contemporary lights he admittedly has strange views about the value and disvalue of earthly things as a result of which he isn't into pitying people for worldly ills. He does not pity himself either but treats himself equally (I.4.15, 24–25). Nor is the purely intellectual activity in virtue of which he is happy something he engages in in order to reach some kind of ecstasy, oblivious of everything but himself and his self-centered enjoyment. Actually, by perfecting himself he is improving the universe (see III.2. 14). Nor is the sage grudging in sharing his experiences and assisting others on the path to wisdom. Schniewind (2003) has persuasively argued that the sage and his ways as described in "On happiness" serves as a model that is supposed to appeal not only to those who are already philosophers but also to ordinary people.[34] The Life indicates that Plotinus entertained hopes that others would become philosophers, and in one place says that the soul which has been in the company of the One and, so to speak, conversed with it, must "announce, if it could, to another that transcendent union" (VI.9.7, 21–23).

The preceding point leads us to further aspects of Plotinus' ethical thought.[35] As already noted several times, the intelligible realm is unified to a much higher degree than the sensible: there are individual distinctions there but the intelligibles are "all together" and each of them reflects every other. This holds also for the undescended part of our souls, which are members of the intelligible realm (cf. VI.4.4, 1 ff.). Embodiment means a narrowing of focus and a weakening of contact with the totality of intelligibles. The sage who ascends to the intelligible realm is reintegrated into the harmonious whole to which his higher self has always belonged. He is not alone there: "But one ought to try to become as good as possible oneself, but not to think that only oneself can become perfectly good—for if one thinks this one is not yet perfectly good" (II.9.9, 26–29). Thus, arguably, the sage's ascent represents the opposite of egoism: the sage transcends the limited self-centered view of embodied life and gains a holistic view of the world in which he lives in peace and harmony with like-minded natures who are admitted as equals.

4 Chapter summary

In this chapter we have considered three central ethical themes: Plotinus' views on virtue, his views on happiness, and finally his views on the ethics of everyday life. His position as regards these three topics is coherent in all its essentials—even if it will in some respects strike modern readers as extreme and outlandish. The baseline of his ethics is that we humans have a soul that is of divine origin. It has descended into the sensible world where it is set over and, in a sense, inhabits a particular body. The cohabitation with the body may lead the soul to forget its origin and become preoccupied with the body and the sensible to the extent of setting the body over itself. The soul should rule over the body and not be ruled by it. It ought to free itself from the life of the body and the compound to the extent possible. Metaphysically this means that the soul should identify itself with, or perhaps rather rejoin, its intelligible source and make its life its own. This is the happy life for human beings and Platonic philosophy is the way to it.

These basic beliefs are the background of Plotinus' account of the virtues and happiness. He distinguishes between grades of virtue in his treatise on the virtues: there are the paradigms of the virtues as Forms in intellect, the intellectual virtues possessed by the sage, and what Plotinus calls the "political virtues" possessed by the decent but unphilosophical citizen. Plotinus differs from Aristotle in holding that only the intellectually illuminated, the sage, is happy: the decent citizen does not make it into that rank. Various questions arise about the character of the sage. In the treatise on happiness Plotinus describes the sage as quite detached from his bodily existence and unaffected by the so-called evils of this world. This should not come as a surprise as the doctrine of virtue clearly indicates that true virtue consists in letting go of the hegemony of the body and its demands.

The question then arises of how the sage deals with everyday life. Scholars' views differ on this question. Some hold that the sage is minimally concerned with states of affairs in the sensible world— including the well-being of other people. Thus, Plotinus' position has been described as egoistic. Others have pointed out that indeed the soul is in the sensible world for a reason and has an obligation there to take care of what it is set over. Moreover, it is noted that several passages suggest Plotinus was indeed concerned with the state of the sensible world, including other people. The line taken here is generally in accordance with the latter view.

Further readings

Primary sources

Ennead I.2. (19) "On virtues."
Ennead I.3. (20) "On dialectic."
Ennead I.4. (46) "On happiness."
Ennead I.5. (36) "On whether happiness increases with time."

Secondary sources

John M. Dillon, "An Ethic for the Late Antique Sage," in L. P. Gerson (ed.), *The Cambridge Companion to Plotinus* (Cambridge: Cambridge University Press, 1996), 315–335.
Andrew Smith, "The Significance of Practical Ethics for Plotinus," in J. J. Cleary (ed.), *Traditions of Platonism: Essays in Honour of John Dillon* (Aldershot: Ashgate, 1999), 227–236.
Charles Brittain, "Attention Deficit in Plotinus and Augustine: Psychological Problems in Christian and Platonist Theories of the Grades of Virtue," *Boston Area Colloquium in Ancient Philosophy* 18 (2003), 223–275.
Dominic J. O'Meara, *Platonopolis: Platonic Political Philosophy in Late Antiquity* (Oxford: Clarendon Press, 2003), especially the introduction.

Pauliina Remes, "Plotinus's Ethics of Disinterested Interest," *Journal of the History of Philosophy* 44, 1 (2006), 1–23.

John M. Cooper, *Pursuits of Wisdom: Six Ways of Life in Ancient Philosophy from Socrates to Plotinus* (Princeton: Princeton University Press, 2012), chapter 6.

László Bene, "Ethics and Metaphysics in Plotinus," in F. Karfík and E. Song (eds.), *Plato Revived: Essays on Ancient Platonism in Honour of Dominic J. O'Meara* (Berlin: Walter de Gruyter, 2013), 141–161.

Suzanne Stern-Gillet, "Plotinus on Metaphysics and Morality," in P. Remes and S. Slaveva-Griffin (eds.), *The Routledge Handbook of Neoplatonism* (London: Routledge, 2014), 396–420.

Alexandrine Schniewind, "Plotinus' Way of Defining 'Eudaimonia' in Ennead I 4 [46] 1–3," in Ø. Rabbås, E. K. Emilsson, H. Fossheim and M. Tuominen (eds.), *The Quest for the Good Life: Ancient Philosophers on Happiness* (Oxford: Oxford University Press, 2015), 212–221.

László Bene, "Ethics and Metaphysics in Plotinus," in F. Karfík and E. Song (eds.), *Plato Revived: Essays on Ancient Platonism in Honour of Dominic J. O'Meara* (Berlin: Walter de Gruyter, 2013), 141–161.

Notes

1 Porphyry's work, the so-called *Sententiae* (*Aphormai*, meaning "starting points"), is a short work presenting some basic tenets of Neoplatonic philosophy. It depends heavily on the *Enneads*.
2 On this and the implication for Plotinus' general account of the image-paradigm relation, see Dillon 1996.
3 A thoughtful account of the civic virtues is to be found in Remes 2006, see also Cooper 2012: ch. 6.
4 For a criticism of Plotinus' reading of Plato on the virtues, see Cooper 2012: 149–160.
5 Practical wisdom (*phronēsis*) replaces wisdom (*sophia*). *Phronēsis* is the term Plato uses in *Phaedo* 69b ff. on which Plotinus is drawing. Presumably, he intends "practical wisdom" here to be just what Plato means by wisdom in Book IV of the *Republic*.
6 On such pre-emotions in Stoicism, see Knuuttila 2004: 63–68.
7 In *On Abstinence* I.41, 6–18 Porphyry makes the same point very explicitly.
8 Cf. Aristotle, *Nicomachean Ethics* VI, 13, 1144b3–1145a2. Plotinus' Platonist predecessors also entertained a notion of "good natural dispositions"; cf. Alcinous, *Handbook of Platonism* 30, 183.17.
9 On the Plotinian sage, see Schniewind 2003, which gives a detailed analysis of the notion and discusses virtually all the passages in Plotinus mentioning the sage.

10 The account of the contents of *Ennead* I.5 here is excerpted from Emilsson 2011 and 2015 with modifications.
11 See Epicurus, *Vatican Sayings* 22 = *Principal Doctrines* 3; Cicero, *On Ends* II, 27–28. And for the Stoics, Plutarch, *On Common Notions* 1061f–1062a; Cicero, *On Ends* V, 28, 83; Seneca, *Letter* 32, 3; Marcus Aurelius, *Meditations* II, 14; XII, 36.
12 We may note, in passing, that Plotinus makes here a distinction between everlastingness and timelessness; Plato's word in *Timaeus* 37d is "eternity" (*aiōn*). Whittaker (1971) argues that this distinction was not made by Plato, Aristotle or the Hellenistic philosophers—a claim questioned on Plato's behalf by Linguiti (2007: 28, n. 36). However this may be, we may here have the first explicit formulation of it. In the tradition before Plotinus it is generally unclear whether it is a question of something outside time or merely everlasting in an unchangeable state.
13 By "the undividedness of time" Plotinus presumably means the instant. See Linguiti's (2007) commentary *ad loc.*
14 The classical article on ordered series in Aristotle is Lloyd 1962.
15 On homonymy in Aristotle, see Irwin 1981.
16 III.8. (30) 10, III.9. (13) 17–18 and V.3. (49) 16, 38–42 seem to speak against the Good having life whereas VI.8. (39) 7, 51 attributes "a sort of life" to it. As Schroeder (1997: 216) notes, the denials may only be meant to underscore that "life" is a different sort of thing in the case of the One.
17 Plotinus wrote a very short treatise, perhaps better described as a note, on suicide: "On going out of the body" (I.9. (16)). Here he argues against suicide on the ground that a violent departure will harm the soul.
18 On what there is of an emotional life for the sage (and it is there in a positive sense of "emotional life") see Schniewind 2015.
19 See *Apology* 30c–d, 41c–d; *Gorgias* 470e; and *Republic* 354a.
20 See e.g. Cicero, *Tusculan Disputations* V.40–41 and Marcus Aurelius, *Meditations* VII. 27.
21 This problem was first noted and discussed in detail by Rist 1967: 142 ff.
22 This change in the soul is of course not an affection of it in the sense Plotinus objects to, see Chapter 7, Section 3.3, "Feelings and Emotions."
23 For elaborate discussions of the sage's levels of consciousness and in general the relationship between his theoretical and practical life, see Smith 1978 and Brittain 2003. Smith argues for consciousness at two levels for the sage, Brittain seeks to resist that conclusion. Wilberding (2008a) seeks to make a case for the sage acting automatically in the sensible world, like the divine souls, which implies that the sage doesn't have to deliberate much or focus his attention on his worldly doings: they flow automatically according to virtue while his focus is elsewhere.
24 In *Republic* VI, 505a Plato calls the Good "the greatest study." There is, however, no reason to suppose that Plotinus restricts his meaning to the study of the Good (the One). It is more likely that he is thinking of the whole intelligible realm.
25 The brazen bull of Phalaris was a kind of torture chamber applied by the tyrant Phalaris of Acragas (sixth century BC). Kalligas (2014) notes *ad loc.*: "An insistent tradition makes out Epicurus to have declared that the sage is to such

a degree imperturbable, that even if he were to find himself in the bull of Phalaris, he would still be capable of calling out: 'how pleasant this is!' (see Epicurus, fr. 601)." The last lines of the quotation allude to this tradition.
26 Both questions are addressed at length in Brittain 2003.
27 See Emilsson 2012 and Bene 2013.
28 Wilberding admits as much in the conclusion of his article (2008a). The question is presumably how much and how often the sage must resort to deliberation and focus his attention on states of affairs in the sensible world.
29 See McGroarty 2006: xvii–xviii; 2005.
30 See McGroarty 2006: xvii, with a number of references in n. 9.
31 See e.g. Bussanich 1990, Smith 1999, O'Meara 2003, Schniewind 2003, Remes 2006, Caluori 2011 and Bene 2013, who, however, differ significantly on a number of details.
32 The citation is from Homer's *Odyssey* IX, 178–179. It is also cited in the pseudo-Platonic dialogue *Minos*, which is probably Plotinus' source here. See Stern-Gillet 2014: 412.
33 I am grateful to Dominic O'Meara for reminding me of this in a private conversation.
34 I find this persuasive even if I hesitate to embrace fully Schniewind's division of "On happiness" into sections aimed at different audiences.
35 In this paragraph I am indebted to Bussanich (1990: 172 ff.), Remes (2006: 17 ff.) and, not least, to Bene (2013: 152 ff.).

Ten
Ethics II
Mystical experience, theodicy, freedom and beauty

1 Mystical experience

It is frequently asserted that Plotinus is a mystic. The Oxford dictionary/thesaurus that I have on my iPhone defines mysticism as "1. The belief that knowledge of God and truths beyond human understanding can be gained by prayer and meditation. 2. Religious or spiritual belief that is not clearly defined." Other dictionaries give similar definitions but also other ones suggesting that the term is used in several rather different senses.[1] Neither one of the definitions above, for instance, would apply to Plotinus' thought. The former is not altogether off, but Plotinus' mysticism is only partly about gaining knowledge. Surely prayer has nothing to do with it, and, depending on what exactly is meant, it is questionable whether it employs meditation. Does Plotinus' mysticism have God as an object? The answer must be "yes, it does" because it is directed at the One and Intellect, which are deities (see Chapter 2, pp. 39–40). To say that it is about knowledge of God can, however, mislead, because these Plotinian deities do not quite fit common conceptions of God and because there is no knowledge to be had of the One.

There are two related spheres where we might appropriately talk about Plotinus' mysticism: there is the human experience of Intellect that transcends ordinary human reason and there is a human "experience" of a kind of union with the One. O'Meara (1993: 103) helpfully distinguishes between three stages in the soul's ascent: (1) the return to one's true self as soul, (2) attaining the life of Intellect, and (3) union with the One. I shall address each of these in turn. We might apply the term "mysticism" to stages (2) and (3) because the experience of these transcends ordinary discursive consciousness.

In the *Life* Porphyry says: "To Plotinus 'the goal, ever near, was shown';[2] for his end and goal was to be united to, to approach the god who is over all things. Four times while I was with him he attained that goal, in an unspeakable actuality" (23, 14–17). From this we might be tempted to infer that the goal for Plotinus, and hence presumably the natural goal for human beings, is to become one with the One, for this must be the god who is over all things. This, however, does not sit well with the evidence of the *Enneads*. Clear references to the soul's direct experience of the One are few. So far as I can tell, only in two treatises, "On the Good or the One" (VI.9) and "How the multitude of the Forms came into being, and on the Good" (VI.7, especially chapter 34), does he attempt to describe such an experience. More frequent are references to an experience of Intellect in which the soul seems to transcend its status as soul and become one with its intelligible source at the level of Intellect. This sort of experience also transcends ordinary discursive thought. We saw in Sections 1 and 2 of the previous chapter that Plotinus identifies happiness with the contemplation that the sage's soul is engaged in at the final stage of cathartic virtue. This contemplation is definitely an activity of soul (see I.2.4, 23; I.4.14, 4–6). As noted in the previous chapter, this is not the pure kind of intellection in which the soul has rejoined its source in Intellect, but an activity of soul in which it lets itself be informed by Intellect by "gazing" at it. Intellect itself is still something external to the soul in this kind of contemplation. The upshot of these observations is that though unquestionably there, the mystical unification with the One is by no means a cornerstone of Plotinus' philosophy. Even the experience of Intellect, which at times appears as a kind of mystical experience—i.e. a striking personal experience which transcends ordinary rational thinking—is not a cornerstone of Plotinus' philosophy either: if what we saw in the previous chapter is true about the nature of the sage's thought by which he or she is virtuous and happy, the soul need not ascend any higher than to the limits of soul: neither virtue nor happiness depends on ascending further, even if some sages unquestionably do.

It is noteworthy that where Plotinus describes the experience of Intellect or of the One, the subject of the experience is generally the individual human soul. This is somewhat baffling: as we saw in Chapter 2, there is a hierarchy of the One, Intellect and Soul. Each of them is characterized by their particular degree of unity and at least Intellect and Soul are essentially thinkers differentiated by the degree of unity of their thought. The human soul belongs to the realm of souls and has as such, at best, the most unified kind of thought that souls are capable of. So—and here comes the question—how could the human soul transcend the level of soul and become one with Intellect, not to mention the One, and still remain a soul? Commentators have spoken of the human soul as a great traveller between the ontological spheres. That is fine so long as we stay within the realm of Soul: the human soul may ascend beyond the sensible realm to the intelligible sphere occupied by pure souls. But if the soul goes beyond that, would it still be a soul? This would seem to be impossible: if souls are distinguished from Intellect primarily by having a less unified form of cognition, how could a soul assume Intellect's mode of cognition and still remain a mere soul? Yet, it is the individual soul which is said to experience the One itself. I think this puzzle must be resolved by supposing that referring to the subject of these supra-psychic experiences as souls is a figure of speech. It is understandable, however: the subject that begins the journey is the individual soul and this is also the subject who comes out of it and reports on it afterwards. The experience is one the soul reports as its own, so it seems natural to think of the soul as the subject of the experience.

When the soul rises to the level of Intellect, it is no longer a soul, at least not strictly speaking. In one way such an ascent seems to make perfectly good sense within Plotinus' metaphysics: the soul has its roots in Intellect and ultimately in the One. We discussed in Chapter 4 whether each soul has a distinct, individual source in Intellect, i.e. whether there are Ideas of individuals, and left the question without a clear answer. Whichever way this may turn out, there is definitely a source of each soul there, the question is only whether it is individual or common. Given that the human soul can ascend at all, raise itself beyond the mode of thought characteristic of embodied life, why shouldn't it rise even higher? Well, why not? Still, there is something puzzling about this. Everything has a source in Intellect and ultimately in the One; only the human soul, however, ascends above its own status, its own hypostasis, to use Neoplatonic jargon. The hypostasis Soul and the World-Soul are eternally illuminated by Intellect and intelligible beings but there is no hint that they ever seek to become Intellect or enter into a union with the One.

With all this in mind let us turn to the non-discursive experience of Intellect. Plotinus begins his treatise "On the descent of soul into bodies" with the following remarkable passage describing his own experience:

> Many times, after waking up to myself away from the body, having come outside everything but myself, after seeing an extraordinary beauty and feeling assured that especially then I belong to the better part, living actively the best life, becoming one with the divine and seated in it coming to that activity placed above every other intelligible being, and after this rest in the divine descending from intellect to discursive reasoning, I have puzzled how I ever and now came down, and how my soul has come to be in the body when it is what it has shown itself to be by itself, even while embodied.
>
> (IV.8.1, 1–11)

This passage has often been taken to refer to the soul's union with the One rather than with Intellect.[3] Plotinus does not tell us here how he comes to have an experience such as the one he describes. Does it come over him out of the blue? Is it the result of some trickery with the body (fasting, special breathing)? Drugs? Very predictably it is none of these. In so far as there are some indications, the route is quintessentially Platonic: after studying the mathematical sciences the philosopher will take up dialectic and study "what Plato calls 'the plain of truth'" (cf. *Phaedrus* 248b). Here the soul

> uses Plato's method of division to distinguish the Forms to determine what each one is, and to find the primary kinds, and weaving together by the intellect all that issues from these primary kinds, till it has traversed the whole intelligible world; then again it resolves the structure of that world into its parts, and comes back to the starting point; and then, keeping quiet (for it is quiet

in so far as it is present there [in the intelligible]) it busies itself no more, but contemplates, having arrived at unity.

(I.3.4, 12–18)

There is a gradual transition from discursive reasoning about the intelligible realm to quiet contemplation of it. There is no hint here of an ecstatic experience including a strong feeling of self, like in the previous passage. The reason may of course be that this is not meant to describe a soul that has fully ascended to the level of Intellect. As we have seen in the previous chapter, pure souls too contemplate Intellect and are informed by it but they do so, so to speak from the outside and without rising fully to that level. The reference to quietness and unity here, however, suggests that the soul is contemplating Intellect from the internal point of view. In the former passage Plotinus speaks about waking up, which surely indicates a sudden transition into a different state. We see no suggestion of anything like this in the latter passage.[4] There is no hint anywhere in the *Enneads* that anything other than philosophical thinking can prepare the way for this sort of awakening. Elsewhere, in connection with an experience of the One, he actually speaks of "awakening from reasonings to the vision of it [the One]" (VI.9.4, 13–14). This suggests that the new "waking state" is something the soul enters into as a result of a good reasoning process. There is, however, no suggestion that this is a guaranteed result. On the contrary, the language of awakening and other indications in the texts suggest that the soul has little control over whether this happens or not.

What is the soul's experience of Intellect like when it has fully ascended to that stage? There are several passages that attempt to describe Intellect from an internal point of view. Though generally not explicitly told in the first person, these passages often have the air of describing an experience: even if the language is factual and does not refer to a subject of the experience, the reader cannot help feeling that it is somebody's experience. One such passage is to be found in "On the intelligible beauty" (V.8) (already considered in Chapter 4, p. 134):

For all things there [in the intelligible world] are transparent, and there is nothing dark or opaque; everything and all things are clear to the inmost part to everything; for light is transparent to light. Each there has everything in itself and sees all things in every other, so that all are everywhere and each and every one is all and the glory is unbounded. ... the sun there is all the stars, and each star is the sun and all the others. A different kind of being stands out in each, but in each all are manifest.

(V.8.4, 4–11)

Here is another passage, from "On the presence of being, one and the same, everywhere as a whole (I)," which describes the intelligible world from the viewpoint of a soul who has ascended to it:

So if you now should take hold of an ever-flowing infinity that is contained within it [the life of Intellect], a nature in itself tireless and indefatigable, in no way falling short of itself, like a life boiling over, you will not find it there by gazing somewhere or staring at something particular. Quite the opposite will happen to you: for neither will you miss it in passing nor, again, end up experiencing it as small as though it could no longer give by falling short in terms of smallness: either you are able to run along with it, or better: you will come to be in the whole, and no longer seek anything, or else you will give up and will pass from it to something else and you will falter, failing to see what is present because you are looking at something else. But if you no longer seek anything, how does this happen to you? It is because you have come to the whole and did not merely remain in a part of it; you did not say "I am this much," but you abandoned the "this much" and in so doing you became the whole.

(VI.5.12, 7–19)

These passages taken together show the main characteristics of non-discursive thought. As the former passage makes clear, different part–whole relations hold in Intellect than in the sensible realm and this is reflected in the experience of it: as opposed to what is generally the case in the sensible realm, here every item contains in itself a reference to every other so that to grasp a single one involves grasping all: "in each all are manifest." The second passage emphasizes that if one is to grasp Intellect internally, one must let go of oneself as an individual and become one with the whole intelligible realm. It is difficult to say precisely what this means but at least this involves a farewell to isolationism: "you did not say 'I am this much,' but you abandoned the 'this much' and in so doing you became the whole." This must somehow involve giving up thinking that "this is I and that over there is something other than me" and instead seeing oneself as the whole. Does that mean that an individual point of view is completely lost, and the experience of Intellect is a kind of view of the whole from nowhere? Perhaps this is what Plotinus wishes to convey. Perhaps—and I think it more plausible—he means something slightly different. We might think that an individual point of view is not so much abandoned as expanded: I am now including the whole intelligible realm in what I see as myself. That does not mean that there isn't a particular point of view, rather that what I see as included in me is everything. As the former passage (V.8.4, 4–11) has it: "A different kind of being stands out in each." This clearly implies that each thing in that realm is something in itself but this something reflects all the others. There are no closed borders. If we transfer this to the latter passage (VI.5.12, 7–19), it turns out that there still is a point of view from which the visitor sees himself in the realm of Intellect, but from that point of view he, himself, includes this whole realm.

Let us turn to the mystical union of the human soul with the One. The early and fairly short treatise, "On the Good or the One" (VI.9. (9)) is Plotinus' first exposition of the full doctrine of the One. In the fourth chapter he notes that "our awareness (*synesis*) of [the One] is not by way of understanding (*epistēmē*) or by way of intellection as in the case of the other intelligibles, but by way of presence superior to knowledge" (VI.9.4, 1–3). In the three final chapters we get an account of what it is like for the soul to experience the One. He says:

> On the contrary, we must put away other things and take our stand only in this, and become this alone, cutting away all the other things in which we are encased; we must hasten away from here and be annoyed at being bound to the others, so that we may embrace him [God] with the whole of ourselves and have no part with which we do not touch God. There one can see both him and oneself as it is right to see: the self glorified,

full of intelligible light—but rather itself pure light—weightless, floating free, having become or rather being a god; set on fire then, but the fire seems to go out if one is weighted down again.
(VI.9.9, 50–60)

We see here the same idea as we could also note in the passage from "On the descent of soul into bodies" quoted above: ascending essentially involves leaving behind, letting go of the body and the sensible, in fact letting go of everything below the stage to which the soul is about to enter: the soul that is to approach the Good, must even leave behind understanding and intellection and whatever comes with this. It is useless to seek to achieve a higher, more unified stage by means of mental modes that do not apply there.

In talking about the modes of awareness at the level of Intellect and in the soul's experience of the One, Plotinus invariably uses perceptual metaphors: there is no discursive reasoning going on here, everything that is apprehended is apprehended immediately, which makes perceptual metaphors natural and handy. The language of vision and touch is especially prominent. Indeed, sense perception is immediate and vision especially has the feature of grasping many things at once, which makes it particularly apt to convey an important aspect of intellection (see Chapter 4, p. 131). Even here, however, vision comes short.

A central aspect of thought at the level of Intellect is that it is self-thought at the same time as it is the thought of the whole intelligible realm. As the last passage quoted indicates, this is also the case in the experience of the One: it is at once an experience of the One and of oneself. This is not easily captured by visual metaphors without stretching the ordinary notion of vision considerably. In the passage above, which is about the experience of the ultimate principle, we have, however, both visual and tactual metaphors. Plotinus speaks of touching God with the whole of oneself. In "On the cognitive hypostases and what is beyond," he says in describing the relation between Intellect and the One (here referred to as "the partless") that "there will not be an intellection of it but only a touching (thixis) and a kind of contact (epaphē) without word or thought" (V.3.10, 42–43). Interestingly, Aristotle uses tactual metaphors when describing a firm intellectual grasp of essences.[5] Plotinus, on the other hand, tends to reserve tactual metaphors for the experience of unity, which is beyond understanding.

Nevertheless, also in the case of experiencing the One Plotinus keeps referring to vision. This has no doubt to do with the Analogy of the Sun in Plato's *Republic*, which, as we noted, is one of Plotinus' main sources for his notion of the One (the Good) (see Chapter 1, p. 54). His account of the way in which the Good is light and how it is seen as light goes, however, far beyond anything we find in this passage in Plato, yet it constitutes an interesting interpretation of it. The sight of the light that is seen in the passage above is no ordinary vision. By this I don't just mean that it is vision in a transferred sense, which is obvious, but that what the vision of the One is likened to is no ordinary vision.

The fullest account of this is to be found in chapter 7 of "That the intelligibles are not outside Intellect, and on the Good" (V.5). Here Plotinus, points out that we generally see light "based upon something different [i.e. the sensible things that become visible by the light], but if it is alone and not resting on something else the sense is not able to grasp it. For even the light of the sun would escape our sense of sight if a more solid mass did not lie under it." Intellect sees the intelligibles as illuminated by an analogous intelligible light. It does not thereby see the light that illuminates the intelligibles in its pure form. The light of the sun is an external light but Intellect must not see this light as external. This motivates Plotinus to return to the human eye and abandon the analogy of the sun as the model for illustrating the mode of apprehension at this level. He continues:

> [The eye] itself will sometimes know a light which is not the external, alien light, but it momentarily sees before the external light a light of its own, a brighter one. It either springs out from itself in the dark of night or, when the eye does not want to look at anything else, it lowers the eyelid before it and all the same sends out light, or the eye's possessor squeezes it and it sees the light in itself. For then, in not seeing, it sees, and sees then most of all: for it sees light. The other things were luminous but they were not light. Just so Intellect, veiling itself from other things and drawing itself inward, when it is not looking at anything

will see a light, not a distinct light in something different from itself, but suddenly appearing, alone by itself in independent purity, so that Intellect is at a loss to know whence it has appeared, whether it has come from outside or within, and after it has gone away will say "It was within, and yet it was not within."

(V.5.7, 23–35)

Let me offer a few comments on this. Both the context and language of this passage strongly suggests that it is not a question of a human soul's ascent to Intellect, but rather the topic is the hypostasis Intellect's relation to the One. (Given this and that Intellect is timeless, it is somewhat strange to read as we do here about the light suddenly appearing as well as about its going away; the temporal language as elsewhere in such contexts is not to be taken literally.) It is a debated issue among scholars whether in its ascent to the One the individual soul follows entirely in the footsteps of the inchoate intellect in its reversion towards its source or whether this is a significantly different affair. Bussanich (1988: 231–236), criticizing earlier interpreters, holds that the two ascents differ, pointing out that the soul's ascent is alone characterized by erotic metaphors: the soul is described as yearning and being excited by the nearness of the One.

However this may be exactly, it is clear that in "seeing" the One the soul "sees light" (cf. the previous passage from VI.9.9 cited above). It seems reasonable to take the sense in which it sees light to be the sense indicated by the latter passage cited above (VI.5.12, 7–19), i.e. as a glimpse of the ordinarily invisible intelligible light that makes the intelligibles intelligibly visible. Moreover, the intelligible light that makes the intelligibles visible and which may itself be seen comes from Intellect itself: the soul's way to the One is from within through Intellect. Like Augustine and Descartes and many others later, Plotinus is convinced that the way to understanding and ultimately to the One (God) begins in introspection. For him the final step of the kind of union human beings are capable of having with the ultimate is also the final step in the soul's search into itself. It is important to emphasize that there are no shortcuts on the soul's path towards the One: it will have to go through the stages described above. Armstrong (1974: 183) aptly captures this by saying: "It is only Intellect which can surpass and fulfill itself by becoming unintelligent. One cannot pass beyond thought except by going through with one's thinking to the end."

Does the soul virtually become the One in its experience of it? This question is related to the other issue mentioned just above of whether the soul goes in the footsteps of the inchoate intellect in its ascent: the inchoate intellect's conversion at the ontological level is not a complete union (see Chapter 3, p. 58); if the human soul's ascent just copies the conversion of the inchoate intellect, it is not a complete union either. If, on the other hand, the soul's ascent is different and goes further than the inchoate intellect in its conversion, the question is open as to whether this is rightly called a complete union. Another controversial aspect of this same issue is whether the soul keeps or loses its identity in its encounter with the One. Presumably, this is at bottom the same question as the previous one: if the soul virtually becomes the One it loses its identity in the union; if it doesn't, it doesn't. Let us have a look at VI.9.10, the chapter following the passage quoted on pp. 341–342. Here we see the soul's experience of the One described in language more strongly suggestive of a union than anywhere else in the *Enneads*:

> When therefore the seer sees himself, then when he sees, he will see himself as like this,[6] or rather he will be in union with himself as like this and will be aware of himself as like this, since he has become single and simple. But perhaps one should not say "will see" but "was seen," if one must speak of these as two, the seer and the seen, and not both as one—a bold statement. So the seer does not see and does not distinguish and does not imagine two, but it is as if he had become someone else and is not himself and does not count as his own there, but has come to belong to that [the One] and so is one, having joined, as it were, center to center. For here too when the centers have come together they are one but there is duality when they are separate. This also is how we now speak of "another." For this reason the vision is hard to put into words. For how could one report as about another when one did not see, there when one saw, another, but one with oneself?
> (VI.9.10, 9–21)

Even if Plotinus speaks here of vision and seeing, the experience he is trying to convey entirely defies the logic of ordinary vision, a key aspect of which is that there is a difference between seer and seen. Surely, there is much here that suggests a union: the seer sees the One and he sees himself, and there is no difference between seer and seen, the subject–object distinction is no longer applicable; "it is as if [the seer] has become someone else and is not himself" but "has come to belong to the One." But does the soul lose its identity in this kind of experience? This is a tricky question whose very meaning may not be entirely clear. In the experience Plotinus describes the soul has no consciousness of itself as anything distinct from the One, in fact, it has no consciousness of itself as anything distinct from anything at all. Nor do I think Plotinus means to say that this unity is only a kind of seeming, that in fact the soul and the One are two but that during this experience this duality escapes the soul. At least it is not a seeming in the sense that it *merely* appears to the highest power of the soul which alone would join the One that it is one with it: it really is while this experience lasts.[7]

On the other hand, this highest power of the soul is something distinct from the One even if they may temporarily coalesce. We see this from the beginning of the chapter where Plotinus asks how it is "that one does not remain there [in the so-called mystical union]" (VI.9.10, 1). The answer is that "one has not totally come out of this [sensible] world" (ll. 1–2). He implies that the body may disturb the union. All this shows that the soul that joins the One is still the soul (or the principle of the soul-power) that animates the body and does other things that souls normally do. This is, I think, also confirmed by the analogy with the two superimposed centers, which Plotinus likens to the soul's relation to the One within VI.9.10, 17–18: clearly, the two centers coalesce but they are separable. Rist (1967: 227) notes that "two dots superimposed on a piece of paper would not seem two but they would in some sense be two." I agree in so far as Rist is implicitly appealing to the two points' separability and hence distinctness. As indicated above, I disagree with what he seems to suggest about their merely appearing one. Perhaps we can conceive of the matter as follows (I am not suggesting that this is in every detail a perfect model for the relationship between the soul and the One, only as concerns identity and difference in the union): think of two paper circles, a small and a big one, each with a hole in the center; we superimpose the small one on the large one so that the holes meet. Clearly, their holes not only *seem* to merge into one; they *are* one so long as the superimposition lasts. I would suggest that this applies to the soul temporarily merging with the One: they are one so long as the merging lasts but the soul's hole belongs to another piece of paper, so to speak.

2 Theodicy and freedom

Quite a few of Plotinus' treatises discuss or at least bring up freedom and related concepts. The treatise "On autonomy and the will of the One" (VI.8. (39)), which we have had occasion to mention a number of times, has Plotinus' most extensive treatment of these notions but other treatises, in particular "On providence (I) and (II)" (III.2. (47) and III.3. (48), cut in two by Porphyry) and "On destiny" (III.1. (3)), also contain significant passages. Plotinus' discussion of freedom in VI.8 is interestingly different from what we find in other treatises: here his primary concern is to elucidate the conditions for calling something free. This leads him to speak more openly and positively about the One than anywhere else. The One turns out to be the free agent par excellence. Human beings can be said to be free in a limited sense, in so far as they resemble the One. In the other treatises, those on providence and on destiny, in particular, he considers questions about human freedom in the context of theodicy and divine predetermination of events and actions in the sensible world. Unfortunately, these two concerns about freedom are nowhere fully treated together. I shall proceed by first considering Plotinus' views on freedom, providence, fate and theodicy, which indeed is an ethically relevant topic in its own right, and then turn to the issues dealt with in VI.8.

2.1 Providence, fate and human responsibility

In the presentation that follows I shall rely primarily on Plotinus' late treatise "On providence." It provides his most extensive discussion of these issues and it is, needless to say, his last word on the subject. This treatise and the treatise "On destiny" add to a long list of works on the same topics by Hellenistic authors—Stoic, Platonic and Aristotelian.[8] In his excellent introduction ("Notice") to "On providence" in his edition, Bréhier (1924–38) identifies a number of influences and background views on Plotinus' account in this treatise. First, there is a great deal that agrees with Stoic doctrine. This is particularly obvious in the case of the theodicy proclaimed in the treatise but the debt to the Stoics also cuts much deeper (cf. Frede 2011: ch. 8). Secondly, though ultimately Stoic in origin, the notion of the grand *logos* of the cosmos, which plays a quite central role in this treatise, bears a strong resemblance to *logos* in Philo of Alexandria and in Origen. Thirdly, as is to be expected, Plato sets the premises: in *Timaeus* 30b–c Plato says that in creating the world the god "wanted to produce a piece of work that would be as excellent and supreme as its nature would allow" and that this is how "divine providence brought the world into being." In *Theaetetus* 76a he says that "evils can never be done away with" and that "they have no place among the gods but haunt our mortal nature and this region forever." It is fair to say that these two discordant but logically compatible claims set Plotinus' agenda about our topic. In Books IX and X of the *Laws* (870d–e, 872e, 881a, 904 ff.; cf. *Timaeus* 42b–c) Plato also refers to punishments for wrongdoings in previous lives through new incarnations and emphasizes the detail in which the god has devised the world. These passages too provide an important background for Plotinus' discussion.

In "On providence" Plotinus appears to identify providence with the *logos* of the world—I say "appears to" because he does not explicitly identify them but it is fairly evident that he does. What is this *logos*? We have seen that Plotinus posits the three hypostases, the One, Intellect and Soul. After Soul comes the sensible world. It has puzzled interpreters where to fit this *logos* into this scheme. In "On providence (I)" he says that "Intellect, by giving something of itself to matter, made all things in unperturbed quietness; this [what is given by Intellect] is the *logos* flowing from Intellect" (III.2.2, 15–17). There is no mention of soul here. Later in the treatise, however, he says that the *logos* is an "outshining of both, Intellect and Soul" (III.2.16, 15) and also that "the *logoi* are an activity of a universal soul, and the [activities of their] parts [the activities] of soul parts" (III.3.1, 4–5). He also seems to imply that some *logoi* are souls in their own right and others not (III.2.18, 28–29). Thus, souls have not at all dropped out of the picture. Though *logoi* have an even more prominent place in the treatise on providence than in general in the *Enneads* there is nothing here that conflicts with Plotinus' normal doctrine: as we have seen in previous chapters (see especially Chapter 2, p. 46 and Chapter 5, p. 341), *logoi* are commonly soul-powers that operate in the sensible world and as such are closely akin to nature, the immanent phase of the World-Soul.

The *logos* of the world is structured like a tree (see III.3.7). It begins as one and then divides itself into branches, which are partial *logoi* in charge of parts of the cosmos. It arranges everything in the sensible world for the best. Everything is coordinated: providence is likened to a general who is in perfect control of everything, giving orders to obedient subordinates, who pass them on to their subordinates. The general not only directs and controls the war but also the supply of food and weapons (III.3.2). In fact, if we can imagine a general who not only controls his own army but also that of the enemy, the image would be almost perfect (III.3.2, 13–15). There is a difference, however. A human general would deliberate his way to the optimal results. Providence, by contrast, does not have to deliberate.

The questions that occupy Plotinus in connection with providence are primarily of two kinds. First, there is the fact of evil: obviously a lot in the sensible world is less than ideally good (human wrongdoing and folly are a part of this). How is this compatible with a providence that arranges everything for the best? In particular, are the bad sides of the world also according to the will of providence? Secondly, there are questions relating to the place for human freedom within a generally providentially ordered cosmos. Plotinus insists both in the treatise on providence and elsewhere that we are not nothing (III.1.8; III.1.9, 1–2). He objects to any theory about the world which makes us mere puppets who do nothing on our own accord, and is adamant about our moral responsibility. The question is how this is compatible with providence arranging everything.

In addressing the first question Plotinus notes that it is a striking fact about the sensible world that there is war and conflict there: fire extinguishes water, animals fight and eat each other, and human beings fight each other too. In general, the sensible world is full of opposites. There is a general explanation of such facts:

> For from that true universe [the intelligible world], which is one, this universe comes into existence, which is not truly one; for it is many and divided into a multiplicity, and one part stands away from another and is alien to it, and there is not only friendship but also enmity because of the separation, and in their deficiency one part is of necessity at war with another.
> (III.2.2, 1–6)

Thus, the discord and conflicts are due to the great distance from the intelligible realm or, in other words, closeness to matter (cf. Chapter 6, p. 198 ff.). There being a great distance is just a different way of saying that we have reached a greater multiplicity, which in turn means more isolation and individuation: "each part is not self-sufficient, but in being preserved is at war with the other by which it is preserved" (III.2.2, 6–7). There is unity, however. There is a single universal *logos* which includes both good and bad things (III.3.1, 1–2). "For all things sprung from a unity come together into a unity by natural necessity, so that, though they grow out different and come into being as opposites, they are, all the same, drawn together into a single common order by the fact that they come from a unity" (III.3.1, 9–12). So the opposites form a unity administered by the universal rational principle. There is nothing haphazard about this. The universal *logos* arranges things in the best possible way. This means that given the nature of material things and the general situation in the sensible realm, there will be opposites and there will be things devouring each other. But this is as it should be, given the conditions: just imagine how it would be if organisms lived and procreated forever (see III.2.4, 17–18).

The fact that individual things vary in goodness and beauty is explained along the same lines with some significant additions:

> We are like people who know nothing about the art of painting and criticize the painter because the colors are not beautiful everywhere, though he has really distributed the appropriate colors in each place ... or we are like someone who censures a

play because all the characters in it are not heroes but there is a servant and a yokel who speaks in a vulgar way; but the play is not a good one if one expels the inferior characters, because they too help to complete it.

(III.2.11, 9–16)

We may summarize these ideas by saying that due to the separation that results in individuation and lack of self-sufficiency, the sensible world is characterized by internal conflicts. Such conflicts are, nevertheless, included in a larger scheme and are indeed a necessary part of an optimal sensible world. A further consequence of this is that beings in the sensible world differ in rank: a being that is in itself insignificant and even bad may nevertheless necessarily be included in the best possible sensible world. It is needless to say that Leibniz's views about this being the best of all possible worlds—most explicitly expressed in his *Theodicy*, and ridiculed in Voltaire's *Candide*—bear a strong resemblance to those of Plotinus. Leibniz too explains the apparent badness of particulars as a necessary part of the best whole.

The views we have just expounded give rise to a host of ethical questions. First, is Plotinus really saying that the bad is good? In other words, is he saying that badness of particular details, whether people, events or states, is only apparent and that if we considered the matter from the viewpoint of the whole we would see that they are good after all? It may seem that Plotinus is saying just that. In comparing the universe to a play he says, justifying the presence of evil: "For there is fitness and beauty in the whole only if each individual is stationed where he ought to be—the one who utters evil sounds in the darkness of Tartarus: for to make these sounds *there* is beautiful" (III.2.17, 64–67). Despite remarks of this kind, it would be a misrepresentation of Plotinus to say that according to him crime, brutality and vice generally are really good: providence makes use of such vicissitudes but this does not make them good. Things are good or bad according to where they stand on the scale reaching from the Good to matter; the apparent evils are really on the low side of this scale and hence not merely apparent but real evils. Their being necessary parts of the best world does not change their status in this respect.

In this connection it is appropriate to make a note about Plotinus' use of the terms "good" and "evil." In the sections on the virtues and on happiness above we saw that no event or state in the sensible world is good or evil in an absolute sense: nothing that happens there can make a happy person unhappy or happier, nor will anyone be truly well off just on account of some such event or state. Nevertheless, as we saw in Chapter 6, matter is the primary evil and things are evil to the extent they have a share in matter. And in discussing providence and fate he often uses the words "good" and "bad" in the ordinary way, i.e. he uses them about states and events in the sensible world we would ordinarily consider good or bad. This does not mean that he thinks such things are "good" or "bad" in the sense he denies in the other treatises. Being poor, for instance, is from the viewpoint of Plotinus' account of virtue and happiness a morally neutral fact: nothing follows from it about a person's real qualifications with respect to goodness. On the other hand, from the viewpoint of providence and the doctrine of matter as the root of evil, poverty can be considered to be an evil, to be something anyone would naturally prefer to be without. Thus, we may say that things and states in the sensible world may be metaphysically evil without, however, being morally evil: moral evil is peculiar to human souls. Some 150 years after Plotinus St. Augustine in his *Freedom of Choice* accounted for moral evil, sin, as the soul's subordination to something naturally inferior to itself, as, so to speak, a failure to stay in its rank in the hierarchy of beings. Plotinus' has essentially the same view. This is the moral evil of human souls.

Is providence blameworthy in allotting bad fates to people? No. Again we must look at the cases from a wider perspective: destinies such as being taken slave, suffering poverty and being murdered are no accident but in order to see the reason for them we must look beyond the present life; the ones who are now slaves, paupers or murder victims are likely to be guilty of having been bad masters, exploiters and murderers in previous lives (III.2.13, 4–8). So in allotting such fates the *logos* is only rectifying the past wrongs and is not unjust. In this, as in most other things in this sphere, he can cite Plato for support of his views (cf. *Phaedrus* 248c; *Laws* IX, 872e). Thus, if such fates may appear unjust from a narrow perspective the broader view will reveal that there is good reason for them.

It is noteworthy in this connection that the bona fide examples of bad destinies—being taken slave, being poor, being murdered—are all passive undergoings. I don't think Plotinus ever describes something active, murdering someone, for instance, as a part of providence. This is something the person him- or herself does. This last-mentioned fact may resolve an issue that has puzzled scholars: they have wondered whether by referring to sins in previous lives Plotinus isn't just postponing the question: if Josephine suffers now because of something she did in a past life, which in turn she did because in the life before that she did something which made her deserve that fate, which again she deserves because of yet another misdeed in yet another life, and so forth infinitely (see Clark 1943 and Rist 1967: 130–131). If I am right in what I just said that bad fates have to do with what happens to people rather than with what they actively do, there may be an "original sin," of which a particular past wrongdoer is the original agent and responsible for it. Providence did not make her do it. We do not necessarily have to go back to infinity or even very far back, but a wider scope than the present life may be necessary.

Let us now address human freedom and responsibility in the context of providence and fate. It seems that Plotinus believes in all the following propositions relating to this area and thinks that they make up a fully consistent set:

1 Providence does not *produce* evils, including evil actions, but it *includes* them (III.3.1, 3–4; III.3.5, 24–27).
2 Everything that happens is included in providence and is in principle predictable (III.3.6).
3 Bad people are reasonably subject to blame (III.3.4, 5).
4 People are themselves the agents of their actions, both good and bad (III.2.10, 10–11; III.1.9, 9–12).
5 When people act in accordance with providence they are free (III.3.4, 7–8).

The meaning of (1) and (2) is perhaps not entirely lucid. We have seen Plotinus' explanation of why there must be both better and worse things in the world, why there are not only splendid heroes but also snails and worms and people of different characters, some bad. In the treatise he sometimes speaks as if all this is the work of providence. So why does he say that providence does not produce evils? Presumably, a distinction he makes in III.3.5 between providence and fate is relevant here. He suggests that there is "one providence; but it is 'fate' beginning from the lower level; the upper part is providence alone" (III.3.5, 15–16).[9] Evil deeds are a part of fate and a consequence of the higher providence but "they follow by necessity" from providence (III.3.5, 33). He does not explain the distinction between fate and providence proper in any sort of detail but he describes what is attributed to fate as "consequences." I think he has in mind unintended consequences of providence and the chain of physical causes which providence makes use of in implementing the good order. Think of a city planner who wishes to set up a truly excellent city. This will, let us suppose, necessarily include several quite high buildings. These buildings will block an excellent view the inhabitants in nearby low-rises otherwise would enjoy. This blocking follows upon the plan for the city but is not as such a part of it. Similarly, necessary but unintended consequences of providence are fated but they are not, as it were, as such a part of the plan—I speak of a "plan" as Plotinus sometimes does himself in "On providence," even if there is no plan in the ordinary sense of a plan being the result of deliberation. Elsewhere, Plotinus says explicitly that as compounds of body and soul we are a part of the causal nexus of the cosmos ("On whether the stars are causes," II.3. (52) 9). This in turn implies that our physical character as well as bodily desires and impulses are subject to the chain of causes that constitutes fate. It is these together with the sequence of events in which we find ourselves which prompt our evil-doing. As much is also clear from the previous discussion of Plotinus' ethics.

Let us consider the propositions (3), (4) and (5) above, starting with the last one, which says that wicked people are blameworthy for their wrongdoings. Plotinus divides humankind into three groups, the virtuous, the vast mediocre majority and the vicious. Even the mediocre are to be blamed and can blame themselves if they suffer at the hands of the wicked: they failed to prepare themselves and to be courageous (III.2.8, 13–16). The virtuous, on the other hand, who act in accordance with providence, are free and are truly the agents of their actions. I shall have more to say about this last claim shortly when we come to *Ennead* VI.8, but let it be said here that the virtuous act in accordance with providence without being made to act by providence: they act of themselves. It is of course no accident that the virtuous act in accordance with providence: virtue and providence have the same source, Intellect and ultimately the Good. Moreover, the virtuous person acts from what is most truly himself or herself: as we saw in previous sections, this person has become identical with his or her intelligible self. This intelligible self is not subject to anything alien to it. Since to be free means for Plotinus essentially to be autonomous and the intelligible self is autonomous, the intelligible self is free.

How is it then with bad or mediocre people? They are in some sense ruled by their bodily nature and at least their higher self is not the agent of their actions. Given what has just been said, it would seem that they are not truly the agents of their vicious or careless acts. How can they then be justly blamed for what they do? Let us see how Plotinus deals with this question:

> For if man was simple—I mean in the sense that he was nothing but what he was made and acted and was acted on accordingly—there would be no responsibility leading to reproach, just as there is none in the case of other living creatures. But, as it is, man, the bad man, is uniquely subject to blame and no doubt rightly so. For he is not only what he was made but has another free principle, which is not separated from providence or that logos of the whole.
>
> (III.3.4, 1–8)

So every human being has the principle of right and wrong but only some use it. This is, of course, just what we saw in Section 2 of the previous chapter: every human being is potentially virtuous and happy. Slightly later in the discussion we learn that this principle does not act in some people (III.3.5, 40 ff.). The further question naturally arises whether people can help themselves in making the choice they make between the path of virtue and the way of gratifying the demands of the composite. This is the fundamental choice a human being faces according to Plotinus. He, however, nowhere addresses the problems that either a positive or a negative answer to it raises, but he seems to assume that people can help themselves and are responsible for their choice: blameworthiness in general comes with the fact that man, as a species, is not a mere animal but has "another free principle." That would not be of much help unless it is assumed that those who fail to make use of this principle can do so. Plotinus' whole discussion in "On providence" and elsewhere assumes that they can.

But how can Plotinus insist that vicious people are the agents of what they do, given that only the virtuous ones truly act from themselves? The composite of soul and body of the vicious of course causes what happens but in what sense are they more the agents of this than animals are of what they do? Plotinus does not address this question directly but I think the answer must be that they are "agents" and certainly morally responsible very much in the sense that someone who lets something happen by failing to intervene can be said to be the agent of it. In other words, they are agents in a transferred sense by failing to act from the "free principle" given to them.

He holds these views in spite of the fact that he believes our choices, along with everything else, to be in some sense causally determined: "Suppose you say 'I am empowered to choose this or that'. But the things that you will choose are included in the universal order, because your part is not a mere casual interlude in the All but you are counted in such as you are" (III.3.3, 1–3). The account of prophesy in III.3.6 and several other remarks suggest the same. This makes Plotinus a compatibilist with respect to determinism and freedom. He does not, however, discuss the questions that the compatibilist view as such may give rise to in any sort of detail. He, however, makes an interesting and relevant remark. In "On providence (I)," he asks about the wicked whether they have become such by necessity by the stars or the principle (presumably providence). The answer is very brief: "As for necessity, this does not mean that it comes from the outside but only that it is universally so (*pantōs*)" (III.2.10, 11–12). This is first of all meant to exclude the view that the wicked person is at all forced. Plotinus seems to admit that the wicked action can be described as necessary but says that this just means that it is "universally so." This in turn must mean something like: given such and such a character, situation and so forth, such and such a type of action invariably follows but it does so neither by force nor logical necessity. Such a compatibilist position is a commonplace in the history of philosophy.

2.2 Freedom and what is up to one

Let us turn to *Ennead* VI.8, "On autonomy and the will of the One," Plotinus' most informative treatise on freedom and related notions. He begins this treatise by raising the question whether we can ask about the gods if there is something that is in their power or

> whether this kind of enquiry is proper in dealing with human impotences and dubious powers, but we must attribute to the gods omnipotence and say that not just something but everything is in their power? Or is it true that omnipotence and having everything in his power is indeed to be attributed to the One but with the other gods we should say that some things are this way and some the other, and of which each is true?
> (VI.8.1, 2–8)

He then begins by discussing the human case. Since it turns out that human freedom depends on Intellect and ultimately on the One, he is led to raise the question of the freedom of a god, Intellect and ultimately the One itself, the discussion of which takes up more than half of the treatise. Opinions are somewhat divided among scholars as to what is Plotinus' primary aim in this treatise. Is he discussing the human case, only to move on to that of Intellect and finally and most importantly to that of the One? Or is he discussing the divine cases mainly in order to teach a lesson about human freedom? The truth of the matter is probably some of both: the case of the One is interesting for its own sake but it is, as Michael Frede (2011: 132) puts it, "a dark and obscure matter for us." Hence, it has to be approached gradually, beginning with the more familiar case of human freedom. He does not return to human freedom in the treatise. Clearly, however, what is said about divine freedom is relevant to the correct understanding of the human case: it turns out that human freedom is a bleak image of divine freedom, just as the human being itself is a bleak image of the One. Thus, we must consider the One if we want to know what freedom really is. The treatise is designed to show us how limited human freedom is in comparison with true freedom. At the same time it becomes evident that we are indeed free to the extent we manage to be like god.

In the first few chapters, where he deals with the human case, Plotinus brings in all the notions in terms of which his predecessors had carried out their debates in this area: the voluntary (to *hekousion*), mastery (*kyrios einai*), autonomy or self-determination (to *autexousion*), and freedom (*eleutheria*). The central notion, however, is that of having something in one's power, a notion that had been introduced by Aristotle and had assumed a central role in Stoicism. Here is Plotinus' initial characterization of this notion:

> I myself think that, when we are pushed around among opposite chances and compulsions and strong assaults of passions subdue our soul, we acknowledge all these things and we are enslaved to them and carried wherever they take us, and so are in doubt whether we are not nothing and nothing is in our power, on the assumption that whatever we might do when not enslaved to chances or compulsions or strong passions, *because* we willed it (*boulēthentes*) and with nothing opposing our will (*boulēsis*), this would be in our power. But if this is so, our notion of what is in our power would be something enslaved to our will and would come to pass to the extent to which we willed it.
>
> (VI.8.1, 22–33)

The issue here is under what conditions we might be said to be free, to have something in our power. Nothing is excluded among possible things that may interfere with our freedom: not only the demands of despots and all sorts of external circumstances might interfere, but also our own passions. Thus, at stake here is what has been called freedom of the will—"positive freedom" in Isaiah Berlin's (1958) phraseology—rather than external, "negative freedom." The language and with it crucial aspects of the content of the central concepts derive, however, from the social and political sphere. Thus, "to be master" and "not to be enslaved" is quite central to Plotinus' understanding of freedom as indeed it was for his predecessors, both Stoic and Peripatetic. As we might guess, it turns out that the One alone is in no way whatsoever enslaved. It should not come as a surprise at all that this is due to its being truly one and truly good.

The upshot of the preceding quote is that for X to be in our power two conditions must be satisfied: nothing must stand in the way of our will to make X happen; and it must not be settled by the course of the world whether X happens or not. I may, for instance, want to cross a river but the current is too strong. The obstacle may also just as well be internal: it is not that the current is really so strong but rather that I get a panic attack whenever I set out to cross the river, and have to return. That is to say, X must happen *because* I will it to happen. If it had to happen anyway, it would not have been in my power. My will must be the cause of its happening (cf. Frede 2011: 134).

The preceding of course raises the question what it is to will something and what the will is. Rather than addressing this immediately and directly Plotinus asks in chapter 2 of VI.8, to what in us should we ascribe this "in our power." He discusses and rejects several candidates: it cannot be impulse or desire, because then the insane, children and animals would have something in their power, which they in his view obviously do not. Nor is it simply desire combined with reasoning (*logismos*). For what should we say if the reasoning goes wrong somewhere? What gets done then would not be something in our power, would not happen because we willed it to happen. So perhaps what is done from correct reasoning accompanied by correct desire is in our power. In that case it is proper to ask "whether the reasoning set the desire in motion or the desire the reasoning" (VI.8.2, 11–12). He does not believe that what is done as a result of reasoning that has its premises from the desires of the compound of soul and body can be up to us. In that case we are being led rather than taking the lead. Admittedly, reason may set a stop to what desire craves, but in that case reason is rather a principle of inaction than of action (VI.8.2, 34–35).

In general Plotinus rejects anything as in our power that does not originate in ourselves. Given his views on what is really we ourselves (see Chapter 8, Section 4, "The Soul and We Ourselves"), the identification of the self with reason, only that which originates in our reason is in our power. This, of course, also conforms to what we have seen about his views on virtue and happiness: only the virtuous, happy person is self-determined and free. Though they definitely differ about the relationship between virtue and happiness as well as about many other details, Plotinus' views on autonomy are notoriously close to Kant's: both thinkers insist that what is free or autonomous is reason alone and what Plotinus says about the desires corresponds closely to Kant's views on inclination.

In chapter 5 he raises the question whether "self-determination (*to autexousion*) and being in one's own power" is "only in intellect when it thinks, i.e. in pure intellect," or "also in soul when it is active according to intellect and engaged in practical actions according to virtue" (VI.8.5, 1–3). He responds to this by noting that at least the success of the action (*hē teuxis*) is not up to us (l. 5). What he has in mind is presumably cases of the kind when someone or something interferes with the action: a sudden wind sways the arrow off its course, for instance. Someone might say, however, that even if success is not up to us, self-determination may be attributed to us with respect to how we act, i.e. whether we act well (*kalōs*) or not. Against this, Plotinus points out that virtuous action depends on external circumstances. Courage, for instance, requires a certain situation such as war in which it may be exercised, and the same is true for justice. These contingent external circumstances, Plotinus notes, are in general not up to us, and hence it is not up to us to engage in courageous or just actions at will (VI.8.5, 7–13).

Plotinus also points out that when the situation arises, virtue demands a certain action from us. So, not only is it the case that we depend on situations and events over which we may seem to have little or no control for our exercise of virtue in action, we may seem to be compelled to specific actions by virtue when such situations arise. He doesn't think virtue enslaves us, however. He notes that virtue is "a kind of other intellect" (VI.8.5, 34–35) and intellect is not forced by external circumstances or passions. Even when these occur, it "will retain its autonomy (*to eph' hautē*)" (VI.8.6, 13). To illustrate this he says that virtue, i.e. the virtuous soul

> will not follow the lead of the facts (*tais pragmasin*), for instance by saving the man who is in danger, but, if it thinks fit, it will sacrifice him and command him to sacrifice his life and property and children and even his fatherland, having in view its own excellence and not the existence of what is subject to it; so that

also in practical actions self-determination and being in our power is not referred to practice and outward activity but to the inner activity of virtue itself, that is, its thought and contemplation.[10]
(VI.8.6, 14–22)

I take it that the main point of the illustration is to bring home the point of the remark from the Myth of Er (*Republic* X, 617e) that "virtue has no master"—a Platonic text Plotinus has referred to a few lines above in the discussion. He wishes to insist that virtue considers only itself, i.e. in acting virtuously it is only concerned with its own excellence, which the context shows to consist in rationality. The latter part of the quote describes external virtuous action as an external act of the internal activity of the intellect. But how does it follow from this that self-determination belongs primarily to the "internal activity" of virtue and not to practice and its external activity? Plotinus' answer, put succinctly, is that internal activity is free because the activity itself is identical with the agent; the external activity—the action in the sensible world—may be said to be self-determined too in so far as it flows without hindrance from the internal one, but its freedom or autonomous character is parasitic on that of the internal activity.

It turns out, not surprisingly, that the remainder of the treatise is largely devoted to the freedom of the One, which was discussed in Chapter 3. We may add to that discussion here that what Plotinus has to say about the will and freedom of the One aims at establishing the One as self-determined. In contemporary terminology we might say that his whole discussion of freedom aims in general at giving an adequate account of agent causality: how can something truly itself determine what it is and does? It turns out that only the One fully satisfies the conditions for being self-determined. This, of course, has to do with its perfect unity: there is no distinction to be made between the One and its will, it and what it does. Human self-determination is not like that, nor is even the self-determination of Intellect: the latter is dependent on the One (the Good), which is something it has to aspire to (and will) but is not an integral part of its nature. This is so because, as we noted in Chapter 4 (p. 105), there is an element of imperfection and need in thought, even the non-discursive thought of Intellect.

3 Beauty and the fine arts

Outside philosophical circles Plotinus may be best known for his views on beauty, which have had considerable influence on artists (see Chapter 11, p. 379). He wrote two treatises that have beauty in their Porphyrian titles, "On beauty" (I.6. (1)) and "On the intelligible beauty" (V.8. (31)), and the notion of beauty is relevantly present in many other treatises. Yet, as noted in Chapter 4 (p. 113), the metaphysical status of beauty is far from clear. There are passages suggesting an identification of the primary beauty with the Good itself, others affirming that beauty is posterior. Plotinus may well be ambivalent about its status as Plato also presumably was, or for some reason Plotinus failed to write a text that gives us his fully considered view. What is clear, however, is that there is beauty in the intelligible realm. Each of the Forms and the intelligible world as a whole share in it. So does the sensible realm but to a much lesser degree. In what follows, I shall focus on the role beauty plays for us and in particular for the aspiring philosopher.

The word for beauty (or "the beautiful") in ancient Greek is *to kalon*. It is well known that the Greek term has a wider application than "beautiful" is normally considered to have in English. *To kalon* was definitely also what we would consider a moral term. (I say "normally considered to have" because I suspect that actual usage relating to beauty and that whole realm of words in English and other modern languages is closer to the ancient Greek usages than estheticians and moral philosophers generally recognize; we have no problems speaking about beautiful persons, souls or minds; usually, this is not meant to apply just to what meets the eye.) In general it seems fair to say that what is *kalon* is that which will evoke admiration and attraction. To think of *to kalon* as "the splendid" or "the attractive" may give some of the right connotations. As such beauty is the natural object of love.

Plotinus' very first treatise, "On beauty," can be seen as a retelling of the account of the ladder of beauty in Diotima's speech in the *Symposium*, supported by other Platonic insights, especially from the *Phaedrus*. The outcome is, however, markedly Plotinian and original. He begins by talking about beauty in the sensible realm, attending not only to visual beauties but also to those of music. Plato, Aristotle and especially the Stoics had located beauty in the harmony or good proportion (*harmonia*) of the parts of the beautiful object. Plotinus objects: "On this theory nothing single and simple but only a composite thing will have beauty" (I.6.1, 25–26). And he goes on to give examples of simple things that are evidently beautiful: the light of the sun, gold, the lightning in the night and the stars. The same holds for sounds: "Often, in a composition, which is beautiful as a whole each separate sound is beautiful" (I.6.1, 35–36).

It is not that Plotinus entirely rejects any connection between good proportion and beauty. He is mainly objecting to defining beauty in terms of good proportion and especially to reducing it to particular, supposedly fine proportions. Such accounts are narrow in that they do not capture some evidently beautiful sensible phenomena and they do not apply to spheres such as that of the soul, virtue and scientific theorems. He does not think the beauty in these can be reduced to beautiful mathematical proportions.

In chapter 3 of the treatise Plotinus raises and answers the following question:

> How does the architect declare the house outside to be beautiful by fitting it to the form within him? The reason is that the house outside, apart from the stones, is the inner form divided by the external mass of matter, without parts but appearing in many parts. When sense-perception, then, sees the form in bodies binding and mastering the nature opposed to it, which is shapeless, shape riding gloriously upon other shapes, it gathers into one that which appears dispersed and brings it back and takes it in, now without parts, to the soul's interior and presents it to that which is within as something in tune with it and fitting it and dear to it.
>
> (I.6.3, 6–15)

This passage is about how we judge something perceptible, and hence dispersed and manifold, to be beautiful. We do this by seeing the outside object, which by now has been internalized, as something akin to, in tune with and dear to what is within the soul's interior. This means that the prior beauty is within the soul, the recognition of external beauty is presented as a kind of acceptance on the part of the soul: "here I recognize something akin to what I possess." This should not come as a surprise at all, since any beauty sensible objects may possess is given them by soul, be it that of the world or a human soul. Further along, he speaks of "the melodies in sounds, too, the imperceptible ones which make the perceptible ones, make the soul conscious of beauty in the same way, showing the same thing in a different medium" (I.6.3, 28–31). So the soul may be awakened to a beauty it already possesses by perceiving and taking in an external expression of it.

The rest of the treatise deals with non-perceptible beauty. The beauty of souls is accounted for as purification since its opposite, ugliness, is due to the association with bodily nature and matter. The soul, freed of this, becomes intellect and becomes truly itself. In this it also becomes godlike (I.6.6). The soul in this state will aspire even higher towards "the Good, which every soul desires. Anyone who has seen it knows what I mean when I say that it is beautiful" (I.6.7, 1–3). How does one go about this? The answer is that the soul must be trained, starting from "beautiful ways of life" (I.6.9, 3), and ascend. This is, so far, basically Diotima's account in the *Symposium*. But here comes a new element:

> When you see that you have become this, then you have become [intellectual] sight; you can trust yourself then; you have already ascended and need no one to show you; concentrate your gaze and see. This alone is the eye that sees the great beauty. But if anyone comes to the sight blear-eyed with wickedness, and unpurified, or weak and by his cowardice unable to look at what is very bright, he sees nothing, even if someone shows him what is there and possible to see. For one must come to the sight with a power of seeing made akin to what is seen. No eye ever saw the sun without becoming sun-like, nor can a soul see beauty without becoming beautiful. You must first become all godlike and all beautiful, if you intend to see God and beauty.
>
> (I.6.9, 22–34)[11]

What is new here in relation to the sight of beauty itself in the *Symposium* and the Analogy of the Sun in the *Republic*, which Plotinus also draws on, is the emphasis (which really is implicit in Plato) on the godlikeness of the seer. In maintaining this Plotinus makes effective use of a maxim in many ancient Greek theories of perception, including the Analogy of the Sun in the *Republic*, that (only) like perceives like. The purified soul has been made godlike and then and *only then* will it see the beautiful. But what is this beauty that the soul sees? Plotinus says it is the good. Is he then describing an experience that transcends Intellect, a "mystical experience" of the Good here? Some interpreters understand this in such a way (cf. Meijer 1992: 299). In my view this is for several reasons doubtful. Let us see how he concludes the treatise in direct continuation of the previous quotation:

> First the soul will come to its ascent to Intellect and there will know the Forms, all beautiful, and will affirm that, the Ideas, are beauty; for all things are beautiful by these, by the products and the being of Intellect. That which is beyond these we call the nature of the Good, which holds beauty as a screen before it. So in a loose and general way of speaking the Good is the primary beauty; if one distinguishes the intelligibles [from the Good], one will say that the place of the Forms is the intelligible beauty, whereas the Good is that which is beyond, "the spring and origin" of beauty;[12] or one will place the Good and the primal beauty on the same level: in any case, beauty is in the intelligible realm.
>
> (I.6.9, 34–43)

There are several things to note here. Primarily, Plotinus does not seem at this early stage to have firmly made up his mind whether the Good is to be raised above the intelligibles as something transcending them. He toys with the idea without embracing it fully as he does in later treatises. The treatise makes no reference to the One as something possibly transcending both the Good and the Beautiful. Assuming that there is no such notion of the transcendent One in the background, Plotinus is undecided as to whether the Good is at a level above the intelligibles. In any case, the passage suggests that the beautiful is the way the Good appears to the purified soul and to Intellect. Something like this seems to be the meaning of "holding beauty as a screen before it." This translation is Armstrong's, who obviously and I think rightly is exploiting the sense of "covering oneself" of the Greek verb, *proballein*, whose basic meaning is "to throw before oneself." So, the Good does not show itself as it is in itself but throws out beauty as a kind of cover, which is the way it appears to anyone able to approach it.

It is evident from these passages from "On beauty" that beauty is there in the intelligible world. Moreover, it seems to have a status above the realm of Ideas, as something in between them and the Good. The question is only what exactly is its status there. Some passages suggest that beauty is yet another name for the first principle. Stern-Gillet (2000) has made a convincing case for this being so in VI.7.32–33. And she also convincingly shows that beauty never appears as just a regular Platonic Idea in Plotinus. Elsewhere, however, Plotinus insists that the Beautiful is posterior to the Good (V.5.12). In VI.2.18, where he raises the question whether the beautiful should count as one of the primary kinds (and denies that it should), he does not commit himself on the question of whether it should be identified with the first principle or with being.

The other treatise "On the intelligible beauty," V.8, contains much the same message as I.6 about the intelligible origin of beauty and it is an important treatise in other respects as well: it has been cited in previous chapters in connection with Plotinus' holism and non-discursive thought. As regards beauty, however, it is especially remarkable for its doctrine about the relation between beauty and the arts.[13] In the first chapter of this treatise Plotinus notes that the beauty of sensible things is due to their form rather than their matter. For instance a stone that has been made beautiful by art has not changed its matter but it has been given form by the art. That form was previously in the thought of the artist prior to being in the stone:

> Now the material did not have this form, but it was in the man who had it in his mind even before it came into the stone; but it was in the craftsman, not in so far he had hands and eyes, but because he had a share in art. So this beauty was in the art and it was far better there; for the beauty in the art did not come into the stone, but that beauty stays in the art and another comes from it into the stone which is derived from it and less than it.
>
> (V.8.1, 15–21)

He continues, arguing in a familiar way that the beauty in the artist's soul is stronger and superior to the one in the product because the latter is spread out in a spatial magnitude, and loss of unity always involves a loss of strength.

We can glimpse behind these claims several principles of Plotinian metaphysics. One of them is in fact quite explicit here: (1) More unified means stronger and better. Spatial dispersion is a sign of a very low degree of unity. Hence, the beauty in spatially extended things has a low degree of unity. (2) Causes are more unified, hence stronger and better, than their effects. The cause of the sensible beauty of a statue, say, is more unified, hence stronger and better, than the beauty of the statue. (3) We have here also a version of the Platonic–Aristotelian Principle of Prior Possession: what is to become F, becomes so through the agency of something which is actually F (see Chapter 2, Section 4). At least the Platonic version of this insists that the cause is somehow more fully F than the effect which has a status as a mere image or imitation of an F. (4) We see here Plotinus' particular version of this kind of causation, namely the doctrine of double activity (see Chapter 2, Section 4). This is evident from the statement that "the beauty in the art did not come into the stone, but that beauty stays in the art and another comes from it into the stone which is derived from it and less than it." As we may recall, this is something characteristic of double activity: the internal act itself isn't transferred to the effect. It gives nothing out of itself in its external causation but nevertheless produces the external act as a weaker image of itself.

So Plotinus sees something like double activity going on in the relationship between the arts and their products. In this case he focuses on one property in particular, namely beauty. Let us see how he continues:

> But if anyone despises the arts because they produce their work by imitating nature,[14] we must tell him, first, that natural things are imitations too. Then he must know that the arts do not simply imitate what they see, but they run back up to the forming principles from which nature derives; then also that they do a great deal by themselves, and, since they possess beauty, they make up what is defective in things. For Phidias

too did not make his Zeus from any model perceived by the senses, but understood what Zeus would look like if he wanted to make himself visible.

(V.8.1, 32–40)

A few comments on this. To begin with, let us note that it is clear from the context, where beauty is the theme, that even if Plotinus speaks about the arts generally, he has primarily in mind arts that aim at making beautiful objects. The imitative arts such as sculpture and painting would be prime examples of these. We see here that the artists may ascend to the *logoi* of the sensible things they express in their art, presumably *logoi* of the sort the transcendent World-Soul thinks in terms of. Put somewhat boldly, perhaps, but I hope understandably, we might say that the claim is that the imitative artist can grasp the intelligible nature of things, the very intelligible content from which the World-Soul makes the sensible features of things. These artists thus have access to the intelligible beauty which pervades the Forms. Moreover, he says that the arts can even improve on what nature has produced. What does he have in mind by that? He might have in mind arts such as agriculture and medicine, which he says help nature to stay intact. In this context, however, he more probably means that the World-Soul, well organized and clever though she is, leaves some things less beautiful than they could be. Stones, for instance: there is ample evidence that Plotinus thinks little of stones and that they would be benefited by some artistic treatment.

As has been noted numerous times, this account definitely differs greatly from that of Plato in Book X of the *Republic*. According to that account arts such as poetry and painting imitate sensible things and events, which in turn are imitations of the Ideas. Plotinus must have realized this but he does not address this deviation from his master. There was in antiquity a rival theory to Plato's about the nature of the imitative arts. We see it expressed for instance by Philostratus in *The Life of Apollonius of Tyana* VI.19.2, where it is suggested that the artist does not simply imitate what he sees but uses his imagination to supply what he does not know about. This is of course especially relevant in the case of representations of the gods, which few, if anyone, have seen. The idea seems to be that the artist, using his or her memory and power of imagination, forms a mental image, that is not a copy of anything they have directly experienced, and seeks to convey this image in the work of art.

The view Plotinus expresses here goes much further than this in the sense that it grants the artist access to the intelligible paradigms of sensible things and holds that it is these the artist imitates. In the words of Rich (1960: 236): "Whereas in Cicero, Seneca and Philostratus, the artist's immanent concept is something purely 'imaginary' as we would say, a mere concept based on the memory of the physical world, in Plotinus the sculptor's 'imagination' is more solidly grounded in so far as it is to be interpreted as a vision of Ideal Beauty." With this view he widened the concept of artistic imitation, and, apparently, his views on this topic were influential, already in antiquity.[15] They certainly were very influential later, in the Renaissance. Michelangelo, in particular, echoes Plotinus' philosophy of art in his letters and poems.

4 Chapter summary

Plotinus' view that the human soul may have an experience of the intelligible realm, including experience of the One itself, which surpasses ordinary rational reflection is among the most famous aspects of his thought. There are, however, fewer passages than one might expect that unambiguously describe such an experience. We have presented and discussed some of those there are. Indeed, Plotinus is in no doubt that such experiences are possible and real, even if some doubts were raised about how fundamental the alleged fact of such experiences is to his philosophy.

We also addressed Plotinus' views on freedom, divine justice, moral responsibility and related themes. His take on these issues has a Stoic flair. Yet he sees his view as different from that of the Stoics, the great difference being that the individual human soul is according to Plotinus in some sense above the causal nexus of nature (of which the body is a part). Yet, even at the intelligible level of souls the descents and destinies of individual souls follow a rigid pattern of higher justice and providence. It turns out that the autonomy of individual souls consists in their ability to act in accordance with what is already prescribed by providence, which also coincides with what is rational.

The account of Plotinus' views on beauty and the fine arts primarily addressed two topics: the metaphysical status of beauty (also addressed in Chapter 4) and Plotinus' views on the arts and the artist. Strangely, as much as Plotinus is wont to describe the intelligible world as beautiful and the experience of it as an experience of extraordinary beauty, the very status of beauty in this realm is unclear. Sometimes it may seem that beauty simply is yet another name for the first principle, at other times it is given a lower status. Beauty is, however, unquestionably there as an objective feature of the intelligible realm. Plotinus suggests that at least some artists have access to intelligible beauty itself and convey its beauty without the mediacy of sensible models in their works.

Further readings

Primary sources

Ennead I.6. (1) "On beauty."
Ennead III.1. (3) "On fate."
Ennead III.2–3. (47–48) "On providence (I) and (II)."
Ennead IV.8. (6) "On the descent of soul into bodies," chapter 1.
Ennead V.8. (31) "On the intelligible beauty."
Ennead VI.9. (9) "On the Good or the One."

Secondary sources

John M. Rist, *Plotinus: The Road to Reality* (Cambridge: Cambridge University Press, 1967), chapter 16, "Mysticism."
John R. Bussanich, "Mystical Elements in the Thought of Plotinus," in W. Haase (ed.), *Aufstieg und Niedergang der römischen Welt*, pt 2, vol. 36.7 (Berlin: Walter de Gruyter, 1994), 5300–5330.
Erik Eliasson, *The Notion of That Which Depends on Us in Plotinus and Its Background* (Leiden: Brill, 2008).
Audrey N. M. Rich, "Plotinus and the Theory of Artistic Imitation," *Mnemosyne* (4th series) 13 (1960), 233–239.
Michael Frede, *A Free Will: Origins of the Notion in Ancient Philosophy* (Berkeley: University of California Press, 2011), chapter 8.

Panayiota Vassilopoulou, "Plotinus' Aesthetics: In Defence of the Lifelike," in P. Remes and S. Slaveva-Griffin (eds.), *The Routledge Handbook of Neoplatonism* (London: Routledge, 2014), 484–507.

Notes

1 Rist 1967: ch. 16 has an interesting discussion of the various meanings of "mysticism," as does Meijer 1992: 294–298 and Bussanich 1994.
2 The words "the goal, ever near, was shown" are quoted from Apollo's oracle about the fate of Plotinus' soul, which Porphyry has just cited. Amelius consulted the oracle about this (*Life* 22, 8).
3 See e.g. Rist 1967: 56–57 and Meijer 1992: 294. As O'Meara (1993: 105) notes, it is rather a union with Intellect that is described here. Though a kind of activity and life are occasionally ascribed to the One, the emphasis put on activity and life suits Intellect rather than the One.
4 For a fuller discussion of the process leading to supra-discursive experience, see Bussanich 1994.
5 See *Metaphysics* IX, 1051b23–24. See also XI, 1072b21, where Aristotle appeals to contact in explaining how thought and its object are the same.
6 The words "like this" (*toiouton*), which are repeated three times here, refer to what was said in the preceding lines. There Plotinus speaks of the vision of the One as involving a state beyond discursive knowledge.
7 See Rist 1967: 226–227 and Meijer 1992: 277.
8 There are treatises on fate or similar topics from most of the philosophical schools in the period before Plotinus (excepting the sceptics, naturally): there is such a treatise by Cicero (incomplete) rendering the different Hellenistic positions on this topic; Alexander of Aphrodisias wrote a treatise on fate from an Aristotelian point of view and there are treatises by Pseudo-Plutarch and by Pseudo-Galen on the same topic, presumably representing Platonistic positions. Unfortunately the original Stoic works on this are lost. For further reading see Eliasson 2008 and D'Hoine and van Riel 2014 about this material and its relevance to Plotinus.
9 A similar distinction between providence and fate was made before Plotinus by Pseudo-Plutarch, *On Fate* IX, 572f–573b and Apuleius, *On Plato* I, 12.
10 For further comments on this passage, see Emilsson 2012.
11 In the introduction to his *Theory of Colors* Goethe renders Plotinus' thought here in verse, referring to "an ancient mystic": "Wär' nicht das Auge sonnenhaft / Wie könnten wir das Licht erblicken? / Lebt' nicht in uns des Gottes eigne Kraft, / Wie könnt' uns Göttliches entzücken?" ("If the eye was not sunny, / how could we see the light? / If the god did not live in us / how could the divine delight us?"). On the relevance of Plotinus' doctrine in "On beauty" and "On the intelligible beauty" for Michelangelo, see Panofsky 1939: ch. 6.
12 The words "the source and spring" come from Plato, *Phaedrus* 245c; see Chapter 2, p. 53.

13 A fine account of Plotinus' views on artistic imitation is given in Rich 1960; see also Anton 1967, and the more recent Kuisma 2003 and Vassilopoulou 2014.
14 Let us also note that Plotinus uses the word nature, *physis*, in a somewhat unusual way here: here it clearly means the sensible object or the sensible features of things. Most often in contexts such as this one nature is an internal intelligible principle that produces the sensible features. As such, normally, it is the same as the *logos* some sort of elicitation of nature, not the other way around. But, as I said, here he is using the word in an atypical way.
15 For a reserved evaluation of the novelty of Plotinus' aesthetic views, see Kuisma (2003), who argues for the closeness of Plotinus' position to Plato's.

Eleven
Plotinus' legacy and influence

The question of Plotinus' influence is an extremely complex one. For one thing, the matter is insufficiently studied, even if a lot has been written on some aspects of it, for instance about the relationship between Plotinus and Augustine or Plotinus and later Neoplatonists. There is to date to my knowledge no substantial work, however, that seeks to account for Plotinus' presence in the history of thought throughout the ages. The problem is aggravated by the fact that where one sees something in later thinkers that has a Plotinian ring this need not at all mean that Plotinus is the immediate source of it. After all his ancient Platonist successors, whom he undoubtedly greatly influenced, were often quite influential in their own right. St. Augustine (354–430), Proclus (412–485) and Pseudo-Dionysius (fifth–sixth century), a Christian Neoplatonist strongly influenced by Proclus—all had great impact on later thinkers. They were all, so to speak, marked for life, by Plotinus. More often than not one of these would be responsible for a Plotinian trait in later thinkers. Any claim about influence, if it is to count as anything more than free armchair association of ideas, has to be based on research that at least establishes who is likely to have read what. Naturally, this is often difficult. My suspicion is that Plotinus' impact cuts much deeper than has generally been recognized. However, I shall not seek to justify this hunch in what follows but, at least for the most part, stick to what is obvious and well known.

Plotinus transformed Platonism in late antiquity: all the subsequent Platonists followed his example in positing a first principle like Plotinus' One and shared his basic views of a hierarchically ordered reality with the same basic divisions. They also maintained and effectively made use of most of Plotinus' fundamental assumptions such as were outlined in Chapter 2. There are two very significant differences between Plotinus and the late ancient pagan Platonists, however: for them the human soul is thoroughly embodied. It follows that the path of "salvation" through philosophy, involving the possibility of an ascent, is rejected. The other is that the later Platonists adopted and incorporated the Aristotelian ontology of the sensible world as presented in the *Categories* into their Platonic metaphysics in a way Plotinus would not have approved of. This trend may have started with Porphyry himself if not before (see Chapter 6, Section 4).

At the same time as Neoplatonism established itself as the ideology of the educated elite in the Roman Empire, Christianity spread among the masses and ultimately won the day. The earliest, pre-Plotinian Christian theologians adopted both vocabulary and elements of doctrine from the pagan philosophers, Plato and the Stoics in particular, but after Plotinus his and other Neoplatonist thinkers' ideas left strong marks on Christian thought. Some of Plotinus' and Porphyry's writings were translated into Latin by Marius Victorinus (fourth century). These translations have not survived and we do not know exactly what he translated, but they are generally supposed to be what Augustine is referring to in his *Confessions* VII.9.13, where he speaks about "the books of the Platonists," which helped turn his soul towards Christianity.[1] The Plotinian influence on St. Augustine cuts deep. For one thing, he claims to have found the doctrine of the Trinity in the triad of the One, Intellect and Soul, which, however, is puzzling because the relationships of the Neoplatonic hypostases and the persons of the Augustinian Trinity are quite different: Plotinus' three intelligible hypostases clearly come in an order of priority, whereas the persons of the Trinity are somehow at the same level. More significant presumably is Augustine's acceptance of the incorporeality of true reality, of God's changelessness and his status as absolute first cause, the division of reality into different spheres to which different degrees of being are attached, a metaphysical doctrine of evil closely akin to Plotinus', and finally and especially a firm belief in the divine origin of the soul and the sequel of this doctrine that the way to the truth is to be found by looking inward. All these views were widely, if not universally, accepted in the West in the Middle Ages and beyond.

In the East, Neoplatonism also pervaded the Greek Church fathers. Plotinus deeply influenced the Cappadocian fathers (fourth century AD), but the theology in the East (and eventually in the West as well) was in the end very significantly shaped by the aforementioned Pseudo-Dionysius.[2] When Islam took over in large sections of the south-eastern part of the Roman Empire, the conquerors met in some places with cultures of high learning, especially in Egypt and Syria. Soon philosophy flourished again under Islamic rulers. The medieval Islamic philosophers became very fond of Aristotle but this was an Aristotle with a high dose Neoplatonism. There was a piece of work that circulated in the Muslim world under the name of *The Theology of Aristotle*. This was in fact an excerpt from Plotinus' *Enneads* IV–VI. Likewise the so-called *Liber de causis*—the Arabic title was *The Book of the Pure Good*—was attributed to Aristotle but was in fact an excerpt from Proclus and inspired by Plotinus. This work was translated into Latin and initially taken to be a work of Aristotle, even in the West—St. Thomas Aquinas was the first to dispute its authenticity having got in his hands a translation of Proclus' *Elements of Theology*. Jewish philosophy also flourished under Islamic rule in the Middle Ages, and the Jewish philosophers generally adopted the same Neoplatonist approaches to the relation between God and the creation as their Islamic brethren. This meant in particular that they adopted an emanationist interpretation of creation and did not necessarily see a conflict between creationism and emanationism.[3]

In the West knowledge of Greek disappeared during the Middle Ages and very few ancient Greek philosophical texts existed in translation. No text of Plotinus—Victorinus' translations seem to have vanished early—was known in the West. Yet, as we have seen, he and subsequent late ancient pagan Platonists had already set very clear marks on the Christian tradition that took over.

There are threads connecting Plotinus and later thinkers such John Scottus Eriugena (c.800–c.877), Meister Eckhart (1260–1328) and Nicholas of Cusa (1401–1464). Plotinus' impact on these thinkers is, however, indirect and mainly through Pseudo-Dionysius; it is primarily through him that Plotinus' doctrine of the One is echoed in medieval thinkers in the West.

It was not until the Renaissance that the *Enneads* again became directly known in Western Europe. One can even say that during the Renaissance his kind of philosophy had a renaissance: it first became popular in Italy and spread from there to the rest of Europe, still in Christian dress, of course. The most important figure in this movement was Marsilio Ficino of Florence (1433–1499). He translated the whole of Plotinus (and Plato and many other ancient Greek works) into Latin. Ficino's translation appeared in 1492 and was republished numerous times during the next two centuries. This revived Platonism, which venerated Plotinus and other Neoplatonists almost as much as Plato himself, had great impact. It inspired the great artists of the Italian Renaissance. This Platonism eventually reached England. In the middle of the seventeenth century we find there a formidable group of the so-called Cambridge Platonists with Henry More (1614–1687) and Ralph Cudworth (1617–1688) as the best-known representatives. The latter depends heavily on Plotinus in his *True Intellectual System of the Universe* (1678). It is said that the modern sense of the word "consciousness" partly develops from Cudworth's translation of Plotinus' *synaisthēsis* ("together-perception," "consciousness"; see Chapter 8, p. 376) (see Hutton 2013).

The Platonism of Ficino and Cudworth was superseded in the late seventeenth century by Cartesianism, empiricism, and other new philosophical positions. Plotinus was still read, at least in some places, but he hardly had what we can call close followers any more. Still, there are plenty of early modern thinkers such as Descartes, Spinoza, Leibniz, Berkeley and Kant who have, as it were, a Plotinian signature in a new context. Unfortunately, this has been relatively little studied. A valuable attempt to improve our understanding of the impact of Platonism on early modern thought is to be found in Hedley and Hutton (2008), where Platonism—Plotinus of course included—is discussed in relation to various Renaissance and early modern philosophers.

According to Menn (1998), Descartes adhered to a Platonic–Augustinian line of thought, heavily influenced by Plotinus, which consisted in turning away from the sensible world, directing attention inwards to one's soul, and thence "upwards" towards God. To this we may add that some aspects of Descartes' anthropology resemble Plotinus' and are no doubt of Neoplatonic origin. Descartes' second argument for the essential distinction between soul and body in the sixth *Meditation* draws on the same intuitions about the nature of the soul as we have seen in Plotinus: it is an entity to which spatial attributes do not apply; for instance, the soul is present as a whole in different parts of the body.

Kristeller (1984) points out Spinoza's several likely debts to Neoplatonism, in some cases to Plotinus in particular. Among the latter he mentions their respective views on two sorts of human lives: "the unfree life of the passions and the free life of the intellect" (p. 8), about which he sees Spinoza echoing Plotinus, without, however, claiming that he read Plotinus first-hand. He further mentions their respective notion of divine love and of God as *causa sui*. As Kristeller notes, the possible routes of transmission are many and complicated. So far as I know there is no direct evidence that Spinoza read Plotinus, even if he undoubtedly could have. In his case the lines of transmission are more probably indirect through Renaissance Platonists and perhaps the Jewish tradition.

Leibniz's affinity with Plotinus has many times been noted.[4] In his case, there is no doubt that he had direct knowledge of Plotinus' texts—exactly to what extent, however, remains uncertain. Over a century ago Rodier (1902) argued that Plotinus was a source of Leibniz's view that each substance contains or expresses all the others from its particular point of view,[5] and more recently Wilson (1989: 4) writes that Plotinus was perhaps "Leibniz's closest philosophical relative." In Emilsson (2013) I point out several common traits and offer some speculation about Leibniz's relationship to Plotinus.

Berkeley too read Plotinus and refers to him a number of times in the *Siris*. In a recent book, Bradatan (2006) argues that Berkeley is to be seen as essentially a Christian Platonist in the tradition of Ficino and Plotinus. There is little doubt that there are intricate connections between the two thinkers but many of the details remain to be scrutinized.

Kant may never have read any Plotinus, at least he does not find reason to mention his name. There are, however, a number of common features, some of which at least are no doubt due to a frame of ideas highly influenced by Platonic and Neoplatonic thought that Kant inherited: Platonism and Neoplatonism are generally hard to distinguish and especially at this time when Plato was read through Neoplatonic lenses.[6] We have already had occasion to mention their similar understanding of the human condition and freedom (see Chapter 10, p. 360) and that each of these philosophers grounds existence in a principle that lies outside the reach of our knowledge (see Chapter 3, p. 82). The historical connections here, however, remain obscure. To this we may add that the distinction between a sensible world and an intelligible world, or phenomena and noumena, plays a crucial role in Kant's philosophy. Such a distinction is of course Platonic but the way it appears in Kant suggests a Neoplatonic background. The expression "intelligible world" (*kosmos noētos*) is not to be found in Plato but appears for the first time in Philo of Alexandria and is frequent in Plotinus. The distinction appears in the very title of Kant's pre-critical Inaugural Dissertation, *De mundi sensibilis atque intelligibilis forma et principiis* (*On the Form and Principles of the Sensible and the Intelligible World*)[7] and recurs a number of times in his critical period. These terms and the distinction were no doubt quite commonplace in the school tradition Kant belonged to but it is noteworthy that he censures his predecessor Christian Wolff for ruining it by turning it into a merely logical distinction, "to the great detriment of philosophy, *that very noble enterprise of antiquity* [emphasis mine] of discussing the nature of phenomena and noumena, turning us from the investigation of these to what are frequently but logical trifles" (*Inaugural Dissertation* 11). Kant does not explain what he has in mind by this very noble enterprise of antiquity but clearly he is looking beyond the immediate school tradition in asserting this and must, in fact, have Plato or Platonist thinkers in mind. It is of course true and well known that from the *Critique of Pure Reason* on Kant held that intelligible intuition is impossible for us humans. He, however, never abandoned the notion of an intelligible world as a possibility and it continued to play a crucial role for him, not least in his account of freedom.

The German idealists after Kant were more directly engaged with Plotinus and the Platonic tradition than Kant had been. The conceptual framework of Fichte and Hegel, for instance, in which such notions as that of the Absolute, Self-Consciousness, Identity and Otherness play a central role, clearly owes a lot to the Neoplatonists (see Halfwassen 2004a: 12). The general Platonic/Neoplatonic background of post-

Kantian German idealism is well accounted for by Beierwaltes (1972) and more recently in Mojsisch and Summerell 2003. In the chapter "Plotin im deutschen Idealismus" (Plotinus and German idealism) Beierwaltes (1972) discusses Plotinus' presence in Novalis, Goethe, Schelling and Hegel, seeking to establish these thinkers' actual encounter with Plotinus' texts. As regards Plotinus in particular, Goethe and Schelling were positively influenced by him. We noted Goethe's verse, which paraphrases some lines from "On beauty" (see Chapter 10, note 11). According to Beierwaltes (1972: 93 ff.), Goethe found in Plotinus' thought a congenial spirit, especially the relation between nature and art and the origin of both in the Idea and contemplation. Evidently, the doctrine of III.8, "On nature and contemplation and the One," especially appealed to him. Even if the evidence does not reveal Schelling as an industrious student of Plotinus' texts, Beierwaltes is able to point to close parallels in their thought, a similarity that was also noted by contemporaries and cannot be a coincidence (Beierwaltes 1972: 100–144; cf. also Halfwassen 2004a).

In the nineteenth and twentieth centuries we see less of Plotinus, at least at the center of the philosophical scene. In the English-speaking world he indeed continued to inspire poets and artists,[8] but mainstream philosophers to a much lesser extent. Bertrand Russell, however, is surprisingly appreciative of Plotinus in his *A History of Western Philosophy*. The most notable thinker of the nineteenth century under considerable Plotinian influence is no doubt Henri Bergson, who repeatedly lectured on Plotinus and took up aspects of his thought in his own philosophy, while distancing himself from him in some other respects. Somewhat like Goethe before him Bergson was attracted to Plotinus' account of the ensouled sensible world: the dynamic conception of life and the rational principles that proceed from the simple and intensive to the more diverse and extensive in a harmonious way (see Narbonne and Hankey 2006). Bergson had an early influence on the great Plotinian scholar and historian of philosophy, Émile Bréhier, who in turn helped shape the interests of a generation of French scholars. As a result Neoplatonism has probably been more present in French thought than elsewhere (cf. Hankey 2006).

Several commentators see a resemblance between Plotinus and Heidegger, who, however, only mentions Plotinus or other

Neoplatonists in general terms (Beierwaltes 1980: 134; Narbonne 2001: 149). This perceived affinity has primarily to do with Plotinus' elevation of the One as something beyond being and as something which is not "one of the many," something that should not be reduced to a mere existent thing. This is something it may be tempting to compare with Heidegger's distinction between *Sein* (being) and beings (*Seiende*). Whatever similarities there may be, Plotinus' influence on Heidegger is most probably very indirect.

Notes

1. For Augustine and Plotinus with further references, see Moran 2014.
2. On this and Neoplatonic influences on the Eastern Church, see Dimitrov 2014.
3. On Neoplatonism in Islamic and Jewish philosophy, see Pessin 2014.
4. See Mercer 2008 and Emilsson 2013 with references.
5. This is repeated almost *ad nauseam* in the Leibnizian corpus. See e.g. *Discourse on Metaphysics* 8 and 13, and *Monadology* 57.
6. Emilsson and Serck-Hanssen 2004 and Rescher 2013.
7. See para. 2 of *Kant's Inaugural Dissertation* of 1770, trans. William J. Eckoff (1894), Wikisource, https://en.wikisource.org/wiki/Kant%27s_Inaugural_Dissertation_of_1770#Paragraph_2.
8. On Plotinus and Shelley, see Notopoulos 1949; on Plotinus and Blake, see Raine 1969; on Plotinus and Yeats, see Pittock 1989.

Glossary

In this glossary brief explanations are given of some of the more technical terms Plotinus employs. Generally, words of everyday usage are not included, even if Plotinus may hold idiomatic views on the phenomena they refer to. Thus, there is no entry for "soul," "happiness," "sense-perception" or "virtue." Usually, if Plotinus expressed substantial views on the topics such words refer to, the reader will find a chapter or a section of a chapter dealing with them. With the exception of some of Plotinus' more peculiar technical terms, I have not included notions that appear in chapter or section headings. Explanations of such terms are readily obtainable through the table of contents and the general index.

activity, act, actuality (*energeia*) Plotinus borrows the notion of activity from Aristotle. He distinguishes between internal and external activity. The internal activity of anything is identified with its **being** or essence, which Plotinus conceives of as active, whereas the external activity is a byproduct of the internal. This doctrine of double activity is expounded in Chapter 2, Section 4 ("Emanation and Double Activity") and Chapter 3, Section 5 ("The Emanation from the One: Viewpoint of the Emanation"). The external activity is the same as **emanation**. The two acts are also related to Plotinus' Platonic doctrine of paradigms and images in that the external act is an image of the internal one, which then has the role of a paradigm. In every case the external act is less unified than the internal one.

being, essence, substance (*ousia, on*) Plotinus' views on being generally reflect Plato's: true or real being is to be found only at the intelligible level, **sensible** things are mere shadows of being, a kind of false being. In his theory of Intellect he adopts the five "greatest kinds" of Plato's *Sophist* as the highest kinds or **Forms** in the intelligible realm. Though he distinguishes between *ousia* (essence, substance) and *on* (**being**) in II.6.1, he tends to use these words interchangeably. Sometimes, however, his usage reflects Aristotle's, not least when he is discussing the latter's views such as in VI.1. and VI.3. In such contexts it may be appropriate to translate *ousia* by "substance" as is customary in the context of Aristotelian philosophy.

contemplation (*theoria*) *see* **conversion**.

conversion (*epistrophē*) There is not only an unfolding from the principles but also a kind of turning of that which has gone out towards the principles. This is what is meant by "conversion"; it has a similar function in Plotinus to imitation in Plato. Conversion is generally assumed to be some sort of mental or psychological act directed at the principle from which it came. Such an act is often referred to as contemplation (*theoria*). As a result the **emanation** is informed by the superior principle and settles in a new **hypostasis** that is the **internal activity** of the stage below.

discursive thought (*dianoia, logos*) *see* **Intellection**.

double activity *see* **activity**.

emanation Plotinus often describes the unfolding of the levels of reality from the One, through Intellect and Soul, by means of physical metaphors such as light, heat from a fire or water flowing from a spring. Such outgoing process is what is meant by emanation. There is no single word for emanation in his vocabulary, however. The most general term he uses for this unfolding is "process" (*proodos*). Emanation is discussed in II.4. See also **activity**.

external activity *see* **activity**.

Form *see* **Idea**.

form (*eidos, morphē*) In addition to the original paradigmatic **Ideas** or **Forms** in Intellect, there are forms in souls and even forms in matter (enmattered forms). The latter are the **sensible** features of bodies, such as colors and shapes, whereas the forms in souls are **concepts** or **rational formulas**. These **forms** are descendants of the original **Forms** and may even be said to be the **Idea** at a lower stage of ontological derivation.

formative principle (*logos poiētikos*) *see* **logos**.

hypostasis is a technical expression Porphyry adopted to refer to the levels of reality in Plotinus' philosophy, especially the One, Intellect and Soul, as is shown in the treatise titles, "On the three primary hypostases" (V.1) and "On the cognitive hypostases and what is beyond" (V.3). Subsequent scholarship on Plotinus has assumed this practice. Plotinus himself does not use the word systematically in this way. Within each such level except the One there are different items, particular **Ideas** within Intellect and particular souls within Soul. Sometimes "hypostasis" is used to refer to a given such level as a whole. At other times "hypostasis" refers to the underlying substance of each level, which gives it its essential characteristics.

Idea, Form (*eidos, idea*) Plotinus adopts Plato's theory of **Ideas** (**Forms**), which are unchangeable paradigms of which the phenomena of common experience are images. Though Plotinus undoubtedly takes himself to be presenting authentic Platonic views, there are some notable differences between his version of the theory of Ideas and Plato's, at least as the latter is commonly interpreted. The Ideas in Plotinus are internal to a universal mind, Intellect: they are its thoughts. They arise in the **conversion** of the external act of the One towards the One, which this **emanation** from the One is, however, unable to apprehend as it is in itself. Thus, the Ideas may be said to be the One as it appears to Intellect. Another difference is that Plotinus emphasizes more than Plato the unity of the whole realm of Ideas: though each is something distinct, the Ideas form a system in which each part presupposes every other and the whole. Plato may not have disagreed but this sort of holism is not as pronounced in his dialogues as it is in Plotinus. There are other items in Plotinus called **forms** (*eidē*) than the **Forms** in Intellect. When the latter are referred to, "Form" and "Idea" are written so, with an initial capital.

Impression (*typos*) is most importantly used in connection with the human mind, which is often said to contain impressions (see e.g. I.1.7 and IV.3.26). It may be somewhat confusing that Plotinus also firmly rejects the Aristotelian and Stoic view that the memory is effected by retaining impressions from the senses. As he explains in IV.3.26, however, what he is rejecting is a view according to which impressions are conceived as virtual stamps on a corporeal organ. The impressions which he admits are incorporeal.

Intellection (noēsis) is the kind of thought Intellect is engaged in. It is characterized as a veridical and certain grasp of its objects all at once. Presumably, Plotinus does not conceive of this kind of thought as propositional, even if this point has been debated. Intellection is contrasted with discursive thought (*dianoia, logos*), which is propositional and at least in the case of the human soul involves inferences and the search for knowledge.

intelligible (noētos, to noēton) Plotinus follows Plato (and Aristotle) in making a sharp distinction between **sensible** and intelligible phenomena. Originally, the distinction is based on the difference between modes of cognition: intelligible things are apprehended by the intellect, sensible things by the senses. This original sense is sometimes alive, but often "intelligible," especially when used with the definite article, refers to the higher regions of Plotinus' world collectively: the undescended soul, Intellect and even the One, which is not apprehensible at all. Similarly, the **sensible** may be used of the whole consisting of bodies, their properties, and matter, the latter being as such not graspable by the senses. In the context of Intellect the intelligible often refers to the object of Intellect's thought, which are the **Ideas**.

internal activity *see* **activity**.

life is a pervasive notion in Plotinus, closely related to **being**. It seems that what truly *is* according to him is alive, that what is not truly is not alive. Clearly, his notion of life is much wider than what we would recognize as life according to the current science of biology: matter, bodies and their features are not as such alive but everything else is; the One is sometimes said to be beyond life, occasionally life is attributed to it. Everything that Plotinus describes as alive is characterized by self-sufficiency, even if this self-sufficiency comes in degrees and is much lesser for living bodies that have to maintain themselves by nutrition and procreation than Intellect, which is eternally sustained and fecund by its closeness to the One.

logos (pl. logoi), rational formula Already with Plato *logos* had acquired a number of meanings and shades of meaning. When we come to Plotinus' time its uses are even more complex because it has been a key term in most of the philosophical schools in the intervening centuries. Among its translations in philosophical literature we find "reason," "account," "formula," "explanation," "statement," "discussion," "utterance," "argument," "law," "word" and so forth, all depending on context. Presumably, the ancient Greek-speaking philosophers saw just one concept here with some shades of meaning. We find most of these senses in the *Enneads* but in the most common and characteristic use *logos* is the logos of something. The *logos* of X is something that expresses the content of X but in a more detailed and explicit form than this content has in X itself. This use fits that of *logos* in Aristotle according to which it is an account or a formula making explicit what something is. As a cosmological notion, the Plotinian *logos* also owes much to Stoicism. As such *logos* is closely related to soul, which is the bearer of the *logoi*. Thus, the World-Soul contains the *logos* of the human body, for instance, a kind of formula according to which human bodies are made. Such *logoi* may in turn contain more particular *logoi*. The *logos* of the human body will, for instance, contain, the *logoi* of the eyes and the hand. *Logos* in this sense is often interchangeable with **form**. Such *logoi* as generate **sensible** items are sometimes referred to as formative principles in translations of Plotinus.

multiplicity *see* **unity**.

nature, vegetative soul (*to phytikon, to threptikon, physis*) These expressions refer to the lowest phase of soul. We can distinguish between three main functions of this type of soul: (a) the generation of matter; (b) the generation of **sensible** features of bodies; (c) in the context of psychology, nature is a specifically animating principle, not that which makes bodies but that which makes them alive by endowing them with a **trace of soul**. Presumably, Plotinus conceives of these as parallel functions and that at bottom there is only one kind of nature. See Chapter 6, Section 1 ("Matter"), Chapter 7, Section 1 ("The

Human Being I: The Lower Soul–Body Compound") and 3.3 ("Feelings and Emotions").

plurality *see* **unity**.

power, potency, potentiality, faculty (dynamis) is a concept Plotinus has primarily from Aristotle; even Plato also makes use of it. Aristotle distinguishes between active and passive powers. An active power is the power to do something: fire has, for instance, the power to heat. A passive power is the ability to be acted on and receive in a certain way: a stove has the power to become hot. All this is to be found in Plotinus but in his metaphysics and cosmology he primarily speaks of active powers. Thus, he says about the One, that it is the power of everything, meaning that the One has the power to produce everything, not that it can passively receive everything. This use of power is closely linked to **activity**: in general, what has (or is) the power to produce is an internal activity; that which is produced by such a power is an external activity. In the context of psychology *dynamis* is often translated as "faculty" (or again, "power"). Thus, Plotinus speaks of the faculty (or power) of sense perception or the faculty of representation (*phantasia*). Plotinus wrote a little treatise on activity and power.

principle, source, origin (archē) means in non-philosophical Greek "beginning," "origin," "source." It is primarily Aristotle who turned *archē* into an important philosophical term and Plotinus' usage of it largely reflects his. The principle of X is that which enters into the explanation of X. Thus "principle" and "cause" are nearly synonyms.

purification is a notion Plotinus takes over from Plato, not least the *Phaedo*. Plotinus calls real virtue, such as a Platonic sage possesses, purification. What is purified is the human soul which by means of (true Platonic) philosophy is cleansed of the influence of the body on its thoughts. See Chapter 9, Section 1 ("Plotinus' Doctrine of Grades of Virtue").

rational formula *see* **logos**.

sensible (aisthētos) A basic division in Plotinus' philosophy is that between the sensible and the **intelligible** realms. The main characteristic of the sensible as opposed to the intelligible is the loss of unity characteristic of the intelligible realm: at the sensible level the whole is no longer present in the part and each part is something isolated. This low degree of unity at the sensible level is connected with advent of time and space at this level.

trace (of soul), *ichnos* (*psychēs*), *indalma* (*psychēs*) is the **external activity** of nature by which bodies are alive. This corresponds to what we would call the biological activities of the bodily organs, the beating of the heart and metabolism, for instance. It is important to note that even if there is no trace of soul without the presence of a soul, the trace is not a kind of soul and that it is perishable. See Chapter 7, Section 1 ("The Human Being I: The Lower Soul–Body Compound").

unity/one and **multiplicity/plurality** are among the most fundamental concepts in Plotinus' philosophy as one may surmise from the fact that he calls his first principle "the One." The One is sheer unity, does not allow for plurality in any way whatsoever. The subsequent levels and the items on those levels are unified but at the same time plural in some ways. In fact the different levels or **hypostases** and the items belonging to them are distinguished by their degrees of unity, which diminishes the further away from the One a level is placed. Furthest removed is matter, which has no unity whatsoever. As for Aristotle, **being** and unity go hand in hand: to be is to be unified. An apparent exception is the One itself which is said to be "beyond being" but then again the One is not something unified but rather sheer unity. Hence, it is in a sense not correct to say that the One is one, as this may seem to imply that it is something which is made one.

vegetative soul *see* **nature**.

General bibliography

Alfino, M. R. 1988. "Plotinus and the Possibility of Non-propositional Thought," *Ancient Philosophy* 8: 273–284.
Anton, J. 1967. "Plotinus' Conception of the Functions of the Artist," *Journal of Aesthetics and Art Criticism* 26: 91–101.
Armstrong, A. H. 1937. "'Emanation' in Plotinus," *Mind* 46: 61–66.
Armstrong, A. H. 1940. *The Architecture of the Intelligible Universe in the Philosophy of Plotinus: An Analytical and Historical Study.* Cambridge: Cambridge University Press.
Armstrong, A. H. 1955. "Was Plotinus a Magician?," *Phronesis* 1: 73–79.
Armstrong, A. H. 1960. "The Background of the Doctrine 'That the Intelligibles Are Not Outside the Intellect,'" in *Les sources de Plotin* (Entretiens sur l'Antiquité classique 5). Vandœuvres: Fondation Hardt, 391–425.
Armstrong, A. H. 1967. "Plotinus," in A. H. Armstrong (ed.), *The Cambridge History of Late Greek and Early Medieval Philosophy.* Cambridge: Cambridge University Press, 195–268.
Armstrong, A. H. (ed.) 1967. *The Cambridge History of Late Greek and Early Medieval Philosophy.* Cambridge: Cambridge University Press.
Armstrong, A. H. 1974. "Tradition, Reason and Experience in the Thought of Plotinus," in *Atti del Convegno internazionale sul tema: Plotino e il Neoplatonismo in Oriente e in Occidente.* Rome: Academia Nazionale dei Lincei, 171–194.
Armstrong, A. H. 1982. "Two Views of Freedom: A Christian Objection in Plotinus *Enneads* VI, 8 [39] 7, 11–15?," *Studia Patristica* 17.1: 397–406.
Atkinson, M. 1983. *Plotinus: Ennead V, 1: On the Three Principal Hypostases.* Oxford: Oxford University Press.

Aubry, G. 2004. Plotin: Traité 53 (I, 1): Introduction, traduction, commentaire et notes. Paris: Les Éditions du Cerf.
Aubry, G. 2008. "Individuation, particularisation et détermination selon Plotin," Phronesis 53.3: 271–289.
Beere, J. 2009. Doing and Being: An Interpretation of Aristotle's Metaphysics Theta. Oxford: Oxford University Press.
Beierwaltes, W. (trans.) 1967. Plotin: Über Ewigkeit und Zeit (Enneade III 7), with introduction and commentary. Frankfurt am Main: Vittorio Klostermann.
Beierwaltes, W. 1972. Platonismus und Idealismus. Frankfurt am Main: Vittorio Klostermann.
Beierwaltes, W. 1980. Identität und Differenz (Philosophische Abhandlungen 49). Frankfurt am Main: Vittorio Klostermann.
Beierwaltes, W. 1991. Selbsterkenntnis und Erfahrung der Einheit: Plotins Enneade V 3: Text, Übersetzung, Interpretation, Erläuterungen. Frankfurt am Main: Vittorio Klostermann.
Beierwaltes, W. 2002. "The Legacy of Neoplatonism in F. W. J. Schelling's Thought," International Journal of Philosophical Studies 10.4: 393–428.
Bene, L. 2013. "Ethics and Metaphysics in Plotinus," in F. Karfík and E. Song (eds.), Plato Revived: Essays on Ancient Platonism in Honour of Dominic J. O'Meara (Beiträge zur Altertumskunde 317). Berlin: Walter de Gruyter, 141–161.
Berlin, I. 1958. "Two Concepts of Liberty," in I. Berlin, Four Essays on Liberty. Oxford: Oxford University Press, 1969.
Blumenthal, H. J. 1971. Plotinus' Psychology. The Hague: Martinus Nijhoff.
Blumenthal, H. J. 1976. "Plotinus' Adaptation of Aristotle's Psychology: Sensation, Imagination and Memory," in R. B. Harris (ed.), The Significance of Neoplatonism. Norfolk, VA: International Society for Neoplatonic Studies, 41–58.
Blumenthal, H. J. 1996. "On Soul and Intellect," in L. P. Gerson (ed.), The Cambridge Companion to Plotinus. Cambridge: Cambridge University Press, 82–104.
Bradatan, C. 2006. The Other Bishop Berkeley: An Exercise in Re-enchantment. New York: Fordham University Press.
Bréhier, É. (ed., trans.) 1924–38. Plotin: Ennéades; Texte établi et traduit par Émile Bréhier. Paris: Les Belles Lettres.

Brisson, L. 1991. "De quelle façon Plotin interprète-t-il les cinq genres du *Sophiste?*," in P. Aubenque (ed.), *Études sur le Sophiste de Platon*. Naples: Bibliopolis, 449–473.

Brisson, L. 2000a. "Le logos chez Plotin," in N. L. Cordero (ed.), *Ontologie et dialogue: Mélanges en hommage à P. Aubenque avec sa collaboration à l'occasion de son 70e anniversaire*. Paris: Vrin, 47–68.

Brisson, L. 2000b. "Entre métaphysique et physique: Le terme ὄγκος chez Plotin, dans ses rapports avec la matière (ὕλη) et le corps (σῶμα)," in M. Fattal (ed.), *Études sur Plotin*. Paris and Montréal: L'Harmattan, 87–111.

Brisson, L. (ed.) 2005. *Porphyre: Sentences: Études d'introduction, texte grec et traduction française, commentaire*, 2 vols. Paris: Vrin.

Brisson, L., M.-O. Goulet-Cazé, R. Goulet and D. O'Brien. 1982. *Porphyre: La vie de Plotin*, vol. 1: *Travaux préliminaires et index grec complet*. Paris: Vrin.

Brisson, L., J. L. Cherlonneix, M.-O. Goulet-Cazé et al. 1992. *Porphyre: La vie de Plotin*, vol. 2: *Études d'introduction, texte grec et traduction française, commentaire, notes complémentaires, bibliographie*. Paris: Vrin.

Brittain, C. 2003. "Attention Deficit in Plotinus and Augustine: Psychological Problems in Christian and Platonist Theories of the Grades of Virtue," with a commentary by Carlos Steel, *Boston Area Colloquium in Ancient Philosophy* 18: 223–275.

Bröcker, W. 1966. *Platonismus ohne Sokrates: Ein Vortrag über Plotin* (Wissenschaft und Gegenwart 33). Frankfurt am Main: Vittorio Klostermann.

Brouwer, R. 2015. "Stoic Sympathy," in E. Schliesser (ed.), *Sympathy: A History*. Oxford: Oxford University Press, 15–35.

Bussanich, J. R. 1987. "Plotinus on the Inner Life of the One," *Ancient Philosophy* 7: 163–89.

Bussanich, J. R. 1988. *The One and Its Relation to Intellect in Plotinus: A Commentary on Selected Texts*. Leiden: E. J. Brill.

Bussanich, J. R. 1990. "The Invulnerability of Goodness in the Ethics and Psychology of Plotinus," *Proceedings of the Boston Area Colloquium in Ancient Philosophy* 6: 151–184.

Bussanich, J. R. 1994. "Mystical Elements in the Thought of Plotinus," in W. Haase (ed.), *Aufstieg und Niedergang der römischen Welt*, pt. 2, vol. 36.7. Berlin: Walter de Gruyter, 5300–5330.

Bussanich, J. R. 1996. "Plotinus's Metaphysics of the One," in L. P. Gerson (ed.), *The Cambridge Companion to Plotinus*. Cambridge: Cambridge University Press, 38–65.

Caluori, D. 2011. "Reason and Necessity: The Descent of the Philosopher Kings," *Oxford Studies in Ancient Philosophy* 40: 7–27.
Caluori, D. 2015. *Plotinus on the Soul*. Cambridge: Cambridge University Press.
Carroll, W. J. 2002. "The Origin of Matter," in M. F. Wagner (ed.), *Neoplatonism and Nature: Studies in Plotinus' Enneads* (Studies in Neoplatonism, Ancient and Modern 8). Albany: State University of New York Press, 179–207.
Catana, L. 2013. "The Origin of the Division between Middle Platonism and Neoplatonism," *Apeiron* 46.2: 166–200,
Chiaradonna, R. 2002. *Sostanza, movimento, analogia: Plotino critico di Aristotele* (Elenchos 37). Naples: Bibliopolis.
Chiaradonna, R. 2004. "The Categories and the Status of the Physical World: Plotinus and the Neoplatonic Commentators," in P. Adamson, H. Baltussen and M. Stone (eds.), *Philosophy, Science and Exegesis in Greek, Arabic and Latin Commentaries*, vol. 1. London: Institute of Classical Studies, University of London, 121–136.
Chiaradonna, R. 2009. *Plotino*. Rome: Carocci.
Chiaradonna, R. 2012. "Plotinus's Account of the Cognitive Powers of the Soul: Sense Perception and Discursive Thought," *Topoi* 31.2: 191–207.
Clark, G. H. 1943. "Plotinus's Theory of Empirical Responsibility," *New Scholasticism* 17: 16–31.
Cooper, J. M. 2012. *Pursuits of Wisdom: Six Ways of Life in Ancient Philosophy from Socrates to Plotinus*. Princeton: Princeton University Press.
Corrigan, K. 1996. "Essence and Existence in the *Enneads*," in L. P. Gerson (ed.), *The Cambridge Companion to Plotinus*. Cambridge: Cambridge University Press, 105–129.
D'Ancona, C. 1996. "Plotinus and Later Platonic Philosophers on the Causality of the First Principle," in L. P. Gerson (ed.), *The Cambridge Companion to Plotinus*. Cambridge: Cambridge University Press, 356–385.
D'Ancona, C. 2002. "'To Bring Back the Divine in Us to the Divine in the All': *Vita Plotini* 2, 26–27, Once again?," in Th. Kobusch and M. Erler (eds.), *Metaphysik und Religion: Zur Signatur des spätantiken Denkens; Akten des Internationalen Kongresses vom 13.–17. Marz 2001 in Würzburg*. Munich: K. G. Saur, 517–565.
Davidson, D. 1970. "Mental Events," in L. Foster and J. W. Swanson (eds.), *Experience and Theory*. London: Duckworth, 79–101.

de Haas, F. A. J. 2001. "Did Plotinus and Porphyry Disagree on Aristotle's Categories?," Phronesis 46.4: 492–526.

Descartes, R. 1985. The Philosophical Writings of Descartes, vol. 1, trans. J. Cottingham, R. Stoothoff and D. Murdoch. Cambridge: Cambridge University Press.

D'Hoine, P. and G. Van Riel (eds.) 2014. Fate, Providence and Moral Responsibility in Ancient, Medieval and Early Modern Thought: Collected Studies in Honour of Carlos Steel (Ancient and Medieval Philosophy—Series 1). Leuven: Leuven University Press.

Dillon, J. M. 1977. The Middle Platonists: 80 B.C. to A.D. 220. London: Duckworth.

Dillon, J. M. 1983. "Plotinus, Philo and Origen on the Grades of Virtue," in H.-D. Blume and F. Mann (eds.), Platonismus und Christentum: Festschrift für Heinrich Dörrie. Münster: Aschendor, 92–105.

Dillon, J. M. 1996. "An Ethic for the Late Antique Sage," in L. P. Gerson (ed.), The Cambridge Companion to Plotinus. Cambridge: Cambridge University Press, 315–335.

Dillon, J. and H. J. Blumenthal (trans.) 2015. Plotinus: Ennead IV.3–4.29: Problems concerning the Soul, with introduction and commentary. Las Vegas: Parmenides Publishing.

Dimitrov, D. Y. 2014. "Neoplatonism and Christianity in the East: Philosophical and Theological Challenges for Bishops," in P. Remes and S. Slaveva-Griffin (eds.), The Routledge Handbook of Neoplatonism. London: Routledge, 525–540.

Dodds, E. R. 1928. "The Parmenides of Plato and the Origin of the Neoplatonic 'One,'" Classical Quarterly 22: 129–143.

Dodds, E. R. 1965. Pagan and Christian in an Age of Anxiety: Some Aspects of Religious Experience from Marcus Aurelius to Constantine. Cambridge: Cambridge University Press.

Dörrie, H. 1955. "Ὑπόστασις: Wort- und Bedeutungsgeschichte," Nachrichten der Akademie der Wissenschaften in Göttingen 3: 35–92 (Göttingen: Vandenhoeck & Ruprecht).

Eliasson, E. 2008. The Notion of That Which Depends on Us in Plotinus and Its Background. Leiden: Brill.

Emilsson, E. K. 1988. Plotinus on Sense-Perception: A Philosophical Study. Cambridge: Cambridge University Press.

Emilsson, E. K. 1990. "Reflections on Plotinus' Ennead IV.2," in S.-T. Teodorsson (ed.), Greek and Latin Studies in Memory of Cajus Fabricius

(Studia Graeca et Latina Gothoburgensia 54). Gothenburg: Acta Universitatis Gothoburgensis.

Emilsson, E. K. 1991. "Plotinus on Soul–Body Dualism," in S. Everson (ed.), *Psychology* (Companions to Ancient Thought 2). Cambridge: Cambridge University Press, 148–165.

Emilsson, E. K. 1995. "Plotinus on the Objects of Thought," *Archiv für Geschichte der Philosophie* 77.1: 21–41.

Emilsson, E. K. 1996. "Cognition and Its Object," in L. P. Gerson (ed.), *The Cambridge Companion to Plotinus*. Cambridge: Cambridge University Press, 217–249.

Emilsson, E. K. 1998. "Plotinus on the Emotions," in T. Engberg-Pedersen and J. Sihvola (eds.), *The Emotions in Hellenistic Philosophy*. Dordrecht: Kluwer Academic Publishers, 339–360.

Emilsson, E. K. 2007. *Plotinus on Intellect*. Oxford: Oxford University Press.

Emilsson, E. K. 2011. "Plotinus on Happiness and Time," *Oxford Studies in Ancient Philosophy* 40: 339–360.

Emilsson, E. K. 2012. "Plotinus and Plato on Soul and Action," in R. Barney, T. Brennan and C. Brittain (eds.), *Plato and the Divided Self*. Cambridge: Cambridge University Press, 350–367.

Emilsson, E. K. 2013. "Plato, Plotinus, Leibniz," in F. Karfík and E. Song (eds.), *Plato Revived: Essays on Ancient Platonism in Honour of Dominic J. O'Meara* (Beiträge zur Altertumskunde 317). Berlin: Walter de Gruyter, 54–70.

Emilsson, E. K. 2015. "Plotinus on *Sympatheia*," in E. Schliesser (ed.), *Sympathy: A History*. Oxford: Oxford University Press, 36–60.

Emilsson, E. K. and C. Serck-Hanssen. 2004. "Kant and Plato," *Sats: Northern European Journal of Philosophy* 5.1: 71–82.

Emilsson, E. K. and S. K. Strange (trans.) 2015. *Plotinus: Ennead VI.4 and VI.5: On the Presence of Being, One and the Same, Everywhere as a Whole*, with introduction and commentary. Las Vegas: Parmenides Publishing.

Fleet, B. (trans.) 1995. *Plotinus: Ennead III.6: On the Impassivity of the Bodiless*, with commentary. Oxford: Clarendon Press.

Frede, M. 1983. "Stoics and Skeptics on Clear and Distinct Impressions," in M. F. Burnyeat (ed.), *The Skeptical Tradition*. Berkeley: University of California Press, 65–93.

Frede, M. 1987. "Substance in Aristotle's *Metaphysics*," in M. Frede, *Essays in Ancient Philosophy*. Minneapolis: Minneapolis University Press, 72–80.

Frede, M. 2011. *A Free Will: Origins of the Notion in Ancient Philosophy* (Sather Classical Lectures 68, ed. A. A. Long). Berkeley: University of California Press.

Friedman, M. 1974. "Explanation and Scientific Understanding," *Journal of Philosophy* 71.1: 5–19.

Ganson, T. S. 2005. "The Platonic Approach to Sense-Perception," *History of Philosophy Quarterly* 22.1: 1–15.

Gerson, L. P. 1994. *Plotinus*. London: Routledge.

Gerson, L. P. (ed.) 1996. *The Cambridge Companion to Plotinus*. Cambridge: Cambridge University Press.

Gerson, L. P. 2002. "Plotinus against Aristotle's Essentialism," in M. F. Wagner (ed.), *Neoplatonism and Nature: Studies in Plotinus' Enneads* (Studies in Neoplatonism, Ancient and Modern 8). Albany: State University of New York Press, 57–70.

Gerson, L. P. 2005. *Aristotle and Other Platonists*. Ithaca: Cornell University Press.

Gerson, L. P. (ed.) 2010. *The Cambridge History of Philosophy in Late Antiquity*, 2 vols. Cambridge: Cambridge University Press.

Gerson, L. P. 2012. "Plotinus on Logos," in J. Wilberding and C. Horn (eds.), *Neoplatonism and the Philosophy of Nature*. Oxford: Oxford University Press, 17–29.

Glymour, C. 1980. "Explanations, Tests, Unity and Necessity," *Noûs* 14.1: 31–50.

Goulet-Cazé, M.-O. 1982. "L'Arrière-plan scolaire de la *Vie de Plotin*," in L. Brisson, M.-O. Goulet-Cazé, R. Goulet and D. O'Brien (eds.), *Porphyre: La vie de Plotin*, vol. 1. Paris: Vrin, 229–327.

Graeser, A. 1972. *Plotinus and the Stoics: A Preliminary Study*. Leiden: E. J. Brill.

Grmek, M. D. 1992. "Les maladies et la mort de Plotin," in L. Brisson, J. L. Cherlonneix, M.-O. Goulet-Cazé and D. O'Brien (eds.), *Porphyre: La vie de Plotin*, vol. 2. Paris: Vrin, 335–353.

Gurtler, G. M. 1988. *Plotinus: The Experience of Unity*. New York: Peter Lang.

Gurtler, G. M. 2002. "Sympathy: Stoic Materialism and the Platonic Soul," in M. F. Wagner (ed.), *Neoplatonism and Nature: Studies in Plotinus' Enneads* (Studies in Neoplatonism, Ancient and Modern 8). Albany: State University of New York Press, 241–276.

Hadot, P. 1968. *Porphyre et Victorinus*, 2 vols. Paris: Études Augustiniennes.

Hadot, P. 1996. "La conception plotinienne de l'identité entre l'intellect et son objet: Plotin et le *d'Anima* d'Aristote," in G.

Romeyer-Dherbey and C. Viano (eds.), *Corps et Âme: Études sur le De anima d'Aristote*. Paris: Vrin, 367–376.

Halfwassen, J. 2004a. "Freiheit als Transzendenz: Zur Freiheit des Absoluten bei Schelling und Plotin," in J.-M. Narbonne and A. Reckermann (eds.), *Pensées de l'"Un" dans l'histoire de la philosophie: Études en hommage au professeur Werner Beierwaltes*. Paris: Vrin, 459–481.

Halfwassen, J. 2004b. *Plotin und der Neuplatonismus*. Munich: C. H. Beck.

Ham, B. (ed.) 2000. *Plotin: Traité 49: V.3*. Paris: Les Éditions du Cerf.

Hankey, W. J. 2006. *One Hundred Years of Neoplatonism in France: A brief Philosophical History*, in J.-M. Narbonne and W. J. Hankey, "*Levinas and the Greek Heritage*" Followed by "*One Hundred Years of Neoplatonism in France: A Brief Philosophical History*" (Studies in Philosophical Theology 32). Leuven: Peeters.

Hedley, D. and S. Hutton (eds.) 2008. *Platonism at the Origins of Modernity: Studies on Platonism and Early Modern Philosophy*. Dordrecht: Springer.

Helleman, W. E. 2010. "Plotinus as Magician," *International Journal of the Platonic Tradition* 4.2: 114–146.

Helleman-Elgersma, W. 1980. *Soul-Sisters: A Commentary on Enneads IV 3 (27), 1–8 of Plotinus* (Elementa 15). Amsterdam: Rodopi.

Horn, C. 1995. *Plotin über Sein, Zahl und Einheit: Eine Studie zu den systematischen Grundlagen der Enneaden* (Beitrage zur Altertumskunde 62). Stuttgart: Teubner.

Hubler, J. N. 2010. "Moderatus, E. R. Dodds, and the Development of Neoplatonist Emanation," in J. D. Turner and K. Corrigan (eds.), *Plato's Parmenides and Its Heritage*, vol. 2. Atlanta: Society of Biblical Literature.

Hutton, S. 2013. "The Cambridge Platonists: Ralph Cudworth," in E. N. Zalta (ed.), *The Stanford Encyclopedia of Philosophy* (Winter 2013 edition), http://plato.stanford.edu/archives/win2013/entries/cambridge-platonists/#RalCud.

Ierodiakonou, K. 2006. "The Greek Concept of *Sympatheia* and Its Byzantine Appropriation in Michael Psellos," in P. Magdalino and M. Mavroudi (eds.), *The Occult Sciences in Byzantium*. Geneva: La Pomme d'Or.

Igal, J. 1979. "Aristóteles y la evolución de la antropología de Plotino," *Pensiamento* 35: 315–346.

Iozzia, D. 2015. *Aesthetic Themes in Pagan and Christian Neoplatonism: From Plotinus to Gregory of Nyssa*. London: Bloomsbury.

Irwin, T. H. 1981. "Homonymy in Aristotle," *Review of Metaphysics* 34.3: 523–544.
Kalligas, P. 1997. "Logos and the Sensible Object in Plotinus," *Ancient Philosophy* 17.2: 397–410.
Kalligas, P. 2000. "Living Body, Soul, and Virtue in the Philosophy of Plotinus," *Dionysius* 18: 25–38.
Kalligas, P. 2011. "The Structure of Appearances: Plotinus on the Constitution of Sensible Objects," *Philosophical Quarterly* 61: 762–782.
Kalligas, P. 2014. *The Enneads of Plotinus: A Commentary*, vol. 1, trans. E. K. Fowden and N. Pilavachi. Princeton: Princeton University Press. Originally published in Greek 1991–2004.
Karamanolis, G. E. 2006. *Plato and Aristotle in Agreement? Platonists on Aristotle from Antiochus to Porphyry.* Oxford: Oxford University Press.
Karfík, F. 2012. "Le temps et l'âme chez Plotin: À propos des Ennéades VI 5 [23] 11; IV 4 [28] 15–16; III 7 [45] 11," *Elenchos* 33.2: 227–257.
Karfík, F. and E. Song (eds.) 2013. *Plato Revived: Essays on Ancient Platonism in Honour of Dominic J. O'Meara* (Beiträge zur Altertumskunde 317). Berlin: Walter de Gruyter.
King, R. A. H. 2009. *Aristotle and Plotinus on Memory* (Quellen und Studien zur Philosophie 94). Berlin: Walter de Gruyter.
Knuuttila, S. 2004. *Emotions in Ancient and Medieval Philosophy.* Oxford: Oxford University Press.
Kosman, A. 2000. "Metaphysics Lambda 9," in M. Frede and D. Charles (eds.), *Aristotle's Metaphysics Lambda.* Oxford: Clarendon Press, 307–326.
Kristeller, P. O. 1929. *Der Begriff der Seele in der Ethik des Plotin.* Tübingen: J. C. B. Mohr.
Kristeller, P. O. 1984. "Stoic and Neoplatonic Sources of Spinoza's Ethics," *History of European Ideas* 5.1: 1–15.
Kühn, W. 2009. *Quel savoir après le scepticisme? Plotin et ses prédecesseurs sur la connaissance de soi.* Paris: Vrin.
Kuisma, O. 2003. *Art as Experience: A Study on Plotinus's Aesthetics.* Helsinki: Societas Scientiarum Fennica.
Lavaud, L. 2006. "La *dianoia* médiatrice entre le sensible et l'intelligible," *Études Platoniciennes* 3: 29–55.
Lawrence, M. 2005. "Hellenistic Astrology," J. Fieser and B. Dowden (eds.), *Internet Encyclopedia of Philosophy,* www.iep.utm.edu/a/astr-hel.htm.

Leibniz, G. W. 1981. *New Essays on Human Understanding*, trans. and ed. P. Remnant and J. Bennett. Cambridge: Cambridge University Press. Originally published in French 1765.

Lennon, T. M. 2008. "Cudworth and Bayle: An Odd Couple?," in T. M. Lennon and R. J. Stainton (eds.), *The Achilles of Rationalist Psychology* (Studies in the History of Philosophy of Mind 7). New York: Springer, 139–158.

Lennon, T. M. and R. J. Stainton (eds.) 2008. *The Achilles of Rationalist Psychology* (Studies in the History of Philosophy of Mind 7). New York: Springer.

Leroux, G. 1990. *Plotin: Traité sur la liberté et la volonté de l'Un [Ennéade VI, 8 (39)]: Introduction, texte grec, traduction et commentaire*. Paris: Vrin.

Linguiti, A. (trans.) 2007. *Plotin: Traité 36, I. 5*, with introduction and commentary. Paris: Les Édition du Cerf.

Lloyd, A. C. 1962. "Genus, Species and Ordered Series in Aristotle," *Phronesis* 7.1–2: 67–90.

Lloyd, A. C. 1970. "Non-discursive Thought: An Enigma of Greek Philosophy," *Proceedings of the Aristotelian Society* 70: 261–274.

Lloyd, A. C. 1986. "Non-propositional Thought in Plotinus," *Phronesis* 31: 258–265.

Lloyd, A. C. 1987. "Plotinus on the Genesis of Thought and Existence," *Oxford Studies in Ancient Philosophy* 5: 155–186.

Lloyd, A. C. 1990. *The Anatomy of Neoplatonism*. Oxford: Oxford University Press.

Long, A. A. and D. N. Sedley. 1987. *The Hellenistic Philosophers*, 2 vols. Cambridge: Cambridge University Press.

McGroarty, K. 2005. Review of *L'Éthique du sage chez Plotin: Le paradigme du spoudaios*, by Alexandrine Schniewind, *Classical Review* 55.1: 94–95.

McGroarty, K. 2006. *Plotinus on eudaimonia: A commentary on Ennead 1.4*. Oxford: Oxford University Press.

McGuire, J. E. and S. K. Strange. 1988. "An Annotated Translation of Plotinus *Ennead* III 7: On Eternity and Time," *Ancient Philosophy* 8.2: 251–271.

Magrin, S. 2010. "Sensation and Scepticism in Plotinus," *Oxford Studies in Ancient Philosophy* 39: 249–297.

Makin, S. 1991. "An Ancient Principle about Causation," *Proceedings of the Aristotelian Society* 91: 135–152.

Matson, W. I. 1966. "Why Isn't the Mind–Body Problem Ancient?," in P. K. Feyerabend and G. Maxwell (eds.), *Mind, Matter, and Method:*

Essays in Philosophy and Science in Honor of Herbert Feigl. Minneapolis: University of Minnesota Press, 92–102.

Meijer, P. A. 1992. Plotinus on the Good or the One (Enneads VI, 9): An Analytical Commentary (Amsterdam Classical Monographs 1). Amsterdam: J. C. Gieben.

Menn, S. 1998. Descartes and Augustine. Cambridge: Cambridge University Press.

Menn, S. 2001. "Plotinus on the Identity of Knowledge with Its Object," Apeiron 34.3: 233–246.

Mercer, C. 2008. "The Platonism at the Core of Leibniz's Philosophy," in D. Hedley and S. Hutton (eds.), Platonism at the Origins of Modernity: Studies on Platonism and Early Modern Philosophy. Dordrecht: Springer, 125–138.

Merlan, P. 1953. "Plotinus and Magic," Isis 44: 341–348.

Merlan, P. 1967. "Greek Philosophy from Plato to Plotinus," in A. H. Armstrong (ed.), The Cambridge History of Late Greek and Early Medieval Philosophy. Cambridge: Cambridge University Press, 14–134.

Mojsisch, B. and E. F. Summerell (eds.) 2003. Platonismus im Idealismus: Die Platonische Tradition in der klassischen Deutschen Philosophie. Munich and Leipzig: K. G. Saur.

Moran, D. 2014. "Neoplatonism and Christianity in the West," in P. Remes and S. Slaveva-Griffin (eds.), The Routledge Handbook of Neoplatonism. London: Routledge, 508–524.

Narbonne, J.-M. 1999. "'Henōsis' et 'ereignis': Remarques sur une interprétation heideggérienne de l'Un plotinien," Études Philosophiques 1: 105–121.

Narbonne, J.-M. 2001. La métaphysique de Plotin. Paris: Vrin.

Narbonne, J.-M. 2007. "La controverse à propos de la génération de la matière chez Plotin: L'énigme résolue?," Quaestio 7: 123–163.

Narbonne, J.-M. and W. J. Hankey. 2006. "Levinas and the Greek Heritage" Followed by "One Hundred Years of Neoplatonism in France: A Brief Philosophical History" (Studies in Philosophical Theology 32). Leuven: Peeters.

Nebel, G. 1929. Plotins Kategorien der intelligibilen Welt. Tübingen: J. C. B. Mohr.

Nikulin, D. 2005. "Unity and Individuation in the Soul in Plotinus," in R. Chiaradonna (ed.), Studi sull'anima in Plotino (Elenchos 42). Naples: Bibliopolis, 275–304.

Noble, C. I. 2013. "How Plotinus' Soul Animates His Body: The Argument for the Soul-Trace at Ennead 4.4.18.1–9," Phronesis 58.3: 249–279.
Noble, C. I. and N. M. Powers. 2015. "Creation and Divine Providence in Plotinus," in A. Marmodoro and B. D. Prince (eds.), Causation and Creation in Late Antiquity. Cambridge: Cambridge University Press, 51–70.
Notopoulos, J. A. 1949. The Platonism of Shelley: A Study of Platonism and the Poetic Mind. Durham, NC: Duke University Press.
O'Brien, D. 1971. "Plotinus on Evil: A Study of Matter and the Soul in Plotinus' Conception of Human Evil," in P.-M. Schuhl (ed.), Le néoplatonisme: Royaumont, 9–13 Juin 1969 (Colloques internationaux du Centre national de la recherche scientifique, Sciences humaines 535). Paris: CNRS Éditions, 113–146.
O'Brien, D. 1977. "Le volontaire et la nécessité: Réflexions sur la descente de l'âme dans la philosophie de Plotin," Revue Philosophique de la France et de l'Étranger 167.4: 401–422.
O'Brien, D. 1991a. "Platon et Plotin sur la doctrine des parties de l'autre," Revue Philosophique de la France et de l'Étranger 181.4: 501–512.
O'Brien, D. 1991b. Plotinus on the Origin of Matter: An Exercise in the Interpretation of the Enneads (Elenchos 22). Naples: Bibliopolis.
O'Brien, D. 1996. "Plotinus on Matter and Evil," in L. P. Gerson (ed.), The Cambridge Companion to Plotinus. Cambridge: Cambridge University Press, 171–195.
O'Brien, D. 1999. "La matière chez Plotin: Son origine, sa nature," Phronesis 44.1: 45–71.
O'Daly, G. J. P. 1973. Plotinus' Philosophy of the Self. Dublin: Irish University Press.
O'Meara, D. J. 1990. "Le problème du discours sur l'indicible chez Plotin," Revue de Théologie et de Philosophie 122: 145–156.
O'Meara, D. J. 1992. "The Freedom of the One," Phronesis 37.3: 343–349.
O'Meara, D. J. 1993. Plotinus: An Introduction to the Enneads. Oxford: Oxford University Press.
O'Meara, D. J. 1998. "Evil in Plotinus," chapter 9 of D. J. O'Meara, The Structure of Being and Search for the Good: Essays on Ancient and Early Medieval Platonism. Aldershot: Ashgate. [The book retains reprint pagination.]
O'Meara, D. J. 2000. "Scepticism and Ineffability in Plotinus," Phronesis 45.3: 240–251.

O'Meara, D. J. 2003. *Platonopolis: Platonic Political Philosophy in Late Antiquity.* Oxford: Clarendon Press.

O'Meara, D. J. 2005. "The Metaphysics of Evil in Plotinus: Problems and Solutions," in J. M. Dillon and M. Dixaut (eds.), *Agonistes: Essays in Honour of Denis O'Brien.* Aldershot: Ashgate, 179–185.

O'Meara, D. J. Forthcoming. "Explaining Evil in Late Antiquity: Plotinus and His Critics," in A. Chignell and S. MacDonald (eds.), *Evil: A Philosophical History.* Oxford: Oxford University Press.

Oosthout, H. 1991. *Modes of Knowledge and the Transcendental: An Introduction to Plotinus Ennead 5.3 [49] with a Commentary and Translation.* Amsterdam: B. R. Grüner.

Opsomer, J. 2001. "Proclus vs. Plotinus on Matter (De Mal. Subs. 30–7)," *Phronesis* 46.2: 154–188.

Opsomer, J. 2007. "Some Problems with Plotinus' Theory of Matter/Evil: An Ancient Debate Continued," *Quaestio* 7.1: 165–189.

Opsomer, J. and C. Steel (trans.) 2003. *Proclus: On the Existence of Evils* (Ancient Commentators on Aristotle). London: Duckworth.

Panofsky, E. 1939. *Studies in Iconology: Humanistic Themes in the Art of the Renaissance.* Oxford: Oxford University Press.

Pereboom, D. 2002. "Robust Nonreductive Materialism," *Journal of Philosophy* 99.10: 499–531.

Pessin, S. 2014. "Islamic and Jewish Neoplatonisms," in P. Remes and S. Slaveva-Griffin (eds.), *The Routledge Handbook of Neoplatonism.* London: Routledge, 541–558.

Phillips, J. F. 2009. "Plotinus on the Generation of Matter," *International Journal of the Platonic Tradition* 3.2: 103–137.

Pigler, A. 2001. "La réception plotinienne de la notion stoïcienne de sympathie universelle," *Revue de Philosophie Ancienne* 19.1: 45–78.

Pittock, M. 1989. "Yeats, Plotinus, and 'Among Schoolchildren,'" *Irish University Review* 19.2: 213–219.

Raine, K. 1969. *Blake and Tradition.* London: Routledge & Kegan Paul.

Rappe, S. 2000. *Reading Neoplatonism: Non-discursive Thinking in the Texts of Plotinus, Proclus, and Damascius.* Cambridge: Cambridge University Press.

Reale, G. 2005. *La Scuola di Atene di Raffaello.* Milan: Bompiani.

Remes, P. 2006. "Plotinus's Ethics of Disinterested Interest," *Journal of the History of Philosophy* 44.1: 1–23

Remes, P. 2007. *Plotinus on Self: The Philosophy of the "We."* Cambridge: Cambridge University Press.

Remes, P. 2008. *Neoplatonism*. Berkeley and Los Angeles: University of California Press.
Remes, P. and S. Slaveva-Griffin (eds.) 2014. *The Routledge Handbook of Neoplatonism*. London: Routledge.
Rescher, N. 2013. "Kant's Neoplatonism: Kant and Plato on Mathematical and Philosophical Method," *Metaphilosophy* 44.1–2: 69–78.
Rich, A. N. M. 1960. "Plotinus and the Theory of Artistic Imitation," *Mnemosyne* (4th series) 13: 233–239.
Rist, J. M. 1967. *Plotinus: The Road to Reality*. Cambridge: Cambridge University Press.
Rodier, G. 1902. "Sur une des origines de la philosophie de Leibniz," *Revue de Métaphysique et de Morale* 10: 552–564.
Rorty, R. 1979. *Philosophy and the Mirror of Nature*. Princeton: Princeton University Press.
Rutten, C. 1956. "La doctrine des deux actes dans la philosophie de Plotin," *Revue Philosophique de la France et de l'Étranger* 146: 100–106.
Saffrey, H. D. 1992. "Pourquoi Porphyre a-t-il édité Plotin? réponse provisoire," in L. Brisson, J. L. Cherlonneix, M.-O. Goulet-Cazé et al., *Porphyre: La vie de Plotin*, vol. 2. Paris: Vrin, 31–57.
Sambursky, S. 1959. *Physics of the Stoics*. London: Routledge.
Santa Cruz, M. I. 1997. "L'Exégèse plotinienne des ΜΕΓΙΣΤΑ ΓΕΝΗ du *Sophiste* de Platon," in J. J. Cleary (ed.), *The Perennial Tradition of Neoplatonism*. Leuven: Leuven University Press, 105–118.
Schäfer, C. 2004. "Matter in Plotinus's Normative Ontology," *Phronesis* 49.3: 266–294.
Schliesser, E. (ed.) 2015. *Sympathy: A History* (Oxford Philosophical Concepts). Oxford: Oxford University Press.
Schniewind, A. 2003. *L'Éthique du sage chez Plotin: Le paradigme du spoudaios*. Paris: Vrin.
Schniewind, A. 2007. *Traité 5 (V, 9): Introduction, traduction, commentaires et notes*. Paris: Les Édition du Cerf.
Schniewind, A. 2015. "Plotinus' Way of Defining 'Eudaimonia' in *Ennead* I 4 [46] 1–3," in Ø. Rabbås, E. K. Emilsson, H. Fossheim and M. Tuominen (eds.), *The Quest for the Good Life: Ancient Philosophers on Happiness*. Oxford: Oxford University Press, 212–221.
Schroeder, F. M. 1987. "Ammonius Saccas," in W. Haase (ed.), *Aufstieg und Niedergang der römischen Welt*, pt. 2, vol. 36.1. Berlin: Walter de Gruyter, 493–526.

Schroeder, F. M. 1992. *Form and Transformation: A Study in the Philosophy of Plotinus*. Montreal: McGill-Queen's University Press.

Schroeder, F. M. 1997. "Plotinus and Aristotle on the Good Life," in J. J. Cleary (ed.), *The Perennial Tradition of Neoplatonism*. Leuven: Leuven University Press, 107–220.

Schürmann, R. 1982. "L'Hénologie comme dépassement de la métaphysique," *Les Études Philosophiques* 3: 331–350.

Schwyzer, H.-R. 1960. "Bewusst und unbewusst bei Plotin," in *Les sources de Plotin* (Entretiens sur l'Antiquité classique 5). Vandœuvres: Fondation Hardt, 341–390.

Sedley, D. 1998. "Platonic Causes," *Phronesis* 43.2: 114–132.

Seigel, J. 2005. *The Idea of the Self: Thought and Experience in Western Europe since the Seventeenth Century*. Cambridge: Cambridge University Press.

Smith, A. 1978. "Unconsciousness and Quasiconsciousness in Plotinus," *Phronesis* 23.3: 292–301.

Smith, A. 1996. "Eternity and Time," in L. P. Gerson (ed.), *The Cambridge Companion to Plotinus*. Cambridge: Cambridge University Press, 196–216.

Smith, A. 1999. "The Significance of Practical Ethics for Plotinus," in J. J. Cleary (ed.), *Traditions of Platonism: Essays in Honour of John Dillon*. Aldershot: Ashgate, 227–236.

Smith, A. 2006. "The Object of Perception in Plotinus," in S. Gersh and D. Moran (eds.), *Eriugena, Berkeley, and the Idealist Tradition*. Notre Dame: University of Notre Dame Press, 95–104.

Sorabji, R. 1982. "Myths about Non-propositional Thought," in M. Schofield and M. C. Nussbaum (eds.), *Language and Logos: Studies in Ancient Greek Philosophy Presented to G. E. L. Owen*. Cambridge: Cambridge University Press, 295–314.

Sorabji, R. 1983. *Time, Creation and the Continuum*. London: Duckworth.

Sorabji, R. 1990. "Perceptual Content in the Stoics," *Phronesis* 35.3: 307–314.

Stamatellos, G. 2013. "Plotinus on Transmigration: A Reconsideration," *Journal of Ancient Philosophy* 7.1: 49–64.

Stern-Gillet, S. 2000. "Le principe du beau chez Plotin: Réflexions sur Enneas VI.7.32 et 33," *Phronesis* 45.1: 38–63.

Stern-Gillet, S. 2014. "Plotinus on Metaphysics and Morality," in P. Remes and S. Slaveva-Griffin (eds.), *The Routledge Handbook of Neoplatonism*. London: Routledge, 396–420.

Strange, S. K. 1987. "Plotinus, Porphyry, and the Neoplatonic Interpretation of the *Categories*," W. Haase (ed.), *Aufstieg und Niedergang der römischen Welt*, pt. 2, vol. 36.2. Berlin: Walter de Gruyter, 955–974.

Strange, S. K. 1994. "Plotinus on the Nature of Eternity and Time," in L. P. Schrenk (ed.), *Aristotle in Later Antiquity* (Studies in Philosophy and the History of Philosophy 27). Washington, DC: Catholic University of America Press, 22–51.

Struck, P. T. 2007. "A World Full of Signs: Understanding Divination in Ancient Stoicism," in P. Curry and A. Voss (eds.), *Seeing with Different Eyes: Essays in Astrology and Divination*. Newcastle: Cambridge Scholars Publishing.

Szlezák, T. A. 1979. *Platon und Aristoteles in der Nuslehre Plotins*. Basel: Schwabe.

Taormina, D. P. (ed.) 2010. *L'Essere del pensiero: Saggi sulla filosofia di Plotino*. Naples: Bibliopolis.

Tornau, C. 1998. "Wissenschaft, Seele, Geist: Zur Bedeutung einer Analogie bei Plotin (Enn. IV 9, 5 und VI 2, 20.)," *Göttinger Forum für Altertumswissenschaft* 1: 87–111.

Tornau, C. and A. Michalewsky. 2009. "Qu'est-ce qu'un individu? Unité, individualité et conscience de soi dans la métaphysique plotinienne de l'âme," *Les Études philosophiques*, no. 3, "Plotin et son platonisme" (July 2009): 333–360 (Paris: Presses Universitaires de France).

Vassilopoulou, P. 2014. "Plotinus' Aesthetics: In Defence of the Lifelike," in P. Remes, and S. Slaveva-Griffith (eds.), *The Routledge Handbook of Neoplatonism*. London: Routledge, 484–501.

Wagner, M. F. 1996. "Plotinus on the Nature of Physical Reality," in L. P. Gerson (ed.), *The Cambridge Companion to Plotinus*. Cambridge: Cambridge University Press, 130–170.

Wagner, M. F. (ed.) 2002. *Neoplatonism and Nature: Studies in Plotinus' Enneads* (Studies in Neoplatonism, Ancient and Modern 8). Albany: State University of New York Press.

Waterlow, S. 1982. *Nature, Change, and Agency in Aristotle's Physics: A Philosophical Study*. Oxford: Clarendon Press.

Whittaker, J. 1971. "God, Time, Being in Philo of Alexandria," *Symbolae Osloensis* (Supplement) 23: 33–57.

Wilberding, J. 2005. "'Creeping Spatiality': The Location of *nous* in Plotinus' Universe," *Phronesis* 50.4: 315–334.

Wilberding, J. (2006) *Plotinus' Cosmology: A Study of Ennead II.1 (40): Text, Translation, and Commentary*. Oxford: Oxford University Press.

Wilberding, J. 2008a. "Automatic Action in Plotinus," *Oxford Studies in Ancient Philosophy* 34: 373–407.
Wilberding, J. 2008b. "Porphyry and Plotinus on the Seed," *Phronesis* 53.4–5: 406–432.
Wilberding, J. 2011. *Porphyry: To Gaurus on How Embryos Are Ensouled and On What Is in our Power*. London: Bristol Classical Press.
Wilberding, J. n.d. "The World-Soul in the Embryological Theories of Porphyry and Plotinus," unpublished.
Wilson, C. 1989. *Leibniz's Metaphysics: A Historical and Comparative Study*. Princeton: Princeton University Press.

Index

An asterisk (*) indicates a full or introductory discussion, and so a good place to begin. Page numbers in **bold** indicate glossary entries.

Academy, Plato's 24, 36n9
accident 206–8
act *see* activity
activity (*energeia*) 84, 90–9, **381**;
  double 48–57*, 74, 93, 100, 167, 324, 367; external 59, 91–2, 100, 175, 221, 234, 239, 323–4, 326–7, 361 *see also* emanation; internal 84, 91–2, 97–8, 167, 361
actuality *see* activity
actualization *see* activity
affection(s) 161–5, 188, 230, 244–6, 254–6, 259, 275 *see also* emotions; elimination of 261–2
agency 52, 57, 218 *see also* activity, double
Alcinous 25, 60, 114, 116, 123–4
Alexander of Aphrodisias 23, 55, 102n11, 119–20, 173–4, 180, 247, 371n8
Amelius ix, 12, 15–16, 18, 61, 124, 371n2
Ammonius Saccas ix, 10–11, 18, (29), 33–4
Anaxagoras 32, 71, 128
anger 235, 254, 257, 260*, 262
Aquinas, Thomas 94, 375
Archesilaus 24
Aristotelianism 23, 25, 119–20, 204

Aristotle 28, 30–1, 47, 50–2, 119–20, 204–5, 312, 314, 325, 375
art(s) 362–70, 376, 379
attribute *see* accident
Augustine 298, 344, 352, 373–4
autonomy *see* freedom

Bayle, P. 180
beauty: in art 362–70*; in the intelligible world 52–3, 113–15, 125
being *see* substance
Bergson, H. 379
Berkeley, G. 216, 224, 376–7
body 38–42, 185–8, 199–204*; characteristic of *see* extension; impact of 218–19; qualified 228, 230–3, 246, 255, 262
bulk *see* extension

categories 110, 115, 204–6
causality *see* activity, double
cause 49, 53, 55–7, 210–11, 213–24, 222 *see also* activity, double
change (*kinēseis*) 50, 188, 192–3, 200, 210, 217, 242, 248–9
Chrysippus 268n38
Cicero 24, 161, 310, 369, 371n8
color 202, 251

compatibilism 238, 356–7
composite (compound) of soul and body *see* living being
consciousness 111, 122, 175, 177, 181, 227n24, 268n34, 284, 291–2*, 318–19, 322, 346, 376, 378
contemplation (*theoria*) 158, 220–1, 323, 339 *see also* conversion
conversion (*epistrophē*) 57–9*, 94–6, 222, 345, **382**
cosmos 32, 101n1, 150–1, 153, 156, 162–3, 165, 233, 349
courage 298, 301–2, 354, 360
Craftsman 25, 31, 52, 59, 90, 147, 150, 162, 174
Cudworth, R. 180, 376

Demiurge *see* Craftsman
Descartes, R. 178, 216, 219, 224, 226n18–19, 227n24, 256, 285, 344, 376
desire 58, 85, 95–7, 105, 236, 254–62, 303, 354, 359–60 *see also* longing
determinism 214, 238, 356 *see also* freedom
dialectic 128, 306*
difference *see* otherness
divination 14, 161, 163–4 *see also* sympathy
divine principles *see* hypostasis
double activity *see* activity, double
dualism 38, 42, 197, 226n18, 228; Cartesian 215–16, 219

elements 44, 189, 200–1, 210
emanation 48–57*, 59, 93–6, 151, 166–7, **382** *see also* activity, double
emanationism 93, 375
embodiment of the soul 38, 148, 156, 174–5, 228, 234, 238–9, 241, 291
emotion(s) 242, 254–60*, 268n38, 298, 302–3, 305
Enneads 18–22*
Epicureans 23, 41, 181, 220, 310–11
Eriugena, John Scottus 375

essence *see* substance
eternity 168–72, 209, 311, 333n12
ethics 296–7*, 325–6, 330
Eunapius 11–12
Eusebius 36n8
Eustochius 15, 36n8
evil 42, 187–9, 194–9, 223, 317, 351–4
extension 38, 158, 178–9, 190–2, 223
external activity *see* activity, external
existence: of the One 76

faculty *see* power
fear 230, 254, 257, 271
feelings *see* emotions
Ficino, Marsilio 36n8, 376–7
first principle *see* One, the
Form *see* Idea
form(s) (*eidos, morphē*) 47–8, 173, 189–94, 246, 251–2, 273, 281, 288, 292, **382–3** *see also* logos; in matter 190–2, 199, 202–3, 211, 214, 223
formative principle (*logos poētikos*) *see* logos
freedom 238, 347*, 361; human 353–8*; of the One 85–6, 361

genus (pl. genera) of being *see* Idea
Gnosticism 15, 21, 27, 39
god(s) 32, 38–9, 58, 60–2, 69n5, 74, 77, 93, 119, 216, 335
Goethe, J.W. von 20, 371n11, 379
Good, the *see* One, the

happiness 297, 308–18*, 325, 330, 336, 352, 359–60
harmony 32, 41, 363 *see also* beauty
Hegel, G.W.F. 378–9
Heidegger, M. 77, 131, 379–80
Heraclitus 8, 32
holism 61, 134–40*, 277
Hume, D. 183n12, 292
hypostasis 9, 29, 34, 37*, 67, 92, 374, **383**

Idea (*eidos, idea*) 47, 70–3, 116–17, 123–5, 140–1, **383**; the five highest

110–13*, 140, 194; of the Good 52, 63, 75–6
idealism 215–17, 219, 222–4; German 378–9
image(s) (eikōn, eidōlon) 48*, 51, 60, 65, 91–2, 125, 131, 145, 147, 196–7, 253, 265n7, 323; mental 269–73, 281, 292, 369 *see also* power of representation; of the One 95–7, 105, 357; in the sensible world 125, 148, 151, 157, 196–8, 210, 253, 257–61, 263; of soul *see* soul, middle
imitation (mimēma) 55–8, 95, 120, 222, 367–9 *see also* image(s)
impression (typos) 72, 124, 220, 231, 246, 248, 250, 266n19, 266–7n21, 268n34, 269–70, 271*–4, 282–3, 289, **383–4** *see also* image(s)
indefiniteness: and matter 186–7, 191–2, 195–6
Intellect, the 59–62, 65, 71, 81, 104–9, 111–14, 117–38, 140–1, 300–1, 313–14, 336–9; self-thinking of 118–23
intellect: particular 137–8*, 152; universal 106, 137–8*, 140, 151
intellection (noēsis) 96, 100, 104, 127–8, 146–8, 220, 318–19, **384** *see also* thought
intellectual vision *see* intellection
intelligible (noētos, to noēton) 38, **384**; realm 38, 113–17, 134–6, 141, 244, 329
intelligibles 60, 123–7, 129, 343–4, 365
internal activity *see* activity
intuitive thought *see* thought, non-discursive

justice 30, 54, 280, 284, 298, 300–2, 360, 369

Kant, I. 82, 128, 180, 285, 293, 360, 376–9
knowledge 64–5, 119, 121, 127, 131–2, 140

language: Plotinus' 17, 32, 34, 64–6*, 93, 131, 133, 219, 237, 254, 266–7n21, 339, 342, 344–5, 358, 362
Leibniz, G. W. 134–5, 140, 180, 227n24, 276–7, 285, 294n4, 351, 376–7
life **384–5**
life, Plotinus' ix, 9–18
living being 228–32*, 235, 237, 239, 241–3, 246, 262–4
logos (pl. logoi) 31–2, 45–8, 116–17, 154, 185–6, 208, 211–14, 223–4, 252, 348–50, **385**
longing 96–7, 104, 107
Longinus of Athens 15–16, 18, 34, 124

magic 14, 161, 164, 183n10
magnitude *see* extension
materialism 31, 41, 154, 175, 177, 180–1; non-reductive 217, 219, 224, 226–7n20
matter (hylē) 42, 47, 67, 157–8, 185–200*, 223–4, 225n5, 352; intelligible *see* potential intellect
memory 159*, 235, 273–4, 282
mental 63, 89, 100, 214–23, 227n24, 272, 276, 285; and supervenience 217–18
Michelangelo 20, 369
mind 215–17 *see also* consciousness
monism 26–7, 93–4, 195, 216
motion 107–12, 140 *see also* activity
multiplicity 68, 112, 122–3; and spatial and temporal dispersion 38, 42, 168, 223, 367
mysticism 82, 335–6*

nature (physis, to phytikon, to threptikon) 155, 157–8, 181, 185–6, 210, 220–1, 231–5, 257–8, 268n34, 372n14, **385–6**
negative theology (via negativa) 26, 80–1*, 88
Nemesius 163
Nicholas of Cusa 375

408 Index

non-being *see* matter
Neoplatonism 9, 23, 36n9–10, 373–9
Neo-Pythagoreans 26, 94
nous 106, 128 *see also* intellect
Novalis 379
Numenius 18, 25, 26, 33, 60, 147, 186, 222

object *see* subject/object distinction
Olympius of Alexandria 183n10
One, the 59–64, 70–5*; as beyond being (*epekeina tēs ousias*) 63, 75–7, 89, 100, 109, 189, **387**; mystical union with 82, 335, 341, 344–6, 365; will of *see* will, of the One
opinion 220, 240, 261–3, 268n38, 290
organism *see* living being
Origen 11, 33, 348
origin (*archē*) *see* principle
otherness 107–12, 171, 193–4, 171, 378

pain 176–7, 229, 255–7*, 267n29, 316–17
paradigms 55, 48, 51, 57, 115, 300–2
parallelism 215–16, 219, 224
Parmenides 8, 32, 70, 126, 128, 143n15
participation *see* emanation
perfection *see* unity
Peripatetics *see* Aristotelianism
Philo of Alexandria 348, 378
Philo of Larissa 24
philosophy 306; role of 262, 304, 374 *see also* purification
Philostratus 368–9
physical *see* sensible
Plato 198, 297–9, 300–1, 328, 348, 361–8
Platonism 9, 23, 25, 373, 376–7; Middle 23, 25–7, 29, 123; pre-Plotinian 22–8
pleasure 39, 219, 255–7, 261, 264, 267n29, 303, 317 *see also* emotions
plurality *see* unity
Plutarch of Athens 222, 283

pneuma 32, 162–3 *see* soul
Porphyry ix, 10–21*
potency *see* power
potential intellect 96–100 *see also* emanation
potential subject *see* potential intellect
potentiality *see* power
power (*dynamis*) 228, **386**; nutritive/vegetative 181, 257, 265n4, 266n11 *see also* nature; perceptive/sensitive 228, 256; rational *see* logos; of representation 269–75*, 281, 289–92
prayer 160–1, 164, 335
pre-Socratics 1, 23, 32, 132
principle 32, 43–5, 60, 66, 70–5, **386**
Principle of Prior Possession 43–5*, 50, 52, 60, 66, 69, 87, 98–9, 119–20, 197–8, 367
Principle of Prior Simplicity 70
privation *see* matter
Proclus 195, 197, 226n6, 373, 375
Protagoras 23
providence 212, 347–56*, 369
providential thought 147–9
Pseudo-Dionysius 373, 375
Pseudo-Galen 268n38, 371n8
Pseudo-Plutarch 371n8–9
psychology: Plotinus' 228–9, 241, 264
purification 262, 298, 300, 302–4, 327, 364, **386**
Pythagoras 26
Pythagoreans 18, 26–7

quality 113, 206, 252–3 *see also* form(s), in matter
quantity *see* extension

rational formula *see* logos
realism 249–53, 289
reason: discursive (*dianoia*) 145–9, 253, 277, 279, 301, 324, 339 *see also* logos
reasoning *see* logos
reincarnation *see* transmigration
religion 39–40
representation (*mimēma, phantasia, to phantastikon*) 91, 193, 270–4, 282

Index 409

responsibility: human 349, 353, 355–6, 369
rest 107–12, 140
Rogatianus 328–9
Russell, B. 379

sage 308, 315–27*, 329–31
sameness 107–12, 140
scepticism 23–5, 124, 127, 132, 143n14, 253, 267n27, 283–4, 309; perceptual 253; Pyrrhonian 24–5
science 115, 338; analogy of 137–40*, 153
self 285–8, 290–3; intelligible/noetic 43, 303, 318, 320–1
self-knowledge see self-thinking
self-thinking 120–4, 141
sense-perception 124, 219–20, 242–9*, 251–4, 257–60, 263, 269, 272–84, 288–90
sensible (aisthētos) 38–40, **386–7**; world 59, 151, 153, 156
Sextus Empiricus 24–5, 178
shadow (eidōlon) see image(s), sensible world
Simplicius 26–7, 194
Socrates 16, 23–4, 30, 206–7, 317
Soul, the 144, 149–52*
soul: and body 173–80*; descent of 38, 173, 236–8*; divine 158–61*; impassivity (apatheia) of 254–5, 262–3; individual human 38, 42, 116–17, 144–5, 149–50, 153, 157, 165, 181, 228; middle 229, 235, 237, 239–40, 263, 265n1, 284, 289–90, 304; power(s) of 67, 157, 159, 170–2, 175, 181, 234, 237, 239, 253–4, 269, 346, 349; productive activity of 60, 220–1 see also contemplation; intellection; pure 235–6, 240, 263, 290–1 see also reason; and time 167–72*; thought of see reason, discursive; trace of 228–35, 255, 257, 265n5, **387**; unity of 152–4, 163, 165, 167; vegetative see nature
source (pēgē) see principle

space see extension
species 109; specific difference 206 see also accident
Spinoza 128, 216–17, 227n24, 376–7
spring (archē) see principle
Stobaeus 255
Stoicism 23, 31–2, 117, 154, 162–3, 178, 317, 348
subject/object distinction 63, 67, 78, 97, 107, 110, 129, 346
substance (ousia, on) 47, 103n14, 115, 173, 195, 204–9, 216, 224, **382**
suicide 20, 316, 333n17
Sun, Analogy of the 54, 56, 127, 343, 364–5
sympathy (sympatheia) 160–7*, 181, 183n12, 245–6, 250–1

teleology 149, 151
Thales 22
theodicy 347–8
thought: activity of 59–61, 63, 65, 80, 105–6, 110–12, 120, 148, 210, 220–1, 236; discursive thought see reason; duality of 62, 78, 122; non-discursive 60–1, 127–30*, 141, 340 see also intellection; object of 62–3, 107, 110, 120; plurality of 62, 78, 89, 107; subject of 59–62, 107, 110
thinker see thought, subject of
thinking activity see thought, activity of
time 115, 167–72* see also soul, time; as image 147, 168, 171
trace (ichnos) of soul see soul, trace of
transmigration 284, 294
truth 125–6, 130–1, 215, 278, 374

unity 45, 63, 71–3, 185, 350, **387**; and multiplicity/plurality 66–7, 71, 73, 78
up to us (in our power) see freedom

vegetative soul see nature
vice 199–200, 219, 254, 351
Victorinus, Gaius Marius 374

virtue 296–308*; cathartic 301–5, 314–15, 323, 336; civic 298–302, 304–6, 308; intellectual 298, 301–2, 304, 307; paradigms of 300–1, 330; political 298, 330
vision 96–7, 100, 131–4*, 148, 160, 242, 245, 250–1, 267n30, 281, 342–3, 371n6; intellectual *see* intellection

we *see* self
wickedness 238, 354, 356
will (*boulēsis, thelēsis*): of the One 74, 82–9*, 94

wisdom 115, 298, 300–3, 306–8, 325, 328–9, 332n5; practical (*phronēsis*) 300–1, 306, 332n5
Wittgenstein, L. 82
Wolff, C. 378
World-Soul 25, 40–2, 44, 59, 67, 144–5, 147, 150–1, 154–8*, 160, 162–3, 168, 170–3, 181–3, 209–10, 232–5, 238, 327, 338, 349, 368

Xenophanes 70

Zeus 40